ÉMIGRÉ FEMINISM:
TRANSNATIONAL PERSPECTIVES

 P9-EDQ-830

Edited by Alena Heitlinger

Bringing together the views of expatriate, exiled, and émigré feminists from various parts of the world, this collection explores themes of exile, home, displacement, and the practice of feminism across national boundaries.

The thirteen articles presented here originated with a conference on émigré feminism held at Trent University in October 1996. The authors, most of them now living in Canada, are scholars from South Africa, Uganda, Chile, Trinidad and Tobago, Greece, Hungary, the Czech Republic, Poland, Turkey, Iran, Finland, and New Zealand. Their views have been shaped by their experience of specific political and economic changes, such as the dismantling of communism and apartheid, the rise of religious fundamentalism, and rapid marketization. Together the essays offer a rich diversity of intellectual, political, cultural, and religious perspectives.

This book adds a new dimension to our understanding of expatriation by putting a feminist face on the émigré experience.

ALENA HEITLINGER is Professor of Sociology, Trent University.

EDITED BY ALENA HEITLINGER

# Émigré Feminism: Transnational Perspectives

UNIVERSITY OF TORONTO PRESS
Toronto Buffalo London

© University of Toronto Press Incorporated 1999
Toronto  Buffalo  London
Printed in Canada

ISBN 0-8020-0929-8 (cloth)
ISBN 0-8020-7899-0 (paper)

Printed on acid-free paper

**Canadian Cataloguing in Publication Data**

Main entry under title:

Émigré feminism : transnational perspectives

Based on a conference held at Trent University,
Peterborough, Ont., Oct. 3–6, 1996.
Includes bibliographical references and index.
ISBN 0-8020-0929-8 (bound)      ISBN 0-8020-7899-0 (pbk.)

1. Feminism – Cross-cultural studies – Congresses.
2. Feminism – Canada – Congresses.   3. Women
immigrants – Canada – Congresses.   I. Heitlinger, Alena.

HQ1106.E44 1999      305.42      C98-932078-2

ᴾᵒᶜ

University of Toronto Press acknowledges the financial assistance to its publishing program of the Canada Council for the Arts and the Ontario Arts Council.

This book has been published with the help of a grant from the Humanities
and Social Sciences Federation of Canada, using funds provided by the Social
Sciences and Humanities Research Council of Canada.

AUGUSTANA LIBRARY
UNIVERSITY OF ALBERTA

# Contents

# Acknowledgments

This book is based on papers presented at an interdisiciplinary conference entitled 'Émigré Feminism,' which was held at Trent University, Peterborough, Ontario, 3–6 October 1996. The conference was organized by the editor of the present volume, with the help of a small organizing committee.

I would like to thank each of the contributors, whose commitment and support for this project made this book possible.

Financial assistance for the conference from Trent University and from the Social Sciences and Humanities Research Council of Canada (Aid to Occasional Research Conferences and International Congresses in Canada Program) is gratefully acknowledged.

# Contributors

**Sedef Arat-Koc** came to Canada as a graduate student. She teaches women's studies and sociology at Trent University, Peterborough, Ontario. She is the co-author of *Through the Kitchen Window: The Politics of Home and Family,* and the co-editor of *Maid in the Market: Women's Paid Domestic Work.* Her work on Canada focuses on immigrant women and citizenship, and on Turkey on the relationship of different groups of women to the project of modernity.

**Yvonne Bobb Smith** is a Caribbean woman, born in Trinidad and Tobago, where she gained a national reputation for linking women's issues with public adult education. She has a wide experience both in Canada and the Caribbean in gender issues and empowerment, as well as in transformative community organizing. Her doctoral thesis is entitled 'A Caribbean Woman's Identity in Canada: Agency and Resistance in Community Organizing.'

**Alena Heitlinger** is professor of sociology at Trent University, Peterborough, Ontario. The author of five books and numerous articles, she has published widely on feminist, demographic, health, employment, and child care issues in the former Soviet Union, former Czechoslovakia, Canada, Great Britain, Australia, and postcommunist Czech Republic.

**Nóra Jung** left her native Hungary in 1982. In Toronto she has worked with immigrant and refugee women and done counselling on wife abuse. As an undergraduate at York University, she focused on community development among immigrant women. She wrote her MA thesis on community-based services for immigrant women. For her PhD research, she studied newly emerged women's groups in Hungary.

**Eva C. Karpinski** has a doctorate in American literature from her native Poland. She has published articles on postmodernist fiction, immigrant writing, feminist theory, and pedagogy. She is the editor of *Pens of Many Colours*, an anthology of Canadian multicultural writing. She is currently completing her PhD in women's studies at York University in the area of women's autobiography and translation.

**Smaro Kamboureli** teaches Canadian literature and diaspora theory at the University of Victoria, British Columbia. She is the author of *in the second person* (1985) and *On the Edge of Genre: The Contemporary Canadian Long Poem* (1991). She co-edited (with Shirley Neuman) *A Mazing Space: Writing Canadian Women Writing* (1986), and is the editor of *Making a Difference: Canadian Multicultural Literature* (1996). Her book, *Scandalous Bodies: Diasporic Literature in English Canada and Its Contexts*, will appear in the spring of 1999.

**Linzi Manicom** is currently completing a doctoral dissertation entitled 'Re-making State and Gender in South Africa's Political Transition' at the University of Toronto. She co-edited (with Shirley Walters) the book *Gender in Popular Education*, and works freelance as a teacher, writer, and consultant in the areas of women, globalization and transnational feminism.

**Haideh Moghissi** is the author of *Populism and Feminism in Iran: Women's Struggle in a Male-Defined Revolutionary Movement*. She is an associate professor of sociology and women's studies at Atkinson College, York University, Toronto. Before leaving Iran in 1984, she was a senior researcher with the Iran National Archives. She was a founder of the National Union of Women and member of its first executive board and of the editorial boards of *Barabari* (Equality) and *Zanan Dar Mobarezeh* (Women in Struggle).

**Nakanyike Musisi** is an associate professor of history at the University of Toronto, where she teaches African and women's history. She has published on a variety of women's issues in Uganda and among Africans in metropolitan Toronto, and on the social origins of violence in Uganda and the impact of religion on policy formulation in East Africa.

**Verónica Schild** is an assistant professor of political science at the University of Western Ontario, London. She has published on the Chilean women's movement as well as on the problematic treatment of civil society in democratization debates. She is working on a book on women and the neoliberal state formation in Chile.

**Yeshim Ternar** is a writer and researcher with a PhD in anthropology. Her books to date are: *Orphaned by Halley's Comet* (1990) (short stories); *The Book and the Veil* (1994) (nonfiction, an original study of feminism in Turkey at the turn of the twentieth century); *True Romance with a Sailor* (1996) (short stories); and *Rembrandt's Model* (1998) (historical novel). All but the first were published by Véhicule Press in Montreal. Yeshim Ternar has also published widely in literary journals in Canada, the United States, and Europe.

**Jacqui True** is a doctoral candidate in the Department of Political Science, York University, Toronto. Her most recent publication is a comprehensive review of feminist international relations in *Theories of International Relations* (1996). She is currently doing a dissertation on gender and political-economic transformations in postcommunist East Central Europe.

**Vappu Tyyskä** obtained her PhD in sociology from the University of Toronto in 1993. She has taught sociology in many southern Ontario universities, and is currently an assistant professor of sociology at Ryerson Polytechnic University, Toronto. Her research interests include social and family policy, women and the welfare state, and the women's movement in a comparative perspective.

ÉMIGRÉ FEMINISM:
TRANSNATIONAL PERSPECTIVES

1

# Émigré Feminism: An Introduction

## ALENA HEITLINGER

This book explores various aspects of the cross-cultural conveyance and translation of feminist ideas and practices as these are mediated by exiles, émigrés, and/or expatriates. Emigrants frequently move with equal facility among several perspectives, seeing each one simultaneously from within and from without, seeking to make visible to each culture and political tradition both its own preconceptions and those of others. This enables émigrés to adopt liminal and multiple perspectives, defying a single world-view. Caught between different systems of values, beliefs, languages, discourses, and identities, émigrés who are feminists can develop a distinct capacity to translate feminist ideas and practices across cultures. Their fluency in more than one culture makes very apparent the situatedness of different feminisms – in time, space, and a specific political culture. This critical awareness discourages viewing one particular national feminism as hegemonic. It also promotes an understanding of the contingency of the seemingly universal concepts of feminism such as 'women' or 'gender.'

The essays in this book bring together the views of expatriate, exiled, and émigré feminists from various parts of the world. The collection includes authors from countries with oppressive regimes; countries in transition to democracy from communism, apartheid, or military dictatorship; countries where military dictatorship is a more distant memory; countries whose democratic future is somewhat uncertain; countries belonging to the British Commonwealth; and countries with long-standing democratic traditions.

The book is a product of a conference that was held at Trent University, Peterborough, Ontario, Canada, 3–6 October 1996. The participants, all of whom currently reside in Canada, are themselves emigrant, exiled, or expatriate feminists. Thus, all the essays draw on the participants' personal emigrant–immigrant knowledge and experience. The self-reflective methodology that is evident throughout the book is congruent with contemporary developments in feminist and postmodernist thought. Both feminism and postmodernism insist that location is central to the production of knowledge and that this should be made explicit. Contributors to this collection were specifically invited and challenged to explore the interrelationship between their émigré experience and their intellectual work.

This book also makes a contribution to existing Canadian literature on immigrant feminists. Much of this literature has focused on questions of race and racism, tending to elide categories of the 'immigrant' and 'visible minority.' This book shows that there is, in fact, enormous variation in the specific class, ethnic, national, and religious perspectives brought to the Canadian feminist movement by immigrant feminists.

The immigrant literature also tends to focus on immigration as a one-directional experience of accommodation and acculturation. The essays in this book implicitly challenge that perspective. They reveal that immigrants are involved in an ongoing cultural negotiation on identity formation and realignment between their emigrant and immigrant knowledge and experience. This process is also shaped by specific political and economic changes in both the home and the host country, such as the dismantling of communism and apartheid, the rise of religious fundamentalism, or rapid marketization.

For the contributors to this book, these historical changes are viewed and experienced through the prism of feminism. 'Famous' émigrés who have written about their experience have generally been men. This book adds a new dimension to our understanding of expatriation by putting a feminist face on the émigré experience.

### Defining Exiled, Émigré, Expatriate, and Diasporic Feminists

This diverse category of feminists includes (1) immigrant feminists who have established 'permanent' active lives in 'host' (often 'Western') countries, (2) feminists working in international organizations and aid agencies, (3) 'temporary' exiles, expatriates, refugees, students, or contract workers who intend to return permanently to their countries of origin, (4) Canadian (or other Western) feminists who have lived in other countries, and, in some cases, (5) descendants of any of the above (Heitlinger and Manicom, 1996).

Émigrés, exiles, and expatriates, therefore, constitute distinct yet over-lapping groups of people. The main differences among them lie in the circumstances leading to the decision to emigrate; their ability to return 'back home'; age and marital status at migration; reception in the host country; the embeddedness and connection to their respective diasporic communities; the extent of economic, cultural, and social displacement; the period of time spent in emigration; attitudes towards exiles and expa-triates in the country of origin; and where and when, that is, at what historical moment, and with what prevailing discourses, the émigrés encountered feminism.

Exiles are often defined quite narrowly, as involuntary refugees who left their country of origin for political reasons, and who cannot go back. Over time, some exiles move into the expatriate or émigré category, while others become what Linzi Manicom terms 'post-exiles.' Both groups typi-cally become permanent residents or citizens of their country of immi-gration, and, if they so desire, they can visit or return to their country of origin.

A broader definition of exile typically encompasses other types of exile than those directly created by oppressive regimes. For example, many people classified as economic refugees are, in fact, exiles who emigrated for both economic and political reasons. Moreover, as Eva Karpinski and Verónica Schild point out in this volume, the decision to become an exile could also be motivated by the politics of gender. Women who choose exile often do so in order to escape from oppressive nationalist, religious, and patriarchal discourses and laws.

There is no guarantee of 'safe arrival,' however. As Eva Karpinski puts it, 'Wherever I went, I began to discover multiple patriarchies, or "scattered hegemonies" – tangible reminders of the ubiquity of oppression based on gender, class, race, ethnicity, or sexuality ... It seems that choosing femi-nism makes me an exile anywhere, with the possible exception of women's studies departments, or other openly feminist-identified communities.'

Thus, the best way to conceptualize the notion of exile is to see it as a spectrum or a continuum of varieties of conditions, identities, and meta-phors, with powerful historical, political, literary, and epistemological connotations.[1] Several authors in this collection (Karpinski, Manicom, Schild, Heitlinger, and Moghissi) deconstruct the various meanings of exile and then reconfigure them to deal with the subtleties of different circumstances under which exiles leave, adopt new countries and identi-ties, return 'back home,' and/or engage with various nationalist, reli-gious, and feminist discourses.

Returning from exile, be it permanently or only temporarily, is often a highly problematic and emotionally charged experience. The ending or redefinition of formal exile creates what Manicom terms a 'dilemma of return' and 'post-exile': 'Both post-exiles and "returnees" are indelibly inscribed by the exilic experience; but distinguishing them are the different places and paths of their realignments in relation to the designations of "home." For returnees, this dilemma, while not necessarily resolved, is enacted bodily in their geographical resettlement back home. For post-exiles, "return" takes the form of an obligatory remaking of self and identity, a process both banal and profound, not dramatic as was the entry into exile. National identity and, significantly here, the terms of political-scholarly engagement, must be renegotiated and reconstructed.'

Moreover, not all exiles and expatriates are eagerly welcomed when they return home. Some may be resented for their relative wealth or for the very fact that they 'got away' and did not really 'suffer' like those who stayed behind. No matter how hard they fought from the outside against their respective oppressive regimes, they are often perceived to 'have had it easy,' and to have lost the nuances of the local situation. The specific reactions to 're-émigrés' (feminist and otherwise), and the often painful experiences of 'post-exile,' are explored in more detail by Manicom, Schild, and Heitlinger in chapters 3, 4, and 6.

For the purposes of this book, the common denominator for all these 'femigrant' categories (to use Eva Karpinski's term) is the migrants' ongoing attachments to feminism, the adopted country, and the country of origin, however ambivalent these attachments might be. Émigré feminists, therefore, draw on at least four distinct traditions: (1) the history and culture of their country of origin, (2) the history and culture of their adopted country (or countries, if the current country of residence was not the first host country), (3) the history and politics of local, regional, and international feminist movements, and (4) the diasporic experience of migration, displacement, and ethnic minority status.

Salman Rushdie (1991:277–8) has argued that 'full-fledged' migrants suffer a triple displacement: loss of roots, loss of language, and loss of cultural codes. It is on those grounds that migrants and their perspectives are seen as so important, 'because roots, language and social norms have been three of the most important parts of the definition of what is to be a human being. The migrant, denied all three, is obliged to find new ways of describing himself, new ways of being human.' In Rushdie's view (1991:124–5), these generically male, 'radically new types of human beings [are] people who root themselves in ideas rather than places, in memories as much as in material things; people who have been obliged to define themselves – because they are so defined by others – by their otherness; people in whose deepest selves strange fusions occur, unprecedented unions between what they were and where they find themselves. The migrant suspects reality: having experienced several ways of being, he understands their illusory nature. To see things plainly, you have to cross a frontier.'

Rushdie's celebration of the new 'hybrid subjects,' rooted 'in ideas rather than places,' reflects a strong class bias. The new types of human beings Rushdie referred to tend to be successful, highly educated professionals and entrepreneurs, with fluency in English (or some other 'world' language) and a strong cosmopolitan orientation. Their experience of migration has been usually quite positive and has typically included new and exciting business and professional opportunities. The favourable positioning of this group of upper middle-class people within the transnational culture and economy sets them apart from the more common and less privileged migrants and refugees whose experiences of migration tend to be more negative. Rather than success and hybridity, the migrant experiences of the latter group are typically marked by prejudice, discrimination, under- or unemployment, and poverty. When one therefore talks about émigrés as 'hybrid subjects' or as intercultural translators, one has to add the migrants' class location to the translation process.

Thus, among female emigrants it is educated émigré feminists who have acquired the special qualities and competencies that Rushdie is talking about and    who embody the feminist notions of 'the politics of location,' 'world-travelling,' or the 'nomadic,' 'migratory,' 'resident alien,' or hybrid subjects. Elaborated by feminist and postmodernist theorists such as Adrienne Rich (1986), Lata Mani (1990), Rosi Braidotti (1994), Christine Sylvester (1995), and Janet Wolff (1995), these conceptualizations grapple 'with ways of representing women and feminism that do not reproduce the dominance of "Western feminist" issues but reflect and embrace cultural, social, and power differences among women. Building on insights of postmodernism and postcoloniality, the emerging theory of transnational feminism acknowledges both the specific local and national forms of patriarchy, as well as the ways in which global economic restructuring and transnational cultural influences shape and link the material and cultural lives of women around the world. Inderpal Grewal and Caren Kaplan (1994) offer a strong argument for the need to trace the production, circulation, reception, and mobilization of key feminist

concepts and discourses within and across different political contexts'
(Heitlinger and Manicom, 1996).

The orienting document for the 'Émigré Feminism' conference also
stressed the need for comparison of 'various national, regional and global
feminist frames of reference. Émigré feminists, who "live," and are agents
for, intercultural encounters, hybridity and transmigration of feminist
ideas and practices, can play a crucial role in this process' (Heitlinger and
Manicom, 1996).

## The International Context

Contrary to popular wisdom created by the writings on the globalizing
world economy, transnational links involving women and feminism are
not a phenomenon that has arisen only towards the end of the twentieth
century. As Schild points out in this volume, cross-border connections
between various women's organizations within Latin America can be
traced to the nineteenth century, as can Latin American memberships in
a number of international women's organizations. In a similar vein, True
(in Chapter 14) describes how both New Zealand feminism at the turn of
the century and Czech feminism during the late Habsburg monarchy
were deeply embedded in transnational feminist organizations and personal networks.

Similar developments also occurred in Asia and what we now call the
Middle East. As Kumari Jayawardena (1986:17) has argued, 'With the
spread of education and literacy, feminist literature in the form of books,
journals and magazines became an important aspect of the women's
movement. In several Asian countries, there was a flowering of books,
novels, journals and articles in the late 19th and early 20th centuries, written both by women and men and dealing with issues concerning women's
role in society. While many of these publications discussed traditional
"women's" topics, they could not avoid getting involved in the ongoing
debate on women's subordination. In many cases they reported developments in the sphere of women's emancipation in other countries. Egyp-
tian women, for example, were told of innovations and legislative reforms
in Turkey; such journals also informed their readers about the suffragist
and feminist struggles in Europe.'

Moreover, then as now, transnational feminism was not simply a matter
of flow of ideas, but also a question of flow of money and power relations.
Making funds available for bringing women from poorer countries to
attend conferences in the West, translating and reproducing locally pam-

phlets and documents produced by activists in the United States and Europe, and organizing national tours by foreign activists are, therefore, practices of some historical standing. The power and influence of different national feminisms are far from equal: historically and now, the transnational dialogue has been heavily dominated by mainstream feminist discourses and superior financial resources in the wealthier and more powerful Western countries. Hester Eisenstein (1991:65) noted, 'However reluctantly, that feminism in fact grows out of Western tradition. It is well and truly a daughter of Western theory and Western patriarchal categories of thought.'

However, Jayawardena's (1986) book on feminism and nationalism in several countries of the 'East' in the late nineteenth and early twentieth centuries argued strongly against this position. She argued persuasively that 'feminism was *not* imposed on the Third World by the West' (p. 2) and that constructing feminism as Western works against women and feminists in Third World contexts. Tyyskä, in this volume, is also highly critical of the all-consuming concept of 'Western feminism.' Her study of the women's movements in Canada and Finland revealed important ideological and structural differences, which have rendered problematic attempts to fit Finnish feminist organizations into the typical Anglo-American categories of radical, liberal, and socialist feminisms. Significant differences *within* Anglo-American feminist traditions are also noted by Heitlinger and True (in chapters 6 and 14).

In contrast, Jung's analysis in Chapter 5 of postcommunist feminist discourses in East Central Europe reveals that there is 'a small but growing number of women who are enthusiastic about the idea of importing feminism to Eastern Europe. Writers who usually argue along these lines tend to talk about feminism in general. They pay little or no attention to the fact that they themselves are influenced by a specific kind of feminism. Only a few authors in this group seem to be aware about the diversity within feminism ... Women activists and scholars who develop a positive attitude towards feminism (in both a general or a more specific form) tend to accept feminism without criticism. I would argue that this uncritical acceptance of Western feminist ideas often entails an uncritical acceptance of Western norms and values.'

As we noted, the tendency in the literature has been to regard practices of 'exporting' and 'importing' feminism as a form of Western domination, because Western feminists have been able to take advantage of their countries' greater media, publishing, and distribution capacities. However, as Schild notes in this volume, 'for those at the receiving end, involved in the multiple and complex, and hierarchically ordered, organizations and practices that constitute local feminisms, these connections have a different meaning.'

The historical and cross-national record also suggests that local and transnational feminisms can be equated not only with oppositional practice, but also with numerous class-based projects. These include the various middle-class-dominated suffragist movements and the socialist feminisms of the Second International or the Third Communist International (Comintern). In turn, the recognition of the class dimension of various feminisms enables us to make a clear distinction between transnational feminisms of the powerful and the powerless and between the subversive and the order-maintaining aspects of feminism. As True notes (in Chapter 14), transnational feminisms are *not* inherently transformative, though this is not to imply that 'transnational feminist cooperation and reciprocal, equitable, exchange does not exist.'

The transposition of Western middle-class feminism into different social, economic, and political contexts of the Third World or postcommunist East Central Europe, and its engagement or confrontation with varying feminist traditions, cultural constructions of gender, and conceptualizations of women's equality and emancipation, have created a constructive tension, which has forced a rethinking of feminist discourses and practices. The explicit challenges to Western conceptualizations of feminism by non-Western, Third World women, and by anti-racist and postcolonial feminists residing in the Western countries, have led to the contestation of the very definition of feminism (Mohanty et al., 1991).

One of the first public confrontations between 'First World' and 'Third World' feminists took place at the first World Conference for Women, held in July 1975 in Mexico City in conjunction with the United Nations International Women's Year. Third World women made it very clear 'that they were opposed to feminism that ignored problems of poverty and underdevelopment, and that rendered invisible male experiences of oppression ... Since then, western feminists have learned to be less ethnocentric, and to listen more carefully to what women in developing countries and minority women in their own countries have to say about the relationship of gender to class, race/ethnicity and (neo)colonialism' (Heitlinger, 1996:89). Thus, Yvonne Bobb Smith notes in Chapter 8 that 'for a Caribbean woman a feminism that seeks only equality for men and women offers an insufficient basis for action as the brand of feminism which was *learned* from "home" was always rooted in wider social relations.'

Each chapter in this collection gives a different twist to the meaning of feminism, against the cultural and political context of the writer. Moreover, the strongly divergent and at times contradictory versions of feminism presented in this book suggest that in order to fully comprehend the varieties of local, regional, and transnational feminisms, we have to overcome the current opposition between Western and non-Western feminist movements. The developments of national, regional, and global feminist movements, therefore, 'reflect both appropriation and transformation of ideas and practices from "outside" as well as their particular "internal" socioeconomic and political conditions and histories. Thus, the transnational dissemination, mediation, and regulation of feminist discourses and practices in diverse national and cultural political sites have taken place in complex, uneven, and varied ways. International feminist networks, personal encounters (at conferences and elsewhere), United Nations organizations, and various national and international funding agencies have played an important role in this process' (Heitlinger and Manicom, 1996).

The fourth United Nations World Conference for Women held in September 1995 in Beijing was 'only the most recent international forum to expose the ways in which the hegemony of particular feminist discourses has organized international exchange, thus regulating and constraining the representation of national feminisms. For example, U.N. documents on the advancement of the status of women disallow all issues which do not fit their criteria, and in this way dictate the kinds of categories which local women's movements and government policies must measure themselves by' (Heitlinger and Manicom, 1996).

However, international standard-setting activities should be also seen in a positive light. International instruments could be helpful in creating alternative political spaces for local feminists and in legitimating certain types of public protests, advocacy, and lobbying. By using U.N. instruments as standards by which to evaluate governmental actions and policies, local women's groups are engaging in legitimate democratic activity to hold their national governments accountable.

Equally powerful in the regulation of national feminisms, and equally embedded in transnational links, are the conditions imposed by funding agencies. The practices of funding agencies and non-governmental organizations (NGOs) can be also seen in both a negative and a positive light. On the one hand, they might impose some overly restrictive criteria and agendas to which local groups are forced to orient their activities (such as making funding available for action research with poor women but not for the development of Chilean feminist theory), but, on the other, they might create valuable alternative spaces which otherwise would not exist.

## The Organization of the Book: Themes, Perspectives, and Writing Styles

The authors included in this collection represent not only a broad spectrum of émigré experiences, but also a range of ages and a variety of feminist and disciplinary discourses. The theme of subjectivity of émigré feminists is present in one form or another in all of the contributions, but the writing styles and approaches vary considerably. Some contributors opt for a more personal approach, while others problematize and theorize the personal and their use of it. The way in which feminism is conceptualized, and the extent to which it is framed in academic terms as scholarship, as a political struggle for a better future, or as a means of self-discovery and search for an identity, also vary from one author to another.

The differences in approaches, orientations, and styles of writing are also dependent on the various roles the authors have played as intellectuals or as activists in local and transnational feminist movements. The authors' personal confrontations with different feminist ideas and practices, the subject matter of their individual contributions, their current institutional and disciplinary locations, and the specifics of their personal biographies are also significant.

As a literary writer, Yeshim Ternar is interested in exploring the impact that the experiences of growing up, migration, travel, feminism, and marginality have had on her writing and self-development. As Janet Wolff (1995:9) has argued, the experience of 'displacement (deterritorialization) can be quite strikingly productive. First, the marginalization entailed in forms of migration can generate new perceptions of place and, in some cases, of the relationship between places. Second, the same dislocation can also facilitate personal transformation, which may take the form of "re-writing" the self, discarding the lifelong habits and practices of constraining social education and discovering new forms of self-expression.'

Specific biographical events (such as the range of strong female personalities Ternar has met in her formative years) may also motivate the desire for escape and self-reflection. One's class and ethnicity are also important in influencing vocabularies of travel and literary writing. As Wolff (1995:116) pointed out, 'Gender is not, of course, the only dimension involved in travel. Disparities of wealth and cultural capital, and class differences generally, have always ensured real disparities in access to and modes of travel. In addition, it is clear that the *ways* in which people travel are very diverse, ranging from tourism, exploring and other voluntary activity to forced mobility of immigrant and guest workers in many countries, and to the extremes of political and economic exile.'

The traditional notion of travel rests on the 'Western, middle-class idea of the chosen and leisured journey.' Current notions of travel, however, are much more diverse and market oriented. As one of the world's fastest growing industries, travel now includes a whole plethora of adjectives, such as 'business travel,' 'conference travel,' 'sex tourism,' 'package holidays,' 'road movies,' 'year abroad educational programs,' or the Australian / New Zealand notion of 'the big OE – overseas experience.'

Thus, the metaphors, ideologies, and actual experiences of travel and migration have to be situated in the broader context of the global economy and in an analysis of the positionality of both the travellers and those left 'back home.' Smaro Kamboureli's critical reading of Karen Connelly's *One Room in a Castle* suggests that one needs to analyse the specific location of the literary critic (in Kamboureli's case, a Greek-Canadian émigré feminist, who is both a 'native informant' and a tourist in and of Greece), the writer and her discourse (in Connelly's case, a Canadian 'nomadic' travel writer), and the reception of the writer's publication in her native country, in Connelly's case, Canada.

The naming of the impact that our different geographical and class locations have on the production and reception of knowledge is a theme that permeates this whole book. For example, Jacqui True, in her contrapuntal analysis, explores the counternarratives to mainstream Anglo-American liberal feminism that have emerged from inside New Zealand, Australia, Oceania, and East Central Europe. Vappu Tyyskä's essay focuses on problems created by attempts to homogenize Western feminisms; her analysis has important implications for our understanding of key feminist concepts, especially their usefulness and limitations in comparative and cross-national research.

Émigrés can experience unique problems in conducting cross-national research, because their exile location may determine the type of data to which they can gain access. Thus, during the communist period, Heitlinger stayed away from conducting interviews to avoid drawing official attention to her research. Manicom's doctoral research on South Africa relied heavily on 'official' government documents which were available externally. Schild used her research fieldwork in Chile as a 'way of going back home,' but once she got there, she could no longer find her 'home.' Thus, paradoxically, 'returning home' turned into confirmation of her émigré identity as a Chilean living abroad. Musisi's fieldwork experience in her native Uganda transformed her from a position of 'a data collecting instrument' for her doctoral thesis to a 'data collecting instrument for those whose lives were being researched.'

Nakanyike Musisi's and Yvonne Bobb Smith's accounts (in Chapters 7 and 8) focus on the African-Canadian and Caribbean-Canadian experiences of migration and feminism and on the centrality to that experience of racism, classism, and the problems of daily survival. At the same time, however, Musisi warns us not to fall in the trap of essentialism: 'Every immigrant and refugee "African woman" in Canada has her own story. One is not simply an African woman, but a woman with multiple and cumulative identities (Muganda, Ugandan, Somali, middle class, employed, lesbian, straight). This position subverts or displaces all notions of group commonality (as woman, African, immigrant). Nevertheless, it is vital that we acknowledge that the internal differences among women as Africans, immigrants or otherwise, are as great as those that separate us from men and from both women and men of other races. Which of our particular identities asserts itself at any particular contestation is what we each have to live with day in and day out.'

The evolution of feminist movements and scholarship in contemporary South Africa, Chile, Hungary, the Czech Republic, Turkey, and Iran, and their respective diasporic and transnational links, are explored in Chapters 3, 4, 5, 6, 9, 10, and 14. All of the authors discuss both their own émigré positions (and in some cases also those of their émigré colleagues) and the paradoxes involved in writing for a largely North American readership. While Jung, Heitlinger, and True offer broadly similar perspectives on the growing body of literature on Central and East European women, Arat-Koc and Moghissi approach the overlooked agency of Muslim woman from radically different frameworks. Thus, the points of view vary from one chapter to another – sometimes reinforcing and sometimes contradicting each other.

All of the authors raise the issue of accountability and responsibility of émigré feminists, both in the exile and post-exile milieux. Many also address the problem of multiple reception identified by Mani (1990), which involves analyses of diverse audiences and communities with different traditions, understandings, and needs of feminism.

Émigré feminism is a broad and diverse topic, which brings together issues of globalism, multiculturalism, development, nationalism, civil society, migration, travel, displacement, marginality, acculturation, hybridity, ethnicity, race, religion, language, literature, production and reception of knowledge, standpoint methodologies, biographical self-reflexivity, identity, and human rights. Our hope is that the book's specific focus on émigré feminism, and on its relationship to the transnational flow of feminist discourses and political practices, will make a contribution to the development of feminist thought and practice locally, regionally, and globally.

NOTE

1 See, for example, Eagleton (1970), Said (1990) and Kolakowski (1990), who all hold that the social marginality associated with exile produces specific cognitive advantages not available to indigenous observers. For a critique of this position, see Manicom's essay in this volume.

REFERENCES

Braidotti, Rosi (1994) *Nomadic Subjects: Embodiment and Sexual Difference in Contemporary Feminist Theory.* New York: Columbia University Press.
Eagleton, Tery (1970) *Exiles and Émigrés: Studies in Modern Literature.* New York: Schocken.
Eisenstein, Hester (1991) *Gender Shock: Practicing Feminism on Two Continents.* Boston: Beacon Press.
Grewal, Inderpal, and Caren Kaplan (eds.) (1994) *Scattered Hegemonies: Postmodernity and Transnational Feminist Practices.* St Paul: University of Minnesota Press.
Heitlinger, Alena (1996) 'Framing Feminism in Postcommunist Czech Republic.' *Communist and Post-Communist Studies* 29 (4) (March) 77–93.
Heitlinger, Alena, and Linzi Manicom (1996) 'Orienting Document for Participants of the Interdisciplinary Conference on "Émigré Feminism"' held at Trent University, Peterborough, Ontario, Canada. 3–6 October.
Jayawardena, Kumari (1986) *Feminism and Nationalism in the Third World.* London: Zed Books.
Kolakowski, Leszek (1990) 'In Praise of Exile.' In *Modernity on Endless Trial.* Chicago: University of Chicago Press.
Mani, Lata (1990) 'Multiple Mediations: Feminist Scholarship in the Age of Multinational Reception.' *Feminist Review* 35:24–39.
Mohanty, Chandra Talpade, Ann Russo, and Lourdes Torres (eds.) (1991) *Third World Women and the Politics of Feminism.* Bloomington: Indiana University Press.
Rich, Adrienne (1986) *Blood, Bread and Poetry: Selected Prose, 1979–1985.* New York: W.W. Norton.

Rushdie, Salman (1991) *Imaginary Homelands: Essays and Criticism, 1981–1991.* London: Granta Books.

Said, Edward (1990) 'Reflections on Exile.' In Russel Fergusson, Martha Gever, Trinh T. Minh-Ha, and Cornel West (eds.) *Out There: Marginalization and Contemporary Culture,* 357–66. New York and London: New Museum of Contemporary Art and MIT Press.

Sylvester, Christine (1995) 'African and Western Feminisms: World-Traveling the Tendencies and Possibilities.' *Signs* 20(4):941–69.

Wolff, Janet (1995) *Resident Alien: Feminist Cultural Criticism.* London: Polity Press; New Haven: Yale University Press.

# 2

# Choosing Feminism, Choosing Exile: Towards the Development of a Transnational Feminist Consciousness

## EVA C. KARPINSKI

Exile is an uncomfortable situation, though it is also a magical situation. I am not making light of the experience of exile. But we can endure it differently. Some exiles die of rage, some transform their exile into a country ... Some exiles can draw joy from rage ...

Hélène Cixous (1993:120)

Coded in personal terms, the title of this essay contains a mini-narrative of my life as a feminist and a migrant, and it can be read as the shortest autobiographical statement of a 'femigrant.' Like many other Poles in the 1980s, I became an internal exile before actually leaving Poland. My narrative was not exactly one of political or economic migration, although both these factors undoubtedly played a role in my decision to emigrate. Ten years ago, I did not have the language or the conceptual apparatus of feminism to identify what I had found most oppressive in my life in Poland. Today I can say that, in my case, the separation was motivated as much by the rejection of the political regime as by the politics of gender. I decided to emigrate when I was two months' pregnant and no longer able to protect my body from the male-dominated gynecological establishment and from the claims of nationalist, religious, and cultural traditionalist discourses of femininity and motherhood. I refused to be a 'mother' in a country where motherhood, both literal and symbolic, has historically been national property. The official worship of the Polish Mother, a proud producer of sons destined to become cannon fodder, did not assuage the difficulties of real mothers who, in the socialist state, were expected to act as super-women, combining multiple domestic and employment duties in the ever-crumbling economy, while never losing their feminine charm. Therefore, my leave taking was painless and virtually undramatic. If anything, it was accompanied by the joy and exhilaration of new beginnings.

At that time, the choice of exile simply meant opting out of the hateful, pervasively paternalistic system that operated on so many levels of women's lives in Poland, both communist and post-Solidarity. However, as I was soon to learn, there was no arriving at a safe place. Wherever I went, I began to discover multiple patriarchies, or 'scattered hegemonies' (Grewal and Kaplan, 1994) – tangible reminders of the ubiquity of oppression based on gender, class, race, ethnicity, or sexuality. Even in my college teaching in Canada, I am discouraged from identifying as a feminist, either openly or via interventions into course content, supposedly in order not to alienate the students. It seems that choosing feminism makes me an exile anywhere, with the possible exception of women's studies departments, or other openly feminist-identified communities. In this climate, where embracing feminism is a transgressive gesture, one has to recognize that the necessity to leave 'home' can be transformed into a productive site of exile.[1]

In what follows, I want to think around the three terms brought together by the title of this chapter, relating to feminist, exilic, transnational consciousness. But before I can try to tap in this way the creative tension between the personal and theoretical frameworks, which is what I think often happens when a person writing is a feminist, I should situate myself *vis-à-vis* feminism, or rather feminisms, as this highly contested term tends to be used nowadays. Even the mini-narrative produced above hints at a trajectory of my own development, of the intermittent passage through the stages of anti-sexist, anti-capitalist, and anti-racist consciousness, marked by my exposure to liberal, socialist, Black, and postcolonial feminisms, including also a long detour via academic poststructuralist feminism.[2]

So what do I choose today when I say 'choosing feminism'? In its different guises, feminism remains an emancipatory project that I see as characterized broadly by an active interest in and commitment to women's issues in multiple contexts and locations; a sense of 'togetherness,' shared responsibilities, and – despite power differentials – 'overlapping concerns' (Grewal, 1994:237); a willingness to sustain dialogue among women; an alertness to different forms of oppression, injustice, and inequality; and a utopian belief in the possibility of a better world. Even if feminism is articulated from the local, national basis, and women in different geographical locations may have a vital investment in a national struggle against a particular racist and imperialist oppression, feminism still remains committed to the cause of building women's solidarity across race, class, nation, ethnicity, religion, ability, and sexuality.

In this context, exile – whether as an existential condition or as a metaphor – can be viewed as a useful concept. However, because the concept of exile has been traditionally coded in masculinist terms, its usage within the nationalist and postmodernist frames needs to be deconstructed before it can be embraced as a feminist condition. 'Choosing feminism, choosing exile' would thus refer to an open invitation to break the frame and step out of any discourse of containment. It could help us discover new loyalties transcending the boundaries of nationhood and tribal ties. It would open up the possibility of new coalitions, new understandings, and new identities, and lead to the formation of a transnational feminist consciousness. For this to happen, feminism must be driven not only by a revolutionary impulse to end all kinds of oppression, but also by an exilic energy that would give it mobility.

I realize that in choosing 'exile' I have slightly moved away from 'émigré' feminism, but this minor linguistic displacement reflects my discontent with the latter term and my search for a more inclusive category, less tainted by associations with privilege. Perhaps to settle the question of the range of exile, of whether it is forced or voluntary, willed or imposed, one can use the metaphor of a spectrum, which, according to Frances Bartkowski (1995:85), allows for 'speculation about processes of differentiation without suggesting a telos. There is mobility to identity across this spectrum that is arrayed not as a colour chart, but a prism.' Such an image would constantly remind us of the 'inequalities' of exile and prevent using it as a totalizing concept. Contradictions within the spectrum, for example, a different construction of exile by refugee women as opposed to émigré academic critics, can be fruitful and necessary in provoking feminists to further questions. As I have suggested before, one has to make a distinction between the use of exile in reference to an experiential as opposed to metaphoric condition. Despite the obvious spillover between the two, in my discussion I concentrate on exile as a discursive construct, not as a lived experience. I am looking at exile primarily as a recurrent figuration of subjectivity and knowledge in different postmodern discourses. Of course, the question of what aspects of the 'real' experiences of exile are appropriated into the construct and how they inform the theorizing will not be easily dismissed. Inevitably, all metaphors of exile are haunted by the spectre of the body in exile.[3]

In addition to 'exile,' metaphors of 'nomadism' and 'world travelling' have been used by critics looking for adequate figurations of diasporic postmodern subjectivities.[4] As territorial images, they seem to be part of the remapping of discourses of identity, accompanied by a more general shift from the temporal to the spatial paradigm of knowledge (Said, 1993:49). In the context of globalization, this widening of spatial boundaries of knowledge has been marked by a notable move away from the tradition of Eurocentrism, so as to include knowledges produced in 'new' geographical locations (for example, postcolonial theories) and in 'marginal' spaces of metropolitan cultures (for example, feminism, Black theory, or queer theory).[5]

More than the other two models of transnationalism, exile comes with the heavy baggage of modernist ideas. As a trope, exile activates the whole series of semantic associations with separation, loss, dispossession, discontinuity, homelessness, uprootedness, foreignness, otherness, death, and mourning. It seems that as long as we conceptualize exile in terms of nationalist patriarchal discourse, the exilic energy remains locked in negativity. One can clearly see this process at work in psychoanalytic accounts of exile (Grinberg and Grinberg, 1989). Theorized through a psychoanalytic model, exile is predicated on absence. One can analyse different types of object relations as a series of 'attachments' and 'separations.' Moreover, like travel, exile can be viewed as regression, and, as such, it may carry 'the phantasm of unmediated bliss, wonder, solitude, and wordless communication' (Bartkowski, 1995:85), or, alternately, it may bring 'the reality of complex mediations of shame, fear, despair, loneliness, and the disempowered experience of an unshared tongue' (Bartkowski, 1995:86). The fact that some psychoanalysts pathologize exile as a form of neurosis suggests an attachment to 'home' and 'country' as a healthy patriarchal norm.[6]

Similarly, Edward Said's (1990:366) reflections are framed within the context of nationalism, said to be essential to exile: 'Exile is predicated on the existence, love for, and bond with, one's native place; what is true of all exile is not that home and love are lost, but that loss is inherent in the very existence of both.'

Although Said gives a more political meaning to exile when he contemplates the ironic contrast between famous modernist exiles such as Joyce and Nabokov and 'the unaccountable masses for whom U.N. agencies have been created,' he also tends to romanticize the condition of exile as carrying with it 'a touch of solitude and spirituality' (1990:359, 362), resulting probably from a mournful loss of home, identity, dignity, and origin experienced by exiles. Interestingly, Said's (1993) probing of exile

evolves into a celebration of nomadic mobility and migrant consciousness, which – from the gendered perspective (characteristically absent
from his work) – comes very close to the fulfilment of a male fantasy of
the free, unencumbered, independent self.[7]

In contrast to patriarchal discourses of postcoloniality (Said, 1993,
1994; Goldman, 1995) and psychoanalysis (Grinberg and Grinberg,
1989), feminist writers have been trying to detach exile from nationalism,
to de-masculinize exile, and to reclaim it as a 'female' metaphor. When
exile's association with nationalism is made to be 'essential,' as in Said,
women's experiences usually tend to be erased. However, one can say as
well that exile, linked to passivity and waiting, has already been feminized
in patriarchal discourses which have often practised exclusion through
feminization. There is a whole tradition of feminist interpretation, going
back to Virginia Woolf, that views nationalism as male and juxtaposes it
with female exile, epitomized by Woolf's (1938, 1978) famous figure of
woman as an outsider who says, 'In fact, as a woman, I have no country. As
a woman I want no country. As a woman my country is the whole world.'
This tradition is continued by such feminist critics as Hélène Cixous
(1980), Luce Irigaray (1985, 1993), Caren Kaplan (1987), Julia Kristeva
(1991), or Gerardine Meaney (1993), who have embraced exile for its
subversive potential. Kristeva uses Greek mythology to associate the very
origin of the concept of exile and foreignness with women. She interprets
the stories of Io and the Danaides as prototypical figures of female exiles,
fleeing sexual entrapment and choosing their own bodies over their
native land. Considering the Greek wedding ritual, which stipulated that
the bride be treated as a foreign suppliant, Kristeva recognizes sexual
difference itself as accountable for women's exiled condition in relation
to patriarchy. A closer look at three different applications of exile by
Cixous, Benhabib, and Braidotti will further illuminate its usefulness and
dangers in the context of feminist philosophy.

The motif of exile has many avatars in Hélène Cixous, who has spent
years thinking around exile.[8] She invokes exile as a metaphor of women's
economic condition under phallocentrism, as well as women's alienation
from their bodies, their exclusion from history, language, and the symbolic. A discovery of sexism and discrimination coincides for Cixous's
woman (1986:75) with her fall into homelessness: 'Where am I to stand?
What is my place if I am a woman?' In her early texts, Cixous (1980:250)
urges women to return to their bodies, to reclaim their territory by initi-
ating the feminine practice of writing. In her calls for *écriture féminine* one
can detect the same motif of separation and return characteristic of exile:

'By writing her self, woman will return to the body which has been more than confiscated from her, which has been turned into the uncanny stranger on display – the ailing or dead figure, which so often turns out to be the nasty companion, the cause and location of inhibitions.'

Moreover, Cixous (1986:72) emphatically positions herself on the side of otherness, allying herself with 'history's condemned, exiled, colonized and burned.' As a 'Jewoman' growing up in French-colonized Algeria, Cixous has been 'cured' of any compensatory sense of belonging to imagined entities such as countries or nations. In her later texts, Cixous (1990) elaborates an ethic of alterity based on her experience of exile, the chief components of which can be identified as refusal of mastery, celebration of love and life, and movement towards the other.

If in Cixous the trope of exile leads to a rethinking of an ethical stance in relation to difference, in the writings of another feminist philosopher, Seyla Benhabib (1992), exile becomes a prerequisite for finding a utopian space of exteriority from which the feminist subject can conduct a critique of the dominant order. According to Benhabib, the vocation of the social critic, which is 'like the vocation of the social exile and the expatriate' (Benhabib, 1992:227), presupposes a necessary distancing of oneself from one's everyday certitudes: 'The vocation of social criticism might require social exile, for there might be times when the immanent norms and values of a culture are so reified, dead or petrified that one can no longer speak in their name. The social critic who is in exile does not adopt the "view from nowhere" but "the view from outside the walls of the city" ... It may indeed be no coincidence that from Hypatia to Diotima to Olympe de Gouges and to Rosa Luxemburg, the vocation of the feminist thinker and critic has led her to leave home and the city walls' (Benhabib, 1992:228).

This figuration of exile aims to articulate a critique of current epistemological norms and values. Interestingly, Benhabib's assumption – that exile might constitute a privileged epistemic position – can be supported by the curious coincidence that poststructuralist knowledge has been produced to a large extent by 'exiles' such as Derrida, Kristeva, Cixous, and Irigaray. Benhabib's project, however, like other feminist projects, is not limited to the sphere of epistemological theory. Her goal is twofold: 'to situate reason and the moral self more decisively in contexts of gender and community' (Benhabib, 1992:8). Working from within the paradigm of communicative or discourse ethics, she is trying to elaborate moral theory that would inform feminist practice.

The final example of how the metaphorics of exile can be adapted to suit feminist goals is Rosi Braidotti's (1994) figuration of nomadic subjects. Reminiscent of Said's postmodernist celebration of the exilic, migratory, nomadic, anti-systemic energy of our time, Braidotti's treatment of exile and nomadism illustrates the dangers of postmodernist feminism unrestrained by moral and ethical concerns. Her case exposes the limitations of Western constructions of subjectivity and agency when confronted with non-Western models.

Braidotti develops her radically anti-essentialist model of feminist subjectivity by choosing an image of intercultural otherness – the nomad. The nomad is a subject 'who has relinquished all idea, desire, or nostalgia for fixity' (Braidotti, 1994:22). This figuration is about deconstructing identity; it is made of 'transitions, successive shifts, and coordinated changes, without and against an essential unity. The nomadic subject, however, is not altogether devoid of unity; his/her mode is one of definite, seasonal patterns of movement ... repetitions, cyclical moves, rhythmical displacements.' Braidotti describes nomadism as transgressive, heterogeneous, deterritorialized, anti-conventional, polyglot, performative, and affirmative. To her, nomadism is also an 'existential condition' of a transnational individual who refuses to settle into established modes of thought and behaviour. Cutting across the boundaries of race, gender, class, ethnicity, and sexual practice, the nomad as 'a situated, postmodern, and culturally differentiated understanding of the subject' (Braidotti, 1994:4), offers a way out of the phallocentric vision of the subject. Braidotti (1994:8) sees in the nomadic state 'the potential for positive renaming, for opening up new possibilities for life and thought, especially for women.' As she herself said: 'I am interested only in systems of thought or conceptual frameworks that can help me think about change, transformation, living transitions. I want a creative, nonreactive project, emancipated from the oppressive force of the traditional theoretical approach. I see feminist theory as the site of such a transformation from sedentary logocentric thinking to nomadic creative thought' (Braidotti, 1994:30).

Throughout her argument, Braidotti is reworking Deleuze and Guattari's concept of nomadism. I would argue, however, that her reading can be seen as orientalist romanticizing of a minoritarian position, against which Giles Deleuze and Felix Guattari (1986:49) warn in *Nomadology*. The most significant difference between their 'nomad science' and Braidotti's 'nomadic feminism' is that, in Deleuze's terms, institutionalized feminism represented by Braidotti ceases to be 'nomad science.' Her figuration can be seen as 'cannibalistic' in that she uses the object (nomads, homeless, disabled) as a source of her metaphors for the feminine.[9] Braidotti speaks from the site of white, middle-class privilege, forgetting that those multilingual voices she hears while traversing as a nomad the streets and ghettoes of Australia, Europe, and the United States, often negotiate their languages from the position of powerlessness. Moreover, in her case the nomadic pace of travelling has become jet-fast also in the sense of becoming nomads of ideas: Braidotti incorporates allusions, references, aphoristic quotations, gliding through glittering surfaces of transnational, transdisciplinary discourse.

I find it troubling that Braidotti's eclectic feminism can be construed as a new commodity to be sold to women, one more product promising self-transformation and self-fulfilment, marketed as 'an object of desire for women,' 'a joyful, affirmative passion' liberating in women 'their desire for freedom, lightness, justice, and self-accomplishment' (Braidotti, 1994: 167). She is drawn to the style of thinking that opens up the possibility of 'living at a higher degree, a faster pace, a multidirectional manner' (Braidotti, 1994:102). Such rhetoric reminds one of the polyglotic jouissance and the ecstatic speed of Braidotti's own transnational nomadism. With her shift from 'the body' to 'bodies,' we are left with sexually differentiated postmodern subjectivities, multiple, subversive, parodic, transient, from which paradoxically all differences seem to have been evacuated.

Analysing how the motif of exile has been taken up by the writers discussed here, one can see that the 'male' modernist concept of exile as deterritorialization has been reterritorialized in feminist thought and given a new validation. There has been a notable change of attitude in feminist critics' thinking about exile. From reading women's exile as a stigma of marginality, they have moved on to embracing exile as a 'privileged' location from which to question the dominant order. At the same time, there has been a semantic shift among the meanings connoted by exile: what used to be associated with marginality and displacement is now more often linked to transnationality and nomadism. It shows that exile is no longer seen as a passive condition of being in the margin, being homeless, but it becomes a dynamic state suggesting movement across discursive and geographical spaces. In other words, the shift has occurred from an 'ontological' mode to an 'epistemological' stance, as reflection on how the modes of being an exile enables new ways of knowing the world. It might be a formula characterizing any social movement, provided that the next step would lead to the mode of acting. I would say that this change corresponds with the female exiles' redefinition of subjectivity and their recognized need of agency.

I have already mentioned the connection between exile and transnationality. I think it would be useful to make a distinction between transnationality and transnationalism, echoing the one between postmodernism and postmodernity (Grewal and Kaplan, 1994). The confusion between the two renders suspect the adjective 'transnational' used to define the feminist diasporic consciousness. The term 'transnational,' like 'global,' can be celebratory when applied to feminist consciousness; however, both terms can be perceived as threatening because of their relation to capitalism. In the context of global capitalist economy, transnationalism suggests itself in a rather sinister way as a neo-imperialist project. By contrast, transnationality would refer to postmodern cultural, political, economic, and demographic flows and can be seen as closer to the cosmopolitanism of exile. For example, Caren Kaplan (1992:116), discussing the terms 'global' and 'transnational' in conjunction with feminism, chooses the latter term 'to express the possibilities for links and affiliations, as well as differences, among women who inhabit different locations.' A transition from the local to the transnational feminist consciousness is also envisioned by Inderpal Grewal (1994:234), who frames her argument around the possibility of solving the paradoxes of identity politics: 'For some feminists of color, identity politics remains central, though the identity may be multiple. One may position oneself or be positioned in many different groups for different reasons. One may belong to different groups by gender, sexuality, class, race, ethnicity, and so on. There can be syncretic, "immigrant," cross-cultural, and plural subjectivities, which can enable a politics through positions that are coalitions, intransigent, in process, contradictory. Such identities are enabling because they provide a mobility in solidarity that leads to a transnational participation in understanding and opposing multiple and global oppressions operating upon them.'

So far theorists of transnational feminism have not moved very far beyond declarations of the need for alliances, coalitions, collaborative projects, community building, and cooperation. Our conference on 'Émigré Feminism' can actually be seen as one such collective project: a kind of practical workshop in transnational feminism. What took place there is part of a larger context of social practices and discourses of solidarity: listening, translation that goes beyond language, transformation of selves and ideas; in other words, learning how to sustain an ongoing conversation from within our differences. We may not yet know what kinds of understanding will emerge from meetings like this. But we would probably all agree on a few dos and don'ts of 'transnational feminist consciousness': it should not be hegemonic; it should not be a mere 'fashionable' stance; it should always be related to concrete bodies whose histories have been scripted differently by race, class, ethnicity, nationality, and sexuality. Finally, it should not be transformed into an absolutist position or freeze into a dogma, but should always try to cultivate the exilic and revolutionary spirit of feminist movement.

To conclude, I want to turn to Homi K. Bhabha (1994:269), who also postulates moving beyond the critique of the subject and concentrating instead on building collective identifications: 'What is theoretically innovative, and politically crucial, is the necessity of thinking beyond initial categories and initiatory subjects and focusing on those interstitial moments and processes that are produced in the articulation of "differences" ... It is at the level of interstices that the intersubjective and collective experiences of nationness, community interest, or cultural value are negotiated. How are subjects formed "in-between," or in-excess of, the sum of the "parts" of difference (usually intoned as race/class/gender etc.)? What collective identifications become possible in the overlapping, or displacing, of domains of difference?'

Inasmuch as exile, especially in the postcolonial framework, can be seen as a model of this interstitial space of interrogation of identity,[10] feminism can use a vantage point of exile also in the sense of shifting its positioning in relation to all kinds of borders, boundaries, and frames. But rather than embracing exile as a sign of marginalization or exteriority, feminists might discover that the transnational, interstitial space, the space 'in between' borders and identities, is a better place to think from. Then it will turn out that the questions posed by Homi Bhabha are the ones that transnational feminist critics will have to pursue if they want to explore further the mechanisms of coalition making and solidarity building.

NOTES

1  I am referring here to the well-known problematizing of 'home' in recent feminist discourse, especially in bell hooks (1990) and Caren Kaplan (1987). For a postcolonial perspective on 'home' and 'homelessness,' see Abdul JanMohamed (1992).
2  Peggy McIntosh (1990:4) makes a good point that, in the process of outgrowing what she calls 'single-system seeing,' no one person 'exists in complete fixity in a given phase.'
3  This leads to a larger problem of what happens when terms such as 'exile,' 'colonization,' 'nomadism,' or 'homelessness' are used as metaphors. Is it really

an insensitive or parasitic use? Censoring metaphors does not seem to be the best answer. Are we not assuming that all exile is painful, that we are better off than the nomads, that the homeless and the colonized are always less than subjects? Are we not imbuing metaphors with our emotions of guilt? Forbidding us the use of such metaphors might simply cause further 'disappearing' of those forms of experience from our view. Perhaps these figures of alterity can also be evoked out of identification, empathy, and love.

4 See, for example, Said (1993), Benhabib (1992), Braidotti (1994), Lugones (1987). Philosophical ideas of Deleuze and Guattari, as well as some concepts of Paul Virilio, have been greatly influential in developing the notion of nomadism.

5 Ironically, globalization has taken a slightly different turn in my native country, where the cultural, economic, and military pull of 'Europe' is felt more than ever. Poland has a long-standing Manichean tradition of identifying with Western as opposed to Eastern Europe.

6 Grinberg and Grinberg (1989:157) recognize the traumatic effects of exile in that 'it segregates important sectors of the population from national life.'

7 I find it rather ironic that Said, who pioneered the interrogation of orientalism in Western discourse, allows this bit of orientalist imagination to play in his figure of the nomad.

8 Her doctoral dissertation on James Joyce, published in 1969, focused on the motif of exile.

9 Kaplan (1987:191) criticizes Deleuze and Guattari for 'theoretical tourism' with respect to deterritorialized minorities, including nomads. I suspect, however, that at the time she wrote her article, Kaplan's knowledge of their *Thousand Plateaus* was second-hand at best, as can be judged from her bibliography.

10 Similarly to Homi K. Bhabha, Abdul R. JanMohamed (1992:97) in his discussion of exile explores the possibility of interstitial cultural space 'as a vantage point from which to define, implicitly or explicitly, other, utopian possibilities of group formation.'

REFERENCES

Bartkowski, Frances (1995) *Travelers, Immigrants, Inmates: Essays in Estrangement.* Minneapolis: University of Minnesota Press.

Benhabib, Seyla (1992) *Situating the Self: Gender, Community and Postmodernism in Contemporary Ethics.* New York and London: Routledge.

Bhabha, Homi K. (1994) 'Frontlines/Borderposts.' In Angelika Bammer (ed.), *Displacements: Cultural Identities in Question* 269–72. Bloomington: Indiana University Press.

Braidotti, Rosi (1994) *Nomadic Subjects: Embodiment and Sexual Difference in Contemporary Feminist Theory*. New York: Columbia University Press.

Cixous, Hélène (1980) 'The Laugh of the Medusa.' In Elaine Marks and Isabelle de Courtivron (eds.), *New French Feminisms: An Anthology*. Translated by Keith Cohen and Paula Cohen, 245–64. New York: Shocken.

– (1990) *Reading with Clarice Lispector*. Translated by Verena Andermatt Conley. Minneapolis: University of Minnesota Press.

– (1993) *Three Steps on the Ladder of Writing*. Translated by Sarah Cornell and Susan Sellers. New York: Columbia University Press.

Cixous, Hélène, with Catherine Clément (1986) *The Newly Born Woman*. Translated by Betsy Wing. Minneapolis: University of Minnesota Press.

Deleuze, Giles, and Felix Guattari (1986) *Nomadology: The War Machine*. Translated by Brian Massumi. New York: Semiotext(e).

Goldman, Anita Haya (1995) 'Comparative Identities: Exile in the Writings of Franz Fanon and W.E.B. du Bois.' In Mae Henderson (ed.), *Borders, Boundaries, and Frames: Cultural Criticism and Cultural Studies*. New York: Routledge.

Grewal, Inderpal (1994) 'Autobiographic Subjects and Diaspora Locations: *Meatless Days* and *Borderlands*.' In Inderpal Grewal and Caren Kaplan (eds.), *Scattered Hegemonies: Postmodernity and Transnational Feminist Practice*, 231–54. Minneapolis: University of Minnesota Press.

Grewal, Inderpal, and Caren Kaplan (eds.) (1994) *Scattered Hegemonies: Postmodernity and Transnational Feminist Practice*. Minneapolis: University of Minnesota Press.

Grinberg, Leon, and Rebecca Grinberg (1989) *Psychoanalytic Perspectives on Migration and Exile*. Translated by Nancy Festinger. New Haven: Yale University Press.

hooks, bell (1990) *Yearning: Race, Gender, and Cultural Politics*. Toronto: Between the Lines.

Irigaray, Luce (1985) *This Sex Which Is Not One*. Translated by C. Porter and C. Burke. Ithaca, NY: Cornell University Press.

– (1993) *Je, Tu, Nous: Toward a Culture of Difference*. Translated by Alison Martin. New York: Routledge.

JanMohamed, Abdul R. (1992) 'Worldiness-Without-World, Homelessness as Home: Toward a Definition of the Specular Border Intellectual.' In Michael Sprinker (ed.), *Edward Said: A Critical Reader*, 96–120. Oxford: Blackwell.

Kaplan, Caren (1987) 'Deterritorializations: The Rewriting of Home and Exile in Western Feminist Discourse.' *Cultural Critique* 6 (Spring): 187–98.

– (1992) 'Resisting Autobiography: Out-Law Genres and Transnational Feminist Subjects.' In Sidonie Smith and Julia Watson (eds.), *De/Colonizing the Subject: The Politics of Gender in Women's Autobiography*, 115–38. Minneapolis: University of Minnesota Press.

Kristeva, Julia (1991) *Strangers to Ourselves*. Translated by Leon Roudiez. New York: Columbia University Press.

Lugones, Maria (1987) 'Playfulness,'World-Travelling, and Loving Perception.' In D. Soyini Madison (ed.), *The Woman That I Am: The Literature and Culture of Contemporary Women of Color*, 626–38. New York: St Martin's Press.

McIntosh, Peggy (1990) *Interactive Phases of Curricular and Personal Re-Vision with Regard to Race*. Working Paper No. 219. Wellesley, Mass: Wellesley College, Center for Research on Women.

Meaney, Gerardine (1993) *(Un)like Subjects: Women, Theory, Fiction*. London: Routledge.

Said, Edward (1990) 'Reflections on Exile.' In Russel Fergusson, Martha Gever, Trinh T. Minh-Ha, and Cornel West (eds.), *Out There: Marginalization and Contemporary Culture*, 357–66. New York and London: New Museum of Contemporary Art and MIT Press.

– (1993) *Culture and Imperialism*. New York: Knopf.

Woolf, Virginia (1938, 1978) *Three Guineas*. New York: Penguin Books.

# 3

## *Afastada* Apprehensions:[1] The Politics of Post-exile Location and South Africa's Gendered Transition[2]

### LINZI MANICOM

In early 1993 I took up a short-term fellowship at the University of Natal, South Africa, my alma mater of some twenty years before, to investigate women and gender in the discourses of political transition. There was an exciting immediacy to this topic at that time of interregnum between the apartheid regime and the promised 'democratic, non-racial, non-sexist South Africa.' The multiparty negotiations were the focus of national political energies. The talks were charged with setting up a transitional government and procedures for overseeing the first democratic elections, in April 1994, and with establishing the basic ethico-political principles that would govern the post-apartheid political process. Women activists perceived and seized the moment as one of historic opportunity for asserting their claims and concerns within the procedures of formal democracy: they were demanding representation in the negotiating fora and on party electoral lists; they were debating the most women-friendly and effective forms of government; and they were pushing for the inclusion of the principle of gender equality as a fundamental right in the constitution.

The Women's National Coalition, a broad-spectrum coalition of some seventy women's organizations, had been convened and was in the process of gathering the views, demands, and mandates of women all over the country in order to produce the Women's Charter for Effective Equality (Women's National Coalition, 1994). This document (published a couple of months prior to the elections) was intended to orient policy in post-apartheid South Africa. 'Feminist politics' (a term not widely deployed at that time within the popular democratic movement, largely because of its perception as white, 'Western,' and middle class) had, during the anti-apartheid struggle, largely been subsumed or marginalized by the overarching project of national liberation. Now the prospect of a democratic transition opened up rhetorical space for 'women' as subjects of a state-oriented feminism couched in a discourse of equality and rights. My findings and interpretations of the instating of women in the transition – that is, the gendered constructions of women's citizenship that were being promulgated and regulated as official categories of ruling – were synthesized and presented at a seminar at the end of my stay (Manicom, 1993).

To call it a seminar from hell would be an exaggeration; besides, it was the coolness, rather than the heat, of the debate that seared the experience in my mind. While there were a few resounding notes, the presentation had clearly not struck a chord. I wanted and needed to understand why, for it was not for want of agonizing about the tone, pitch, and content of the recital, as I will go on to describe. Unfortunately, the deciphering of the lessons of this dissonant moment could not happen in situ, at the time. In mostly failing to make my analysis intelligible within local framings and formulations of issues, my talk yielded few openings for a dialogical exchange. Dissent and discontent were expressed rather obliquely, with intimations of political inappropriateness and inapposite theoretical discourse. As I returned to Canada a few days later, the process of learning from this encounter has been rather more conjectural, less mutual and collective, than I would have preferred. Nevertheless, the scant but pointed responses at the seminar compounded my own uncertainty about how effectively to mediate my multiple locations both in relation to the subject matter and to the context of presentation and reception. I was pushed and motivated to clarify the grounds and limits of my investigation and interpretation, to disclose and confront more openly the tensions and challenges of transnational, or more specifically, diasporic inquiry.

This essay documents and deliberates that exploration. I discuss the questions that were evoked and implicitly engaged in during the seminar – of deconstructive methodology, of travelling theory, of disjunctive sites of feminist theorizing and struggle. At the same time, I reflect on the influence and inscription of location(s) on feminist investigation by situating myself in relation to such work. The facets of my location and identities – as a formerly exiled, diasporic, and Canada-based, fortysomething, white South African feminist and political sociologist – were intricately implicated in the way I conceived and represented my analysis of feminism and democratic transition. 'Locations,' as Mary John (1996:104) has argued, 'play a constitutive role in structuring the frames of reference within which we develop our projects, a role that deserves to be more fully analyzed. This includes our institutional and disciplinary affiliation, the milieu of intellectual debate, the "background practices" and grain of everyday life, not all of which can be rendered explicit. Indeed, the very nature of ongoing intellectual production could be described as an interplay between what becomes a problem for thought and what is allowed to go without saying.' Most salient and expressive in this instance, often subsuming and suffusing the range of related positionalities, was the composite location of the diasporic subject, or as I will elaborate, the 'post-exile.'

In exploring these questions, I seek ways to practise feminist analysis that speaks to and mediates transnational and local concerns, in this case those related to gendered political democratization. At the same time, I am concerned to acknowledge and account for relations of hegemony and inequality in intellectual production, but in terms that are less simplistic and binary, and more nuanced and reflective of complex politics than those (like 'Western / Third World,' 'black/white') that have tended to prevail in the debates. In this, I subscribe to the project of John and others[3] of working to delineate 'an alternative internationalism for feminist theorists who wish to be equally accountable to unequal places' (John, 1996:4).

### *Afastada* Apprehensions

The preoccupations that prompt and shape this essay were crystallized by a few responses in the seminar discussion (which I return to below). Perhaps inadvertently, they pinpointed the nodes of my apprehension about this project.

I was circumspect about how my conceptual approach would transpose into the context of struggles to democratize – specifically to engender – the South African state. My research project and its questions had taken shape quite explicitly within the discursive parameters of a particular genre of feminist, poststructuralist political theory.[4] Having been studiously immersed for several years in this predominantly North American literature, I had a degree of investment in its capacities to elucidate.[5] Was I then merely 'reading' South Africa as text to inform metropolitan curiosities and nuance conceptual contests? Was I hearing the local formulations of the issues sufficiently in their own terms?

I had pondered these questions long before my research trip. Like all those whose formative experience jarred with the assumptions of theoretical inclusion, I read 'Western feminist theory' in and against national–

cultural sensibilities and filtered it through related political–intellectual concerns. What had sparked my critical attention in the earlier writings in feminist poststructuralism was in fact its apparent inadequacy to the challenge of theorizing gender in South Africa, where race was clearly so fundamental to the construction of political subjects and citizenship.

There were two central planks of this feminist poststructuralist critique of political theory: one was the disclosure of the liberal democratic construct of rights-bearing citizenship as being masculinist (for example, Pateman, 1989; Mouffe, 1992); the other involved debates about equality (assimilation to a male norm) and difference (the valorizing of an essential womanhood) as strategies for redressing the exclusion of women from the polity (for example, Scott, 1988; Bock and James, 1992). A problem in much of this work was its failure to theorize liberal democracy as (white) racialized and (hetero-)sexualized. This critique was then only starting to be addressed through, for example, arguments about the need to make visible the embodiedness of political subjects (Jones, 1990:790–7). Since then, of course, feminist political theory, particularly as developed by postcolonial theorists, has gone a long way in addressing this lacuna (for example, Mohanty et al., 1991; Alexander and Mohanty, 1997; Dhaliwal, 1996).

Feminist critiques of democratic citizenship rely centrally on an exposure of the gendering of public and private spheres. The starkly racialized, 'classed,' uneven, and shifting state regulation of public and private in South Africa provided the basis for a sound critique of the gender essentialist assumptions of this approach. The South African situation suggested an argument for taking into account race, ethnicity, nationality, and sexuality in a far more complex appreciation of notions of citizenship, equality, and gender. In other words, the 'reading' of gender and transition in South Africa through the lens of feminist poststructuralist political theory was not a one-way affair; that body of work was liable to significant challenge and revision in encounter with South African realities.

Another source of apprehension was my identity as a white South African feminist (and sometime) academic. There were several reasons for this; they did not include my feeling exposed or uncomfortable as a feminist on the university campus. Though feminist scholarship was (and remains) very much ghettoized within the South African academe, there was no overt antagonism to its precepts within the progressive academic community at the 'historically white university,' where I was based.[6] More problematic for me, in that context, were the identities of 'white,' on the one hand, and 'South African,' on the other.

Let me pre-empt the likely impression that the politics of reception of my presentation were framed in the binary, oppositional terms of 'white' versus 'Black' feminism. The dynamics of this particular seminar exchange were not explicitly racialized, although the context of feminist academic production in South Africa is, of course, profoundly structured by the politics of race. A conference that I had attended a couple of years previously on this same campus had erupted in a flood of charges, defences, and tears between women of different racial, sexual, professional, and political identities – combinations of these often elided – around issues of representation, appropriation, and exclusion. This milestone conference has been subject to substantial dissection; I will not recapitulate or extend it here.[7] The tenor, tensions, and themes of the struggles were very reminiscent of the politics of identity and difference that had been taking place in various arenas of Canadian feminist politics for several years. Besides the issues mentioned, in both contexts vital questions were being raised about the hegemony and universalization of constructs and issues of what was in fact a particular, though dominant, 'feminism.'

Though cognizant of how my 'whiteness' signified and delivered privilege in that context, I did not subscribe to the essentialist assumption that the theoretical validity or political implications of my analysis could be read off on the basis of my racial identity. My apprehensions here concerned the more intractable intrusions of ethnocentrism, logocentrism, and dominant knowledges in my methodological and conceptual approach. Was there a tension and hierarchy between 'Western' versus 'South African,' or 'imperial' versus 'indigenous' academic feminisms that I was blindly exacerbating? Were there inherent relations of inclusion and exclusion – along axes of gender, race, class, and culture – in the questions I was asking, the categories I was deploying? The reproduction of hegemonic stereotypical constructions of racial and gendered subjects and relations, as Mohanty (1991a) reminded us, are as much an issue for theorists who share social, cultural, and/or geographical space and time with their 'subjects' and subject matter, as for those who do not, that is, who are 'outsiders.' The scholarship of postcolonial and Western subjects, white and black, is imbued, in complex, differentiated ways, with varying tenets and traditions of 'metropolitan' theory which no claiming of authentic and native status (or, in my case, a fractured national identity) will automatically eradicate as an issue for reflection.

Wary and aware of how exacting were the issues of transnational and cross-cultural analysis, I had chosen, for this short-term project, to focus my analysis on official and state-oriented discourses of transition, rather than undertake an ethnography or a study of women's organizations. In these latter my lack of familiarity with the political culture would presumably be more of an impediment. (This choice was also in keeping with my ongoing project of a feminist analysis of 'the South African state' as a study of gendered discourses of ruling, the framing of which had been dictated by the strictures of exile and lack of access to primary research.) In this way I was hoping to avoid some of the methodological pitfalls of (mis)appropriating indigenous experience and (mis)representing subaltern voices.

The other identification causing me consternation was that of 'South African' feminist. On the few occasions of return visits to South Africa since 1990, when the transition process was initiated, I had come to see how contingent and anomalous was the national identity that I had assumed so unquestionably during my years in exile. Being a South African feminist on 'home ground' became uneasy and problematized. I was largely unrehearsed in the forms, conventions, and discourses of feminist politics as these were practised within the country's territorial borders. My changing identification as 'South African feminist' had occurred mainly outside of, though of course with reference to, South Africa, in several quite distinctive geopolitical and temporal contexts of exile, informed by various and changing feminist and nationalist discourses. Some quick examples: the texts for the women's sociology course I had taught to a 'whites only' university class in South Africa in the mid-1970s blatantly reflected narrow but dominant middle-class and Anglo-American constructions of gender and 'women's issues.' Within the South African refugee community in Tanzania in the late 1970s, the rhetorical space of feminism reached little beyond the drawing of attention to the specific, experiential problems for women refugees. Analysis of 'women under apartheid' was in terms of an arithmetic or pyramidal model of triple oppression, where women's oppression was attributed to the system of racial supremacy rather than masculine dominance. In the 1980s, my feminist identity was configured by solidarity activism in international non-governmental organizations (NGOs) and in the Canadian anti-apartheid movement.

In this latter site, despite discomfort, I generally felt constrained to represent 'South African women' in terms that called upon a strategic gender essentialism and a rather uncontradictory and unproblematic rendering of the political accomplishments of courageous, militant women. In the North American context, this positive and racially homogenizing representation had been a deliberate move to counter the liberal, colonialist depictions within anti-apartheid and even academic discourses. These portrayed 'women under apartheid' as downtrodden and pitiable victims. The contrasting, triumphalist, and undifferentiated subject of 'women's struggles' was appropriate for public consumption – and accommodating to media sound bytes – at that time when women's participation and gender issues were being overlooked and undervalued both within the South African democratic movement and among its overseas supporters. However, counterposing victor to victim neither challenged nor displaced the dichotomization of these one-dimensional and exoticized images. It worked merely to reproduce the 'othering' of women 'over there' in the South African townships and rural reserves.

My relationship to contemporary South African feminist politics was thus thoroughly forged in the conditions of exile. Moreover, my encounters with the developing strands of the national women's movement(s) had been filtered through a select set of conversations, meetings, interviews, popular media, published texts, and, prior to the political liberalization, co-exiles, friends, and contacts with those South Africans privileged to travel abroad.

Re-situated, if briefly, in South Africa, I supported and identified deeply with the feminist politics of the process I was investigating – for after all, the 'liberation of South African women,' however conceived, had been for many years, unabashedly 'my' struggle. Yet, here, now, I was definitively *afastada* – an outsider. I could not adopt the convention of address I had noticed among home-based South African activist–academics, which posited a collective and inclusive 'we' as subject. Befitting an emergent movement and a dynamic, consequential political moment, it was mildly exhortatory in tone and programmatic in content – along the lines of 'we need to do this, women must do that.'[8] I was not of that 'we,' and in any case, had been vehemently tutored out of its homogenizing assumptions by North American anti-racist feminist politics. In trying to find a 'voice,' a stance, from which to present my work in South Africa, I was struggling to shed habituated and anachronistic narratives of political struggle, striving to exorcise the inappropriate inflections of theory, and floundering about in search of a way to mediate and express the contradictions of this place of 'post-exile.' How was national identity or political orientation at issue in this academic research? From what political-intellectual and accountable space(s) should I venture critique? Where was my reference group and constituency located: among 'émigré feminist theorists' gathered in the cold climes of Canada or with colleagues and comrades in South Africa? On the face of it – in appearance, accent, and attire – I was 'a local girl,' at home in my home town, but in relation to my work and its theoretical and political referents, I was 'other.' Was there a way I could reconcile what John (1996) called these 'discrepant dislocations'?[9]

### Disparate Registers, Dissonant Responses

These apprehensions translated into the troubled, bifurcated form of my presentation and its incoherence. As a way of engaging my putative positioning as 'South African feminist' – within the confines of academic address – I talked first about 'women's politics.' I saw features of the actual form of the state-centric process of political transition as both enabling and constraining in relation to feminist politics. Although formal transition without doubt presented a propitious set of possibilities for the redress of women's disadvantage, it at the same time compelled a focus on centralized, national-level, and rather exclusive juridical politics. It actively shaped feminist agendas in the terms of constitutional debates and rights; it promoted and privileged those categories of women (white and black middle class) who were comfortable in the literacy and practices of liberal democratic citizenship; and it reassigned the energies of the limited number of women leaders to the negotiating front at the cost of their input in developing and consolidating the more popular and community-based women's movement.

This was not a particularly new or insightful analysis. What was significant in relation to the dilemmas of dislocation was my choosing to place the burden of explanation for the particular path being followed by dominant South African feminist politics on the structure and strictures of the transitional process. I eschewed the analysis of the political ideologies and choices of local feminist leaders as agents, though they should have been an integral part of the picture. From what I saw, political ideological differences among feminists and women activists (other than those that were presumed to derive from racial identity or party affiliation) tended not to be distinguished and debated as defining alternative feminisms and as offering potentially contending strategies.

I was, in fact, quite dismayed at the prevalence and prominence of state-oriented feminism of a liberal feminist politics that tended to be represented as synonoymous with 'women's position,' as if this was a unitary, and the only, feminist politics. Given the important and extensive gains that have been made for many women around the world by liberal demands for the extension of citizenship rights, it was difficult to know whether, when, and how to frame a critique of the limits of liberal feminism. I came to the issue jaundiced by the Canadian women's movement's experience of the costly, socially skewed, and inadequate realizations of the promises of the Charter of Rights and Freedoms. On the other hand, that same Canadian exposure had impressed upon me the ways in which a politics of rights and constitutionalism could be deployed, as evidenced by the successful claims of Native Canadian women for cultural and economic rights.

It must be emphasized, though, that there was a strong sector of South African women activists who were determined to find ways of transcending narrow interpretations of equality and rights. This tendency was reflected in parts of the Women's Charter (mentioned above), which claims the indivisibility of social, economic, political, and legal equality rights, thus refusing the confinement of rights to the merely and narrowly political. I must confess, too, to harbouring remnants of a revolutionary romanticism and a persistent attachment to an explicitly socialist and even populist feminist politics. These tendencies were discernible in the popular democratic movement of the 1980s, but their political distinctiveness appeared to be lost in the clamouring for 'women' to enter 'the transitional state' whose gendered and 'class-ed' forms remained largely untheorized.

Shifting, in the second part of the presentation, into a more abstract and esoteric gear, I considered the struggles to include women in the transitional process in terms of two issues within feminist poststructuralism: the binarism and essentialism inherent in notions of gender equality and the fixing of ahistorical and essentialist constructs of women's identity in the attribution of 'women's rights.' Clearly both the discourses and enactment of 'equality' and 'rights' within the post-apartheid constitution and state were crucial and inevitable. Nevertheless, the political-discursive limitations and disciplinary constraints of those constructs had also to be recognized and openly contested, I argued. The construction of 'gender' and 'women' based solely on sex difference within the official discourse of formal transition – the latter including constitutional language, affirmative action programs, quotas of representation, and 'women's machinery' in government – had the effect of suppressing race and class differences within its terms and thus occluding them from the implications of political commitments to, and claims for, equality and redistribution.

There was at hand an example that illustrated the political dangers of conceiving gender in abstraction from race and class and the need to contest the fixities of juridical language. The then South African government (that is, the outgoing apartheid regime) had recently promulgated a set of bills which (among other things) repealed all legislation discriminating against women and proposed equal opportunity measures. The liberal 'equality feminism' with its binary, men–women logic that informed this legislation made possible the legislation of 'gender equality,' even while the majority of South African women were simultaneously excluded from the vote – that most minimal tenet of democracy!

As I mentioned earlier, the seminar underscored the challenges of mediating disparate locations of feminist analysis. At play was a subtle positioning of participants along the familiar axes of tension, such as activist–academic, political–theoretical, insider–outsider, indigenous–foreign, with their various implied weightings of expertise, authority, and authenticity. Certainly the different facets of my location *vis-à-vis* the topic cut across and militated against these binary framings of investigative subjectivity, and this was likely the case for many present. It suggests the general inadequacy of such dichotomizations in understanding the transnational production of knowledge.

Then came discussion. One response queried my interrogation of the categories of 'women' and 'gender' with the riposte: 'I know a woman when I see one!' and 'How is this useful?' This reaction among feminists to the deconstruction of categories of gender representation and identity reflects what Ella Shohat (1995:167) called the 'paradoxical situation in which theory deconstructs totalising myths while activism nourishes them.' South African feminists, too, would seem to have a particularly justifiable antagonism towards the deconstruction of women as the subject of feminism at this moment in (their) history when, within state discourses, women were (finally) becoming citizen-subjects in contrast to being posited as the targets of population programs, the culpable mothers of rebellious youth, or the cheaper workers of tax-exempted industrial zones. Within nationalist discourses, women were making inroads as political subjects other than as mothers, nationalist symbols, and peacemakers. The tension surrounding the choice of an analytical point of departure – whether women or women's politics, or the deconstruction of such categories – is not unique to such historically charged moments. The question raised of the analytical purchase and political utility of deconstruction as methodology is a critical one, and I return to it subsequently.

Another comment criticized my reference to Anglo-American feminist

literature on liberal democratic jurisprudence because it seemed to presume a local familiarity with the debates. There was also a suggestion that
a more indigenized theoretical approach could have been used. The
irony is that I had been exposed to the most sophisticated deployment of
those ideas while actually in South Africa. They were the currency of
debates among the feminist lawyers and political scientists who were then
playing so critical a role in advising and formulating women's interventions in the negotiation process. There had been, in that period, a flurry
of consultations between local advisers and women political leaders and
state feminists and jurisprudential experts from (significantly) Canada
and other northern democracies. These consultations were the medium
for transnational flows of applied feminist theory. What this question
emphasized for me, however, was the need for more appreciation of the
way in which theory travels (Said, 1983). By this I mean a better understanding of what varieties of metropolitan theory find their way to which
of the different academic and political sites, who takes them up, and
to what extent and in what ways are they accommodated and/or
indigenized.

A third intervention raised the difficult issue of how to apprehend different women's struggles in different parts of the world. I was asked my
prognosis – whether optimistic or pessimistic – of 'the future for South
African women.' I trotted out something along the lines of that tired old
idiom of gaps and tension between rhetoric and reality: this had served
for solidarity speeches, but had little to contribute to analysis. An
approach to theorizing women's struggles that was at that time prevalent
in South Africa (as elsewhere) drew on the distinction between practical
women's needs and strategic gender interests, as first proposed by Maxine Molyneux (1985a). The tendency to understand these constructs in
hierarchical terms, and the assumptions involved in classifying struggles
as either practical or strategic, devalued this framework in my assessment
(Walters and Manicom, 1996:13). The seminar question, however, or
rather its implicit subquestions – the future for which women? according
to what political vision? in which site and with what priorities? – underscored for me the acute need for different, new conceptual modalities for
understanding feminism(s) transnationally.

I will revisit these issues in the conclusion. The point here is that these
dilemmas, questions, and responses signify and connect with discussions
in the contemporary politics of location. With the development of postcolonial and postmodern feminist scholarship in recent decades, there
has been increasing challenge to and refinement of conceptualization

and practice of the cross-border production of knowledge about women (where borders may be cultural, geopolitical, temporal, or discursive). The politics of location has itself become a more complex and contested terrain: Chandra Mohanty (1992:74) defined it as 'the historical, geo-graphical, cultural, psychic and imaginative boundaries which provide the ground for political definition and redefinition,' while Rosi Braidotti (1994:21) talked of the 'practice of dialogue among many different female embodied genealogies.' In problematizing not just what is said, but who gets to say, who is embraced by the saying subject, who is being addressed, how and where (Radhakrishnan, 1996:147; Mani, 1990), the politics of location invites the integration of a more explicit methodologi-cal and political self-reflexivity in social inquiry. In the context of that seminar, it was my subjectivity as sojourning former exile that traversed the different aspects of my apprehension. I now turn to reflect more on that issue.

## Problematizing Post-exile

With view to thinking through the implications of my subjectivity and location in relation to the analysis of gender and political transition in South Africa, and building on the lessons of the seminar, I propose the construct of 'post-exile.' I do so with a degree of irony and somewhat as a conceit, for I have significant reservations about both 'post' and 'exile.' Exploring these in engagement with prevailing theoretical and figurative deployments of both these terms will define and delimit the concept in a way that yields potentially useful orientations in transnational feminist analysis.

First, concerning the prefix 'post.' I share, with others, a complaint about 'the ritualist ubiquity of post-' (McClintock, 1995:10), seeing it as oversubscribed and overdetermined within contemporary theoretical dis-course. Yet arguably the currency of 'post' reflects its effective and suc-cinct encapsulation of a relationship that both embraces and moves beyond its referent. But in order to do so, 'post' must be disentangled from a one-dimensional and one-directional conception of history and time (Ahmad, 1995; Radhakrishnan, 1996). The 'post' in post-exile does implicate a concrete historical moment, that is, the conversion from a state of formal exile (defined in narrow, political, even juridical terms) to the more amorphous positionality of post-exile. However, the meaning of 'post' that I want to mobilize here is that which emphasizes the inextrica-ble presence of the past, in this case, the continuities of the conventions and constraints of exilic subjectivity, even after the eradication of its defining conditions. There is another connotation of 'post' circulating within postcolonial theory that I invoke here, too. This is the normative project of finding an intellectual modality – always contingent and subject to revision – that contends with, and aims to transcend, while at the same time invoking the ground of, in this case, the conditions of exile.

The historic shift that inaugurates post-exile (that is, the removal of sanctions or persecution linked with the return 'home') is clearly pivotal, precipitating for exiles a 'dilemma of return.' Both post-exiles and 'returnees' are indelibly inscribed by the exilic experience; but distinguishing them are the different places and paths of their realignments in relation to the designations of 'home.' For returnees, this dilemma, while not necessarily resolved, is enacted bodily in their geographical resettlement back home. For post-exiles, 'return' takes the form of an obligatory remaking of self and identity, a process both banal and profound, not dramatic as was the entry into exile. National identity and, significantly here, the terms of political–scholarly engagement must be renegotiated and reconstructed.

Post-exile can be provisionally defined, then, as a historically produced, contingent identity or location that is an effect of the continuing but constantly re-narrated bearing of a previous political exile on intellectual perspectives, specifically on the home country. In my own case, the unbanning of prohibited organizations in South Africa rendered me, technically, no longer an exile.[10] That change in political–legal status did not so much remove the sway of exile over my subjectivity and scholarship, I am suggesting, as reconfigure it.

Like 'exile,' 'migrant,' 'postcolonial,' and other terms of historical, geographical, and metaphorical dislocation, post-exile may refer not just to the people or the subjects thus defined or identified, but also to the temporal and spatial conditions, the subjectivities, sensibilities, and political relations inferred and embraced by the construct, aspects which I unpack a little, below.

But why problematize post-exile at all? Why not build on the existing conceptualizations of other relevant identities or standpoint locations such as feminist, or post-colonial, for example? There are three broad rationales; they reflect my qualms and quarrels with forms of representations of exile (and by extension post/exile) as a preferred and pristine site for intellectual production.

The first set addresses discourses of social theory in which the theme of exile is both pervasive and prominent. In postmodern and postcolonial currents, exile bears conceptual affinity with the notions of displacement – deracination, migration, nomadism – that abound. These concepts of geographical and cultural dislocation mirror the massive population movements, globalized and fragmented forms of production, the disjunctures between place and identity characteristic of our era. In feminist discourses, exile tends to take on more intrapsychic hues, tracing the constitutive subjective experience of banishment, unbelonging, and marginalization from dominant patriarchal institutions and cultures. Within these fields of intellectual production exile is represented ambivalently. On the one hand, it is drenched in pathos, often with implicit appeal to the moral and victimist claims that currently adhere to notions of marginality and exclusion. On the other hand, exile is romanticized, iconized, and celebrated as a preferred postmodern subjectivity.

These representations jar with my experiences of politically defined exile. The correlative and multiple 'exiles' – gendered and geopolitical – which I, like most exiles live(d), do not allow for the assumed coherence and clarity of the singular position of the exilic or outcast subject. Exile tends rather to be articulated and complicated along different axes, underwritten by varying degrees of choice and consequence. In my case, for example, I was white within a black-majority political movement, socialist within a united-front nationalist politics, and feminist within patriarchal political cultures. Layers of discursive displacement made routine a self-conscious and strategic shuttling between subject positions and voices.

Equally, the unitary representation of exile as outsider fails to give space to the simultaneous belongings, identifications, and insider places that coexist and may mediate exile's circumstances. For example, in contemporary North America, being ethnically white, Anglophone, and culturally middle class makes for points of connection and privilege that redefine and mitigate some of exile's deprivations. From the perspective of the potential of exilic subjectivity in cross-cultural analysis, too much is lost when these ranging disparities are read by the same gauge of 'exile.'

Contradictorily, even as I say this, fully recognizing and acknowledging the different registers, various forms, and inflections of 'exile,' in terms of affect, personal narrative, and self-formation, it is the identity of political exile (and now post-exile) that has prevailed across many fronts of my life. More pertinently here, and as illustrated above, exile has significantly influenced and motivated the focus of my scholarship, infusing the framing of my questions, and sustaining the projection of a putative national intellectual constituency. Some of the durability and intrusiveness of this identification is attributable to the life-defining and life-deferring 'pathology' of political exile, 'one of the saddest fates' (Said, 1994:47). It must also be understood as part of the inexorable pull of the national 'imagined community' (Anderson, 1983). The symbolic profile of South Africa's anti-apartheid struggle within these times of global racism also worked to reproduce and reconfirm an exile identity, as did living in contemporary Canada's 'multicultural' society that rewards display of benign cultural difference, while downplaying the more materially consequential ones of class and race.

## Metaphoric Exile

If enduring the pain of 'real' prohibitions on going 'home' has made me prickly about some of the abstracted and allegorical appropriations of exile, its persistent configuration of my personal, political, and professional life – and that of all the exiles I know, from many regimes and regions – both explains and confirms why exile is such a powerful and much-wielded metaphor. More reason why exile, like all metaphors and figurations, should be scrutinized for its illicit exclusions and promotions.[11] As an unsituated abstraction, it is susceptible to the effects of its suppressed and unmarked elements, and liable to complicity in reproducing dominant representations.

Take the well-ensconced metaphor of exile within feminist writing, referred to previously. As Rosi Braidotti (1994:21) noted, 'The identification of female identity with a sort of planetary exile has since become a *topos* of feminist studies.' From my prejudiced perspective, the conditions of gendered exclusion, on the one hand, and political exile, on the other, diverge too profoundly to make this analogical extension a valid or elucidating one. Braidotti (1994:21) and John (1996:92) rightly, I argue, question the ethnocentric exclusions and assumptions inferred in this metaphorical association. As John (1996:92) put it: 'The figure of exile works by relating the more literal image and knowledge of exiles who have had to leave the second and third worlds and are now in the West, on the one hand, with the relations of otherness that a first-world woman – usually white – experiences from her home, language and sexuality, on the other. The very different and discrepant locations in each case are once again papered over, as are possible ways of articulating the kinds of expatriation at work for women 'at home' outside the West.'

What of the other unmarked sociological and political relations of exile – and potentially, by extension post-exile – that are clandestinely invoked in its metaphorical use? Though the bulk of the substantial literature on exile is to be found in literary criticism and French poststructural feminism, a turn to critical sociological and cultural studies provides the basis for the deconstruction of the category of exile, revealing its racialized and class connotations, along with its implicitly gendered construction (Braidotti, 1994; Kaplan, 1994; Wolff, 1995a).[12] Stark stereotypes illustrate the point made by others (Said 1994, 1996; McCarthy, 1994): within the dominant social imaginary, the contemporary exile figure is singular, masculine, middle class, and prone to intellectuality and creativity. Women exiles, themselves anomalous, are cast as wives with children who have faithfully followed the exile's fate. Such popular representations are backed by official state practices: laws of asylum have only recently started recognizing individual women as political dissidents and refugees in their own right, and the predominant public culture of political opposition remains, in most countries, overwhelmingly masculine. Even more recently and still rarely have women been recognized as refugees on the basis of gender oppression and persecution, a historical development that will, over time, hopefully effect a gendered reconfiguration of the constructs of exile and politics.

The racialization of exile is blatant. Nevertheless, the actual race or ethnicity associated with exile (and, usually, part of what distinguishes exile from refugee) can only be discerned historically. The mass dislocations of peoples who cross regional and national borders are overwhelmingly concentrated among the poor in Third World nations, and they are generally identified as refugees. A South African example serves to illustrate: the young Black men and women of Soweto and other townships who fled South Africa in the mid-to-late 1970s were perceived and treated as refugees, sojourning mainly in neighbouring Southern African countries. The 'whites' (myself included) who left at the same time became exiles, generally with the contacts and resources to claim resident status within other (mostly North Atlantic) countries.

What these staccato comments imply is that the metaphorical figure or condition of exile cannot be innocent of these representations of difference that lurk within the prevailing imaginaries. While I am clearly privileging political exile as the basis for critique of the metaphor of exile, I do not suggest its total abandonment. Rather, I argue for its deconstruction and reflective application in ways that expose and displace, rather than reproduce uncritically the latent politics of representation and exclusion. Publicizing the material conditions and narratives of specifically Third World, subaltern, and women exiles and refugees will help to disrupt the metaphorical associations of exile and to recast them in positive, embodied, historical terms.

## Exilic Vantage Points

This brings me to the second motivation for elaborating a notion of post-exile, namely, a critique of the representation of exile as a particular epistemic vantage point, or, even more strongly, advantage. This contrasts strongly with my own experience, described above, of the inhibitions, dilemmas, and dissonance that post/exile introduced into my work on South Africa.

The promotion of exile as a privileged standpoint is based on the claim that a position 'elsewhere,' excluded from the determinations of dominant knowledges, lends a less invested, more panoramic, and critical perspective which works to disrupt and de-authorize the hegemonic viewpoint. This kind of approach is also pursued through elaborations of positive 'theoretical figurations' (Braidotti, 1994) such as those of nomadic, hybrid, or subaltern subjects. These are understood as made possible by, and as appropriate to, postmodernity.[13] Here I can only outline debates about preferred standpoints and subjectivities for the production of counter-hegemonic knowledge (that which is currently and variously equated with, for example, feminist, non-heterosexual, indigenous, or subaltern knowledges). These have exercised feminist, 'queer,' and postcolonial theorists over the past couple of decades. One of the problems raised is how the boundaries are drawn that designate in or out, marginal or exile status. As suggested above, the binarism and homogenizing of both exile and its 'other' (home, insiders, or indigens) as knowing subjects or epistemic sites occlude and deny the significance of cross-cutting identities or relations of power in the production of knowledge. There is, too, an unwarranted assumption that the exile experience and related knowledge will remain authentic, unaffected, and untainted by the dominant discourses.

Such critiques suggest the need to move out of the language of epistemology and into that of sensibilities and predispositions. The relevant question here then becomes: are there any partial, distinctive ways of knowing that can be seen as characteristic of the condition or subjectivity of feminist post-exile? Consider Said's (1994) depiction of the intellectual propensities of the apparently gender-neutral 'exile intellectual' as an example. The deep sense of historicity that he attributes to this figure along with an understanding of situations as contingent and transformable, a constant counterposing of ideas with others so that both can be seen anew, and the tendency to be intellectually risky and innovative, are capacities that are not unique to exiles. They are arguably characteristic of politically oriented intellectuals generally. They may apply in particular to those who have experienced the discrepancies and mandatory self-reflexivity that comes from cross-cultural adaptation. Extrapolating Said's notion, a feminist exile would blend into these qualities an appreciation of the varying and locally distinctive representations of women across and within different national and transnational feminist discourses.

But Said, here, was representing the optimal features of post/exilic investigative subjectivity. That same location of exile can produce decidedly less generative and less constructive academic propensities. The adulatory portrayals of exilic intellectual practice tend to suppress its negative and deleterious effects. What must also be sketched into the picture (and here again I draw on experience) are the consequences and effects of separation from the content, context, community, and constituency that animate and provide a touchstone for intellectual work. They include scholarly debilitation, a tendency to excessive theorization, and a stultifying, misplaced quest for 'relevance.' There is a certain freedom in being physically *afastada*, out of reach of the drumming and demanding exigencies of an intense political situation and out of range of what can sometimes be parochial preoccupations and concentric theorizing. But on the other side of this is the severance from the immediate terms, textures, and discourses of political–intellectual debate and the distortions that derive from the intrinsically politicized subjectivity of post/exile. Here I am thinking of the constraints of nostalgic party-political loyalties which might, even within a strictly academic format, insidiously translate into blunted (though possibly judicious) analyses of home-country political developments.

I would argue, in fact, that lack of fluency in local idioms of political argument, unfamiliarity with prevailing thematics of analysis, and the lack of knowledge of the genealogies of key concepts within home-country bodies of thought are critical conditions of possibility in post-exile intellectual production. For it is in these spaces of deficiency that dissonances in understandings and discrepancies in conceptual valences arise. The challenge lies in how to perceive and work constructively with the misalignments that result.

As I discovered in the process of investigating gender and transition in South Africa from a post-exile perspective, when apprehended as signalling the boundaries of shared assumptions and as sites of contested meaning, the dissonances can be instructive in calling attention to those places where conceptual explication and deeper reflection on the politics of location is required. My experience confirmed John's (1996:53) point about 'the analytical and political productivity of discrepancies rather than congruencies between colonial or postcolonial concerns and those of the contemporary West.'

**The Salience of Identity?**

The third proviso in the exploration of a construct of post-exile concerns the way in which identity is conceived and deployed in the legitimation of different analytical perspectives. I have argued above against making knowledge claims on the basis of a single-attribute and essentialist identity. But even when understood as a historically generated and contingent identity, post-exile remains susceptible to that convention within the politics of difference in which a slew of social markers of personal identity are declared in prefacing a public intervention. The intention of these self-referencing identities is to indicate awareness of the partiality of one's views and thus presumably vindicate, and absolve oneself of responsibility for particularistic content. Like others (Chow, 1993; Suleri, 1995), I see this confessional mode as playing on a 'political moralism' (Brown, 1995), and as deeply depoliticizing, for it tends to substitute for actual analysis of the multifaceted and unequal power relations that are indexed by race, class, ethnicity, exile, and the like.[14] It reveals little, for it fails to demonstrate the actual salience, relevance, and impact of any particular identity, or facet thereof, on the production of specific knowledge.

The conditions of feminist post-exile, in many ways, tend to foster a self-reflexivity and forge a determinant subjectivity in intellectual work. But this does not happen in abstraction; the identification as post-exile and the sensibilities it engenders are relational. There are clearly some areas of social inquiry where one's identity (or more peripherally, one's biographical footnote) as an exile has no particular or consequential bearing. There are others where it is critically informative and inextricably implicated in the modalities of analysis and interpretation. With the identity of post-exile historically defined by, and narratively imbricated in the terms of political transition in the home country, the diasporic investigation of gender and democratization falls within the latter.

If, as I have been arguing, feminist post-exile can be mobilized metaphorically only in the most vigilant and historically referenced way, can boast no epistemic bonus other than a sensibility which is as liable to insularity as cosmopolitanism, and can claim no determinate and fixed identity, is there any particular conceptual mileage or merit to the notion?

## From Post-exile to Transnational Location

The construct of post-exile can be usefully recuperated when situated within the framework of the politics of location. Location encompasses a broad, composite set of relations, issues, and orientations that inform transnational feminist intellectual practice. These include the interrogation of forms of symbolic representation of social relations; the recognition of uneven and unequal production and flows of feminist social theory; and a questioning and delineation of the effective links between location, modalities of inquiry, investigative subjectivity, and identity. Thus, post-exile should be conceived as a contingent and relational identity within the politics of transnational location, embodied in historical subjects, and embedded in sociopolitical contexts, rather than narrowly affixed to a national politics. Post-exile can edge open different questions and angles, and it can induce distinctive perspectives in transnational feminist inquiry.

The overriding lesson of the seminar encounter in South Africa was the need to make transparent, and to set out for critical and collective consideration, the lineages of theoretical preoccupations and the perceptions of anomaly and difference that excited questioning and pertinent reflections on subject position. I am not suggesting a painstaking and ponderous cartography that overwhelms content, but rather a brief tracing of location in relation to the subject matter. This is at one level a banal point about delivery style. I am suggesting it more as a methodological injunction, not only in speaking and writing, but in formulating the project, interpreting the findings, and developing the analysis..

Such sketching will help to establish conditions for both accountability and solidarity, those key watchwords in discussion of 'working across difference' and transnational feminism. Yeatman (1994:24, 23) has suggested that accountability requires the development of strategies of address that would 'evoke or connect up with publics for whom [her] work may be relevant,' and the promotion of 'the dialogical, rhetorical practices which open up in any particular discursive terrain.' For solidarity to be more than a declaration or gesture, there needs to be a spelling out of the multiple relations of location that might provide a basis for – or alternatively impede – transnational comparative or correlative analysis.

The notion of 'cohort' is useful in elaborating post-exile feminism in terms of transnational location. Katie King (1994) has developed this concept to refer to generational groupings of feminists characterized by their investments in particular political issues and related theoretical questions. In other words, the designation as cohort refers not just to a generation or its historical conjuncture, but also the distinctive political and theoretical discourses that frame analysis. Conceiving contemporary post-exile feminists as a cohort, the following features are relevant. One is a formative involvement in political opposition to previously authoritarian regimes that, as of recent years, have been undergoing political transition and liberalization, along with forms of accommodation to the global capitalist market. What are the gender implications of forms of democratization within the homeland? Under this rubric, the main objectives of critical analysis are the gendering of states, the organization of women in civil society, and shifting representations of gender in the transition process. How are those constructions shaped, historically and contextually, by familial, religious, cultural, class, ethnic, and national relations and identities (West, 1992), and how does this inform and challenge local and transnational understandings of feminism and of democracy?

The broad ideological and political conjuncture of the current cohort of post-exiles equally suggests its place on the cusp of, and embracing, significant changes and transitions. The de-authorization of 'the woman question' approach to feminist politics that was influential in anti-imperialist national movements and prevailed in former communist countries represents a redrawing of the ideological landscape for post-exiles.[15] Ascendant now in the global arena is a human rights feminism. While appeal to rights has provided the moral sanction for vital struggles for survival and dignity for women around the world, the hegemonic status and, indeed, the logic of rights discourse within countries undergoing political transition has had other, more ambiguous effects. There is a blurring and obfuscation of ideological and political differences among feminists in democratic transitions; it has become harder to express and distinguish between transformatory positions and more accommodatory and reformist ones. The labels that previously distinguished the orientations of feminist politics – Marxist, socialist, liberal, radical – have lost their social points of reference. Key terms of feminist struggle – like empowerment, rights, even democracy – appear within and across widely divergent political and ideological frameworks. The affinity between feminist strategies for women's empowerment within civil society and neoliberalism's devolution of responsibility for women's well-being from state to market is being revealed.[16] With rights claims being made on the basis of politicized identities, political difference is now most often assumed and expressed as – and even reduced to – difference in identity. The politics of difference and rights importantly engages with questions of national and ethnic identity, culture, tradition, and religion which were obscured within rigid socialist discourse and ethnocentric feminism. On the other hand, as Nancy Fraser (1995) pointed out, the questions of political economy and the redistribution of resources, critical to a broad and gendered understanding of democracy, have tended to be lost in struggles over recognition and identity.

Along with the legacy of notions of liberation, the predominance of rights talk, and the currency of the politics of difference, there are other political–intellectual tendencies reflected in the popular organization of women in transitional countries. These retain, as points of departure, visions of popular power and women's and men's material needs. The 'empowerment approach,' which is articulated by mainly Third World feminist intellectuals (Sen and Grown, 1987), has been influential within poorer and developing communities in both the North and South. Then there is the body of work on transnational feminist practice that has been referred to above (Mohanty, 1991b; Grewal and Kaplan, 1994).[17] Not surprisingly, in the absence of clearly articulated and widely resonant ideological divisions within feminism, attempts to assert a more rigorous, defined, and radical transnational feminist politics appear to be trapped in the language of opposition. Jacqui Alexander and Chandra Mohanty (1997), for example, argue for an 'anticapitalist,' 'decolonizing,' 'denationalizing,' 'anti-racist' feminism, though through these oppositional attitudes they do elaborate a positive notion of 'feminist democracy.'

These features of the current cohort of feminist post-exiles depicted here in the broadest brushstrokes, are, I am suggesting, loosely transnational but not transhistorical. The bases of solidarity, shared projects, points of mutual reference, commonalities, and differences that emerged in discussion in the 'Émigré Feminism' conference that generated this volume, for instance, can arguably be replicated in other gatherings of contemporary émigrés and exiles. However, there would not be the same resonance with a different historical cohort of exiles and émigrés, their sensibilities and politics having been shaped by different world events and frameworks of understanding.

**Post-exile Sensibilities**

There are two further facets of post-exile location that illuminate the sensibilities brought to bear in intellectual work. The first is also characteristic of other *afastada* positionalities, but it is perhaps more intensely etched in post-exile. It pivots on the notion of what Radhakrishnan (1996:xxii) called 'doubleness.' Doubleness expresses itself in a duality of perspective, looking forward and back, in time and place. In a perceptive article on South African 'returnees,' Nixon (1995:163) referred to 'the exiles' Janus-faced vision.' He saw this bi-directional vision and the cultural 'misfit' status of exiles as a potential symbolic resource in rebuilding South Africa to 'accommodate those vast tracts of culture that have been sidelined, trivialized, or mutilated by the dictates of the apartheid/antiapartheid agon ...'

That doubleness is often traced as an analytical and political strategy, characteristic of certain feminist, postcolonial, and (as demonstrated in this essay) post-exile approaches. There is recognition of the representations and assertions of ethnic, national, gender, and exile identities, but simultaneously there is an interrogation of the exclusions, differences, and relations of power that contest and threaten to fragment those entities. As Braidotti (1994:157) argued in relation to contemporary feminism, 'Feminism is based on the very notion of female identity, which it is historically bound to criticize. Feminist thought rests on a concept that calls for deconstruction and de-essentialization in all of its aspects.'

The very term 'post-exile' flags double tendencies. Exile, like feminism, is embedded within the project of modernity, imbued with notions of progress and emancipation, of futures and reconciliations. Both are being reinscribed by the conditions and discourses of postmodernity. Though there is a strategic politics – as well as an energy and a nostalgia – in working with a clear sense of exile or woman as the subjects of liberation, the complex, cross-hatched identities and relations of power and hierarchy undermine its longer term validity. 'Post' captures the messier, less scripted, non-teleological politics of the present – be it post-apartheid, postcommunism, or a feminism that must yield its unitary subject in recognition of the multiple and often more politically mobilizing identifications of race, nationality, ethnicity, sexuality, and class.

How does the framework of a politics of location in transnational feminist inquiry recast the issues of the post-exile 'dilemma of return'? I portrayed this earlier as the challenge of relocation that is posed for exiles by the fact of political transition. It involves a reorientation or renegotiation of one's physical, emotional, political, and intellectual (perceptual and conceptual) relationship to the home nation and its emergent national and democratic project.

One possibility is to remain *afastada*, clinging sentimentally and anachronistically to the place of exile. This stance constitutes a dislocation rather than relocation, for there is an erosion of the ground upon which the 'situated knowledge' (Haraway, 1988) of exile was previously based and a dissipation of intellectual constituency. Moreover, exile is not merely a displacement from the home country, nor a vacuous conceptual site. It is/was inevitably filled with the political concerns and theoretical relevancies of local affiliations. In terms of analysing and interpreting political processes 'at home,' this unadjusted disposition tends to result in a rather confused and contradictory sense of intellectual constituency, an eclectic shuffling between different political–intellectual projects and theoretical problematics. This was well illustrated in the disjunctive approach in my seminar presentation.

An alternative negotiation of 'return' denotes post-exile as a location within a transnational setting. This position entails the acknowledgment of multiple locations and cross-cutting orientations in social investigation of the home country. It involves taking responsibility for and working with the sometimes contending frames of reference and discordant notes of interpretation. At best, new perspectives and insights are introduced or sparked by aspects of the multi positionality of post-exile. Certainly the political history that is tied to the experience of exile will infect the kinds of questions asked by post-exile scholars. The possibility of certain 'traditional' political ideals and visions will be held up for comparative examination with the complex, current realities, reminding of forgotten or unmined reefs of the national imaginary. Post-exile's double vision will draw connections between the politics of the places of home and residence and hold in critical tension the layered relationship between 'global' and 'local.'

To sum up, as a normative project of feminist transnational intellectual work, post-exile attempts to take account of, and be accountable to, multiple, correlative, and sometimes contending locations.

**In Conclusion: Responses Revisited**

Having discussed some of the issues of post-exile and the politics of location and transnational feminist investigation, let me revisit the debates in the seminar in South Africa. 'Debates' is perhaps not the appropriate term, since they were rather implicit and inferred points of methodological and conceptual misalignment, contention, and sometimes, more strongly, disagreement. As I suggested earlier, the most notable interventions can be seen (taking some licence with extrapolation) as invoking and highlighting some key themes in transnational feminist analysis. These were, first, the methodological sensibility and sensitivity to discrepant conceptual categories and theoretical formulations across different sites of feminist intellectual production, trans- and intra-nationally; second, the uncovering and critique of the uneven travelling and coalescing of hegemonic and indigenous theory; and third, the recognition and conceptualization of differently located, historically-constructed feminist issues, strategies, and struggles. What conclusions and directions are suggested?

First, the political and analytical value of a poststructuralist approach was queried. In my home-town seminar in 1993 the 'usefulness' of deconstructing categories of 'women' and 'gender' at that moment of political transition was disputed. Two years later, in the Canadian seminar where a similar analysis was presented, there was a variant of this same issue. It was expressed from a position of solidarity with the project, and from an identification with its dilemmas: how, it was asked, did one reconcile abstract and abstruse categorical deconstruction with politically engaged inquiry and intervention?

My subsequent reflection prodded by these questions has in fact buttressed my sense of the analytical and interpretive value of a 'deconstructive attitude,' not necessarily in all facets of social inquiry, but particularly and productively in such historical moments as the one that I was investigating. For, as I see it, what was going on at that time was an intense, concentrated, contested, and transparent discursive production of state or ruling categories of women and gender in the politics of transition. South African politicians, and women and men activists, were engaged precisely and very perceptibly in the construction and deconstruction of rights-bearing, national, cultural, gendered political subjects. This political process was occurring in the generalized form of reinscribing the meaning of citizenship. One example was the extension of the space and definition of politics to include, as 'national issues,' those concerns that previously had been defined as 'private' or 'domestic' or as 'women's concerns.' In the more intricate and technical mode of the text of the constitutional drafts, the labels of 'men' and 'women' were substituted for the unmarked category of 'people,' so that the specificities of women's status would not be subsumed to the generalized national subject (Driver, 1991).

In other words, a 'deconstructive attitude' in this context was not just an academic methodology, but rather an effective political strategy. Radhakrishnan (1996:148–9) made this argument in defending a strategic relationship between postcoloniality and poststructuralism: 'The daring and risk-taking that remain merely playful, ludic, epistemological (that is, disjuncted from real politics), and superstructural within poststructuralism take on a sense of constituency and therefore become political in the postcolonial juncture.' In the latter there are a 'concrete set of issues that use and transform poststructuralism.' These include the double affirming and deconstructing of ethno-nationalist or feminist identities and the necessity, in describing postcolonial reality, of 'multiple, nonsynchronous narratives, not a single masterful story.'

A comment on my seminar presentation portrayed my interest in the meanings of 'gender' that I had encountered in popular and official political discourses as a rather esoteric preoccupation. That curiosity on my part had been provoked, some years earlier, by the discrepancies in my analytical understanding of gender compared with those I came across in South Africa at that time. Then, 'gender' mostly overlapped with 'women,' but was also contested and rejected by some popular women's organizations on the grounds that it was not 'a struggle word.' The term was perceived rather as a distraction from 'women's issues,' a ploy that allowed men to retain control in organizations. Within the formal transition discourse that I was now investigating, 'gender' was being instituted and regulated as a state category, where its binary construction was not, as I have indicated above, without consequence. Within state-oriented feminist discourse, gender seemed to imply a feminist equality politics, again binary in its formulation. Today, gender is also used to qualify 'activism,' replacing or contesting 'feminism' and thus eluding feminism's white, middle-class connotations.

This is by no means a comprehensive genealogy or inventory of the concept of gender within South African feminist discourse. It is intended more as an illustration of both the dangers of deploying such key concepts transhistorically and transnationally and the need to discern their political referents and cultural resonances.[18] Leaving a deep impression on me just prior to my departure to South Africa on the 1993 research visit was the story of Rey Chow's response on being asked to do a 'gender reading' of the events of Tiananmen Square soon after their occurrence (Chow, 1991). She turned the question around to ask not what gender could tell us about China but what events in China could disclose about the limits of certain constructions of gender as a category of analysis.

The pliable and multiple meanings of 'gender' in South African political discourses have much to disclose about the flows, influences, institutionalization, and indigenization of different strands of feminism in different sites of gender politics. But as I noted earlier in relation to feminist political theory, deconstructions and genealogies of gender and feminism in South Africa illuminate not only South African realities. Where they are distinct and dissonant, they refract back, throwing light on the constructed boundaries and assumptions of transnational feminisms. They augment the powerful challenges, on the part of non-dominant and postcolonial theorists, to the presumption of universal relevance of hegemonic feminist concepts and theory.

Grewal and Kaplan (1994:9) considered the tracing and mapping of the debates around production and reception of feminist cultural and intellectual production to be an essential aspect of transnational feminist practice. Given the relations of inequality and unevenness between hegemonic, metropolitan-based, academic feminist discourses, on the one hand, and Third World, or non-dominant ones, on the other, some inquisitiveness about itinerary and genealogy should invariably form part of an accountable methodology. Certainly feminist theory should not be allowed to travel incognito, that is, without some reference to its conditions of production and possibility and the national, cultural, and political problematics that motivate and situate its questions and formulations – 'data-laden theory,' as John (1996) calls it. Blind travel that does not check its baggage – or have its baggage checked – can only serve to reproduce those transnational relations of feminist hierarchy in which Third World women and national feminisms are subsumed to Western interpretive schema. The vitality and validity of such mappings lie in the extent to which they help to translate concepts across cultural venues, to mediate between discordant discourses, and usefully recast issues and debates that have become conventionalized, both locally and globally.

This language of 'travelling theory' with its absent voyager is a bit disconcerting, since theoretical travels are, of course, mediated not only by texts, but also by concrete, historical subjects, hierarchically located within, in this case, South Africa and its diaspora. These transnational and national figures are interlocutors of sometimes divergent, sometimes overlapping theoretical and political feminist conversations.

I mentioned above the intellectual and political feminist elite who, via transnational consultations around inserting gender into political transition, mediated the feminist political and jurisprudential theory that has been so influential in shaping post-apartheid's impressive constitution and some of its gender policy initiatives. Not to be forgotten, however (especially in the context of this essay), are those other cohorts of South

African women (and men) who mediated flows of (more loosely defined) feminist practice that has contributed to the shape of popular and state feminism in South Africa. The returning body of exiles and refugees who lived in various locations of displacement during the years of apartheid – in Zambia, Tanzania, Angola, Mozambique, and England, as well, in more singular situations, in former communist countries and in North America – were influenced by a range of gender and feminist politics that they brought home with them. Another important and busy flow of influence in the formation of South African feminism(s) was mediated by international and local non-governmental organizations and formulated within a 'women and development' discourse. The insistence, on the part of international funding agencies, on the inclusion of a 'gender component' in the programs and projects of the local community-based organizations did much to set the terms of feminist discourse in civil society. It consequently contributed to the shapes of both state-oriented feminism and the post-apartheid political transition.

Overall, there remains a pattern of dominance, of a one-way feminist theoretical traffic from former imperial metropoles to previously colonized territories, from North to South, or more specifically in relation to South Africa, of Anglo-American feminist theory. This underscores a need to build alternate transnational feminist highways. These could facilitate connections between, for example, state feminisms in South Africa and in other culturally diverse, post-authoritarian, democratizing nations, where core concerns involve state forms, legislation, and policy for the redress of gender inequality, all couched in and constrained by official state discourse. There are also important links to be formed among grass-roots women's movements that are developing strategies for democratization largely outside the ambit of the state. The grass-roots political struggles and 'feminist' discourses of Native Canadian women and Latin American women seem to me much more congruent with those of the majority of South African women than the liberal democratic feminism that reigned during the political transition. However, these connections are more difficult to make directly, not only because of the lack of funding and official facilitation, but also because local issues and indigenous linguistic and political cultures are more pronounced in these more popular sites of feminist practice. Nevertheless, such alternative links are being made by feminist activists at various sites of 'global feminism,' such as meetings, networks, and workshops. In such sites, there is a need for a critical grasp of the ways in which the transnational and national relations of hierarchy, and the political ideologies within 'global feminism,' unevenly sanction

the voices of some feminisms over others. This has a bearing – transnationally and with reverberations in national women's politics – on the stip-
ulation of which issues come to be regarded and acted upon as 'women's
issues' and the kind of politics that is represented as 'feminist.'

Finally, in the seminar, there was a question about my perceptions of
the prospects for women in post-apartheid South Africa. Much of the
approach that has been elaborated in this essay speaks, not so much to
the actual forecast requested, but to the subtextual questions elicited. In
which and whose terms should an evaluation of the 'engendering of
political transition' be made? Is it possible to do this without imposing a
set of specifications about what constitutes 'feminist progress,' 'democratization,' or even 'better conditions for women'? And if not, what are the
sources, legitimations, and discursive and spatial parameters of any such
evaluative framework? Is there a way of assessing feminist struggles and
possibilities without reflecting the implicit criteria of globally hegemonic
Western feminism as they infuse the dominant feminisms in South
Africa? Could such an assessment be made without privileging a particular historical construction of gender and thereby misrecognizing the lives
of excluded women?

Chandra Mohanty's (1992:87) conception of 'a temporality of struggle'
is useful here. This, she asserted, 'disrupts and challenges the logic of linearity, development and progress which are the hallmarks of European
modernity ... It suggests an insistent, simultaneous, non-synchronous
process characterised by multiple locations, rather than a search for origins and endings.' To Mohanty's emphasis on temporality, I would add
an emphasis on spatiality, specifically the spaces and relationships of
national and transnational feminism(s). These, too, are incommensura-
ble, relative, and shifting in time.

Does this questioning – these challenges to the neat boundaries of the
nation and hence of South African feminism, this unsettling of the uni-
linearity of time – necessarily mean a messy and impossible relativism in
assessing the potential of South African feminists' struggles over the gendered terms of political transition?

Postmodern theory would attribute such anxiety about relativism to
an attachment to an archimedian standpoint (and a dominant white
masculine one at that), to conceptions of absolute time and space, to all-
encompassing explanatory frameworks. These remain intractable questions, and, though relevant, I set them aside here. Rather, let me see what
perspectives are accentuated by the post-exile version of a transnational
location. There are three that emerge strongly for me.

One is the need to apprehend the contemporaneous, ascendant feminist politics in the home country historically. When viewed either in terms of local political priorities, or from an international comparative perspective, it is easy to lose sight of the ways in which the dominant institutional sites of national feminist politics, the related strategies and possibilities, and the prevailing feminist discourses are historically produced and situated. The related ethico-political values, which inform the ways gender struggles are viewed as being successful or otherwise, are also historical products. The national hegemony of a particular feminist politics at any point in time has the effect not only of downplaying other forms and sites of feminist politics, but also of marginalizing and delegitimating the questions they raise.

A related perspective is that of the interfacing of national and transnational feminisms discussed above. Again, an 'internal' reading of feminist politics might overlook the ways in which, and degree to which, the nationally dominant feminism is either supported in its indigenous articulation or, alternatively, colonized by globally dominant feminist trends. At the time of the transition in South Africa, for example, the global hegemony of liberal and human rights feminism (consolidated by the U.N. Decade for Women and the 1993 Vienna Tribunal on Human Rights) made it very difficult to imagine a national feminist political initiative that was not uttered in the language of rights or to conceive of a constitution that did not inscribe gender equality. What did this mean for the articulation of indigenous South African feminisms? How these values and frameworks of evaluation come to prevail, at least officially, must not be occluded from the reach of feminist analysis.

The third dimension that has been accentuated for me in this exploration of post-exile is that of the political and ideological differences among women and feminists and the need to bring these more explicitly into analysis and interpretation. One of the effects of the transition process was that feminist politics became quite technical and instrumental. Debates centred around the most effective ways of adding women's issues to the agenda, getting women into the state. There was surprisingly little debate and contestation of the ideological underpinnings and political implications of this project to augment women's representation in the state.

I suggested earlier that, globally, with the prevalence of rights discourse and the related politics of identity and difference, political ideologies and questions of class and political economy have become murkier and harder to read. Like elsewhere and not surprisingly, given South Afri-ca's history, feminist political differences there tend to be racialized.

Women's politics more broadly show differentiations of class, geographical location (urban and regional), ethnicity, and tradition. Perhaps even more surprising, then, is the extent to which women activists and feminists from very different social locations were able to work effectively together in coalition during the transition period, notably in the Women's Charter campaign. As the limitations of public resources for redressing women's needs and gender inequality become more pronounced, as the effects on poorer women of the new government's neoliberal policies are felt, and as the nitty-gritty policy debates ensue, the resilience of such feminist coalition politics will be tested. Hopefully this will not lead to further politicization of identities and the making of impossible but constitutionally correct claims on a strapped state. I agree with Brown (1995:51) when she argues for moving beyond this globally prevalent feminist practice. She urges, instead, feminist engagement in public debate about different political strategies, 'not to overcome our situatedness, but in order to assume responsibility for our situations and mobilize a collective discourse that will expand them.' Perceived as a strategy of post-apartheid, acknowledging and assuming responsibility for, rather than residing defensively in, apartheid-conferred and patriarchy-defined identities (and this includes post-exile) might open up the space for the collective local elaboration of 'feminist democracy.'

NOTES

1 *Afastada* is the Portuguese word for remote, distanced, even 'out of the loop.' It is one of those words which, having enormous use value and no convenient English equivalent, quickly and tenaciously found its way into the everyday lexicon of the Anglophone 'cooperants' in Mozambique in the 1980s. 'Apprehension' is used here in both senses, that of the grasping of ideas and concepts and the feelings of trepidation, anxiety, and uncertainty.

2 I acknowledge the Centre for Social and Development Studies, University of Natal, Durban, and the Nattrass Visiting Research Fellowship for providing the opportunity and support for generating the material upon which I draw in this essay.

3 Central texts include Alexander and Mohanty (1997), Braidotti (1994), Grewal and Kaplan (1994), Kaplan (1994), Mani (1990), Mohanty (1992), Probyn (1990), Radhakrishnan (1996), and Spivak (1993).

4 It is important to note that in this essay I use the term 'poststructuralist' quite loosely and often interchangeably with deconstruction. Radhakrishnan (1996:48) uses poststructuralism similarly to refer to the following methodo-

logical themes: 'the questioning of representation, the perennial deconstruction of identity, the sensitivity to difference and heterogeneity, the insistence
on autocritique, and a noncoercive attitude to the production of knowledge.'

5 I refer here, among other relevant literature, to Butler and Scott (1992), Fraser (1990, 1995), Haraway (1988), Jones (1990), Pateman (1989), and Scott
(1988).

6 The 'historically white universities' are differentiated from the 'historically
Black universities,' both the legacy of apartheid segregration. Faculty at the
former are still predominantly white, but the student populations are now
more reflective of the country's Black majority demographics.

7 See, for example, Bazilli (1991a), Horn (1991b), Lewis (1996), and Robinson
(1994).

8 See, for example, Horn (1991a) and articles in the collection *Putting Women on
the Agenda*, edited, ironically, by Bazilli (1991b), a Canadian woman.

9 By way of comparison, when I presented a similar paper (Manicom 1995) in a
Canadian context, the politics of reception and constituency differed; there
was, for me, nothing like the same anguished dilemma. First, the disciplinary
site and project were more narrowly defined (i.e., a conference panel on new
directions in feminist political theory) which meant that I could assume a
shared theoretical discourse and common set of objectives. Second, I could
comfortably claim the now more familiar identities of diasporic feminist academic, former anti-apartheid activist, and South African national.

10 Technically, I gained refugee status in Canada in 1991, after it was feasible for
me to return to South Africa (a commentary on bureaucratic tardiness in the
contexts of public service cuts). I remained a citizen of the Republic of Ire-
land, a status gained expediently via marriage, and I now retain an affection-
ate affiliation with Eire though it has no affective claim on my national
identity. 'Home' remains South Africa, my diasporic adulthood notwithstanding. Such cross-hatched national and official categorization is not unusual for
exiles, immigrants, and refugees in Canada (as in other metropoles), particularly non-white, non-Anglo- or non-Francophone ones. Certainly it has been
the norm for the majority of South Africans within the borders of their own
country.

11 See, for example, Wolff's (1995c) critique of travel metaphors in 'On the
Road Again.'

12 There is a genre of South African non- and fictional writing and criticism that
deals with the experience of exile that I cannot reference here. Two recent
texts on exile are by Nixon (1995) and Bernstein (1994), who compiled interviews with South African exiles.

13 For critical discussions of this epistemological strategy, see Wolff (1995a) on

'the female stranger' and Grewal (1994) on 'diasporic autobiographic subjects.'

14 Significantly, in the contemporary global conjuncture, and more pertinent in North America and South Africa, it is racial identity that has assumed definitive and often totalizing status within feminist politics. The 'white guilt' that gets mobilized in this mode, as Butler (1995: 444) has argued, 'is quite useless as a resource in building a political community organized by an affirmative struggle against racism.'

15 While there were distinctive national articulations of 'the woman question,' they also evidenced significant continuities across nation and time. See Molyneux (1985b), Waylen (1996: 75–91), the collection of case studies in Kruks, Rapp, and Young (1989), and Jung, Heitlinger, and True (this volume).

16 But see Schild (this volume).

17 The original elaboration of the 'empowerment approach' by the international feminist research collective, Development Alternatives for Women for New Era (DAWN), remains a crucial political tract that should not be buried within 'development' literature. This transnational feminist literature engages much more explicitly with issues in contemporary feminist theory, such as identity and experience and symbolic and cultural representation, as well as with issues of the global political economy.

18 My comment on the culturally distinctive appropriations and meanings of 'gender' within South African feminist discourses elicited a lively comparative discussion of the different genealogies, translations, and meanings of 'gender' in the various cultural and political contexts represented by participants at the conference on 'Émigré Feminism.'

REFERENCES

Ahmad, Aijaz (1995) *In Theory: Classes, Nations, Literatures.* London: Verso.
Alexander, M. Jacqui, and Chandra Talpade Mohanty (1997) 'Introduction: Genealogies, Legacies, Movements.' In Jacqui M. Alexander and Chandra Talpade Mohanty (eds.), *Feminist Genealogies, Colonial Legacies, Democratic Futures,* xiii–xl. New York: Routledge.
Anderson, Benedict (1983) *Imagined Communities: Reflections on the Origins and Spread of Nationalism.* London: Verso.
Bazilli, Susan (1991a) 'Feminist Conferencing.' *Agenda,* no. 9: 44–52.
– (ed.) (1991b) *Putting Women on the Agenda.* Johannesburg: Ravan Press.
Bernstein, Hilda (1994) *The Rift: The Exile Experience of South Africans.* London: Jonathan Cape.

Bock, Gisela, and Susan James (eds.) (1992) *Beyond Equality and Difference: Citizenship, Feminist Politics, Female Subjectivity.* London: Routledge.

Braidotti, Rosi (1994) *Nomadic Subjects: Embodiment and Sexual Difference in Contemporary Feminist Theory.* New York: Columbia University Press.

Brown, Wendy (1995) *States of Injury: Power and Freedom in Late Modernity.* Princeton: Princeton University Press.

Butler, Judith (1995) 'Collected and Fractured: Response to Identities.' In Anthony K. Appiah and Henry Louis Gates Jr (eds.), *Identities*, 439–47. Chicago: University of Chicago Press.

Butler, Judith, and Joan Scott (eds.) (1992) *Feminists Theorize the Political.* London: Routledge.

Chow, Rey (1991) 'Violence in the Other Country: China as Crisis, Spectacle, and Woman.' In Chandra Mohanty, Ann Russo, and Lourdes Torres (eds.), *Third World Women and the Politics of Feminism*, 81–100. Bloomington: Indiana University Press.

– (1993) *Writing Diaspora: Tactics of Intervention in Contemporary Cultural Studies*, Bloomington: Indiana University Press.

Dhaliwal, Amarpal (1996) 'Can the Subaltern Vote? Radical Democracy, Discourses of Representation and Rights, and Questions of Race.' In David Trend (ed.), *Radical Democracy*, 42–61. New York: Routledge.

Driver, Dorothy (1991) 'The ANC Constitutional Guidelines in Process: A Feminist Reading.' In Susan Bazilli (ed.), *Putting Women on the Agenda.* Johannesburg: Ravan Press.

Fraser, Nancy (1990) *Unruly Practices: Power, Discourse and Gender in Contemporary Social Theory.* Minneapolis: University of Minnesota Press.

– (1995) 'From Redistribution to Recognition? Dilemmas of Justice in a "Post-Socialist" Age.' *New Left Review*, no. 212 (July–August):68–93.

Grewal, Inderpal (1994) 'Autobiographic Subjects and Diasporic Locations: Meatless Days and Borderlands.' In Inderpal Grewal and Caren Kaplan (eds.), *Scattered Hegemonies: Postmodernity and Transnational Feminist Practices*, 231–54. Minneapolis: University of Minnesota Press.

Grewal, Inderpal, and Caren Kaplan (eds.) (1994) *Scattered Hegemonies: Postmodernity and Transnational Feminist Practices.* Minneapolis: University of Minnesota Press.

Haraway, Donna (1988) 'Situated Knowledges: The Science Question in Feminism and the Privilege of Partial Perspective.' *Feminist Studies* 14(3):575–99.

Horn, Pat (1991a) 'Post-Apartheid South Africa: What about Women's Emancipation?' *Transformation*, no. 15:26–39.

– (1991b) 'Conference on Women and Gender in Southern Africa: Another View of the Dynamics.' *Transformation*, no. 15:83–88.

John, Mary (1996) *Discrepant Dislocations: Feminism, Theory and Postcolonial Histories.* Berkeley: University of California Press.

Jones, Kathleen (1990) 'Citizenship in a Woman-Friendly Polity.' *Signs* 15(4): 781–812.

Kaplan, Caren (1994) 'The Politics of Location as Transnational Feminist Critical Practice.' In Inderpal Grewal and Caren Kaplan (eds.), *Scattered Hegemonies: Postmodernity and Transnational Feminist Practices*, 137–52. Minneapolis: University of Minnesota Press.

King, Katie (1994) *Theory in Its Feminist Travels: Conversations in U.S. Women's Movements*. Bloomington: Indiana University Press.

Kruks, Sonia, Rayna Rapp, and Marilyn B. Young (eds.) (1989) *Promisory Notes: Women in the Transition to Socialism*. New York: Monthly Review Press.

Lewis, Desiree (1996) 'The Politics of Feminism in South Africa.' In M.J. Daymond (ed.), *South African Feminisms: Writing, Theory and Criticisms, 1990–1994*, 91–104. New York and London: Galland Publishing.

Mani, Lata (1990) 'Multiple Mediations: Feminist Scholarship in the Age of Multinational Reception.' *Feminist Review*, no. 35:24–39.

Manicom, Linzi (1993) 'In/Stating Women in the Transition Process.' Talk and unpublished paper given for the Centre for Social and Development Studies series, University of Natal, 25 June.

– (1995) 'The New Non-Racial, Non-Sexist South Africa: Gender in the Discourse of Political Transition.' Paper presented at the Canadian Sociology and Anthropology Annual Meetings in Montreal, June.

McCarthy, Mary (1994) 'A Guide to Exiles, Expatriates and Internal Emigres.' In Marc Robinson (ed.), *Altogether Elsewhere: Writers on Exile*. Boston: Faber and Faber.

McClintock, Anne (1995) *Imperial Leather: Race, Gender and Sexuality in the Imperial Context*. New York: Routledge.

Mohanty, Chandra T. (1991a) 'Under Western Eyes: Feminist Scholarship and Colonial Discourse.' In Chandra Mohanty, Ann Russo, and Lourdes Torres (eds.), *Third World Women and the Politics of Feminism*, 51–80. Bloomington: Indiana University Press.

– (1991b) 'Cartographies of Struggle: Third World Women and the Politics of Feminism.' In Chandra Mohanty, Ann Russo, and Lourdes Torres (eds.), *Third World Women and the Politics of Feminism*, 1–47. Bloomington: Indiana University Press.

– (1992) 'Feminist Encounters: Locating the Politics of Experience.' In Michèle Barrett and Anne Phillips (eds.), *Destabilizing Theory: Contemporary Feminist Debates*, 74–92. Berkeley: Stanford University Press.

Mohanty, Chandra T., Ann Russo, and Lourdes Torres (eds.) (1991) *Third World Women and the Politics of Feminism*. Bloomington: Indiana University Press.

Molyneux, Maxine (1985a) 'Mobilization without Emancipation? Women's Interests, the State and Revolution in Nicaragua.' *Feminist Studies* 11(2): 227–54.

– (1985b) 'Family Reform in Socialist States: The Hidden Agenda.' *Feminist Review* 21:47–66.

Mouffe, Chantal (1992) 'Feminism, Citizenship and Radical Democracy.' In Judith Butler and Joan W. Scott (eds.), *Feminists Theorize the Political,* 369–84. London: Routledge.

Nixon, Rob (1995) 'Refugees and Homecomings: Bessie Head and the End of Exile.' In Roman de la Campa, E. Ann Kaplan, and Michael Sprinker (eds.), *Late Imperial Culture,* 149–65. London: Verso.

Pateman, Carole (1989) *The Disorder of Women: Democracy, Feminism and Political Theory.* Stanford: Stanford University Press.

Probyn, Elspeth (1990) 'Travels in the Postmodern: Making Sense of the Local.' In Linda J. Nicholson (ed.), *Feminism/Postmodernism,* 176–89. New York: Routledge.

Radhakrishnan, R. (1996) *Diasporic Mediations: Between Home and Location.* Minneapolis: University of Minnesota Press.

Robinson, Jennifer (1994) 'White Women Researching/Representing "Others": From Antiapartheid to Postcolonialism?' In Alison Blunt and Gillian Rose (eds.), *Writing Women and Space,* 197–226. New York: Guildford Press.

Said, Edward (1983) 'Travelling Theory.' In *The World, the Text, and the Critic,* 226–47. Cambridge: Harvard University Press.

– (1994) 'Reflections on Exile.' In Marc Robinson (ed.), *Altogether Elsewhere: Writers on Exile,* 137–49. Boston: Faber and Faber. Originally published in 1984.

– (1996) 'Intellectual Exile: Expatriates and Marginals.' In *Representations of the Intellectual,* 47–64. New York: Vintage Books.

Scott, Joan W. (1988) 'Deconstructing Equality-versus-Difference: Or, the Use of Poststructuralist Theory for Feminism.' *Feminist Studies* 14:38–47.

Sen, Gita, and Caren Grown (1987) *Development, Crises and Alternative Visions: Third World Women's Perspectives.* New York: Monthly Review Press.

Shohat, Ella (1995) 'The Struggle over Representation: Casting, Coalitions, and the Politics of Identification.' In Roman de la Campa, E. Ann Kaplan, and Michael Sprinker (eds.), *Late Imperial Culture,* 166–78. London: Verso.

Spivak, Gayatri Chakravorty (1993) *Outside in the Teaching Machine.* New York: Routledge.

Suleri, Sara (1995) 'Women Skin Deep: Feminism and the Postcolonial Condition.' In Anthony K. Appiah and Henry Louis Gates Jr (eds.), *Identities,* 133–46. Chicago: University of Chicago Press.

Walters, Shirley, and Linzi Manicom (eds.) (1996) *Gender in Popular Education: Methods for Empowerment.* London: Zed Books.

Waylen, Georgina (1996) *Gender in Third World Politics.* London: Open University Press.

West, Lois A. (1992) 'Feminist Nationalist Social Movements: Beyond Universalism and towards a Gendered Cultural Relativism.' *Women's Studies International Forum.* 15(5/6):563–79.

Wolff, Janet (1995a) 'The Female Stranger: Marginality and Modes of Writing.' In *Resident Alien: Feminist Cultural Criticism*, 1–22. Cambridge: Polity Press.

– (1995b) 'Memoirs and Micrologies: Walter Benjamin, Feminism and Cultural analysis.' In *Resident Alien: Feminist Cultural Criticism*, 41–58. Cambridge: Polity Press.

– (1995c) 'On the Road Again: Metaphors of Travel in Cultural Criticism.' In *Resident Alien: Feminist Cultural Criticism*, 115–34. Cambridge: Polity Press.

Women's National Coalition (1994) *Women's Charter for Effective Equality.* Working document adopted in principle at the National Convention, 25–7 February, Cape Town.

Yeatman, Anna (1994) *Postmodern Revisionings of the Political* (London and New York: Routledge).

# 4

# Transnational Links in the Making of Latin American Feminisms: A View from the Margins

## VERÓNICA SCHILD

The recent transitions to civilian regimes in Latin America have led to important transformations in local feminisms. Commitments that once fuelled massive public demonstrations by women, for example, in protests against human rights violations, in commemorations of International Women's Day, and in actions of defiance by organized grass-roots women, are increasingly being traded in for pragmatic forms of collaboration with the new, civilian governments. Indeed, a new convergence appears to have emerged in countries like Chile, Argentina, and Brazil, between many formerly oppositional practices and legacies of women's movements and those state practices intent on shaping 'modern' neo-liberal democracies. In Chile, for instance, an oppositional discourse of the self, pivoting on the notion of women's self-development, which had been elaborated by feminists during the dictatorship, is now being shaped as a key component of institutional practices promoting new (marketized) citizens. One could argue that such changes in Latin American feminisms are simply the outcome of local responses to what is seen as possible, even desirable, given the constraining contexts of nationally based democratization efforts. To do so, however, would be to underestimate, or ignore altogether, the broader socioeconomic and cultural–political context – associated today with global restructuring – in which geographically and historically specific forms are articulated. I want to suggest that we explore these cultural transformations as one dimension of the articulation of the local and the extra-local, or global, in recent capitalist transformations in Latin America. To this end, I want to argue that the concept of transnational feminist links, in particular, is central to this exploration, one that highlights the webs of relations connecting women across the space–time divide and embodies their active involvement with changing forms of capitalism.

The purpose of this essay is to delineate the notion of transnational feminist links in the making of contemporary Latin American feminisms by exploring in depth the recent transformations of Chilean feminisms and highlighting the networks in which local feminists have been entangled. Transnational links have been implicated in significant ways in the very constitution of Latin American feminisms, making it difficult if not impossible to think about these feminisms as 'uncontaminated' by so-called Northern or Western forms.[1] Surprisingly, scant attention has been paid to the materiality and complexity of these vast women's networks operating across borders and time frames, although important resources, both symbolic and material, circulate through them. The tendency in the literature has been to eye such connections with suspicion, as simply a form of domination by so-called Western feminisms, in collusion with their local counterparts (see, for example, Marchand, 1995). For those at the receiving end, however, involved in the multiple and complex, and hierarchically ordered, organizations and practices that constitute local feminisms, these connections have a different meaning.

My interest in the question of transnational links is not accidental. It stems from my own attempts, deeply embedded in biographical considerations, to come to terms with the history of what I euphemistically refer to as 'women working with women' in contemporary Chile – including here both the sense of solidarity and collaboration as well as the more instrumental sense of 'working over.' Through this work I have become increasingly interested in the impact of ever-shifting, expanding networks of women activists and intellectuals across time frames and borders, which are ultimately also exclusionary networks. Working-class activists, for example, are invariably outside these loops of intellectual production and circulation. This work has led me to insist upon a rather simple observation about transnational links that seems too often to be either downplayed or quite simply overlooked: Transnational links involving women are not a phenomenon of the late twentieth century, but are historically based connections that have been part and parcel of collaboration with, as well as of adaptation and resistance to, processes of postcolonial state formation in Latin America more generally. In other words, transnational links are an old phenomenon; the new element within these networks is their specific configuration at different moments, corresponding to different historical periods.

Judging from the recent historical accounts of women's activism in different countries of Latin America – narratives that portray an incessant flow of bodies and ideas to and from the region – transnational links have helped shape feminisms throughout the postcolonial period.[2] Thus, the experiences and actions of women activists in Latin America have been woven into place with 'borrowed' strands from many Western, women-centred, and feminist discourses for a very long time. Moreover, the cultural effects of these hybrid forms, or the shaping of successive 'modern' Latin American women – always in the plural because these were, and obviously continue to be, highly differentiated, classed, and racialized forms – are equally long-standing.

In the following pages, I first offer a brief overview of the historical dimension of feminist transnational links in Latin America. Then I retrace the evolution and recent transformations of Chilean feminisms, using elements from my ten-year-old explorations of women's organizing in Santiago. In working on both sides of the seeming divide between the 'other' feminisms (in this case, Latin American) and Western feminisms, while ultimately situated in neither, I explore the complexities of transnational links in the Chilean case. My particular focus is the intersections of transnationalized feminisms with local forms, which I conceive of as an expanding embodied network of cultural practices, by which I mean women involved in working relations with one another, through forms like research and action projects, meetings and conferences, policy design and implementation, and others. My approach to the study of transnational links is from the margins looking in, as it were. It is rooted in my own powerful experience of migration and the questions of identity and belonging that such an experience inevitably raises. I write from an 'outsider' position, or as someone who never quite 'belongs,' either in a disciplinary niche or in the comfort of a sense of sameness *vis-à-vis* her surroundings. Moreover, this position of never quite belonging, or of being permanently outside in some sense, has become entrenched. I cannot, I have discovered, ever fully return home. I begin this exploration, then, with a narrative of the personal and intellectual disjuncture that has marked my own trajectory as a scholar negotiating the discursive strategies deemed legitimate for engaging questions pertaining to feminist research in the Latin American context. I live this disjuncture as a more or less permanent fault line that constantly threatens to disrupt the relation between what 'I know' and the various discourses I have access to.

### 'Non-belonging Can Be Hell'

My journey from Chile began at dusk on a soft fall evening in 1971 when I peeked out of the window of the Braniff airplane onto a Santiago carpeted with lights, and my heart beat a final farewell. This violent rupture marked the beginning of a nomadic journey whose end is not in sight. The body, after all, does not forget. In 1971 Allende had just been installed in office, and the women in my family were on the run, not from this unprecedented political experiment but from the oppressive effects of a very old practice: an abusive stepfather who, with Chilean civil law on his side, and with the added power of personal connections, had refused to grant his wife a legal separation. At sixteen I was too young to vote but not young enough to have resisted political activism. I did not want to leave. In twenty-four hours, however, home and roots had vanished. What better reminder of this than the charmingly ignorant reaction of the vacationing older woman in a hotel lobby in Miami Beach to my reply to her question about my place of origin: 'Chili? Chili? Isn't that a place near Boston?' A significant comment this was, in hindsight, because despite my accent and because of my fair skin and my 'European' looks I had become invisible. Thus, began a time of 'passing,' of translating myself to others and to myself.

I returned to Santiago in 1986 after a fifteen-year absence, in the context of fieldwork for my doctoral dissertation. Pinochet's dictatorship had radically transformed the place I still called home. My arrival there marked the end of my search for roots and the beginning of a more or less permanent sense of homelessness. I had, it seemed, arrived through the senses only, matching verbal categories like winter or illness with the smells of rain hitting Santiago's brownish soil, or the smells of lunchtime foods wafting out of restaurants, and home kitchens. And yet, this bodily embrace of 'home' could not undo the facts of dictatorship twisted into shape through the imprisonment, torture, and death of countless Chileans, among them friends, and former classmates and teachers. The fault line, the sense of rupture, had become a permanent feature for me.

In the end, the home I nurtured in my memory was not the place I went back to. How could I match my own adaptive strategies of survival to those of the many who had remained in the country, survived, adapted, and moved on – some friends I knew I would not find, most I simply did not find (these were times of fear and suspicion and one did not ask too many questions). Equally important, however, though not so to me at the time (already having omitted my own class positioning from my own expectations of homecoming), I had fallen off the class-based webs of connections that had allowed middle-class women to climb into the leading ranks of feminists doing intellectual and activist work. My self-made trajectory abroad betrayed important and seemingly insurmountable gaps. For example, missing from it were the steps neatly strung together – the right schooling leading to the right university, followed by the scholarships for postgraduate work in the United States or, preferably, in the capitals of Europe – into a clean line traumatically disrupted, but not permanently broken, by the coup and the massive repression that ensued. What scholars in Canada and the United States were beginning to call 'Chilean feminism' (see, Chuchryk, 1984; Jaquette, 1991) was, as I found out, deeply embedded in a context of class relations and status connections.

Out of this experience of dislocation, the fault line, stemmed my inability to make myself at home – that permanent sense of lived and intellectual marginality – and my stance as a 'permanent outsider.' Rosi Braidotti (1994:14) has characterized the nomad's identity 'as a map of where s/he has already been; s/he can always reconstruct it a posteriori, as a set of steps in an itinerary.' Braidotti forgot to mention, however, that this identity has hegemonic pretensions; it is a map wilfully written and traced over that other one penned through the senses and fleshed out by powerful emotions. It is hard to describe this other map as anything but stones and cracks that keep springing up as if from nowhere, jolting one back, however momentarily – through hurt and pain – to that initial point, to the fault line. We are, after all, to paraphrase Philip Corrigan, always 'embodied selves' and, thus, nomads' identities are anchored to bodies that will not forget.[3]

Not only did I battle with a personal sense of not belonging in this post-Allende Chile, but as a researcher I soon discovered that I was an intruder of sorts. For over three months I travelled a difficult road of knocking on institutional doors and was forced to realize that I was an outsider without connections to the research networks that could give me access to the grass-roots organizations I wanted to reach. The periphery of Santiago, that vast area where most poor and working-class neighbourhoods are located, had been parcelled out by the Church, research institutes, and the non-governmental organizations (NGOs) studying the poor. Clearly, livelihoods depended on having access to certain research constituencies, as it were, and I was seen as competition. On one occasion I was warned by a researcher that, being a student not backed by these institutions, I 'had nothing to offer' (by which she meant tea or sandwiches) to my potential subjects in exchange for information.

After a period of false starts, and overall frustration, I met a community organizer who put me in touch with the women who would become the main focus of my study of women's organizing. Esteban taught me to look beyond the layer of brown dust that limits an untrained middle-class view of poor neighbourhoods. He also taught me to distrust the niceties trotted out for visitors by well-meaning leaders of organizations. Finally, he introduced me to Julia, the coordinator of a women's group in a *poblacion* (poor neighbourhood) in the southern periphery of Santiago. Gradually, through Julia's network of family, friends, and neighbours, as well as through other women active in the Zona Sur, I have come to have a sense of the everyday lives and problems of *pobladoras*, as women in the *poblaciones* call themselves – as highly differentiated a group as any with both common and divergent aspirations and expectations – referring to the one characteristic they do share, namely, their spatial location. Over the years, Julia has taught me a very important lesson: respect for differences, and lasting friendship, counts for more than tea, sandwiches, and 'raw' data.

Although my research has since taken me beyond Julia's neighbourhood, I return to it regularly and to the familylike and friendly relations I have built there over time. My experience of this other Santiago now spans a decade. I am always pulled back to this place and to the life experiences of Julia and her network (itself an expanding one), as if by a magnet that provides the necessary grounding of my research with women. Moving to the core of the city, from the periphery, one is reminded of the profound schism between the two. The vast area covered by the periphery, most of the city in fact, has barely been touched by the patina of modernity covering the newly modern Santiago – an area with islands of supermodernity where turning right on a red light is permitted and where the local branch of Citibank flies large banners advertising services in English. This vast peripheral Santiago is a spatially distinct area – itself a collage of the new and the old, however, touched here and there by mega-shopping malls and run-down repair shops that take credit cards – whose inhabitants live in a kind of apartheid, coming in touch with well-off Chileans rarely, and then mostly during their working day. Old and young, single or attached, mothers or grandmothers, the women in Julia's neighbourhood travel daily – often for more than an hour each way – to the other city to clean, cook, and mother for others, and to serve them in restaurants and stores. Increasingly, many of them have been travelling in the other direction, to the outlying areas south of the capital, to work as *temporeras*, or seasonal workers, in the fruit-exporting businesses, weeding and tending to fruit trees and eventually packing the fruit headed for northern winter markets. A smaller, more privileged group of younger women, like Julia, who managed to finish high school, or who acquired additional skills, have moved into other types of work. Some may work as typists and secretaries, others as assistants to social workers and teachers. These women, and those older, active women who spent the years of the dictatorship involved in community, or more specifically women's, organizing, are increasingly forming a core of poorly paid helpers engaged by state and non-governmental organizations to implement social programs with their less fortunate neighbours, or with those living in some of the newer, dreadfully poor, and downright dangerous, adjacent *poblaciones*.

In my movements through this other Santiago, I am aware of being an outsider. My style of dress, my pattern of speech, my universe of reference, that is, the cultural resources available to me, remind me constantly that I do not belong and that I am empowered in ways that those I come in contact with are not. I am, after all, ultimately free to come and go. I also 'know' that my class belonging and educational background translate into power, which is manifested in subtle, but effective, ways. With most of the men I meet I may transcend the limitations posed by my gender and pass as one of them, for example, in discussions about community matters or party politics. Furthermore, I am more often than not treated by them as a *señora*, or someone who is owed respect, and who is not an explicit (or overt) sexual partner or a target for hostilities. Instead, these typical responses are reserved for us female professionals by fellow male colleagues in academic or political circles – for whom we are, no doubt, transgressors of sorts, and for whom we remain first and foremost women.

With the women I come in contact with in the *poblaciones*, my relation is more complex and contradictory. I am acutely aware of my class-based difference, yet this difference is often masked by a sense of familiarity and complicity, a gender-based complicity, based on our ability to translate for each other in our telling of personal experiences. This sense of sameness, however, is not permanent, for in subtle ways it is subverted, yet constantly renewed. For example, among *pobladora* friends and acquaintances I am often placed, and may inadvertently place myself, in the position of the expert who has something to offer, either with personal advice or with practical tips. In encounters with strangers this distinction is much more explicit.

How ingrained class-based codes of behaviour and power relations are was made dramatically clear to me during a play-acting session I was invited to take part in by a group of *pobladoras* meeting for a personal development workshop at a women's centre in Pudahuel in 1992. The *monitora* of the workshop announced that we, me included, would begin the day's discussion with a session of play acting. The women chose to do a sketch of a visit to the local clinic, to highlight and discuss their problems with health practitioners. As roles were assigned, I was singled out by everyone to play the doctor. I was overcome by an immediate sense of discomfort at the thought of having to play the key, power-wielding role. Yet as I sat down at the assigned place, and my first 'patient' showed up, I slipped without much thought into my role: I listened to her complaints while feigning to clean my fingernails, and tapped on the desk with impatience, repeatedly looking at my watch, before deigning to ask her a few very condescending questions about her symptoms. I finished my performance by sending her home to take some aspirin and to clean herself properly. Throughout I could hear whispers, giggles, and expressions of recognition, 'That's it! That is exactly how they treat us.' At the end, I was thanked profusely for playing the role so convincingly. My own reaction was one of surprise, embarrassment, and the uncomfortable feeling of being exposed, of no longer passing unnoticed.

To suggest, however, that only my class-belonging marks me in fundamental ways would be to ignore the fact that I am, in an important sense, an outsider to the culture I was born into and grew up in. In informal interactions with friends and acquaintances I have often betrayed my less than seamless handling of appropriate cultural codes and have earned, as a result, the nickname of *la gringa*. Having spent my adult life in North America does make me different from other middle-class Chileans. At the same time, this precarious space, this never quite being at home in one cultural context, of always being slightly on the margins looking in rather than fully belonging – both in the Canadian and the Chilean contexts – is precisely the space in which I have built networks of my own. The transition to civilian rule, and the expansion of government-related activities in the past five years, has meant that my own networks of friends and acquaintances have evolved and expanded. Many of these women have moved from grass-roots activities and now work in non-governmental organizations, government agencies, research institutes, and universities. I am, then, myself caught in the expanding webs of Chilean feminisms, and this has facilitated, and restricted, my research efforts.

**Transnational Links of Chilean Feminisms**

The struggle for women's rights in Chile in the first half of this century was built on pre-existing links that brought together the experiences and ideas of women from the region and from the United States and Europe. Those early activities centred on the social rights of women and particularly on women's access to education. During the colonial period, and for most of the nineteenth century, women's education – the formation of proper ladies in private, Catholic schools, and the practical imitations of this education with a focus on moral and vocational training which some poor, urban women received from Catholic charitable organizations – was in the hands of the Catholic Church.[4] Already at the time of the Wars of Independence, Latin American women intellectuals had taken a leaf from European and North American discourses in vogue on the 'rights of man,' borrowed by their male counterparts to support the anti-colonial cause, and extended them to include a serious consideration of the rights of women.[5]

The historical record suggests that the intellectual and organizational work of women also contributed to liberal efforts of the late nineteenth century to construct secular institutions and, more generally, to processes of modern state formation.[6] These contributions were spearheaded by an emerging group of women professionals. It is from this group of educated women that a sustained public critique of the social and political condition of women in Latin America first emerged. Moreover, these efforts cannot be fully understood without recognizing the fact that the activities of this emerging group of women professionals were increasingly embedded in networks extending beyond national and regional boundaries. Latin American feminists, it turns out, have been an integral part of broader feminist debates and struggles for women's social and political rights. In the late nineteenth century and early twentieth century, their participation took the form of local appropriation and circulation of intellectual debates by free thinkers (anti-clerical) and of an avid reception of prominent European women activists touring the region.[7] Increasingly, Latin American women joined regional and international organizations. For example, new middle-class professionals, educators, and health practitioners joined international professional organizations and attended regional and international conferences (Miller, 1991:ch. 3 and 4; Carlson, 1988:ch. 3). Women from the incipient workers' movements formed their own links with activists abroad.[8]

In places like Chile, Argentina, Uruguay, and Brazil the circulation of feminist intellectual and activist production through local papers and newsletters of the labour movement and of concerned middle-class liberal (anti-clerical) reformers became widespread. In the case of Chile, these activities were often backed by labour's incipient political voice –

the Democratic Party, precursor of the Chilean Communist Party – until the 1920s when the Comintern declared the fight for women's rights a bourgeois distraction and ordered greater clarity of focus and commitment from national parties and individuals alike. The circulation of feminisms in Chile was not limited to the local reproduction of the pamphlets and documents produced by activists in Europe and the United States. It also involved extensive national tours by foreign activists. These included, for example, women like the Spanish free thinker (and strongly anti-clerical) activist Belen de Zarraga, who travelled to Chile's far-flung mining and urban manufacturing centres in 1913, urging women to form their own organizations and to struggle for basic rights.

In 1916 in the Northern Chilean mining town of Iquique, the Centro Instructivo de Obreras Librepensadoras 'Luisa Michell' (Female Workers' Free-Thinking Learning Centre Luisa Michell) was established in honour of the Parisian teacher and committed militant of the Association for Women's Rights, Louise Michel, whose name had become a symbol of the Paris Commune struggles of 1871.[9] Clearly, women in Chile and in other countries of the region have been long-standing subjects and objects of projects of emancipatory transformation articulated in the tension between local and internationalized feminisms. As the twentieth century wore on, organized women workers and professionals increasingly became members of international women's organizations. For example, women were active in the International Council of Women (ICW) and the International Women Workers (IWW). Furthermore, their participation in international professional organizations – venues that attracted women pioneering in the fields of health, education, and, later, social work – became more widespread.

The recent re-emergence of Latin American feminisms – paradoxically, in the midst of repressive authoritarian regimes of the late 1960s and 1970s – and their more recent transformations in connection with the present activities of civilian governments throughout the region, raises renewed questions about transnational connections. In fact, Latin American feminisms have entered the broader debate on global feminisms, and this debate has already given rise to a very rich literature (see, for example, Alvarez, 1990; Jaquette, 1991; Radcliffe and Westwood, 1993; Sternbach et al., 1992; and Jelin, 1990). Who are these women embedded in the multiple and different national contexts of South, Central, and southern North America, whom we Latin Americanists habitually render invisible when counterposing Western feminist discourse to its Latin American 'other'?

## Contextualizing Chilean Feminisms of the 1990s

Since my first trip to Chile in 1986, the context in which Chilean feminisms re-emerged has changed significantly. The repressive regime of Augusto Pinochet came to an end in 1989, a time when presidential elections ushered in the first civilian government in seventeen years. Despite some important political changes, the transformations under way do not, by any means, constitute a radical break with the recent past. Indeed, what we are witnessing today is the consolidation of a neo-liberal project of economic and institutional restructuring begun by the military regime, or, put differently, it is the newest class-based modernization project.[10] These transformations have been accompanied by important changes in, and expansions of, the networks of Chilean feminisms.

Transnational links played a fundamental role in the making of a web of Chilean women's organizations in the late 1970s. Women professionals in Santiago organized soon after the military takeover. In 1977 they formed the Asociación para la Unidad de las Mujeres (ASUMA), and soon after the Círculo de Estudios de la Mujer de la Academia de Humanismo Cristiano (the Women's Studies Circle of the Academy of Christian Humanism). These were key contributions to an emerging network through which feminist resources came to be circulated. Feminist scholars and activists wrote books, gave lectures, and participated in exchanges with women from different sectors of Chilean society. They also established and nurtured connections with feminists abroad. Furthermore, women returning from exile made important contributions to the intellectual and activist tasks of local feminisms. Many brought with them the intellectual resources garnered from their own experiences with feminism while abroad, as well as contacts with solidarity NGOs and other sources of funding. Over time, the initiatives stemming from the U.N. Decade for Women (1976–1985) created funding possibilities for action-research with poor women and promoted new discourses of women in development. These new resources merged with the local experiences accumulated on the ground by women professionals engaged in popular education and by explicitly feminist consciousness-raising types of activities – all made possible by the funding from abroad.

Middle-class feminist professionals and activists were not the only ones who mobilized in response to the military coup. Poor and working-class women activists, both party militants and political sympathizers with a long organizational trajectory – often in mothers' centres or in popular education initiatives – organized in their neighbourhoods to cope with the dramatic impact on their families of political and economic repression. Their activities came to be supported, and sometimes simply appropriated, by the neighbourhood church, the only safe space for collective initiatives. Soon after the coup, the Church undertook the role of protector of poor families devastated by the loss of the family income, and by the retreat of the state, and for this it established the Vicaria de la Solidaridad. The Vicaria and its five branches operated in the poor areas of Santiago. Like NGOs, the Vicarias developed programs of action geared to women with funds received from international agencies and from solidarity NGOs. Thus, the Church became an employer of many middle-class and working-class women activists and professionals – mostly social workers, nurses, and educators – who because of their political background were barred from other employment. It also competed for foreign funds with NGOs and developed its own programs with women. A number of women's NGOs that emerged in the late 1980s, and which continued with their activities until very recently, were in fact formed by the former staff of the Vicarias. They opted to leave that institution when it deliberately veered to the right after the Pope's visit in 1987, when it pulled back from social activism.

The return to civilian government has marked a new moment in the struggle of feminists in Chile. Although many accounts of Chilean, and for that matter Latin American feminisms, emphasize rich diversity marked by class and race, that is, the question of 'difference,' they tend to elide questions of power within difference and voice.[11] The ongoing transformations of feminisms in Chile, and more specifically, the fate of different groups of women activists and professionals in the past five years, illustrate these questions of power within difference and of representation.

Critics rightly argue that the imaginary other of Western feminism, namely, Third World feminism, or its subvariant of Latin American feminism in this case, is a gross, homogeneous abstraction made to stand for what are, in effect, women's multiple and complex lives, shaped by relations of class, race, ethnicity, and other powerful markers of difference.[12] This gross abstraction of Western feminism's 'others,' it is claimed, in effect silences the majority of Third World women, namely, poor and working-class women. Others speak on their behalf (Marchand, 1995). But the implicit assumption about transnational feminist links found in this discussion is itself problematic. It relies on rather conventional notions of discourse and culture in pitting a neo-colonial discourse, including its local variant embodied in middle-class, Westernized feminists, against a presumably different (more genuine or more pristine?) discourse embodied in the subordinate others of these local dominant feminisms. Although this analysis allows us to recognize differences within local feminisms, its conception of the cultural effects of transnational links remains rather rudimentary. Infinitely more complex and more contradictory cultural processes are at work in the circulation of resources enabled by feminist transnational links. Indeed, the most effective way of conceiving transnational links is as networks of women differentially located, both nationally and internationally, through which cultural and discursive (for example, academic feminist debates, expert knowledge, activist knowledge) and material (for example, funding opportunities, conferences) resources are circulated that empower some women more than others, but that ultimately contaminate them all.

I would suggest that transnational feminist links are networks that disseminate resources, spinning ever-wider webs that entangle different women, who are nevertheless not some place totally outside it. 'Language,' the singer Laurie Anderson once said, 'is a virus.' Following this linguistic analogy, feminist resources act like a grammar that different women appropriate, and transform for their own purposes, but always within limits. To speak of feminisms as a grammar implies quite literally thinking of discourses as the rules of a language that enable us to speak, rather than as its specific content or meanings. Such a grammar sets parameters that local, both middle-class and popular (the term used by poor and working-class activists themselves), as well as transnational feminisms share. For example, they may all recognize that women are in a subordinate condition, though what this subordination consists in, and how it is to be overcome, is defined by different groups of women depending on their own specific location. In this sense, attempts by those 'others' of Chilean feminisms, poor and working-class activists, to articulate counterfeminisms – a 'popular feminism,' for example, or most recently in Chile, a 'radical popular feminism' – should not be construed as a sign that their minds have been colonized.

Like their middle-class counterparts, local popular feminisms are forged through a constant translating, adapting, resisting, and general working over of cultural resources that circulate through the symbolic and material networks that women have entered into over time, and that extend beyond national borders. Indeed, as already mentioned, appropriations of so-called Western feminisms have been taking place for well over a century. We need to remind ourselves, then, that it is not some raw notion of material conditions that determines the different forms of feminisms emerging in a local context, but conditions that are always mediated by cultural practices. These practices, or means of acting and making sense, are themselves the outcome of a permanent, dynamic relation with dominant forms: they are forged through adaptation to, contestation, and even contradictory appropriation of these forms (and of sedimentations of earlier ones).

Following the elections of 1989, the women's movement in Chile lost its visibility and was pronounced transformed, paralyzed, or quite simply dead.[13] The end of Pinochet's regime eliminated the obvious enemy that united myriad, heterogeneous groupings and organizations. Moreover, the transition to liberal democracy, or to 'normal' politics, exposed the real differences and tensions among women which had been latent in the past. A fundamental divide exists today between those feminists who feel that the struggle for greater equality for women must be fought for within party politics and the state (informally known as the *politicas*) and those who have increasingly come to see this move as leading to a loss of autonomy of the movement (the *autonomas*).

Already in late 1988, the creation of two new coordinating bodies with very different goals, the Concertación de Mujeres por la Democracia and the Coordinación de Organizaciones Sociales de Mujeres, made the tensions between these two basic positions palpable. The Coordinacion de Organizaciones Sociales de Mujeres brought together feminists who chose a strategy of action beyond parties and the state, in the name of preserving the autonomy of the women's movement. On the other hand, those well-known feminists who joined the Concertacion de Mujeres por la Democracia belonged to parties of the centre and left which formed the Concertacion por la Democracia that became the first civilian government after 1989. This women's coalition was formed with the express purpose of presenting women's demands to the new civilian government (Montecino and Rossetti, 1990). Those women who took part in this initiative insist, and without a doubt rightly so, that without the pressure they exerted as a group, and without the pressure exerted subsequently by the few feminist parliamentarians and politicians elected in 1989, the *Concertacion* government would not have a Programa de la Mujer (Women's Program) (interview with Antonieta Saa in Hola and Pischedda, 1994). Clearly, the Concertacion de Mujeres por la Democracia represented the option of those with *doble militancia* (feminists who are also members of parties) who chose to work for change within the parameters established by the political mainstream. But, as such, it also excluded those who did not choose to marginalize themselves politically from this process but whose 'double militancy' played itself out in the Communist party and the Movement of the Revolutionary Left (MIR).[14]

The emerging divisions between feminists manifested themselves in new forms of action. First were the campaign, mounted during the last parliamentary elections, to vote more women in, and the widespread discussions and meetings organized in preparation for the U.N. Beijing Conference on Women in September 1995. Furthermore, two *redes de mujeres* (women's networks) have been created, one that mobilizes women around issues of health and reproductive rights (Foro Abierto de Salud y de Derechos Reproductivos) and the other around issues of male violence against women (Red Contra la Violencia). These networks are sustained by NGOs and women's organizations and their achievements to date suggest that, at least so far, the former has been more successful than the latter. For example, it has successfully organized discussions on abortion, marked the International Day of Women's Health, and acted as a consumer watchdog by producing an exposé of the widespread use in hospitals of an unauthorized, experimental drug to treat women.

Moreover, recent developments suggest that after a period of relative lull, new feminist antagonisms are emerging. The Beijing conference sparked some of them. In addition, the leading role of the *feministas autonomas* in the November 1996 meeting in Chile of the Encuentro Feminista Regional, the meeting that brings together feminists from the Americas every three years, galvanized those sectors of the movement who want to continue advancing the cause of women within existing political structures, as well as those who are increasingly critical of the government but disagree with the radicalism of the *autonomas*. This new feminist radicalism brings together lesbian groups, women from the left, and some groups of *pobladoras* in a strong critique of co-optation of the women's movement by the state.

Beyond these questions of strategy and practice, however, there is the question of the cultural presence and impact of feminisms and, more concretely, of women's movements in Chile. A cursory exploration of the ongoing networks that constitute the movements reveals important continuities and changes. A number of independent women's research institutes, for example, Centro de Estudios de la Mujer (CEM), and its splinter group, Instituto de la Mujer (CEDEM), along with ISIS Internacional, continue to operate, as do a number of NGOs working with women's issues and some women's centres, including the first one to have opened in Santiago during the dictatorship, Casa de la Mujer la Morada.

In addition, the women's radio Radio Tierra, and a number of feminist bulletins, journals, and a newspaper, continue to inform and educate about women's issues. All these efforts continue to be funded from abroad, though increasingly less so than in the past.

Other important legacies are evident in the sociopolitical transformations that have taken place since 1990. Perhaps the most obvious one is the creation of Servicio Nacional de la Mujer (SERNAM or National Women's Bureau). This government agency, created in January 1991, was a response to the demands expressed by the Concertacion de Mujeres para la Democracia during the negotiations for a social pact between a number of the opposition forces – known as Concertacion para la Democracia – that paved the way to the elections.[15] SERNAM's operating budget is limited and, in fact, heavily reliant on foreign funding.[16] This institution has representation in the country's thirteen regional governments, as well as in a number of local, municipal governments, through Oficinas Municipales de la Mujer (OMMs or Municipal Women's Bureaux). Its explicit aim is to 'design and coordinate public policies at sectoral and interministerial levels.' (Servicio Nacional de la Mujer, 1994:15). In other words, SERNAM acts primarily as a watchdog, a ministrylike body created to oversee all other ministries' policy making in areas directly affecting women. In addition, the institution can propose legislation to parliament, promote societywide educational campaigns, and design and implement specific social programs. What it lacks is executive power. Indeed, it is headed not by a minister but by a director with ministerial powers, directly accountable to the president of Chile.

## Shaping 'Poor' Women into 'Active Citizens': Contributions of the Feminist Curriculum

The major task faced by the civilian governments that have followed Pinochet's dictatorship is a moral and formative one, namely, how to translate the terms of the newest version of modernity – pivoting on the key qualities of autonomy, accountability, and responsibility – into the lived behaviours of citizens and of the society at large. This task is being promoted by international aid to bolster neo-liberal democratic polities in Chile and, indeed, in the region more generally, while simultaneously supporting efforts to soften the human impact of economic and institutional restructuring. Thus, for example, a cursory exploration of recent funding for national government programs and NGOs by philanthropic European and North American agencies, as well as by multilateral agencies like the

World Bank, reveals an increasing commitment to projects that aim to strengthen 'civil society' and promote 'citizen participation.'[17]

Autonomy and self-reliance are the two values of the new citizenship being promoted implicitly, and explicitly, by recent social programs and policies. In very concrete terms, this means that, increasingly, certain funds are set aside by ministries for programs that involve the poor in designing and articulating 'projects' aimed at improving their own health, education, or community life. The amount, in dollar terms, of these initiatives may be negligible, but their cultural significance should not be ignored. They are part of a strategy that aims to redefine not only the self-definition of individual citizens but the very terms of the relation between the state and civil society. Thus, while the capacities of poor people to help themselves out of their condition of poverty are being extolled as the latest signs of modernity, the expectation acquired by poor Chileans over the course of nearly three decades, that the state has a responsibility to deliver certain public goods, has become morally suspect.[18]

Ironically, these new projects build on the accumulated experience of, and the networks of clients built by, both domestic and foreign-based solidarity NGOs during the dictatorship. At that time, funds poured in from a range of international agencies, both governmental and nongovernmental, to support displaced professionals and to bolster local NGOs primarily involved with the poor. By the late 1970s, an intricate web of NGOs had emerged with funding from agencies such as the Ford Foundation, Oxfam, Caritas, and other European politically and religiously based foundations. Moreover, these agencies followed the resolutions adopted by the United Nations, under the banner of the U.N. Decade for Women (1976–1985), and increasingly earmarked funds for development work with poor women. Today, the priorities of funding agencies have changed, and most of the remaining funds have been redirected to support the social programs of the civilian governments. Funds are still reaching NGOs, but the direction of funding is firmly in the hands of the Chilean government, and the beneficiaries in the non-governmental sector are those organizations that increasingly act as the executors and/or evaluators of government social programs.[19]

For some feminists the recent changes have created new arenas for action. For example, an ever-increasing number of feminist intellectuals and activists participate today in the processes of knowledge production through which the state constructs a new, modern Chile. Even a cursory exploration of what has happened with feminist professionals in Chile in the past five years reveals an important trend.[20] Many social scientists –

sociologists and economists, as well as social workers and educators –
mostly employed in NGOs during the dictatorship, have joined the various ministries and agencies like Instituto Nacional de Estadistica (INE or
National Statistics Institute). Significant numbers of them have moved to
middle-level positions in SERNAM. In addition to their presence in government agencies, and most importantly in SERNAM, feminist professionals continue to be found in the non-governmental sector of NGOs
and independent research institutes. They are increasingly also found in
universities, where in some cases they have succeeded in establishing
courses in women's and gender studies.

As far as poor and working-class women are concerned, these new
forms of assistance channel their individual and collective efforts, energies, and experiences in certain directions and not others. Activists, and
those engaged in NGOs and local organizations, lack the long-standing
contacts with the smaller network of women professionals regularly
tapped by government agencies and external funding agencies. The centrality of having the right connections is evident in the description by
women in NGOs of their relations with SERNAM. Typically, project ideas
and evaluation of existing projects are commissioned by the agency, not
by inviting NGOs as organizations, but rather individuals within them.
Often, those who are outside the known circles, like women from NGOs
based in the *poblaciones*, are not even aware of the projects in question.
Thus, vital information circulates in a network that is highly stratified and
that has expanded to include women in government ministries and other
agencies, while at the same time marginalizing others who are closer to
the grass roots.

Seen from the margins, a convergence of certain feminist (and other
progressive) discourses and newly emerging state forms of moral regulation is taking place which is reshaping in fundamental ways the terms of
sociality for the majority of Chilean women. Put differently, the focus of
the state on certain categories of poor women as targets of modernizing
efforts has come to crucially *depend* on the many activities of women professionals and activists located in non-governmental organizations, universities, and independent research institutes, as well as women at the
grass roots. Moreover, these activities and the state's gendered social
agenda, more generally, depend to an important extent on material and
intellectual resources made available through transnational links, including transnational feminist networks.

During the dictatorship, feminist struggles to promote new forms of
female identities coincided with other forms of solidarity work with the

poor, and all were funded from abroad. Over the years the myriad organizational activities and educational work that brought professionals working for NGOs and activists together with women at the grass roots crystallized in what has come to be known as a 'feminist curriculum.' This curriculum aimed at bringing women out of their homes, as it were, and helping them change their lives through consciousness-raising activities on matters such as female sexuality, women's rights under Chilean law, parent–child relations, and leadership potential (Schild, 1991, 1994). It consisted in a series of popular education-inspired modules and a strategy for organizing women in their neighbourhoods.

The feminist curriculum recognized the need to attract women into workshops of *desarrollo personal* (personal development) through conventionally feminine activities focused on crafts like knitting and sewing. The assumption was that once the women established a level of trust and comfort with their group, and once they acquired a sense of personal competence, and an incipient sense of self-worth, they would move naturally to an exploration of a different range of questions, for example, about sexuality, parenting styles, women's rights, and life and work skills. The hidden agenda of this stage was to promote women's sense of self-worth and self-esteem. It was expected that the outcome of these explorations, at least for some of the women, would be a desire to join literacy courses, if needed, and leadership and skills training courses. This voyage of self-discovery was undertaken under the guidance of a veritable army of volunteers or *monitoras*. The *monitoras*, mostly working-class women themselves, offered their skills in crafts, or an expertise in the more advanced aspects of the curriculum they had previously learned from other volunteers, or from the staff at the NGOs which coordinated and financed the entire effort.

The workshops constituting the feminist curriculum, understood here as a set of work relations among different women, are the clearest expression of the ever-expanding, contradictory, networks of feminists in Chile. They were inclusionary because they involved ever-increasing numbers of professionals, activists, volunteers, and ordinary poor and working-class women in the circulation of cultural resources through myriad workshops. At the same time, they were also exclusionary because not all had equal access to resources and funding to engage in the production of knowledge.

Generally speaking, the feminist curriculum sought to 'empower' women – here workshops on women's rights and on leadership training were crucial – as political actors. Thus, without calling it such, the women's movement was engaged in undermining Chile's authoritarian political culture by promoting the organization of women across class lines and by calling for a redefinition of women's political identities. Given the important feminist dictum that the personal is the political, it is fair to say that in Chilean society, where acceptable forms of collective and individual identity traditionally placed women as extensions of their families, incursions into the private domain, such as those embodied by the feminist curriculum of NGOs during the dictatorship, have made a difference, if not for how some women live their lives, at least for what they desire for themselves.

Today, the basic elements and assumptions of the feminist curriculum have been retained and adopted by the entire gamut of institutions, organizations, and programs seeking to reach poor and working-class women. Indeed, the focus on strategies for personal development, which was central to the curriculum, has come to be recognized as a necessary component of any work with women. SERNAM (1994), for example, identifies it as a key first step in the project of 'integrating women into development.'[21] Even new organizations, like the Christian Democratic Party-affiliated foundation PRODEMU (discussed below), have identified personal development as a fundamental element in their own, politically motivated interventions in poor neighbourhood organizations. The original aim of the feminist curriculum, to raise consciousness and help generate a movement of women for change, has, of course, been forgotten or deliberately put aside by those funding and otherwise supporting these initiatives locally and internationally.[22] Today, the main goal of *desarrollo personal* (personal development), variously defined depending on the entity that puts it into practice, nonetheless all share the assumption that poor and working-class women must be appealed to as autonomous individuals, not as mothers or as homemakers.

These new forms of social intervention, in the name of 'active women's citizenship' and through an offer of strategies to *improve the self,* are a powerful reminder of the workings of feminist networks extending locally and beyond national borders. They are also, however, part of a renewed strategy to hierarchically integrate poor and working-class women in Chile's latest project of modernization. They are, in effect, being repositioned, and are repositioning themselves, as new types of *clients* of administrable 'needs' – as ones who are being fashioned into certain kinds of individual subjects, those who will develop their individualism through the *marketplace.*[23]

The widespread use of the feminist curriculum is illustrated by Fundación Para la Promoción y Desarrollo de la Mujer) (PRODEMU). This is a private foundation, established in 1990 by the Christian Democratic Party, that fills a vacuum created by the end of the dictatorship in the area of official, politically motivated volunteer work with poor women. PRODEMU replaced Centros de Madres – Chile (CEMA-Chile), the body that coordinated and oversaw traditional forms of women's neighbourhood organizing, the Mother's Centres during Pinochet's rule.[24] The aim of PRODEMU is to promote women's personal development by teaching a version of the feminist curriculum that is compatible with its Catholic underpinnings, including first and foremost the teaching of handicraft skills to be used by women primarily in 'strategies of *autoconsumo*' (self-consumption) and only then for the benefit of their families. Emphasizing 'self-consumption' over family concerns, in the context of a Catholic-based institution, is significant. It suggests a recognition of women as independent subjects rather than as mere appendages of their families. In this appropriation, and transformation, of the link made previously by feminist-inspired work with women between economic necessity and empowerment, PRODEMU has achieved a happy union between women's autonomy and the market. Its handicraft workshops aim to empower women as economic subjects. Approximately 2,500 *monitoras*, a veritable army of poorly paid, mostly poor and working-class women, many of whom had previously worked for non-governmental organizations, are at the forefront of this new initiative. Clearly, this is a rather dramatic instance of the recycling of female bodies, the rearticulation of experiences accumulated by women activists, and of the expansion of women's networks in the service, now, of the new government's own gendered anti-poverty programs as appendages of the marketplace and of new kinds of citizen–clients.

## Understanding Feminist Networks under Global Capitalism: Some Final Thoughts

In the introduction to their edited volume, *Scattered Hegemonies*, Inderpal Grewal and Caren Kaplan (1994:17) warned their readers: 'If feminist political practices do not acknowledge transnational cultural flows, feminist movements will fail to understand the material conditions that structure women's lives in diverse locations. If feminist movements cannot understand the dynamics of these material conditions, they will be unable to construct an effective opposition to current economic and cultural hegemonies that are taking new global forms.'

Grewal and Kaplan equated feminism with broadly understood oppositional practice to existing dominant orders, but, as this essay has shown,
this is a troubling assumption. Although it may hold at a most general
level, we must come to terms with the fact that feminisms have always
been, and continue to be, rooted in class-based projects, unless, of
course, we dismiss much women's activism of the nineteenth and twentieth century as simply not progressive or oppositional. The historical
record painstakingly unearthed by feminist scholars, for example, shows
that in the Latin American case, feminisms have typically embraced,
either critically or welcomingly, the 'modernisms' of the moment. Their
struggles in the name of all women against female subordination have
been shaped by this understanding. In this sense, feminisms have not
only been committed to 'understanding material conditions,' but they
have also actively questioned dominant forms of feminine sociality and
struggled for new, that is, modern ones. Moreover, Latin American feminists have not elaborated these crucial cultural resources in isolation;
they have been woven into far-reaching networks across the divide of time
and space.

At the end of the day, what we learn from a discussion of the transformations of local feminist projects over time is that what is oppositional at
one moment becomes the status quo at another. The progressive forms of
Latin American feminist activism that emerged during the dictatorships,
facilitated by innumerable outside resources, have been taken up by state-
backed and regulated institutional practices and goals. There is another
lesson here. In coming to terms with transnational feminist links, in the
context of the Third World, we must recognize that each part of the postcolonial world is different, if for no other reason than the dates that mark
its formal break with the colonial powers. Hence, attempting to come to
terms with the local and its connection to 'Western' forms, we must take
account of the different settings, each with its own colonial history.
Finally, how are we to understand Western feminist cultural forms and
their appropriation in local contexts? Perhaps the strongest lesson to be
learned from the preceding discussion of the articulation of changing
local discourses and practices and extra-local forms is that feminist discourses are best understood as cultural resources, a social grammar that is
neither inherently oppositional nor oppressive, but always amenable to
be recruited for different projects. In the Latin American context, as in
the West, this feminist grammar rests on the key modernist concept of the
self – self-development – and this concept has a wide range of meanings,
not only one.

NOTES

1 It should be noted that, as everywhere else, the recognition of the very existence of a first wave of Latin American feminisms, associated with the struggle
  for political rights and centred on the fight to obtain the vote, is relatively
  recent. The historical record shows that these struggles were shaped from
  early on, and in fundamental ways, by transnational links, something that
  remains all too often unproblematized. For an exception, see Miller (1991).
  Indeed, the rich literature covering the rise of contemporary feminisms in the
  region does not attribute any importance to transnational links. See, for example, the accounts found in Jaquette (1994), Alvarez (1990), Chuchryk (1984),
  and Radcliffe and Westwood (1993).
2 For a discussion of the activities and ideas associated with the struggle for
  political rights in the countries of the Southern Cone and Brazil, the focus of
  this essay, and for countries that together with Mexico and Cuba possessed a
  similar degree of development, including a sizeable urban, educated, middle-
  class segment of women engaged in reformist activities, see the following: for
  Argentina, Carlson (1988); for Chile, Gaviola et al. (1986); for Brazil, Hahner
  (1980, 1990). For a discussion of the region as a whole, see Miller's (1991) useful overview, especially chapters 5 and 6.
3 Discussions of the body have been central to feminist debates, and it is not my
  intention here to rehearse and assess them. My intention is simply to flag the
  stance that informs my own work. What I mean here, following feminist appropriations of Foucault's work, is that the body is a concrete phenomenon – see,
  for example McNay (1992). Thus, following Donna Haraway, while on the one
  hand the body is not a biological given, that is, the sum total of organs and
  functions, on the other, it is always more than a textlike 'field of inscription of
  sociosymbolic codes' (Haraway, in Braidotti, 1994:103).
4 For a useful overview that pays attention to recent work on women's education
  during colonial times, and thus puts to rest the accepted view that the
  education of women was of little concern during that period, see Miller (1991:
  ch. 3).
5 Mary Wollstonecraft's *Vindication of the Rights of Woman*, for example, was translated into Portuguese by the Brazilian writer Nisia Floresta Brasileira Augusta
  in 1832. This first edition was so well received that it was followed by a second
  one a year later. See Miller (1991:42).
6 For example, already in the late nineteenth century women teachers were central in promoting secular education in countries like Argentina, Mexico,
  Cuba, Brazil, and Uruguay. Indeed, as commentators have suggested, it is
  from this group of women that a consistent feminist critique of society

emerged. For a detailed discussion of the contributions of women to secular education in Latin America, see Miller (1991: ch. 3). In the Chilean case, a unique document commemorating the fiftieth anniversary of the famous *Ley Amunategui*, the legislation passed in 1877 that allowed women into higher education, records the story of the achievements of professional women and offers a sense of the contribution made by these women to the development of public health, education, and welfare. See, *Actividades Femeninas en Chile* (1928).

7 We should not forget to include here the impact made by that fascinating woman, Flora Tristan, who in 1843 wrote, 'Without the liberation of woman there can be no liberation of man.' Tristan, the daughter of a Peruvian father and French mother, was a writer and social critic whose ideas reflect a unique and interesting combination of feminism, socialism, and activism. She toured France extensively in the 1830s and 1840s, calling on working women and men to constitute themselves as a class, as the aristocracy and bourgeoisie had done before. Tristan visited Peru in 1833–34, and she was retrieved by Peruvian feminists as one of their precursors in 1944. See Miller (1991:14–15) for a discussion of this; see also Doris Beik and Paul Beik (1993) for a sample of Tristan's writings and an interesting biographical sketch.

8 See the discussion in Miller (1991) as well as Salinas (1987) for Chile, Carlson (1988) for Argentina, and Hahner (1980, 1990) for Brazil.

9 See Salinas (1987) for a discussion of the European 'free thinkers' who toured Chile and their impact on working-class women's organizing.

10 Today, with its privatized, that is, dismantled education, health, and welfare programs, Chile is a model that other countries, including those in the industrialized world, seek to emulate. Seen from the perspective of the losers – the majority of Chileans – the gains made over a period of roughly thirty years up to the fall of the Allende government in 1973 seem to have been lost forever. The term 'Chileanization of labour,' for example, is increasingly being used as a shorthand for unprecedented levels of labour exploitation; for an increasingly feminized and 'flexibilized' labour force whose wages, when coupled with the meagre fruits of two-tiered education, health, and pension programs, do not translate into a decent life. See, for example, Kelsey (1995).

11 Witness, for example, the tensions and outright acrimony marking successive regional encounters of Latin American feminists, and their subsequent discursive transformation in feminist texts into a seamless whole with many parts. The tensions and discursive transformations are well captured in Sternbach et al. (1992).

12 This variant of the debate is typically associated with Chandra Mohanty's (1988) influential piece.

13 For a recent interpretive account of the evolution and present fate of the Chilean women's movement, see Gaviola, Largo, and Palestro (1994). For more comprehensive accounts see, for example, Chuchryk (1984) and Gaviola et al. (1986).

14 Many feminists felt marginalized from active participation in the so-called reconstruction of democracy. For a critical appraisal of this initiative and its outcomes, see Gaviola, Largo, and Palestro (1994).

15 The *decreto de ley* that established SERNAM was passed after a seven-month-long parliamentary discussion. SERNAM's precursor was the stillborn Ministerio de la Familia, proposed during the Popular Unity period, 1971–3.

16 Since its inception, SERNAM has received funding from a variety of international agencies, ranging from the World Bank, the Food and Agricultural Organization, UNICEF, and the Panamerican Health Organization, to the European Community and the governments of Sweden, Spain, Holland, and Denmark, as well as non-governmental aid agencies. See Servicio Nacional de la Mujer (1994:19).

17 The bank's interest in, and support of, so-called innovative social programs, such as the Fondos de Inversion Social, which have been introduced in a number of Latin American countries, is one example of this shift. Others are the recent projects financed by agencies like Sweden's SIDA and the U.S. Ford Foundation in Chile which aim at 'strengthening civil society.'

18 Perhaps all that distinguishes this Chilean moralizing project from, say, the Canadian one, is that the powerful, by definition amnesiac, discourse of modernization allows Chilean defenders of neo-liberal restructuring to always orient themselves to the future, without having to tangle with the legacies of the past. For example, with one swoop the past becomes unmodern, what held us back, what prevented us from moving to the twenty-first century; and the future, guided by the present, holds the promise of us becoming modern. Meanwhile, in Canada, we must engage in a further piece of moralizing, namely, the chastizing of Canadians, individually and collectively, for 'living beyond our means,' for having been irresponsible – to ourselves, but most importantly, to our children, that is, Canada's future.

19 The government agency that controls the flow of funding from abroad is the Agencia de Cooperacion Internacional. Soon after the Aylwin government came to power, representatives of international agencies stationed in Chile were called to a meeting and told that the government was not interested in 'co-government' (interview with the representative of a Christian funding agency, June 1991).

20 A careful study of feminist professionals in the present period remains to be done. My observations, which are based on discussions conducted since 1991

with feminists found in the myriad organizations and agencies at work in Santiago, reveal a very strong trend, but obviously they are not conclusive.

21 For example, the National Program in Support of Women Heads of Households with Limited Resources, developed by that institution in collaboration with other government agencies, contemplates consciousness-raising sessions as the first step in the work with poor women heads of households. These sessions of so-called collective reflection aim to sensitize women to their condition and promote personal change. For a detailed description of the program, see Valenzuela, Venegas, and Andrade (n.d.).

22 For a discussion of the activities developed by NGOs with organized women from poor neighbourhoods that fit this curriculum, see Schild (1990, 1994).

23 In Schild (1995:143), I linked this positioning of poor and working-class women as clients of administrable needs to Nancy Fraser's discussion of the development of 'expert needs discourses' within feminist practice and its impact on feminist politics. See Fraser (1989).

24 CEMA-Chile, which was itself a latter-day version of much earlier, and equally politically motivated efforts to organize women in poor neighbourhoods, was not dismantled at the end of the dictatorship but remained, through an eleventh-hour legal manoeuvre, in the hands of military wives.

REFERENCES

*Actividades Femeninas en Chile* (1928). Santiago: La Ilustracion.

Alvarez, Sonia E. (1990) *Engendering Democracy in Brazil.* Princeton: Princeton University Press.

Beik, Doris, and Paul Beik (1993) *Flora Tristan, Utopian Feminist.* Bloomington: Indiana University Press.

Braidotti, Rosi (1994) *Nomadic Subjects: Embodiment and Sexual Difference in Contemporary Feminist Theory.* New York: Columbia University Press.

Carlson, Marifran (1988) *Feminismo!* Chicago: Academy Chicago Press.

Chuchryk, Patricia (1984) 'Protest, Politics, and Personal Life: The Emergence of Feminism in a Military Dictatorship, Chile 1973–1983.' PhD dissertation, York University, Toronto.

Fraser, Nancy (1989) *Unruly Practices.* Minneapolis: University of Minnesota Press.

Gaviola, Edda, Ximena Jiles, Lorella Lopestri, and Claudia Rojas (1986) *Queremos Votar en las Proximas Elecciones.* Santiago: Centro de Analisis y Difusion de la Condicion de la Mujer.

Gaviola, Edda, Eliana Largo, and Sandra Palestro (1994) *Una Historia Necesaria:. Mujeres en Chile: 1973–1990.* Santiago: Aki and Aora.

Gerwal, Inderpal, and Caren Kaplan (eds.) (1994) *Scattered Hegemonies: Postmoder-*

*nity and Transnational Feminist Practices.* Minneapolis: University of Minnesota Press.

Hahner, June (1980) 'Feminism, Women's Rights, and the Suffrage Movement in Brazil, 1850–1932.' *Latin American Research Review* 15(1):65–112.

– (1990) *Emancipating the Female Sex: The Struggle for Women's Rights in Brazil, 1850–1940.* Durham, NC: Duke University Press.

Hola, Eugenia, and Gabriela Pischedda (1994) *Mujeres, Poder y Politica: Nuevas Tensiones Para Viejas Estructuras.* Santiago: Centro de Estudios de la Mujer.

Jaquette, Jane S. (ed.) (1991) *The Women's Movement in Latin America: Feminism and the Transition to Democracy.* Boulder: Westview Press.

Jelin, Elizabeth (ed.) (1990) *Women and Social Change in Latin America.* London: Zed Books.

Kelsey, Jane (1995) *Economic Fundamentalism.* East Haven, Conn: Pluto Press.

Marchand, Marianne (1995) 'Latin American Women Speak on Development: Are We Listening Yet?' In Marianne H. Marchand and Jane L. Parpart (eds.), *Feminism/Postmodernism/Development,* 56–72. London: Routledge.

McNay, Lois (1992) *Foucault and Feminism.* Cambridge: Polity Press.

Miller, Francesca (1990) 'Latin American Feminism and the Transnational Arena. In Francesca Miller, Marta Morello-Frosch, Kathleen Newman, and Mary Louise Pratt (eds.), *Women, Culture and Politics in Latin America,* 10–26. Berkely: University of California Press.

– (1991) *Latin American Women and the Search for Social Justice.* Hanover: University Press of New England.

Mohanty, Chandra (1988) 'Under Western Eyes: Feminist Scholarship and Colonial Discourses.' *Feminist Review,* no. 30:61–88.

Montecino, Sonia, and Josefina Rossetti (eds.) (1990) *Tramas para un Nuevo Destino: Propuestas de la Concertacion de Mujeres por la Democracia.* Santiago: Arancibia Hannos.

Radcliffe, Sarah A., and Sallie Westwood (eds.) (1993) *Viva: Women and Popular Protest in Latin America.* New York: Routledge.

Salinas, Cecilia (1987) *La Mujer Proletaria: Una Historia Por Contar.* Concepcion: Ediciones LAR.

Schild, Verónica (1990) 'The Hidden Politics of Neighbourhood Organizations: Women and Local Level Participation in the Poblaciones of Chile.' *N/S: Canadian Journal of Latin American and Caribbean Studies* 30:137–58.

– (1991) 'Gender, Class and Politics: Poor Neighbourhood Organizing in Authoritarian Chile.' PhD dissertation, University of Toronto.

– (1994) 'Recasting "Popular" Movements: Gender and Political Learning in Neighbourhood Organizations in Chile.' *Latin American Perspectives* 21(2): 59–80.

– (1995) 'NGOs, Feminist Politics and Neo-liberal Latin American State Formations: Some Lessons from Chile.' *Canadian Journal of Development Studies*, Special Issue: 123–47.

Servicio Nacional de la Mujer (1994) *Memoria. Servicio Nacional de la Mujer, 1990–1994*. Santiago: Editorial Antartica.

Sternbach, Nancy, Saporta Marysa Navarro-Aranguren, Patricia Chuchryk, and Sonia E. Alvarez (1992) 'Latin American Feminisms: From Bogota to San Bernardo. *Signs* 17 (Winter):393–434.

Valenzuela, M. Elena, Sylvia Venegas, and Carmen Andrade (n.d.) *De Mujer Sola a Jefa de Hogar*. Santiago: SERNAM.

5

# Feminist Discourse on Central and Eastern Europe: Hungarian Women's Groups in the Early 1990s as a Case Study

## NÓRA JUNG

I was born and raised in Hungary and emigrated to Canada in 1982. I remember once in my high school in Budapest we had to fill out a statistical form that included our parents' occupations. The girl sitting next to me did not know what to put down as her mother's occupation, because her mother did not work outside the home. The teacher told her to put down 'housewife.' I was puzzled by why Martha's mother had to stay home. All the adult women I knew at that time had an occupation. Only older women stayed at home, but they were retired. Perhaps her mother had some kind of illness, I thought, and felt sorry for her. As I became friends with Martha, I learned that her mother was fit as a fiddle, but I was too embarrassed to ask why she stayed at home. Women like Martha's mother were the exception in the Hungary I grew up in.

When I arrived in Toronto, I was introduced to a completely different system of values. Although my knowledge of English was rather limited, the immigration officer told us that only my husband was entitled to free English classes. Adding insult to injury, I was also informed that only my husband would be reimbursed for his Metro pass, because he had to travel to look for a job. Not surprisingly, my Canadian experience drew me to women's groups working with immigrant women. In my academic work I also started to focus on problems that immigrant women have to face in Canada.

Doing work with immigrant women, I had to familiarize myself with feminist literature. The debates about anti-feminism and lack of feminist movements in so-called Third World countries[1] made me think about my lack of knowledge about feminist movements in Hungary. I knew that my great-grandmother had some connections to the feminist movement of her time, but when I asked my grandmother about it, all the information

I got was that 'she was a weird woman.' Although Hungarian women have not achieved full emancipation, my mother had enjoyed many of the rights and freedoms that my great-grandmother only dreamt of. She also read Simone de Beauvoir's *The Second Sex* – one of the few feminist texts translated into Hungarian in the late 1960s – but none of those experiences transformed her into a feminist. Why was feminism a pejorative term for two generations of women in Hungary? Why did I have to come to Canada to discover feminism? Then, in the 1990s, what made feminism attractive to some Hungarian women of a younger generation? In my academic work I formulated these questions as a research project.

When I began my research on new women's groups in Eastern Europe I assumed that the term 'new' referred to all women's groups that emerged after 1989, when Eastern Europe underwent fundamental political and social changes. However, I soon discovered that the fact that a women's group was established after the collapse of state socialism does not suffice for a group to be mentioned as a 'new' Eastern European women's group. Although there are a number of new women's groups active in Eastern Europe, Western publications,[2] written by both Eastern European and Western scholars, acknowledge the activities of only a few of them.

In the pages that follow I attempt to point out some of the problems inherent in accounts that systematically ignore some groups and privilege others. I will address how Western publications document the activities of newly emerged women's groups in Eastern Europe. In so doing I will discuss the social consequences of producing knowledge that privileges women's groups that are more familiar with Western academic discourses. I explore some aspects of Western hegemony in the production of knowledge about non-Western women, specifically about women from Central Eastern Europe. Part and parcel of this hegemony is the acceptance of Western feminist scholarship by some Eastern European scholars. Finally, I will reflect on some critical voices that are now emerging in Eastern Europe.

In this collection Vappu Tyyskä correctly calls into question the social construction of Western feminism. I am also aware of the dangers of essentialism in using the terms 'Eastern' and 'Western.' As I have argued elsewhere, 'I have chosen to retain the terms Western and Eastern European, because it helps me to identify historically specific political and economic differences that have had different impact on women's organizing as well as on theorising about the situation of women in these two regions. By Eastern and Western I do not simply refer to geographical locations. These terms also denote the historically specific division between capitalist and formerly socialist countries which in turn signify not only different modes of production but also distinct political systems with their concomitant dominant ideologies' (Jung, 1994a: 195).

Although I retain these terms for the above reason, I do not treat them as diametrically opposed categories. My criticism in this essay is aimed at those Western feminist scholars and activists who are eager to teach their Eastern European sisters, but are unwilling, or unable, to learn anything from them. I challenge feminists who consider knowledge produced in the West superior to knowledge produced by non-Westerners.[3] Similarly I am suspicious of Eastern European scholars who – in harmony with the goals of their countries' political and economic elites – aim to 'catch up with the West.' Eastern Europe needs feminist scholarship and activism. Feminism, however, cannot uncritically be imported from the West. Since my research is focused on Hungarian women's groups, I use for the most part the Hungarian case as an example to illustrate my arguments.

### Lack of Dialogue between East and West

Before 1989 there had been little communication between scholars in Eastern Europe and Western feminists, with the result that each group remained enclosed in its respective theoretical frameworks. During the period of state socialism, East European scholars gave little thought to feminist theories.[4] Since the Soviets allegedly failed miserably in their effort to terminate patriarchy, Western liberal feminists writing about women's oppression rarely contemplated the question of whether they could learn anything from the experiences of women in Eastern Europe.[5] Again in Eastern Europe after the political changes of 1989, the denial of the socialist legacy became the norm. This included discrediting the socialist approach to the woman question, as well as the devaluation and rejection of women's organizations that existed during state socialism.[6]

Following the collapse of state socialist regimes, the number of publications by and about East European women has increased dramatically. Some of these writings discuss differences between women's organizations during state socialism and women's groups that emerged after 1989 (Bishop, 1990; Einhorn, 1993). Western publications on newly emerged East European women's groups tend to focus on few groups, whose names have become known to Western feminists. However, other groups, such as the Hungarian Women's Association, who also define themselves as 'new' (based on the fact that they were established after 1989) are systematically excluded from these accounts. Specifically, based on my research on newly emerged Hungarian women's groups, I found that the activities of the Hungarian Feminist Network generated considerable interest among writers publishing in the West, whereas other new women's groups were excluded from Western accounts. One consequence of rendering some women's groups invisible means that these groups are less likely to get moral or financial support from Western organizations. Women's groups mentioned by Western publications have an advantage over the groups that are ignored when seeking financial and moral support from the West.

I suggest that in order to understand better the literature on women in Eastern Europe, one can draw parallels with feminist accounts of the situation of Third World women. The histories of women's organizing in Eastern Europe and in the Third World differ enormously, as do women's relationships to the state, their control over their bodies, and their rights as workers and citizens. While the priorities of women's struggles in these two regions are also different, there are some similarities in the ways Western publications explore the situation of Eastern European and Third World women.

Western feminist publications have been seen as exhibiting orientalist tendencies in their approach to Third World women, treating them as 'the other' and as a monolithic group.[7] Western traditions are depicted as tolerating (if not nurturing) feminism; the culture of the Third World, on the other hand, is seen as inherently anti-feminist (Lazreg, 1988; Mohanty, 1991). Similar tendencies can also be discovered in the literature on Eastern European women. For example, some authors in the 1970s suggested that Eastern Europe had to imitate postindustrialist countries like the United States if they wanted to provide the necessary preconditions for women's emancipation (Jancar, 1978). More recent studies imply that the change from a planned economy to a market economy was paralleled by the struggle to bring women's rights to a more advanced and more desirable stage of feminist politics (Bishop, 1990). To be sure, Western discourse on Eastern European women is not monolithic, and there are examples of different voices as well (for example, Lapidus, 1978; Molyneux, 1990; Segal, 1991; Einhorn, 1993). However, even the most balanced accounts seem to accept without criticism the premise that the lives of Eastern European women are best defined within a theoretical framework developed in the West. There is also a tacit understanding that Western feminism (of any definition) is superior to any theory or practice that Eastern European women themselves have developed against their own subordination.

## Women's Initiatives to Organize in Hungary

In talking about women's attempts to organize in Hungary, I focus on the period from 1990 to 1994. In this period there were more than two dozen women's groups. Some of these were the women's sections of political parties, while others claimed to be autonomous. The 1990 national elections resulted in a coalition government with the Hungarian Democratic Forum (MDF) as the main governing party. Shortly afterwards, ultra-conservative nationalists emerged from the right wing of the party and the MDF was too slow in excluding this right-wing faction from its ranks. The main opposition party of the time was the Free Democratic Party (SZDSZ), which opposed the MDF's tolerance for antisemitic and nationalist rhetoric within the government. The conservative political climate during the MDF coalition government (1990–94) left little room for women's organizing. Although the right-wing, nationalistic agenda of the MDF was not a choice for most women activists, some conservative women joined the Hungarian Women's Forum, which, in harmony with the MDF politics, is anti-communist, anti-abortion, and anti-feminist. The Women's Forum is an example of a women's section of a conservative party, but other parties such as the Socialist Party, the Labour Party, or the Free Democrats, also have their women's sections.

In contrast to the Women's Forum and its commitment to the (then) governing party and their stress on Christian values, the other group, the Hungarian Women's Association (HWA), is independent of any party or creed. The 1991 membership list of the Hungarian Women's Association lists forty-two women's organizations nationwide, but, based on my discussions with some women from these organizations, I would say that only a few of them were really active. The list of participants at the April 1993 round-table discussions organized by the Hungarian Women's Foundation (MONA) contains the names of twenty-five groups or organizations. This number might be more accurate. The HWA represents Hungary in the U.N. Commission on the Status of Women and was admitted to the International Women's Council (Hungarian Women's Association, 1992). Despite its high profile in international bodies, this group has been ignored or discredited by Western publications, because of the HWA's connection to the Women's Council – the only official women's organization prior to 1989 (Adamik, 1991; Corrin, 1992a; Einhorn, 1993; Molyneux, 1994).

The only women's group that calls itself 'feminist' is the Feminist Network. It was established by about a dozen women, mostly from academia. Although there have been several women's groups active in the early 1990s in Hungary, Western feminist publications tend to focus only on the activities of the this network, which is described as an autonomous women's group, with an active grass-roots base. I want to emphasize that I appreciate the activities of the Feminist Network and support their politics. While it is not my intention to discredit this group, I believe that the dismissal and lack of recognition of other women's groups in the Western literature requires some explanation.

Let us look, for example, at Western accounts on the Hungarian abortion debate. During my research I found reports about public debates on the restrictions on reproductive rights where female MPs (Dorottya Büky, Edit Rózsa), lawyers (Judit Csiha), sociologists (Mária Hercog), and a representative of the Hungarian Women's Association (Ibolya Újvári), participated.[8] I also discovered that at least three women's groups were active in the pro-choice campaign: the Women's Association, the Women's Section of the Socialist Party and, of course, the Feminist Network. The most often quoted Western sources, however, either ignore women altogether (Gal, 1994) or mention only the activities of the Feminist Network (Adamik, 1991; Corrin 1992a; Einhorn, 1993). Rendering all other women invisible in Western accounts raises the question of who is entitled to name the other. Why is the Feminist Network privileged as the only women's group to be mentioned in these accounts?

### Searching for 'New Social Movements' and Identities in Eastern Europe

As I argue throughout this essay, what is considered a 'new' women's group by Western publications is not determined simply by the date a particular group was established. An important criterion in defining an Eastern European women's group is whether or not the group is perceived as 'feminist.' The authors publishing in the West usually assume that there are fundamental differences between women's organizations that existed during state socialism and 'new' women's groups that emerged after 1989. The 'lack of feminist consciousness' among Eastern European women under communism is contrasted with the postcommunist 'mushrooming of feminist movements' (Bishop, 1990) and the 'feminist voices' that are to be heard in Eastern Europe today (Corrin, 1992b;

Einhorn, 1993; Funk and Mueller, 1993). Although being feminist is presumably an important criterion for being mentioned in Western accounts, these writers fail to define what exactly they mean by 'feminist.'

It seems that such Western feminist scholars are looking for their mirror images in Eastern Europe, and they report only on women's groups that resemble Western groups. On the other hand, Eastern European women are often more than willing to imitate what they perceive as the Western model of a women's group. For example, the Feminist Network used an American consultant from California to resolve some of its organizational problems. I would argue also that the process by which an Eastern European women's group becomes labelled as 'new' is also determined by the discourse on identity and cultural politics, which characterizes new social movement (NSM) theories. Most scholars seem to privilege groups that are familiar with Western academic discourses or have contacts with Western scholars. These, in turn, can construct their identities to fit the Western academic discourse. The group that cannot be described within the framework of identity or cultural politics seems to be ignored by authors publishing in the West.

Several writers on social movements have claimed that there is a fundamental difference between traditional, or 'old' social movements, and so-called new social movements (Dalton, Kuechler, and Burklin, 1990; Johnston, Laraña, and Gusfield, 1994). Although it is hard to find a typical group that would exemplify all the characteristics of NSMs, women's movements are mentioned by most authors as an example. Authors examining NSMs agree that while it is hard to capture the essence of these new movements, there is a more or less agreed-upon list of dimensions that characterizes them. The collective search for identity is presumed to be a central aspect of NSMs. Identity-seeking movements 'tend to focus on cultural and symbolic issues that are associated with sentiments of belonging to a differentiated social group where members can feel powerful' (Johnston, Laraña, and Gusfield, 1994:10). Talking specifically about women's movements these authors refer to nurturing their own identity as an important element of women's activities.

In the context of Eastern Europe, however, a search for identity has a different meaning. As whole countries in Eastern Europe re-evaluate their history, so members of women's organizations revise their own identities. 'New' women's groups help women to build new identities. These new identities have to be different from whatever existed during state socialism. A recurrent theme in this search for a new identity has been what I would call the 'masked identity.' This refers to the claim of Eastern

European people that they had to wear a mask in order to survive during state socialism. People who were prominent members in the party and/or were respected public figures during the previous regime became the most ardent critics of socialism. Not surprisingly, in the new context their credibility has been questioned. People with ties to the (then) dissident movement have more credibility when they claim that they were never devoted to the old regime. Although dissociating oneself from the previous regime has become an important aspect of the search for a new identity in Eastern Europe, there are many ways of associating oneself with a new identity. I will focus on some of them – the search for a national identity, the search for a European identity, and the dilemma of rejecting or saving one's past (state socialist) identity – and discuss how these identity-searching activities are reflected in Hungarian women's groups.

The MDF regime (1990–94) was well known for its strong preoccupation with nationalism. The search for a national identity has been prevalent in the program of the Hungarian Women's Forum as well. A leaflet introducing the group proudly described the Women's Forum as a 'women's group of conservative spirit' with a strong dose of nationalism: 'The Women's Forum emphasizes the importance of the Hungarian cultural heritage, it is for the spiritual rebirth of Hungary, for a new patriotism. It fights for giving back to motherhood its dignity and generally to give back to women their dignity lost during the forty years of Soviet-type socialism' (Women's Forum, 1992).

Discrediting the previous regime's approach to the so-called woman question was a favourite topic of authors writing on women's situation in Hungary in the early 1990s. But, by adding a touch of 'Hungarianness' to their program, the Women's Forum became acceptable to the Hungarian Democratic Forum as well.

Several countries, Hungary among them, want to get rid of the notion that former state socialist countries are on the periphery of Europe. Thus, we can see a search for a European identity (as opposed to an Eastern European identity). I would argue that the insistence of Hungarians that they belong to Central Europe is related to a quest for a new identity. This is embraced particularly strongly by the Feminist Network, whose members have close ties to Western feminist scholars and/or activists. Many have participated in feminist conferences and workshops, and some studied for long periods in the West. As they become more and more familiar with feminist academic discourses, they start to use the same language, seeing themselves as 'European' and 'Western.'

Since the Women's Association is often simply equated with the former

Women's Council, the search for a new identity dissociated from the state socialist past is difficult for its members. I talked to an older member of the association, who had no problems acknowledging the historical links between the association and the former Women's Council. She emphasized how much the Women's Council had done for women in Hungary. In contrast, a younger member argued that the Women's Association is distinctly different from the Women's Council and that the activities of the council had no bearing on the new organization.

Social scientists have argued that the politics of the so-called NSMs cannot be explained within the framework of older theories that focus on economic and class interests. During the state socialist period, official representation of women's interests was limited to their roles as workers and mothers. Thus, the politics of former women's organizations were based primarily on family and class identity. These women's organizations had their progressive moments as well, however, especially when they were in conflict with the state regarding women's interests. The best documented case is the history of the *Zhenotdel* in the early years of the Soviet Union (see, for example, Lapidus, 1978:63–73; Heitlinger, 1979:57–63). The Hungarian Women's Council also had its struggle in the 1960s, when the ruling party wanted to declare women to be emancipated (Turgonyi, 1991). Today, it is not acceptable for a women's group to focus on women in their role as workers. The emphasis has shifted to women in their role as mothers, which has been a theme pushed by conservative groups such as the Women's Forum.

With respect to historical continuity, authors writing on NSMs in Western industrialized countries acknowledge that the new movements have links to the past (Johnston, Laraña, and Gusfield, 1994). However, in the case of Eastern European women's organizations, the possibility of a link with the state socialist past is simply not permitted. The fact that historically the Hungarian Women's Association emerged from the Women's Council (which was the only women's organization before 1989) appears to disqualify the association from being included in Western publications on new Eastern European women's groups.

**The East European Voices**

Before I discuss some of the consequences of mentioning or ignoring certain women's groups in Western publications, I would like to discuss how Eastern European scholars commented on the situation of women in their countries. I am specifically interested in how Eastern European scholars interpret the effects of post-1989 political changes on women's lives and in their opinions about importing feminism to Eastern Europe.

Immediately after 1989 no kind word could be said about former regimes. The media portrayed them as communist, thereby suggesting that these societies embodied 'Marxism put in praxis.' Intellectuals or politicians from the left were ridiculed if they had a chance to voice their opinion at all. Although there were many dissidents in the 1980s who criticized the regime from the left, after 1989 most of them disappeared from the political as well as from the publishing scene. After the 1989 anti-communist revolutions, most Eastern European commentators on women's issues focused on a critical assessment of the past. They labelled the commitments of state socialist governments to women's emancipation as 'forced emancipation,' 'pseudo-emancipation,' or even 'over-emancipation' (Šiklová, 1993). Women's organizations that existed during this period were labelled as bureaucratic puppets of the party. The activities of these organizations were interpreted as working for the economic and demographic interests of the country as defined by the communist government, rather than representing women's 'real interests.'

Several Western scholars commented on the lack of feminist consciousness among Eastern European women (Bishop, 1990; Arpad, 1994), and Eastern European authors felt compelled to explain why there is so little enthusiasm about feminism among them. Most explanations have started from blaming the lack of feminist consciousness on the previous regime. There is an allergy towards feminism because it is reminiscent of communist policies. Many authors argue that anything that resembles the state socialist approach to emancipation is rejected by women in Eastern Europe.

Jiřina Šiklová (1993:7), the Czech sociologist and former dissident, whose name is well known to Western feminists, has written:

Most of the men working by our side were not self-confident bosses but people similarly 'downtrodden' by the over-protective Party and government. Thus, men were not our rivals but humble partners working at the next desk or machine. Women did not have to conform themselves to the political regime as men because, as a rule, they were not the main breadwinners of their families and their professional work was not the only form of their 'career.' Women could also use their duties to their children and their family as an excuse, or could even 'escape' to maternity leave.

For these reasons women today in post-Communist countries do not feel such an aversion to men as is the case with a great many Western European feminists.

As women we were not suppressed by men as such, but rather by a political system that lacked distinct sexual characteristics. This is also why, for the moment, proclamations of patriarchy under capitalism tend to evoke memories of political indoctrination. The hatred, the militantly ideological manifestations of some feminists, and the ideological character of feminist trends make us feel the same nausea, which, in the past, we used to experience to 'class struggle.' Today we are unfortunately at the stage of aversion against every 'ism.' And 'feminism' regrettably has this ending.

As these quotations illustrate, hostility towards feminism is usually coupled with lack of knowledge about it. Other authors suggest that women were actually getting a better deal under state socialism than men. An Estonian woman writer, Maimu Berg, even maintains that 'Estonian women have nobody to fight against. Our men are so defenceless and have suffered so from the cruel destiny of our state that the very task of women is to protect them by making stable homes' (quoted in Hallas, 1994:299–300).

**Catching Up with the West**

There is, however, a small but growing number of women who are enthusiastic about the idea of importing feminism to Eastern Europe. Writers who usually argue along these lines tend to talk about feminism in general. They pay little or no attention to the fact that they themselves are influenced by a specific kind of feminism. Only a few authors in this group seem to be aware about the diversity within feminism and without acknowledgment state their preferred version of it. For example, in her article 'Do Czech Women Need Feminism?' Jiřina Šmejkalova-Strickland (1994) maintained that Czech women do need feminism – but the salient question is which kind of feminism should that be. Smejkalova-Strickland's article focused exclusively on postmodern feminism. She suggested that in order to catch up with Western feminism, Eastern Europeans have first to find the missing link to deconstructionist theories. Since she did not explain why postmodern feminism is her preferred version of feminism, one is left with the suspicion that it might have something to do with what is the latest fashion in theory in the West. A more problematic part of her argument is that she seems to take it for granted that Eastern Europe has to catch up with the West.

Women activists and scholars who develop a positive attitude towards feminism (in both a general or a more specific form) tend to accept feminism without criticism. I would argue that this uncritical acceptance of Western feminist ideas often entails an uncritical acceptance of Western norms and values in general.

In the Eastern European women's movements the indoctrination for accepting Western feminist ideas and definitions as the norm is to a large degree promoted by newly emerging women's studies centres. Women's studies courses have been organized in various Eastern European countries, and the teachers are Western or (at best) Western-trained Eastern European scholars. Most of these courses are taught in English, and the reading material is hardly ever written by East European women. Susan Árpád, an American who taught women's studies in Hungary for two years in the early 1990s, described some of her experiences in a way that reminded me at times of missionaries' accounts of teaching the 'barbarians' in some 'exotic' country. Árpád quoted extensively from her students' comments in order to show how misinformed they were about feminism and how traditional their views about men's and women's roles were. In describing the difficulties of teaching women's studies in Eastern Europe, she maintained that 'Women's Studies in Hungary is in approximately the same position in 1993 as Women's Studies was in the United States in around 1968' (Árpád, 1994:490). Apparently Hungarians have quite some catching up to do! Árpád told us that she 'taught the Introduction to Women's Studies classes in essentially the same way that [she] taught [her] classes in the United States ... all of the readings and most of her presentations were about U.S. experiences' (ibid).

Árpád reported that by the end of the course some students 'were forming more positive ideas about feminism.' Certainly, it is the most rewarding experience for a teacher to see her students changing in a way that is perceived as positive by the teacher. From a feminist perspective (which I share), the claim about a need for the development of positive attitudes towards feminist ideas and theories is understandable. However, I wonder how far the development of positive ideas about feminism also means the development of positive ideas about American values. I wonder how many of these students began to undervalue their own culture and feel the need to catch up with Western ideologies.

Maria Todorova's (1994) article 'Historical Transition in Bulgaria: Women's Issues or Feminist Issues?' is a good example of how idolizing American values can become part and parcel of accepting American feminists theories. Todorova used Barbara Jancar's development model to explain the situation of women in Bulgaria. Jancar (1978) apparently believed that all women living under communism faced the same difficulties and that changes in their lives showed similar trends. In Jancar's view, only the postindustrial societies have created the social conditions that support women's demands for emancipation. Interestingly enough, she mentioned the United States and Sweden as examples of postindustrial societies, although in terms of sexual equality these two countries can hardly be mentioned in the same breath. What Jancar suggested is that Eastern European countries have to become postindustrialist – by implication, they have to become more like the United States – if they want to provide the necessary social conditions for women's emancipation. In her conclusion, Todorova (1994:140) maintained that 'the Bulgarian case agrees with many of the characteristics of Jancar's model, and diverges from some others.' Todorova also acknowledged that models have limited value in their predictive capacity. However, she did not even question the value system implied in Jancar's model. Her article clearly showed that the notion of 'West knows best' still has currency in the East.

Several prestigious Hungarian journals devoted space to discussions on feminism and women's studies. The acceptance of Western authority is striking in these publications. The June 1994 issue of *Replika* includes a section called 'Male Dominance' and the lead article in it is an interview with Pierre Bourdieu. The same year, a collection of essays on 'women, men, and feminism' was published by the same team who worked on the *Replika* issue. The title of the book is *Férfiuralom* (Male Dominance), and Bourdieu's article of the same title is both the lead article and the longest of the collection (Hadas, 1994). The collection suffers not only from male dominance, but more than half of its pages are translations from the work of Western scholars. It certainly could be argued that the editors wanted to familiarize the Hungarian audience with the works of Western scholars, but I am afraid that the uncritical acceptance of Western authority also played a role in decisions about content.

This reminds me of the cynical comments of Slavoj Zizek, who maintained that although Western Europe was fascinated by the East, the real object of fascination was the supposed gaze of the East fascinated by Western liberal democracies: 'In the Eastern the West found a sucker still having faith in its values' (Zizek, 1992:25). I am afraid that Zizek's claim can be applied to some of the Eastern European scholars who accept Western feminism without criticism as well.

Lest I convey the depressing impression that all fledgling feminists in Eastern Europe are just accepting the latest wisdom from Western feminists, let me tell you about some Eastern European scholars whom I consider as being truly critical of what has been said about Eastern European women since 1989. With the calming of the first anti-communist wave, we can find some Eastern Europeans who caution against an all-out trashing of the former regime. Dimitrina Petrova is a former dissident and presently politically active in Bulgaria. She challenged the notion, prevalent in the literature, that women until 1989 'were victims of socialist ideology and socialist practice.' As Petrova put it: 'My thesis is that, whereas societies of Eastern Europe were not socialist in any historically legitimate sense, they incorporated, though artificially and mechanically a complex set of measures aimed at formally fulfilling the socialist promise to women (maternity leave, child-care benefits, free medical care, formal equality in employment and pay, etc). Taken in themselves, isolated from the social context, these state organized policies were socialist. But they were distorted by their non-socialist societal context, and therefore they did not fulfil their liberating goals' (Petrova, 1994:268).

Some Western authors have already mentioned that an all-out criticism of socialism in Eastern Europe bears the danger of throwing out the baby with the bath water. Petrova, however, went one step further in her criticism, maintaining that former Eastern European regimes were actually not socialist. Nevertheless, within these non-socialist societies a number of measures were taken that she would accept as progressive (and would call them socialist in and by themselves).

While Petrova focused on the reassessment of women's situation during state socialism, the Russian writer Olga Lipovskaya (1994:275) criticized the way in which Western feminists want to teach Eastern European women: 'It is "trendy" now to help "those poor Eastern European women," just as it previously was with respect to women of the Third World. But, recalling the sometimes bitter experience of Third World women in connection with their Western sisters – the experience of condescending or didactic attitudes on the part of rich and powerful women – we would like to switch from being studied and analyzed as objects to subjects of equal socio-cultural exchange.'

Thus, Lipovskaya implied that Eastern European women should look at the experience of Third World women rather then simply trying to imitate the Western model of feminism.

## Anti-feminism versus Criticism of Western Feminism

As most of us know, it is very difficult for us as feminists to be critical of feminism. I recall my own experience of presenting a paper at an international conference where I was on a panel together with a Hungarian woman who was a member of the conservative Hungarian women's group, the Hungarian Women's Forum. The argument I put forward in that paper was very similar to what I have maintained here. I criticized some Western feminists who tended to define the situation of Eastern European women within a theoretical framework that was not developed in Eastern Europe. Anything that does not fit a Western framework is not considered worthy of recording by Western scholars, I argued. I thought I achieved in my paper a balance between acknowledging the emancipatory potential of feminism and criticizing Western feminists, who only want to see their mirror images in Eastern Europe. While some people from the audience understood my paper the way I intended, my Hungarian colleague interpreted my argument in a way I did not like at all. During the coffee break she congratulated me on my critical comments about Western feminists. According to her, feminists were like the Bolsheviks under state socialism, since they both forced women out of their homes and into the workforce. As with Bolshevism, she elaborated further, there is nothing Hungarian about feminism either. Therefore, she 'agreed' with me that feminism cannot simply be imported into Hungary (Jung, 1995).

This incident illustrates how easily one's critical comments on feminism can be misread as anti-feminist. I have also been misunderstood by some Western feminist colleagues, who felt personally attacked by my criticism, and who accused me of homogenizing Western feminism. I certainly do acknowledge the self-criticism among feminists in the field. However, we still lack the tools that would help us to understand some of the problems that emerge from doing research on East European societies within theoretical frameworks that have been developed in the West.

Chris Corrin (1990:179), who did extensive research on women in Hungary, cautioned us against cultural bias: 'There are obvious dangers here for analysts in imposing Western prescriptions onto different cultures. Feminism is an excellent body of writing from which to make a critique of social policy, but the values of a largely white, Western feminism cannot be neatly transposed into other situation with different historical, economic and cultural backgrounds and a different prioritizing of needs and desires.'

Corrin was correct in reminding us not to commit the same mistake in studying Eastern European women. However, she failed to follow her caution in her own writing (Jung, 1994a).

## The Western Monologue Continues

As I mentioned earlier, doing research on women in Eastern Europe raises the question of who has the opportunity or right to study and thereby name the other? Looking at the literature on women in Eastern Europe, we can discover the predominance of North American and Western European scholarship. Although editors of collections on Eastern European women make an effort to include Eastern European contributors, often these Eastern European authors have to be Western trained in order to meet the criteria of Western publishers.

A look at the list of participants at the Fifth World Congress of Central and Eastern European Studies (held in Warsaw in August 1995) reveals similar tendencies. Most of the presenters were form North America and Western Europe, reflecting the comparative advantage these scholars have in accessing conference funds and other such resources. Among the sessions focusing on some aspects of women's lives and activities in Eastern Europe, the predominance of Western (or Western-trained) scholars was particularly striking.

The dominance of Western scholars in the field suggests that Western (or Western-trained) scholars are more than willing to study women in Eastern Europe. This willingness, however, often stops short of trying to understand Eastern European women outside of a framework that is familiar to Western feminists. As we have seen in the case of accounts on the Hungarian abortion debate, this can result in a distorted production of knowledge.

My goal is not simply to challenge the 'truth value' of these accounts or to call the value of these publications into question. Rather, I am concerned about the consequences of recording and disseminating distorted accounts from a potentially powerful location. The role of researchers does not stop at witnessing and recording something. Given the Western hegemony of cultural production, authors publishing in the West do make political choices when they ignore or decide to witness the activities of certain women's groups. Although there were several Hungarian women's groups active in the abortion debate, their activities have not been recorded by authors publishing in the West. This way their histories remain hidden from Western audiences. The women's groups that are rendered non-existent in these Western publications do exist for women in Hungary. They are visible and audible in the Hungarian media. They are just invisible to those Western academic feminists who are blind to anything but their mirror image and who selectively focus on groups that can be defined within the framework of Western feminist discourse.

It is also important to consider for whom these publications are written. Given that they are published in the West, written in English, and are prohibitively expensive for Eastern Europeans, most of the readership probably consists of Western feminist academics and activists. Feminist organizations interested in assisting Eastern European women's groups would also get much of their information from these writings. Thus, groups excluded from these accounts are less likely to be considered for any financial or moral support.

Since feminism has an even more contested definition in Eastern Europe than in the West, most women's groups are cautious about calling themselves 'feminist.' It also has to be taken into account that women's groups might avoid being called feminist for different reasons. During my discussions with the members of the Women's Association I noticed that they usually do not call themselves feminist in Hungarian, yet they are less hesitant to identify themselves this way when among self-declared feminists. The association is afraid of alienating women who do not have an understanding of the complex definition of feminism. In contrast, the Women's Forum has a conservative view of feminism. The leader of the forum avoids being called a feminist because she equates feminists with what she terms 'fetus killers.' I do not want to bestow the label 'feminist' on women's groups, especially when the self-definition of these groups excludes the term. Whether defined as feminist or not, several Hungarian women's groups have participated in the struggle for reproductive rights, yet their activities have not been reported in Western publications. Excluding their histories from accounts of 'new' Eastern European women's groups denies these groups their role as agents of history. Was this not one of the problems that feminists have had with male-centred historians?

Indeed, the lack of enthusiasm about feminism in Central and Eastern Europe is depressing. During state socialism feminism was officially rejected as bourgeois ideology. After 1989, attitudes towards feminism remain controversial. Most women are suspicious of feminism because it reminds them of what they perceived as 'forced emancipation' during the previous regime. Among conservative women, this suspicion culminates in outright hostility. The handful of Eastern European women who do appreciate feminism tend to ignore the unfortunate tendency for Eastern Europe to become a dumping ground for the West, not only for goods and services, but for ideas as well. The few scholars or activists who embrace feminism tend to accept Western feminist theories without criticism.

However, there are now voices emerging both in Eastern Europe and in the West that challenge the hegemony of Western feminist discourses. One way to overcome the current opposition between Western and East Central European feminisms is to work through transnational networks. One such network is the Washington-based Network of East–West Women, which defines itself as 'an international communication network that supports women in Central and Eastern Europe and the former Soviet Union through dialogue, networking, activism, and information exchange.' Only time will tell how effective such collaborative initiatives will be.

NOTES

1 The term 'Third World' is still rather problematic in its implicit positing of hierarchies. Therefore, I prefer to use it in quotation marks.
2 The term 'Western scholars' refers to scholars from the Western hemisphere, including North America.
3 I used the label 'Western supremacist feminists' to describe this type of scholar (Jung, 1994b).
4 For example, Zsuzsa Ferge (1983), the Hungarian sociologist, is critical of Western feminism, but her critique is based on a simplified and distorted image of feminism.
5 See, for example, Kate Millett (1971:168–76).
6 See contributions in Funk and Mueller (1993).
7 See, for example, Mary Daly's *Gyn/Ecology* (1978). See also the 'Zed Press Women in the Third World' series. List of titles in this series can be found in Mohanty et al. (1991:76f).
8 See, for example, *Magyar Hírlap*, 5 May 1992.

REFERENCES

Adamik, M. (1991) 'Hungary: A Loss of Rights?' *Feminist Review*, no. 39 (Winter): 166–73.
Árpád, S. (1994) 'Teaching Women's Studies in Hungary,' *Women's Studies International Forum* 17(5):485–97.
Bishop, B. (1990) 'From Women's Rights to Feminist Politics: The Developing Struggle of Women's Liberation in Poland.' *Monthly Review*, 42 (November): 15–34.

Corrin, C. (1990) 'The Situation of Women in Hungarian Society.' In B. Deacon and J. Szalai (eds.), *Social Policy in the New Eastern Europe: What Future for Social Welfare?* Aldershot: Avebury; Brookfield, Vt.: Gower).

– (1992a) 'Gendered Identities: Women's Experiences of Change in Hungary.' In Shirin Rai, Hilary Pilkington, and Annie Phizacklea (eds.), *Women in the Face of Change*, 167–85. London: Rouledge.

– (ed.) 1995b) *Superwomen and the Double Burden.* Toronto: Second Story Press.

Dalton, J.P., M. Kuechler, and W. Burklin (1990) 'The Challenges of New Movements.' In J.P. Dalton and M. Kuechler (eds.), *Challenging the Political Order: New Social and Political Movements in Western Democracies* 3–20. New York: Oxford University Press).

Daly, Mary (1978) *Gyn/Ecology: The Metaethics of Radical Feminism.* Boston: Beacon Press.

Einhorn, B. (1993) *Cinderella Goes to Market.* London: Verso.

Ferge, Zsuzsa (1983) 'Változik-e a nők helyzete?' In A. Olajos (ed.), *Tanulmányok a női munkáról,* 230–57. Budapest: Kussoth Kiado.

Funk, N., and M. Mueller (eds.) (1993) *Gender Politics and Post-Communism.* London: Routledge.

Gal, S. (1994) 'Gender in the Post-Socialist Transition: The Abortion Debate in Hungary.' *East European Politics and Societies* 8(2) (Spring): 256–86.

Hadas, M. (ed.) (1994) *Férfiuralom – Irások nőkröl, férfiakrol, feminizmusról* (Male Dominance – Writings about Women, Men, and Feminism). Budapest: Replika Kor.

Hallas, K. (1994) 'Difficulties with Feminism in Estonia.' *Women's Studies International Forum* 17(2/3):290–300.

Heitlinger, A. (1979) *Women and State Socialism: Sex Inequality in the Soviet Union and Czechoslovakia.* London: Macmillan Press; Montreal: McGill-Queen's University Press.

Hungarian Women's Association (1992) 'On the Association of Hungarian Women' (pamphlet). Budapest.

Jancar, B. (1978) *Women under Communism.* Baltimore: Johns Hopkins University Press.

Johnston, H., E. Laraña, and J. Gusfield (1994) 'Identities, Grievances, and New Social Movements.' In H. Johnston, E. Laraña, and J. Gusfield (eds.), *New Social Movements: From Ideology to Identity,* 3–35. Philadelphia: Temple University Press.

Jung, N. (1994a) 'East European Women with Western Eyes.' In Gabriele Griffin, Marianne Hester, Shirin Rai, and Sasha Roseneil (eds.), *Stirring It: Women's Studies and Feminist Practice,* 195–210. London: Francis and Taylor.

– (1994b) 'Importing Feminism to Eastern Europe.' *History of European Ideas* 19(4–6):845–51.

– (1995) 'About Feminism and Nationalism in the Coffee-break.' Paper presented at the annual conference of the Women's Studies Network (U.K.) in Stirling, June.

Lapidus, G.W. (1978) *Women in Soviet Society.* Berkeley: University of California Press.

Lazreg, M. (1988) 'Feminism and Difference: The Perils of Writing as a Woman on Women in Algeria.' *Feminist Studies* 14(1):81–107.

Lipovskaya, O. (1994) 'Sisters or stepsisters: How close is sisterhood?' *Women's Studies International Forum* 17(2/3):273–6.

Millett, Kate (1971) *Sexual Politics.* New York: Avon.

Mohanty, C., A. Russo, and L. Torres (eds.) (1991) *Third World Women and Feminism.* Bloomington: Indiana University Press.

Molyneux, M. (1990) 'The Woman Question in the Age of Perestroika.' *New Left Review,* 183:23–49.

– (1994) 'Women's Rights and the International Context: Some Reflections on the Post Communist States.' *Millennium,* 23(2):287–313.

Petrova, Dimitrina (1994) 'What Can Women Do to Change the Totalitarian Cultural Context?' *Women's Studies International Forum* 17(2/3):267–71.

Segal, L. (1991) 'Whose left? Socialism, Feminism, and the Future,' *New Left Review,* no. 185:81–91.

Šiklová, J. (1993) 'McDonalds, Terminators, Coca Cola Ads and Feminism? Imports from the West.' In Susanna Trnka with Laura Busheikin (eds.), *Bodies of Bread and Butter: Reconfiguring Women's Lives in the Post-Communist Czech Republic,* 7–11. Prague: The Prague Gender Studies Centre.

Šmejkalova-Strickland, J. (1994) 'Do Czech Women Need Feminism?' *Women's Studies International Forum* 17(2/3):277–97.

Todorova, M. (1994) 'Historical Transformation In Bulgaria: Women's issues or feminist issues?' *Journal of Women's History* 5(3): 129–43.

Turgonyi, J. (1991) Interviews with E. Fodor, and N. Jung. August–September.

Zizek, S. (1992) 'East European liberalism and its discontent,' *New German Critique* 57:25–49.

# 6

# The Multiple Locations of a Czech Émigré Feminist: A Biographical Perspective

## ALENA HEITLINGER

The main objectives of this essay are to (1) use the contours of my personal and intellectual biography as a Czech-born, British-trained, Canadian feminist scholar to reinterpret my 'home' and 'adopted' countries' experiences and understanding of gender relations and feminism and (2) explore issues of 'representation,' 'voice appropriation,' and the impact of different geographical and political locations on the production and reception of knowledge.

### The Birth of a Czech Émigré Feminist

I was born in 1950 in Prague, Czechoslovakia, where I lived until 1968. When the Warsaw Pact armies invaded Czechoslovakia in August 1968, I was vacationing in England. Fearing Soviet oppression and the resurgence of antisemitism, my parents urged me not to come back. I agreed, and my life was changed forever. I stayed in the United Kingdom, becoming a full-fledged exile. I suddenly lost my daily immersion in the Czech language and culture, and I did not know when I would be able to return.

At the same time, however, the conditions of my exile could not have been more favourable. I was very young and ready for new adventures. British public opinion was quite sympathetic to the plight of Czechoslovak refugees, and the government gave all Czechoslovak refugees open work permits. Eligible students were able to enrol, with scholarships, in post-secondary educational institutions already in October 1968, less than two months after our exile had begun.

My sense of loss and displacement was soon taken over by a sense of liberation and empowerment. I grieved both the demise of the 'Prague Spring' experiment in 'socialism with a human face,' and the loss of my family and my native city. I also found myself at the age of eighteen free from parental control, a financially independent student at a British university, and in charge of my own life. Instead of embarking on the study of law at Charles University in Prague, I studied sociology at the University of Kent at Canterbury. Having to study and write in English was very difficult, especially during my first year, nevertheless, I found student life exciting and enjoyable.

The years of my undergraduate and postgraduate studies coincided with the emergence of the Women's Liberation Movement (WLM), with whose goals, political style, and membership I quickly identified. As April Carter (1988:53) has argued, 'In the late 1960s and early 1970s, British WLM was primarily young and middle class, drawing on students and women just entering the professions ... local groups sprang up spontaneously among friends and acquaintances and had a fluctuating membership; they enabled women to share their problems and relate their sense of anger or inferiority to a broader awareness of the position of women. The groups therefore emphasised mutual support and consciousness-raising, and tended to exclude men.'

The dissemination of feminist ideas through flourishing women's newsletters, conference papers, magazines, and books, and the growing (if often negative) publicity given to militant feminism by the mainstream national press, radio, and television, gave new saliency to women's issues. The two consciousness-raising groups that I joined at the Universities of Kent and Leicester (where I pursued my doctorate) concretized for me the meaning of the popular slogan 'the personal is the political.' By opening up new areas of debate and creating an alternative ideology emphasizing the imminence of social change, WLM motivated women to action, giving us a genuine sense of being politically active. I was particularly attracted to feminism by the discovery that I did not have to wear make-up, that I had a right to sexual freedom and the control of my own body, that my mother's 'double burden' was not inevitable, and that it was possible for both parents to accept responsibility for domestic labour and child care.

The British WLM had a strong Marxist orientation and included many women who identified themselves as Trotskyists or, more loosely, as socialists. Several of my friends were members of different Trotskyist groups, and their critical ideas about state socialist societies, and about the status of women in those societies, were of obvious interest to me.[1] My new-found ability to go back to Czechoslovakia for temporary visits,[2] and my eagerness to make some use of my knowledge of the Russian language (which I had learned at school in Czechoslovakia), were also influential in my choice of a topic for my doctoral thesis – a comparative study of the position of women in the Soviet Union and Czechoslovakia.

### Revisiting My Research on the Status of Women in Czechoslovakia and the Soviet Union

Given the oppressive political context of post-1968 communist Czechoslovakia, my role as an émigré feminist in conveying ideas and translating cross-culturally feminist concepts and practices was of necessity limited to a one-way flow of information *from* Czechoslovakia and the Soviet Union *to* the United Kingdom and other Western countries. The ruling communist party–state insisted on a monopoly of power and doctrine, and *any* potentially autonomous political force was regarded as a threat to this monopoly. An independent feminist movement of the Western type, therefore, could not *legally* emerge in communist countries to campaign against male domination or demand access to Western feminist literature. Thus, the main audience for my research and publications was in the English-speaking 'West.'

Most of the empirical research for my doctoral dissertation was conducted at the British Library in London and at the Charles University Library in Prague. I spent countless hours in both institutions gathering data from Czech, Slovak, and Russian books, scholarly journals, statistical yearbooks, newspapers, and women's magazines. I stayed away from interviews, largely because I did not want to draw any official attention to my research. As far as Czechoslovak authorities were concerned, my stays in Prague were private family visits. Like most Czechoslovak citizens, I was able to apply for a temporary library card simply by presenting my ID – my Czechoslovak emigration passport. While I could not take any books or periodicals out of the library, I was able to look at them in designated reading rooms.

The printed material offered a rich and valuable source of data. Even though the re-establishment of communist political orthodoxy after 1969 required local researchers and policy makers to frame most of their questions and arguments in acceptable Marxist–Leninist terms, this did not prevent them from producing some useful empirical knowledge. One often had to 'read between the lines,' but this was not a major problem for an émigré scholar familiar with both the local situation and East–West differences. Thus, I was reading various demographic publications with the knowledge that 'socialist' demography differed in important respects from demography as we know it in the West. In the planned socialist societies, the study of demography was much broader in scope, since it included not only formal demography but also related aspects of economics, geography, sociology, and planning (Heitlinger, 1987:34).

Empirical research on a variety of demographic and related women's issues was given substantial state support by Czechoslovak communist elites, and it was sanctioned by the official need to understand the complex set of causes responsible for below-replacement fertility. A 1956 research project on parenting, sponsored by the State Statistical Office in cooperation with the Ministry of Health, was apparently the first such research in a socialist country. Since its establishment in 1957, most of the research on population issues and policy was sponsored by the State (later Government) Population Commission, which was disbanded only after communism collapsed.

Throughout the 1960s, the State Population Commission conducted a number of surveys among married women or couples on family planning and day-to-day problems experienced by employed mothers with small children. The research findings were made available to government and academic bodies (though not to the public at large) and served as a basis for the adoption of an explicit pro-natalist policy in the 1970s (Heitlinger, 1987:30–1). While the Czech-based research and self-understanding offered an important source of data that I could consult, the prevailing official hostility towards émigrés,[3] and towards any broad critiques of the socialist system, prevented any meaningful open exchange of ideas. During the course of researching and writing my doctoral thesis (subsequently revised and published as *Women and State Socialism*), I therefore gave little thought to any potential benefit the book might have for Czech and Slovak women. The book is written in English (as are all but one of my publications to date), and its major intellectual and political concern was assessing the relevance of the state socialist experience for Western feminist theories and practice.

**Moving to Canada**

As my doctoral studies were coming to an end, I began to search for an academic position. My adviser encouraged me to look abroad, and when Trent University in Canada offered me a full-time teaching job in the spring of 1975, I did not hesitate to take it. I came first on a sessional basis (and on a work permit), and the following year as a landed immigrant. I was the first woman hired by the department, and the first to teach a women's course in the regular academic program.

My second emigration did not involve a major displacement, since this time there was no loss of language and only a minimal loss of roots and culture. In fact, there was a basic continuity in my professional life, because my first years in Canada were devoted to revising my doctoral thesis for publication.

In the early 1980s I embarked on a new Czechoslovakian study, focusing on the social and individual management of reproduction. Published in 1987, my second book, *Reproduction, Medicine and the Socialist State*, was once again inspired by Western feminist concerns and by my ongoing association with Czechoslovakia. Since I was at that time very interested in the, by then, growing Western feminist literature on the medical management of childbirth, I decided to extend the Western-based research to Czechoslovakia. Immersion in Czech and Slovak data soon convinced me that 'the topic of medical management of childbirth is too limited and that it would be more fruitful to broaden my focus to the whole reproductive sequence, from coitus to post-partum. In turn, the broadening of focus enabled me to consider in some detail various forms of state intervention in reproduction' (Heitlinger, 1987:xiii). Another source of inspiration for this research can be located in my personal biography: my first child was born in 1980 and my second at the end of 1982.

In my research I again relied mainly on printed sources, but, whenever possible, I supplemented those by 'anecdotal' observations and by information gained from several informal unstructured interviews with medical professionals. These interviews were arranged through personal contacts rather than through any official channels. I also took advantage of my own pregnancy. For example, in the summer of 1982, my, by then noticeable pregnancy enabled me to visit a prenatal clinic (with a friend who was also pregnant at that time) without anybody raising any questions about what I was doing there (Heitlinger, 1987:xiv).

As time went on, I felt more and more at home in Canada. I also found my visits to Czechoslovakia more and more depressing, both because of the political situation there and because I increasingly felt that I had nothing new to say about the situation of women in East Central Europe. I thus began to explore research options that would include Canada and also Britain. To meet the Social Sciences and Humanities Research Council of Canada requirement that research grant applicants demonstrate links with previous research, I came up with the idea of applying my research on socialist women's equality and pro-natalism to the very different social, economic, and political contexts of Canada, Britain, and Australia.

## Revisiting My British Feminist Roots

I embarked on this research during my sabbatical in 1988–9, which I spent with my family in London. The extended stay enabled me both to revisit my British feminist roots and to evaluate British feminism and government policies through a Canadian lens. My comparative research revealed that, with the exception of the local and metropolitan levels of government in the early 1980s, British feminism 'has not been accepted as a legitimate political force that can set a political agenda, participate in a dialogue about specific policy initiatives, monitor the implementation of relevant policies and otherwise engage in interest politics on behalf of women' (Heitlinger, 1993:109). I attributed the British feminist failure to gain meaningful access to the political process both to the unfavourable political opportunity structure of the closed and inflexible British political system and to the localized, fragmented, sectarian, socialist character of the women's liberation movement. British feminist activists have been ambivalent about 'playing the state' and engaging in pragmatic reformist politics, with the result that 'the building up of women's coalitions and networks across a broad spectrum of issues, the creation of links with traditional women's organizations, and the lobbying of the national government are much less developed in the U.K. than in Canada and Australia' (Heitlinger, 1993:109).

I also found that, in contrast to Canada and Australia, the U.N. Decade for Women was largely invisible in Great Britain. The 'strong antagonism to feminist viewpoints and issues by a powerful female prime minister, Margaret Thatcher, has also worked against the interests of women, as has the existence of mostly covert procedures governing appointments to "quangos" (quasi-governmental bodies), which include the Equal Opportunities Commission (EOC). While in Canada and Australia, femocrats and women's groups routinely consult each other and can offer mutual support, EOC femocrats have lacked the supportive political constituency that is necessary for successful bureaucratic confrontationist stance. There is no powerful national women's lobby to press for specific reforms across a range of women's issues and for greater access to elite institutions' (Heitlinger, 1993:307).

Jacqui True has since pointed out to me (in private communication) that the failure of British feminism to become institutionalized also reflects the rigid class structure of the United Kingdom and the difficulty the modern feminist movement has had in surmounting this. As postcolonial 'new world' states and societies, Canada, Australia, or New Zealand defined themselves in opposition to the rigid class structure of the United Kingdom. Egalitarianism was therefore much more legitimate in the 'new world,' giving feminism a space in which it could develop. The postcolonial state formation also meant that suffrage was an issue for all British subjects, including women. In fact, women in New Zealand and Australia got the vote not long after men in those countries, well over twenty years before their British sisters. This historicity of feminism is important for the understanding of subsequent developments of second-wave feminist movements.

**The Aftermath of the Velvet Revolution: Problems of 'Post-exile'**

The timing of the geographical and political shift in my research focus was highly ironic. As I watched the unfolding of the Velvet Revolution on my television screen in Canada, I was about to start writing a book that had nothing to do with East Central Europe. In the spring and summer of 1990 many of my acquaintances visited Prague, but I went to Australia. I did not visit postcommunist Prague until May 1991, although I have gone every year since.

I soon learned from local public debates (though *not* from personal experience) that 'discussion of the problem of emigration ceased to be the preserve of a small circle of former dissidents and became part of national discourse' (Holy, 1996:66–7). Emigrants were now able to return to Czechoslovakia, but they were treated with considerable ambiguity and, at times, outright hostility. Pekárková (1995:79) has argued that Czech re-émigrés, that is, repatriated Czechs coming back from emigration after twenty or forty years, belong to a peculiar category of 'half-foreigners.' While they speak the Czech language, their lifestyles, cultural and ethical values, memories, and political concerns are quite different from those of 'average' Czechs. Many Czechs are quite hostile to the re-émigrés. There is a latent rejection of this group, on the grounds that 'they did not make it in the West, so they came back and now want to give advice to us,' or 'what could they ever know about our experiences, they ran away, while we had to stay here,' or 'they came back and now want to show off their wealth.'

Another reason for the uncomfortable feelings many Czechs have towards émigrés could be that the latter remind them that some personal choices were available even under communism. In their search for new postcommunist identities, most Czechs like to dissociate themselves from the previous regime by seeing themselves as victims of a system where you did as you were told. The presence of émigrés, who physically left the communist regime, challenges the credibility of this construction. Thus, many Czechs, especially those who blame all their personal problems and misfortunes on the previous regime, prefer not to be reminded about emigrants, since thinking about emigrants would force them to think about themselves.

'Post-exiles,' that is, those who came back for temporary visits but who had no intention to return permanently, have also encountered problems. As Holy (1996:67) pointed out, 'On the one hand, emigrants are a source of national pride in that they demonstrate that Czechs can become successful even in the competitive West. Czechs point out with distinct satisfaction that people like Tomáš Bata, Miloš Forman, and Robert Maxwell are or were once Czechs and that in the 1930s Chicago had a Czech mayor. On the other hand, any comparison of the situation in their old homeland with their experiences in the West, which often implies criticism of many practices which Czechs at home take for granted, is detested. Emigrants are expected to display supreme loyalty to the nation.'

Holy (1996:64) attributed the latent hostility towards émigrés to the specific discourse on Czech nationalism, in which national identity is conceptualized as a primary identity. Choosing 'post-exile,' Holy (1996:68) implied, thus goes against the grain of the Czech notion of 'unswerving loyalty to the nation to which any other loyalty and commitment must be subordinated. These emigrants had turned renegades – an idea rendered in Czech by the verb *odroditi se*. The nearest English equivalent is 'to renounce one's birth' but the Czech verb refers not to something people do but to something that happens to them ... If emigrants show divided loyalties or criticise Czech attitudes and practices too strongly (particularly if their criticism does not tally with that expressed by Czechs themselves or goes beyond it), their Czechness becomes suspect.'

These specific precepts are not unique to Czech nationalism; they are typical of nationalist prescriptions in general. All aggressive nationalisms attempt to conceptualize national identity as the primary one. Nationalist constructions always attempt to universalize and homogenize individual identities, thus automatically excluding those who construct their identities on a more pluralistic basis and with a different order of priorities.

In the emerging postcommunist climate of political pluralism, the narrow collectivist discourse of nationalism coexists with, or is being gradually replaced by, Western liberal democratic discourse. Unlike the collectivist nationalist discourse, the liberal discourse valorizes individual choice, personal autonomy, human rights, democratic pluralism, and the market economy. Within this discourse, emigration is a private matter, and as such of no concern to the national collectivity. Cutting across these coexisting discourses is a dominant discourse of Czechs as a democratic, well-educated, and highly cultured nation, open to new ideas and values from other cultures. However, as Holy (1996:168, 172) pointed out, this process is highly selective, 'and it is again the opposition between the naturally constituted and the consciously created that provides the gauge for the acceptance or rejection of new trends. In the past several decades, the two most important trends that have emerged in the West have been the ecological and the feminist movements, and each has had a distinctly different impact on Czech culture ... In contrast to the ecological movement, which began to have its impact long before the final overthrow of the communist regime, the feminist movement came to affect Czech discourse only gradually after the November events.'

### 'Post-exile' and Feminism

Having spent most of my professional career in efforts to explain a variety of women's issues in East Central Europe to Western feminist scholars and activists, I was hoping that, with the fall of communism, I would finally be able to transmit something back *from* Canada and the United Kingdom *to* my country of origin. As a Czech-speaking feminist émigré scholar, I was looking forward to explaining to interested Czech women, and men, the scope and concerns of various Western feminisms. However, my personal experience as a young Czech émigré in the United Kingdom, who in the early 1970s eagerly identified with the goals and political style of WLM, turned out to be a poor guide to the understanding of Czech women's reaction to Western feminism. I soon found out that, like many other long-time émigrés, I am now more Canadian than Czech. My knowledge of local culture has aged, since my life experience, North American middle-class lifestyle, political commitment to feminism and anti-racism, and cosmopolitan multilingual pluralistic orientations are quite different from those of most Czech women and men.

My attempts to comprehend the negative Czech reaction to Western feminism eventually led me to the analytic notions of 'framing,' 'frame resonance,' and 'frame alignment.' I have found that Western and Czech women are approaching a shared problem (of women's inequality) with frames based on very different life experiences, socioeconomic contexts, and ideologies. Feminism does not strike a deep responsive chord with Czech women (and men) 'because most Czechs mistrust utopian and emancipatory ideologies; associate concepts such as "women's emancipation," "women's equality" and "women's movement" with the policies of the discredited paternalistic communist regime; are disinclined to engage in collective action; regard themselves as strong women rather than as victims; assign highly positive meaning to motherhood and the family, and perceive feminism to be anti-male. The world view of Czech women is informed by the social legacy of communism, and as such it currently lies outside the descriptive and theoretical frameworks of Anglo-American feminism' (Heitlinger, 1996:90).

As an émigré feminist interested in the cross-national translation of feminist concepts and practices, I also had to address the issues of 'voice appropriation' and 'representation,' especially the question of how the work of an emigrant is viewed in her country of origin.

**Issues of 'Voice Appropriation' and 'Representation'**

I first encountered these issues in August 1978 at the Ninth World Congress of Sociology in Uppsala, Sweden, where I presented a paper entitled 'The Women's Movement in State-Socialist Czechoslovakia.' During the question period, the male head of the Czechoslovak delegation suggested that only Czech-based (and communist party–state sanctioned) sociologists could legitimately speak at international congresses about the lives of Czechoslovak women. He stated the following: 'We have heard some strange things about Czechoslovakia, *a country we know, because we live there.*' The Czech sociologist then invited the audience (consisting mainly of Western feminist scholars) to visit Czechoslovakia to see for themselves 'our beautiful girls.'

Not comprehending why he was booed and hissed for this remark, and assuming that the audience did not believe him, the Czech speaker then made a complete fool of himself by repeating that 'Czechoslovak girls are truly beautiful,' without addressing any of the issues raised in my paper.

More than a decade later, the events of 1989 finally ended the communist insistence that only 'home-grown,' party-sanctioned researchers could produce legitimate accounts about the lives of women in the region. Since 1989 a variety of approaches to the situation of women in

East Cental Europe has been generated, both in East Central Europe and in the West. Nóra Jung (1994a, 1994b), has found important differences in perspectives among East European scholars who were born, raised, and remained in Eastern Europe, émigrés who left their countries and now live in the West, and Western scholars lacking first-hand knowledge of local languages and culture.

Hiring an interpreter can be expensive. Thus, Western feminist scholars have tended to rely on secondary sources and on interviews with 'key informants.' As Jung (1994b:10) argued, 'Western researchers find it convenient to choose their informants from people who they find through their western contacts. Their "key informants" tend to be the same people who informed (all) other western researchers as well.' Thus, personal ties among Western feminists interested in the postcommunist transition tend to hinder rather than advance the production of knowledge, for, as Jung (1994b:10) pointed out, 'Instead of presenting new information, authors tend to repeat the knowledge produced by previous authors ... Informants who do not speak a western language, or lack connections to western academics, are ignored. As a result, instead of creating new knowledge, the knowledge of a handful of people with western connections is recycled.'

Moreover, the dominance of English in international feminist exchange allows local speakers with proficiency in English greater access to Western audiences. Thus, perspectives of East European scholars and activists who speak English, who are familiar with Western feminist politics and academic discourses, and who have contacts with Western (or émigré) feminists tend to be privileged. Knowledge couched in (inappropriate yet familiar) Western feminist terms not only distorts the complex postcommunist reality; it also perpetuates the hegemony of Western feminist discourses. Moreover, the dominance of Western feminisms also creates a new cadre or elite class of women and feminists in the receiving country, who then have a direct interest in reproducing this hegemony.

Émigré feminists who speak the local language have an important asset with which they can access indigenous documents, journals, and public debates, and interview other than English-speaking informants. However, as noted, émigrés' background knowledge of local culture and politics can age. Over time, émigrés can lose their familiarity with the nuances of the local situation and become, instead, more knowledgeable about the cultural and political environment of their adopted country. Thus, émigré feminists, especially those writing for a Western audience, are not immune to gazing at Eastern Europe only through 'Western eyes.'

With the emergence of a more open political climate of postcom-munism, émigré feminists have also lost their monopoly on rendering simultaneously an indigenous and a Western analysis of gender relations. As new cohorts of Eastern European women come of age, travel and study abroad, acquire the capacity to communicate complex ideas in Eng-lish (say, or German, or French, or Spanish), and as the legacies of com-munism begin to fade, new indigenous feminist self-understandings are bound to emerge. Indeed, as I have noted, 'Another way of interpreting the Czech attitude towards western feminism is to see rejection as a neces-sary first step in women's efforts to develop their own conceptual lan-guage and collective action frames, their own methods of organizing, and their own political priorities' (Heitlinger, 1996:88).

Thus, what started as a misguided effort on my part 'to transmit some-thing back *from* Canada and the U.K. *to* my country of origin' has become a constructive and mutually respectful dialogue between an 'émigré,' those 'who stayed,' and a new generation of feminist activists. I soon dis-covered that I could learn more from my local informants by listening to what they have to say about their lives and experiences than by attempt-ing to enlighten them about Western feminist theory and practice.

During my various post-1989 interviews with government officials at the Ministry of Health and the former federal Ministry of Labour and Social Affairs, leaders of the Czech Association of Nurses and of the Asso-ciation of Home Care, various academics, and several activists associated with the Gender Studies Centre,[4] my Czechness was never suspect. All my informants considered me 'one of them,' and they felt quite free to com-plain to me about some of their frustrating encounters with various West-ern visitors. 'Feeling free to complain' was often more important to them than learning something about Canada. What the Czech informants par-ticularly resented were those Western visitors who 'wasted their time,' either by asking uninformed questions and/or by imposing inappropri-ate research agendas and analytical frameworks.

Šiklová (1994:9) has noted, rather sarcastically, that 'we sometimes get the impression from the questions asked by our Western female visitors that they think that the position of women in our society has considerably worsened since 1989. Women have apparently lost all the advantages given to them by socialism, they can no longer reach leading positions, are discriminated against in the workplace, have lost their jobs, have enormous economic problems, have neither maternity leave nor family allowances, the Catholic church has pushed through legislation criminal-izing abortion, and because kindergartens have been also abolished, women are massively returning to the home. Moreover, we are so wretched that we are not even aware of this situation, are not complaining, and are not defending ourselves!'

While many of these trends may characterize some of the other countries in East Central Europe, they certainly do not apply to the Czech Republic. As Šiklová (1994:9) pointed out, 'Women who took the risk to become entrepreneurs form only one-third of the numbers of male entrepreneurs, but they do exist! Despite the fact that women can now stay at home and devote themselves fully to child care, the total level of female employment decreased by only 3 per cent. We still have one of the highest levels of women's labour force participation anywhere. Research findings have revealed that women are planning to keep their jobs even if their husbands earn high incomes. Only 13 per cent of women are willing to give up their job to a man and only if there is substantial unemployment. Cinderella would not do anything like that!'

Several other women associated with the Prague Gender Studies Centre told me how annoyed they were with both the title and the cover[5] of Barbara Einhorn's book *Cinderella Goes to Market*, which they found demeaning and condescending. They apparently voiced their objections directly to Einhorn, but she chose to ignore them. Šťastná's (1995:120) review of Einhorn's book asked the following questions: 'Why is she calling women Cinderellas? Why does she describe them in the title as going to the market, when she knows very well how long women have already participated in the labour market? In an attempt to find answers to these questions, readers could come up with a hypothetical explanation, suggesting, possibly unfairly, that some western authors are consciously or unconsciously creating a certain symbol and 'ideal type' of a postcommunist woman, which better suits the purposes of their analysis. I would very much hope that in the case of the otherwise successful book by Einhorn, this was only a simple mistake and inconsistency.'

How does one move away from Western dominance of feminist analyses and research agendas and from relying on only a select few key feminist informants (such as Šiklová)? One possible approach is to engage in collaborative research projects. While during the communist period my bi- or even tri-annual research visits were quite sufficient to produce credible knowledge – things changed rather slowly then – this mode of operation is clearly unsuitable for the current situation of rapid social change. I have found my location in North America, and the fact that I do not want to leave my family for more than a month at a time, a real barrier to maintaining an ongoing research association with my 'home' country. The only way I can now conduct meaningful Czech-based research is in collaboration with locally based researchers. They do not have to be Czech-born and raised, but they need to speak the Czech language and have a first-hand *current* knowledge of local culture and politics.[6]

## Conclusion

Émigré perspectives on, and participation in, local and global feminist movements are phenomena that have so far received little attention in scholarly analyses. My biographical self-reflection reveals that the ability of émigré feminists to act as cross-cultural translators and 'ambassadors' is dependent on their ability to return to their 'home' country, on the reception they receive there, both as émigrés and as feminists, and, above all, on their sensitivity to different socioeconomic contexts, ideologies, and life experiences.

NOTES

1 Needless to say, I did not learn much about Trotsky when I lived in Czechoslovakia. He was mentioned only once in my high school history class, as a negative figure who nearly caused the defeat of the Bolshevik revolution. Before my move to the United Kingdom, I was not aware that there was a Trotskyist tradition of critical analysis of Soviet-type 'state capitalist' societies and their new 'ruling class.'

2 My marriage to a British citizen, a 'foreigner' from the standpoint of Czechoslovak communist authorities, retroactively legalized my emigration from Czechoslovakia. Marrying a 'foreigner' enabled me to become a Czechoslovak citizen permanently living abroad, who could from time to time visit her homeland and her family. However, each visit required a special visa from the Czechoslovak embassy in London, and the duration of these visits could not exceed thirty days. My marriage ended up in a divorce well before my emigration to Canada, where I subsequently remarried.

3 As Holy (1996:66) noted, 'The government's attitude to emigration was straightforward: it was a betrayal of the country, the nation, or socialism. Although people may not have always agreed with what the Party construed as being betrayed (particularly if it was socialism), the notion of betrayal was not culturally alien to them.'

4 Jiřina Šiklová, a prominent 'key' Czech informant for many Western feminists, started the centre in 1991 in her apartment with help from what was then the New-York based Network of East–West Women. Šiklová is a well-known Charter

77 dissident who was imprisoned during the communist period for her activities, a sociologist, and the first chair of the department of applied sociology and social work at Charles University in Prague. Since the collapse of communism, Šiklová has given numerous interviews, written many articles, and attended several conferences on feminist issues, both in the Czech Republic and abroad. Her extensive network of friends in many Western countries and her knowledge of several languages adds to her 'attractiveness' as a native feminist informant.

5 The book's cover depicts two women in aprons sitting on motorcycles. As Šťastná (1995:120) asked in her scholarly review of the book, 'If the author wanted to present a sober picture of East Central Europe, does she really think that women wearing aprons and sitting on motorcycles are so typical that they belong on a book's cover?'

6 My most recent research project, on the lives of young, 'ordinary' (as opposed to 'successful') Czech women who came of age in the aftermath of the Velvet Revolution, was conducted in collaboration with Susanna Trnka, a second-generation Czech American, who spent the 1995–6 academic year in Prague. The publication resulting from this project is a collection of interviews with fourteen women of similar age and education, but varying work, marital, and childbearing experiences. Unlike many informants whose voices 'disappear' in random quotes and aggregate statistics and graphs, our respondents – 1989–90 and 1990–1 nursing graduates – speak for themselves and come across as real personalities. The fourteen chapters of interviews are preceded by two background chapters outlining the project, and the social and historical forces that have shaped these women's lives. A concluding chapter analyses common themes that have emerged from the interviews, linking them to legacies of communism as well as to the current postcommunist transition. Both Czech and English editions of the book have been published. See Heitlinger and Trnka (1998a, 1998b).

REFERENCES

Carter, April (1988) *The Politics of Women's Rights.* London: Longman.
Einhorn, Barbara (1993) *Cinderella Goes to Market: Citizenship, Gender and Women's Movements in East Central Europe.* London: Verso.
Heitlinger, Alena (1979) *Women and State Socialism: Sex Inequality in the Soviet Union and Czechoslovakia.* London: Macmillan Press; Montreal: McGill-Queen's University Press.
– (1987) *Reproduction, Medicine and the Socialist State.* London: Macmillan Press; New York: St Martin's Press.

- (1993) *Women's Equality, Demography and Public Policies: A Comparative Perspective*. London: Macmillan Press; New York: St Martin's Press.
- (1996) 'Framing Feminism in Postcommunist Czech Republic.' *Communist and Post-Communist Studies* 29(1) (March): 77–93.

Heitlinger, Alena, and Trnka, Susanna (1998a) *Životy mladých pražských žen* Prague: Slon.
- (1998b) *Young Women of Prague*. London: Macmillan Press.

Holy, Ladislav (1996) *The Little Czech and the Great Czech Nation: National Identity and the Post-communist Transformation of Society.* Cambridge: Cambridge University Press.

Jung, Nóra (1994a) 'East European Women with Western Eyes.' In Gabriele Griffin, Marianne Hester, Shirin Rai, and Sasha Roseneil (eds.) *Stirring It: Women's Studies and Feminist Practice*, 195–210. London: Francis and Taylor.
- (1994b) 'What Is New about the "New" Women's Movements in Eastern Europe?' Unpublished manuscript.

Pekárková, Kateřina (1995) 'Czech Republic: More Liberty, More Hi-Fi Stereos, More Hatred.' In Bernd Baumgartl and Adrian Favell (eds.), *New Xenophobia in Europe*, 68–87. London: Kluwer Law International.

Šiklová, Jiřina (1994) 'Úvod.' In Eva Hauserová (ed.), *Alty a soprány. Kapesní atlas ženských iniciatiu*, 7–10. Prague: Gender Studies Centre.

Šťastná, Jaroslava (1995) 'Ženy v postkomunistických zemích očima západní sociologie.' *Sociogický časopis* 31(1) (March): 119–23.

# 7

# Catalyst, Nature, and Vitality of African-Canadian Feminism: A Panorama of an Émigré Feminist

## NAKANYIKE B. MUSISI

Each of my works is a part of my own biography.

Michel Foucault[1]

### The Chicken in All of Us (Even Tigers)

Writing about my self, my consciousness, my history; subjecting my thoughts, my work, my words, activities, and lived experiences to self-reflection for public consumption has been one of the biggest challenges of my life. Here I am, given a discursive space but wishing it had not been given. The procrastination has proved one thing to me – the depth of my fears of self-exposure, even when I am given a friendly discursive space. This is a rare opportunity. Right now, I am being transformed into a subject of history who is at the same time an object of my own knowledge! This is exciting. Since I accepted the challenge, I work from the conviction and acknowledgment that personal reflection on the conditions, past and present, out of which our discourses and knowledge are produced, is crucial. The version I give is not just a by-product of my cultural milieux of being both African and Canadian, but of how I as an individual within all my other locations (educational background, colonial past, employment) have processed and constructed the knowledge that I give as history and analysis.

### Child of My Parents and the Empire

In the mid-1950s, Uganda, like all other coffee-producing countries, experienced an economic boom as the country's cash crop began fetching a higher value on the world market. I was born during that prosperous time. My parents' fortune, as landed civil servants, suddenly changed. Senior paternal clan members could not ignore the coincidence. During an initiation ceremony (*okwalula abaana*), which saw several babies officially welcomed and acknowledged as rightful clan members, I was named *Munnakutayitwako* – meaning 'the poor cannot be by-passed.' The extension of this: I was lucky. And lucky indeed I grew to be. At a relatively young age, I was taken to an elite girls' boarding school – Gayaza High School. This school was initially founded at the beginning of this century for daughters of the aristocrats. My parents were not aristocrats, but there I was! At this school we were given the education the missionaries thought was fit for our station in life;[2] similarly, the colonial state had appropriated the education given to the British working classes for the colonies. We sang 'Ring around the rosies / A pocket full of posies,' 'London Bridge is falling down,' 'Humpty Dumpty sat on the wall,' 'Jack and Jill went up the hill,' and several other nursery rhymes learned by all children of the British Empire who received our kind of education. We also did Scottish dancing on the grass on the equator as part of our physical education!

Throughout my schooling years, I held various positions of leadership – as a house leader, head girl, deputy head girl, leader of one club or another – I was marked out as a leader. This role became second nature to me. In the holidays I would extend it to my siblings and the village children. In the holidays, I organized almost nightly concerts for my father, who was a very quiet man. I would instruct my younger siblings, line them up, and sing or perform for my father – in the living-room, while my mother was busy finishing off the never-ending chores of a large household. I do not recall ever performing for my mother. I also gave my village an annual concert at least until I was sixteen years of age.[3]

**Defiant in High School**

In my last year at high school I was involved in a controversy, my response to which I think could be seen as proto-feminist. But I did not articulate it that way because I had no such vocabulary, nor had I even ever heard of such people as 'feminists.' One member of my class, and for that matter from my ethnic group, was suspected of being pregnant. The headmaster was afraid to subject this individual to a medical examination, so he opted instead to have all the female students undergo the medical. This was a mixed school that had close to six hundred students, about forty-five of whom were female. I was the deputy head girl. Everybody in the school knew about the impending examination to pin down the 'culprit.' The doctor who was to perform the examination had no direct connection with the school, although complicated cases that our residential medical assistant could not manage were referred to him from time to time. Generally, he had a bad reputation – he was a 'womanizer' – at least we knew him as such in those days; but now I am convinced he was an abuser – a man in a position of power exploiting his vulnerable clients. Rumours that probably started in the boys' quarters, that he was going to do a 'physical hand-in check,' caught fire.

Like most girls at that age, I had been brought up to cherish my virginity. I had a younger sister in the school, and I was concerned for hers, too! The method as described to us was very intrusive, and we had every reason to be concerned. I located the head girl and tried to persuade her that we should all stand together and defy the headmaster's plan. I suggested that we convince all the girls to be uncooperative in the project and that we should present the headmaster with a petition stating why we objected to the examination. The head girl was totally opposed to my strategy because, according to her, it was tantamount to a protest against the school authorities – she was to go ahead and present an example to the girls that it was 'safe for us to be examined.' I was left alone. But I knew I was not alone. I had the boys' support, probably for the wrong reasons, too; and some teachers indirectly expressed their support. I called the girls for a meeting and about thirty turned up. I remember telling them that 'what was about to happen to us was defiling to our bodies,' that 'it was a total disgrace,' that 'no man should touch me or my sister,' and that 'it was up to them to decide what course they would take but I would encourage them to follow my example.'

In the end, the head girl and about seven other girls were examined. The headmaster and his wife[4] were extremely angry with me. I was ethnically different from the majority of the students in the school, and my ethnic group (Baganda) had a notorious reputation among the more modest Western Ugandans. I was labelled rebellious, and a staff meeting was convened to determine my future at the school. What happened afterwards is all history now – I was not dismissed, expelled, or suspended. With the final national examination just around the corner, I concentrated on my studies to embarrass the headmaster and his wife who wanted me expelled. Miss Lucky? – I was the only girl from my school who went to university that year! From this experience, I also obtained my second 'situational' name. My enterprising young admirers, the 'dirty dozen,'[5] corrupted Western Ugandan pronunciation of my name Naka-Niike, to *Maka-Nika*, meaning *mechanic* in popular speech. I had thus become a *mechanic*, who at that time had managed to engineer a successful revolt.

## Mature and Subdued

When I was a student at Makerere University, Idi Amin was in power. I had matured and become less dynamic than in my youth, for good reason. There were several protests, but I held no leadership role, nor did I participate centrally in them. My eldest sister had been picked up from Kampala Road by Amin's police for wearing a skirt that was just one inch below the knee line. She was imprisoned and charged for wearing a mini-skirt and thus being 'idle and disorderly.' This incident instilled fear in me. Yet my adventurous spirit was not completely dead; it only rested on the back burner.

I concentrated on my studies. Not surprisingly, therefore, in my final year, I was among the top five students in the Faculty of Arts. These were the days of scarcity of instructors as several older *gulus* who had made Makerere the Harvard of East Africa fled Idi Amin's Uganda. As one of the best students, I was put into the Staff Development Program to become an instructor. I was only twenty-three, and several of my male students were much older than me.

Within a few months of my graduation Idi Amin's regime collapsed. The period that followed was equally tragic and devastating, as different factions that had participated in the war that overthrew Amin contested for power. The university became a very politicized place once again, and I participated in one of the largest demonstrations in Uganda during the 1980s, marching in support of the 'wrong' (politically and militarily weak) candidate. We were earmarked. An insider who was in the opposite camp, but who had had a relationship with one of my sisters, alerted her that I should disappear from Uganda as soon as possible, for I had been labelled as one of the leaders.[6]

I had to vacate my home country. I had had an offer at Birmingham University, in the United Kingdom, for a postgraduate program, but I had neither money nor sponsorship. I left Uganda in August of 1980. How I obtained money for my studies is another long story; suffice to say that I completed a master of arts degree in 1981, and secured a master of philosophy degree in 1983. In between, I married a medical resident

Toronto. I moved to Toronto in August of 1983 and began my doctorate in September of that year.

My life story had finally led me to where I belonged – studying African women's history and being exposed to a vast literature on, about, and by women. Although I remained excited throughout, I was greatly overwhelmed by my new discoveries.

## Acknowledging My Cumulative and Multiply Hyphenated Identity

During the lengthy period of my doctoral program, my husband graduated as a medical specialist, we had two children,[7] and when I finally graduated, I worked hard to secure a tenure-track position at the University of Toronto.

My long history will tell much about me, *but* – I am also a hyphenated feminist. This lived experience has not surfaced anywhere so far, and yet it is the subject of this essay. Now as I sit back and contemplate the evolution of my feminist consciousness, it is clear that this consciousness has been more of a cumulative process than a conversion or an awakening. Whether in the comforts of my father's living-room, on the grasses of the village compounds, at boarding schools, and even later, I was not a self-acknowledging feminist. I had no language to name my character and convictions. My feminist consciousness began to surface overtly in the mid-1980s during three closely related exercises – my fieldwork in Uganda, the process of writing and defending my doctoral thesis, and, lastly, as a researcher in the Toronto African community. I evolved from an easily intimidated woman during my stay in Britain and two years of doctoral residency, to become a fully expressive, argumentative woman who totally rejected standard norms, especially in academia. Behind the closed doors of my fieldwork – meeting, exchanging notes, and discussing with women, otherwise known as 'interviewing' in social science – I was transformed into a feminist, not just a woman studying 'other' women. Throughout this period, I discovered that 'interviewing' was just like marriage – everybody knows what it is, but behind each closed door lies a world of secrets.

## Field Research, the Most Effective Gospel for Conversion to Feminism

In 1986 I went to Uganda to research the impact of foreign ideologies on Baganda women from the mid-nineteenth century to 1945. Early in the preparatory stage, I had recognized the centrality of oral sources to my project.[8] This required following conventional recipes for fieldwork research and of research reporting, including engaging in a process of depersonalization of both my sources and myself. The sources would be transformed into objects and data-producing machines, while I would be transforming myself into a data-collecting machine. That is not all, as I would be required to assume the role of a psychoanalyst in a hierarchical relationship with my sources.

Standard social science interviewing borrows its questions from the language of psychotherapy. For example, one would be required to ask, 'Tell me more about ... Isn't that interesting ... Do you feel that ...' In this methodology, the 'interviewer' defines the 'interviewee's' role as subordinate and the extraction of information becomes more important than yielding it. In fact, we are warned against yielding information in the process of 'interviewing'; we are trained in techniques of not answering questions from the people we are questioning and expect to get answers from!

My personal experience behind the closed doors revealed that the very issues that social science research reports do not require us to comment on are indeed the central ones to feminist research.[9] I found that my research required more responsibility. There I was, asking too much from the women in terms of time, cooperation, and hospitality, and intruding in the privacy of their lives. They had every right not to entertain me. In fact, I recall vividly a comment one woman made to me. Previously, she had given me much information, but on the third day she said: 'I do not want any more conversation with you. I am poor. I am in the village, and I toil every day possibly until I will drop dead – but for you, you take my words and my sad experience (*ennaku yange*) and will earn a degree, a big name, and big money from it [!] No conversation to-day.'

The wisdom obtained from that fieldwork goes against the standard prescribed recipes of social science methodology. I was brought face to face with reality (which our theorized education tends to draw us away from) – that the so-called interviewees are people. They are *human beings* with considerable potential for sabotaging attempts to research them. Research cannot proceed without a mutual trust and, in fact, interviewees having the upper hand. In my case, I became the subordinate, at the mercy of my sources. I was their guest, on their own terms. I became more convinced that the prescribed interviewing practices were not only morally indefensible and wrong, but exploitative and anti-women. Hierarchical relationships had to be dismantled, and I had to invest my personal identity and knowledge in the relations I was engaged in as a researcher. I had to acknowledge that my personal characteristics mattered and had the potential to determine the type and quality of data I would get. I had to be sensitive to my sources' feelings about being asked questions, respect their objections, and be content with their leading me on. Finally, I had to acknowledge the several ways these women were using and seeing me as a source of information.

My position changed from being a data-collecting instrument for my doctoral thesis, in essence to impress my professor, to being a data-collecting instrument for those whose lives were being researched. Communicating with them became a strategy for documenting their own accounts of their lives. To me, historical research gained a new meaning – that of giving the subjective situation of women greater visibility by not appropriating their voices and historical past, but by being a medium of their voices as they saw and evaluated their past. In the final analysis, I was reshaped intellectually and physically too! The title of my thesis, and hence the questions to ask of my data, even the data I had collected from England, Rome, and the Entebbe Government Archives were all equally reshaped. The time frame for completing the thesis was equally adjusted. Since then, I have engaged in six different research projects.[10]

### Postmodernism and the Question of Location

The world is currently experiencing the emergence of 'new social movements.' As Stuart Hall (1989) observed, we are living in 'new times' that are characterized by the salience of identity politics in the form of racial, gender, and cultural struggles. We cannot deny the international context within which difference is celebrated and the previously marginalized social movements are increasingly recognized. Yet as these social movements are claiming identities, theoreticians are busy deconstructing them – disembodying them of any essentialistic characteristics. The reminder of this essay seeks to analyse the evolution of the conceptualization of African-Canadian feminism. Basically I attempt to show how it has manifested itself in the present transitionary stage of North American 'third wave feminism.'

### Conceptualization of Feminism

Since the late 1960s there has been a flood of literature about feminism in North America, spanning many theoretical interpretations for academic analysis. The conceptualization of feminism in Canada has corresponded to the dominant paradigms within the broader national and provincial political affiliations and parties, namely, conservative, radical, liberal, and socialist. Classifying Canadian feminism into these four broad categories is itself an essentialist enterprise. It tends to homogenize and generalize women who, though having some shared basis of interpretation, may differ from each other. It also tends to create a view of hard boundaries between antagonistic categories that in real life may be softer. Though conceptualizing the categories along a continuum reduces some of this tension, it is not an adequate means by which to do away with the existing classifications. When I use the term 'African-Canadian feminism,' I therefore acknowledge my own entrapment. As stated earlier, every immigrant and refugee 'African woman' in Canada has her own story. One is not simply an African woman, but a woman with multiple and cumulative identities (Muganda, Ugandan, Somali, middle class, employed, lesbian or straight). This position subverts or displaces all notions of group commonality (as woman, African, immigrant). Nevertheless, it is vital that we acknowledge that the internal differences among women as Africans, immigrants or otherwise, are as great as those that separate us from men and from both women and men of other races. Which of our particular identities asserts itself at any particular contestation is what we each have to live with day in day out.

The matter is not so simple, however. As Calhoun (1994:17) has argued: 'Where a particular category of identity has been repressed, delegitimated or *devalued* in dominant discourse, a vital response may be to claim value for all those labelled by that category, thus implicitly involving it in an essentialist way.'[11]

Part of the process of survival in a multicultural state entails negotiating sociocultural space for the multiple identities that constitute the Canadian nation. Canada provides a dynamic case study of attempts to understand and appreciate émigré multicultural feminisms. As Calhoun (1994:10) has further argued, 'The challenges posed by projects of identity cannot be averted simply by asserting that those projects are embedded in essentialist thinking.' Political dynamics that have activated and shaped feminist cultural contentions need to be more seriously probed than they have been. The objective should be to seek holistic approaches that take into account political, economic, and psychocultural as well as social factors. The project is not a simple one. Several contributors in this book agree that any analysis of émigré feminism has to explicitly encompass processes of state formation and state building or disintegration (with all its attendant regulations), for there are inextricable parts of the emergence of class, gender, racial, and ethnic conflict. We need to incorporate the state and the rules and institutions it creates as important variables in explaining how and why feminism will be manifested – as a unitary movement or otherwise.

### African-Canadian Women – Postmodern Identity or Not?

In the summer of 1994 a focus group gathered at New College, University of Toronto, to discuss what would be the most effective research strategy and to develop a pretest questionnaire for a research project that was to be funded by the Social Sciences and Humanities Research Council of Canada (SSHRC).[12] The project was to probe the employment needs of African-Canadian women in Metropolitan Toronto. The group was made up of the research co-investigators, a cross-section of women from the African community, and research assistants. At this meeting I described the African people in Canada as 'postmodern,' characterizing our multiple identities as embedded in multiple sites of oppression (as women, as Blacks, as Africans, as immigrants or refugees, as employed, unemployed, or underemployed). I also explained that our location entailed that as a people (African women) in Canada, we must be prepared for multiple struggles of resistance rather than a straightforward confrontation with society to get employment, or better jobs for that matter.

To use the term 'postmodern' to refer to our identity was in essence challenging the validity of pure categories such as 'Black community, working class, African,' which deny the existence of unstable, diverse, and subjectively recognizable group interests. I concluded by saying that in using the term 'postmodern' we shy away from privileging any one of our identities over the other (race, ethnicity, class, gender, or geopolitical background). Our identity must be seen as subjective, socially constructed, contextually dynamic, and historically specific. It is a sociopsychological image that locates us back in time and space, in history, memory, and territory (Rattansi, 1995:258). As socially constructed, our female immigrant or refugee identity becomes an arena in which hierarchical relations are presented, reproduced, and contested.

At the end of the meeting, one of the research assistants took me aside and chastised me for having used what she termed a 'negative term' – 'postmodern.' I asked her why she felt as she did, and her answers were precise: 'Because it means deconstruction, it means a community without form.' In the process of my listening, I heard a number of adjectives being aired and strong subjective statements – 'It is a language of the privileged, of those angry feminists at ... (a place was mentioned) who have less to do and make one more angry than contemplative.' But as the research progressed, all of us on the team came to terms with the poststructuralist approach that would not freeze the individual African women subjects of the study into the generic African woman. Each woman had a unique way of evaluating and making sense of her situation. Within this plurality of experiences, nevertheless, there existed a remarkable commonality of vision and an understanding as to why it may be difficult to achieve collective political strategies for transforming oppressive (gender, race, or economic) power relations.

In conceptualizing our identity, we recognized that our ethnic or continental identities are not 'backward,' 'traditional,' and hence outmoded forms of representation that do not belong in the era of modernity (in Canada, in North America). We argue that ethnicity (and hence differences among ourselves as African-Canadians) is part of the very process of modernity and thus has the potential to be a legitimate form of political and self-expression – precisely because we cannot afford to privilege one form of identity over another. At any one given time we are all. However, there is a danger. In insisting on a multiplicity and cumulativeness of identities that people can inhabit simultaneously, an unfortunate impression is produced – that the expression of particular identities is largely an individualistic choice. In this conceptualization, feminism for African-Canadian women is but one in a myriad of identities, no more or less important than any other. As far as those characteristics that define us as Africans are concerned, this may be only situationally true. There are situations in which we are given no alternative, where we do not have the luxury of expressing our varied identities – especially in a climate where having an accent, braids, or colour may determine whether you will be accorded an interview for a job offer. In a recessionary economy, where racial and gender differences are mobilized, they become a means through which to gain access to a job or to call upon the Charter of Rights or employment equity (affirmative action) legislation.[13]

**Emergence, Nature, and Vitality of African-Canadian Feminism**

As early as 1991, during an interview, I asked an African-Canadian woman, 'What do you understand by "African" and the term "African feminism"?' The answer was not a definition as I would have expected, but rather, what African feminism *does*. Amina stated: 'African-Canadian feminism challenges the mandate of those with advantage over us.' The African-Canadian feminist consciousness is an inevitable part of the feminist movement, but its perimeters are qualitatively different from the mainstream feminist movement.

The context within which African-Canadian feminism has arisen is one characterized by resistance to racism and other forces of domination and the traditional patriarchal and religious structures. To a large extent African-Canadian feminism is mounted by those who feel opposed to the existing social order, in their homes, at work, and in society at large. In its activist form, it seeks to alter the status quo to ensure social and economic equality between men and women and among women, dismantling the triple burden of gender stratification, economic domination, and racial superiority. We therefore argue that the strains that underlay the development of African-Canadian feminism are structural in nature – inherent in the workings of the social system. The strains are representative of the basic power struggles among groups within the Canadian system. These structural strains range from ambiguity, conflict, tension, discrimination, deprivation, and discrepancies within the social structure. The African-Canadian feminist response is very complex and quite elusive to an eye looking for obvious signs and symbols of its manifestation. Many seek changes in the social structure(s) through grass-roots actions, and there is never a typical 'African-Canadian feminist.'

At the same time, however, the nature and vitality of African-Canadian feminism cannot be seen in isolation from African continental and ethnocultural gender relations,[14] the global economic crisis, Canadian immigration and labour policies, and Canadian national and provincial politics at large. The global economic crisis has been responsible not only for demographic and distributive shifts over different societies; it has had a multiple role in heightening inequalities, disrupting traditional relationships, and altering the usually accepted order. Moreover, the global economic crisis has led to intranational and racial tensions, isolation, and ghettoization in labour markets and elsewhere. The movement of many African women into a racially discriminatory paid labour market has sharpened their analysis of their location; preparing them not to accept and become complacent of other forms of discrimination. Concomitantly, where employment has been steady, it has increased women's economic power in the family, facilitating the challenging of unequal gender relations in the household. Moreover, women's location in an urban environment has exposed them to other women who hold various forms of feminist awareness.

African-Canadian women have also been politicized through a number of different social groups in their countries of origin, in the process of migrating to Canada, and here in Canada. As our research has revealed, a great number of women experience status encapsulation on immigration, which leads to status inconsistency. Many African-Canadian women are highly educated and, yet, because of racism or sexism, they have no access to jobs within their training.

Furthermore, a separate African-Canadian feminist movement has emerged because of the failure of the mainstream feminist movement to address or appreciate this group's needs and demands. African-Canadian feminism therefore advances a critique of the previous discourse of Western feminists, questioning their objectivity and representation of cultural groups. It is dangerous to view mainstream feminism as capable of providing all the answers and a full account of African-Canadian women's oppression. The major contestation against Western feminists(isms) is their ethnocultural Eurocentric subjectivity, which has often unwittingly embraced universalistic categories, concepts, and assumptions of experiences, and hence assumed a universalistic approach and degree of concern. This universalization of subjectivity erases differences of race, age, sexual orientation, ethnicity, and immigration status. In their articulation of their positions and status in the Canadian society, African-Canadian women explore other structures and other power relations in which their identity of difference is entrapped. African-Canadian women emphasize the point that male dominance does not wholly explain their social and economic oppression. Moreover, African-Canadian women perceive the ineffectiveness of the mainstream feminist movement, but equally so the unlawfulness of male domination and the racist social structure. Confronted by real frustrations and despair, these women have analysed their position in Canadian society as beyond the politics of gender.

The female world (especially the African-Canadian) has not fallen short of role models, anti-role models, or standards of judgment and comparison. Perception of relative deprivation in comparison to female members of the white Canadian community has led to a reassessment of the nature of the stratification system and of its contradictions and inequalities that go beyond male dominance and personal self-blame. This, in the long run, has been a powerful tool in fighting what is seen as the system's illegitimacy.

While waging their struggles on a personal front, some African-Canadian women, nevertheless, do recognize that the attainment of group goals will harmonize with their own personal goals. This has called for vigilance, formation of women's organizations, and attending conferences specifically organized by African women. Our strength has been in articulating and approaching our goals as a self-identified group. As one African-Canadian woman so ably put it, 'My feminism is experiential, you have to be me – African woman, to know how I feel now and how in the past I have felt about my constraints' (Eno Egbo Egbo, a self-proclaimed African-Canadian feminist). It is women like Eno Egbo Egbo, who have started from a subjective position and have gone on to become community organizers, serving to heighten awareness of the actual strains that African-Canadian women are feeling in our fragmented and cumulative identities. Such community leaders have helped to convert the condition of apathy into a feminist activism without using much of the jargon in the mainstream feminist movement.

African-Canadian feminism is a field in which traditional notions of womanhood, person, and femininity are being contested and renegotiated. Émigré feminism of an African-Canadian type is interactional, intersecting with other forms of oppositionality (race, class, religiosity, and ethnicity). It is about practical identity discourse and praxis. At once, the topic African-Canadian feminism entails issues of identity, subjectivity, resistance, and agency. One's identity is constituted by a number of social relations and practices in which she is engaged. As African-Canadian women, we are opening up more and more to being sensitive to different forms of domination that operate through mechanisms of subjectification, objectification, and normalization. We feel objectification when we are constituted and labelled by others; subjectification through multiple practices of self-ways of knowing and governing ourselves that are inherited from historical traditions (culture); and normalization when we take the Euro-American approaches, definitions, and experiences as universally applicable. We also acknowledge how often we have participated in normalization through our complicity in patriarchal, racial, and classist practices of victimization – especially when we fail to question them.

Our experiences as African-Canadian women are sometimes contradictory and often destabilizing, giving rise to an identity that is fragmented and dynamic. What emerges is a conflict over loyalties and interests relative to the African–Black and Canadian–white communities. It is exactly the fact of fractured identity conflicts that has made it possible for African-Canadian women to accept coalition politics. Coalition politics, instead of competition or domination, promise a great deal to the women's movement in contemporary Canada. An understanding of feminist liberation based on multiple identities (a by-product of economic, ethnic, racial, and other social relations) requires more than simply a demand for equality with men. In the feminist movement, dialogue between women of different racial or ethnic, religious, economic, and sexual orientation backgrounds, is already under way. We argue that the ultimate goal of such a dialogue should remain educational, learning from each other rather than eliminating our differences and attaining artificial homogenization in which case the dominant will rule over the minority – falling further in the trap of 'universal woman.' This by no means plays down the need to invest in efforts that will reveal what we have in common and building on it for a stronger coalition.

If we understand relations of power as dispersed and fragmented through the social playing field, then we can better appreciate that resistance to power will take the same form. If differences are garbled and veiled and made cloudy in the totalizing theory of feminism, we stand to lose sight of the diverse empowering strategies of resistance. The strongly held feminist convictions by 'other' women point to the need to subject the current feminist knowledge, categories, and concepts to critical analysis in an effort to expose their limitations and biases. The goal of 'other' voices is not to silence (and vice versa) and exclude differences, but rather to positively utilize differences to diversify our strategies and a wide variety of visions for a better and fair future for all us in the struggle.

Equally important, freedom for us as African-Canadian women lies in our capacity to discover the historical links between certain modes of self-understanding and the modes of domination and to resist the ways in which we have already been classified and identified by dominant discourses (Rajchman, 1983:15). This requires that we develop new ways of understanding ourselves and each other, refusing to accept the dominant culture's characterizations of our being, and redefining ourselves from within resistant cultures. In this struggle we, as African-Canadian women do not stand alone. At present, many marginalized groups of people are finally breaking the silence, rejecting their object status within the dominant discourse, and constructing oppositional political subjectivities, theories, and progressive visions of their own.

One way to achieve our goal is to engage in a process of collective consciousness raising. Such consciousness raising would insist on defining ourselves as we want to be defined and claiming for ourselves that special space and power to name ourselves. That, however, need not be the end.

As one African-Canadian feminist declared: 'We must take every opportunity to educate the structures of domination that define us as inferior' (Focus Group Discussion, New College, Summer 1994). For example, the meaning of the term 'African-Canadian' varies from highly positive to victim, to an employment or social service category. Consequently, it is always open to redefinition with shifts in its discursive context. The power of racism is so appalling that to counter all of its forces will require the concerted effort – including the power of naming – of all those affected by domination.

### In Difference We Flourish or Perish?

Questions of identity have become the focal point of profound tensions within the feminist movement. Current discourses on differences among women pose difficult questions about the implications of these differences for the building of a unified feminist theory and practice. The question could also be posed differently: Do women *need* a unified feminist theory and practice – is it even plausible?

As a feminist transcultural group, we stand to gain from utilizing Foucauldian analysis of power, resistance, and freedom. Foucault argued that power is never won once and for all; neither is it ever possessed entirely by one individual or group. It is diffused and perpetually contested. The implication is that there will always be possibilities of resistance. For African-Canadian women, this assures us a spot for our version of feminism. Foucault's analysis helps us to view difference as a resource rather than as a threat to the women's movement. Difference can help us multiply the sources and fronts of resistance to the relations of domination that circulate in the society or community in which we live (Sawicki, 1991:12, 28, 45).

Locating power in a monolithic structure (say, of economics or racism) or in individuals (for example, Western feminists), does not help our cause. Radical feminists have for a long time pointed to the value of politicizing the personal domain. This will free us from the perception that we are perpetual victims of outside power (cultural, economic, or racial). Personal power and freedom could be attained before a full feminist revolution could be achieved. In the meantime, sharing our experiences as sisters in this book is a crucial instrument for growth, reflection, and for building grass-roots coalitions.

Adrienne Rich (1986:144) has rightly stated, 'Breaking the silence, telling our tales is not enough.' A meaningful and political outcome of our individual narratives should aim at analysing them collectively and their finding a receptive place in the feminist theory and struggle to serve both intellectual and practical purposes of the movement. As émigré feminists, we are not necessarily expressing desires for autonomy in a ghetto. What we do, however, seek is group recognition, not in a paternalistic manner, and for the larger family of feminists to sincerely value diversity.

## Conclusion

Émigré feminisms are politically significant because they reveal the short-comings of analyses that seek to create subjects into clear-cut categories. Deficiencies in the women's movement are realized, and a need to accommodate multiplicity, both in terms of identities and the various types of social organizations, is appreciated.

Thinking through African-Canadian feminism as émigré feminism, it has been argued that we cannot stop at only discussing émigré conten-tions on the basis that they are socially constructed. Instead, we need to shift our focus on the current social contests in which different feminist identities have come about, have been and are constructed – the reasons for this and the means though which this is done. Accountability for our actions remaining central to whatever we do and say, we have to seriously ponder the political implications and effects of the claims we make, the questions we raise, and the history we make.

NOTES

1 'Truth, power, self: An interview with Michel Foucault, 25 Oct. 1982.' Quoted in Luther, Gutman, and Hutoton (1988:11).
2 For further detail see, Musisi (1992a).
3 This concert coincided with our Christmas holiday, and it included children from other households. My mother always supported and encouraged us.
4 Up until now I strongly believe that this woman was behind the whole scheme to have us disgraced.
5 The 'dirty dozen' was a group of Grades 9 and 10 students who specialized in teas-ing newcomers either as Grade 12 or Grade 8 students. They had taken a liking to me because I resisted them strongly. Most girls accepted the ritual as some-thing they had to go through. I gave them a challenge, and they liked me for that.
6 Of course, they would not believe me that I was not a leader of any sort, that I just marched with other people. All qualities of leadership were written all over me. I was outspoken, determined, fearless, and articulate.

7 Nalwanga – the goddess of women's affairs, and Lwanga, the disciple of the goddess.
8 Oral history provides a distinctive opportunity for women whose experiences have often been ignored.
9 These include the quality of interaction between the interviewee and interviewer, the interviewee's feelings about being interviewed, the social and personal characteristics of the researcher, hospitality and hostility experienced by the researcher, and attempts to see the researcher as a source of knowledge.
10 These include (1) wife assault among Africans in the metropolitan African community, (2) a biography of Buganda's most controversial Queen Mother, (3) candlelight dinners on suburban Kampala streets, (4) meeting employment needs of African women in metropolitan Toronto, (5) the social origins of violence in Uganda, and (6) the impact of religions on policy formulation in East Africa.
11 Emphasis is mine.
12 Dr Turrittin and I wish to thank the Social Sciences and Humanities Research Council of Canada for having generously funded this research.
13 The progressive employment equity legislation of the previous (socialist) NDP government in Ontario has been eroded since the 1995 election of the Mike Harris Conservative government.
14 It is not surprising that at times our struggle for gender equality has come in direct conflict with the norms of our cultures.

REFERENCES

Anzaldua, Gloria (1988) *Borderlands*. San Francisco: Spinster.
Buijs, Gina (1994) 'Introduction.' In *Migrant Women: Crossing Boundaries and Changing Identities – Cross Cultural Perspectives on Women*, 1–19. Oxford: Berg Publishers.
Calhoun, C. (ed.) (1994) *Social Theory and the Politics of Identity*. Oxford: Blackwell.
Foucault, Michel (1979) *Discipline and Punish: The Birth of the Prison*. Translated by A.M. Sheridan Smith. New York: Vintage/Random House.
– (1980a) *Power/Knowledge: Selected Interviews and Other Writings 1972–1977*. Edited by Colin Gordon. New York: Pantheon Books.
– (1980b) *The History of Sexuality*. Vol. 1. *An Introduction*. Translated by Robert Hurley. New York: Vintage/Random House.
Gupta, Akhil, and James Ferguson (1992) 'Beyond "Culture": Space, Identity, and the Politics of Difference.' *Cultural Anthropology* 7(1):6–23.
Hall, Stuart (1989) 'Ethnicity: Identity and Difference.' *Radical America* 23(4): 9–20.

Kasozi, A.B.K. (1988) 'The integration of Black African immigrants in Canadian society: A case of Toronto, CMA.' Canadian-African Newcomer Aid Centre of Toronto (CANACT) – Report.

Luther, Martin H., Huck Gutman, and Patrick H. Hutoton (1988) *Technologies of the Self.* Amherst: University of Massachusetts Press.

Moussa, Helene (1993) *Storm and Sanctuary: The Journey of Ethiopian and Eritrean Women Refugees.* Dundas. Ont: Artemis.

Musisi, Nakanyike B. (1992a) 'Colonial and Missionary Education: Women and Domesticity in Uganda, 1900–1945.' In Karen Hansen (ed.), *African Encounters with Domesticity*, 172–94. New Brunswick, NJ: Rutgers University Press.

– (1992b) 'Wife Assault in Metro Toronto African Immigrant and Refugee Community.' Canadian-African Newcomer Aid Centre of Toronto (CANACT) – Report.

Musisi, Nakanyike B. and Jane Turrittin (1995) 'African Women and the Metropolitan Toronto Labour Market in the 1990s: Migrating to a Multicultural Society in a Recession.' Social Sciences and Humanities Research Council of Canada. Manuscript.

Peréz-Torres, Rafael (1994) 'Nomads and Migrants: Negotiating a Multicultural Postmodernism,' *Cultural Critique*, no. 26:161–89.

Rajchman, John (1983) 'The Story of Foucault's History.' *Social Text* 3(2):3–24.

Rattansi, Ali (1995) 'Just-Framing: Ethnicities and Racism in a Postmodern Framework.' In Linda Nicholson and Steven Seidman (eds.), *Social Postmodernism: Beyond Identity Politics*, 250–86. Cambridge: Cambridge University Press.

Rich, Adrienne (1986) 'Resisting Amnesia: History and Personal Life.' In *Blood, Bread, and Poetry*, 136–55. New York: Norton.

Sawicki, Jana (1991) *Disciplining Foucault: Feminism, Power and the Body.* London: Routledge.

Seyla, Benhabib (1992) *Situating the Self: Gender, Community and Postmodernism in Contemporary Ethics.* New York: Routledge.

Spivak, Gayatri Chakraworty (1988) 'Can the Subaltern Speak.' In Gary Nelson and Lawrence Crossberg (eds.), *Marxism and the Interpretation of Culture*, 271–313. Chicago: University of Illinois Press.

8

# There Is No Place Like Home: Caribbean Women's Feminism in Canada

## YVONNE BOBB SMITH

Who am I in Canada? I had to take the agency for everything I got involved in – the first move or the last move, nobody came looking for me, I had to take that initiative, so I felt I have used both the experience I have internalized, as I was socialized by mother as well as my aunt, and the belonging to community groups.[1]

I'll tell you something, oftentimes when I look at the risks I have taken, I think that it is the ol' West Indian/Caribbean spunk, I think it is the way I have been socialized. You are socialized so that you don't take shit from anybody, your rights are paramount ...[2]

These are the words of two of forty-five Caribbean women whom I heard repeatedly attribute their strength and survival to childhood socialization and community.[3] Although diverse (racially and by class and country of origin), the Caribbean women I interviewed are nearly all community activists. Most have been either paid or voluntary community workers during some or all of their residency in Canada, which has varied from twenty to thirty years. They reflect the multiracial, multicultural mix of the Caribbean: Aboriginal, African, Chinese, Indian, European, Portuguese, Syrian/Lebanese, and various combinations of these. In response to the question, How did you survive?, they told their stories, beginning with childhood learning to be independent in women-centred households and developing further through encounters with racism, sexism, and issues arising out of economic inequality. I discuss here these stories of survival in Canada over the past thirty years.

Home as a site of learning resistance and empowerment was an important and recurring theme in the narratives I heard. Mabel, of African

heritage,[4] said, 'You learn by seeing how people do things, and sometimes by anecdotes, the Anansi stories, that they tell you, you learn your
culture indirectly. It is still so even now, for my brothers and sisters who
were born here, because my mother, though she has been here for a long
time, she is very much a Barbadian.'[5]

Home exists in the imagination as a site where a Caribbean woman
belongs. It lives in her consciousness as a site of learning resistance. This is
a notion of home not found in other scholarly explorations (Puar, 1996;
Grewal, 1996). The women in my study imagine home to be in the geography of numerous safe spaces. They do not construct it in their minds as
a place from which they have been displaced. Although having resided in
Canada for long periods, they find themselves unable to replace fully the
idea of the Caribbean as home. Instead, they choose to make a distinction
between living in the North as home and home as they carry it with them
in their minds. As Bianca said, 'Funny for the length of time I am here,
with all my family, and others who are important to me, but deep down I
can't say here is home. I still talk about home as Jamaica.'[6]

Although some women were confronted with issues of domestic violence in the home, learning to survive in a colonial world muted the
intensity of issues of gender safety. Sexism, violence, economic deprivation, and an always tenuous claim to nationhood did not prevent them
from constructing 'home' as an empowering space, one for learning
survival.

Another example of the idea of 'home' as a site of learning resistance is
found in a Caribbean woman's story of resistance to the labelling and
divisiveness that is prevalent in Canadian communities. Sumanta, defining herself as of East Indian / South Asian heritage,[7] encountered a
struggle for her identity in community work. She felt pressure to occupy a
position as a South Asian woman, on the one hand, and, on the other,
she found herself gravitating to a multicultural Caribbean group where
she recognized similarities in culture and in efforts of resistance. She
related how she rationalized a solution by recalling in her memory that
'home' was, most of all, a mixture of good and bad incidents of family
and community life, yet she claimed that she learned about diversity
because her family had creolized their Hindu household. Imbued with
those memories, she pursued her desire to return frequently to the site
where she learned to imagine that ethnic and racial harmony exists: 'I
started going back to Trinidad ... every two years ... and that was part of
me finding myself and reconnecting with Trinidad ... because in this
country everybody wants to identify you. Going back to Trinidad helped

me a lot. It made me learn who I was, I never realized how much I had left at an early age, that whole identity was there and you come here and there is the struggle of your parents and yourself to survive.'[8]

Going back 'home' is the continuing education that enabled 'home' to become real in her identity, so she can survive in Canada with the sense of her own security. Lucinda, who identified herself as coming from African, European, and other heritages, migrated to Canada twenty-seven years ago and could only find a low-paying, menial job. After two years, she found another job, more appropriate to her secretarial skills. In spite of meagre earnings and her sole responsibility for four children, she completed an undergraduate university degree. She spoke of her early 'education' in survival, connecting it to a time when circumstances of poverty caused her mother to make creative use of her skills 'to make two ends meet'[9] and provide a livable existence for herself and her children. This, Lucinda noted, her mother did with the help of a community. When she herself discovered how resilient she was to some devastating experiences during her early days as a migrant, she recognized her reliance on the survival skills that her mother had taught her. Lucinda ultimately established and operated on a volunteer basis two newcomer service organizations in a government-subsidized housing project where she lived. In her eyes she brought 'home' with her to Canada, and in this way she could balance self and community the way her mother had. For those and many other community efforts she has earned two prestigious awards. She summed up her reflections about her activism by saying, 'I think where I was raised and where I was born and the type of parent I had gave me strength to achieve my goals in Canada. I can go home, back now, today and you can ask anybody who knows me back home, it's like I never left. Oh yes, I can go back home and I'm a Jamaican, my food, my attitude and I get back into my culture. Like, that's who I am, and you can't take that away from me.'[10]

'Home,' like community and nation, is an *imagined* construct (Anderson, 1991:7). Regardless of the inconsistencies that prevail, individuals believe that they belong to it as an entity that embodies safe and nurturing relationships with several people. Perhaps 'home' is also romanticized by my subjects who recall an inclusionary culture and communal living. Yet 'home' imagined in this way enables a construction of consciousness holding a Caribbean woman responsible first to herself, and then to her community, which defines her. Because 'home' *is* with her, the agency and strength to commit acts of resistance are alive. It is a conscious embodiment of values and practices of things to do. She may establish community services and Black women's organizations, produce newsletters, conduct workshops, lobby governments and institutions, and generate materials to promote positive values about 'visible minority' women. Some of these forms of activism are part of my own story, and I know I could only have undertaken them because of the way I was socialized to learn assertiveness and community in my childhood. My research, therefore, contains stories that are unyielding to victimization and that speak instead of the resilience acquired at home.

### Researching Subjectivity in Caribbean Women

Arriving in Canada with twenty years of experience as a corporate manager, and equally as many years in community work, I felt that the construction of my identity shifted from one of relative power and privilege as a middle-class woman to one of partial dependence and passivity. In the 1970s, during the era of revolutionary politics that swept the Caribbean, I was heavily engaged in feminist work. In the 1980s, similarly active, I focused on adult education, especially leadership development skills. Using the mass media, I was one of the people central to public educational programs for institutional changes in the country.

One can therefore imagine how surprised I was after arriving in Canada when one day, while sitting in a deli and perusing my notebook, a White woman placed a used tray in front of me, as if to suggest that I was the attendant on duty there. She made no effort to acknowledge her error even though I glared at her. Conversely, I have heard people express surprise and comment on the extent of my knowledge of English, or on any critique I have made of Eurocentric art. It does not end there, as some Third World immigrants also hesitate to show confidence in my ability to perform tasks that I had thought nothing of in my birthplace of Trinidad and Tobago. I consider their ambivalence to be a part of the process of acculturation and assimilation to the racism of the industrialized world, where the knowledge and skills produced by people of the Third World are devalued.

Stories similar to my own are familiar to many members of the Caribbean community. Theorized, these stories are examples of the individual racism described by Essed (1990:24) as the prejudice that Blacks (and others who are oppressed) experience every day in informal contexts or in private relationships. In other words, forms of prejudice practised in society have ways of producing difficulties for Caribbean women in their relations with others in Canada.

Many members of the dominant group either do not want to recognize the knowledge of Westernized tools and structures possessed by Third World women, or they appear threatened by their competence. Any exhibition of competence makes it more difficult to place Blacks and other visible minorities in racial categories of unintelligence and dependence. As a Caribbean woman living in Canada, I therefore came to understand that my location in the 'Black' category relegated me to sectors that require cheap labour for reproductive activity. But I know that this could not be the single identity of a Caribbean woman. She is not a homogeneous subject either by race or class, and heterogeneity is central to her subject position.

My Caribbean experience, which was valuable and transferable, thus lost its worth, because my subjectivity was regulated by the dominant perceptions of Third World women. However, it was not long before I recovered my strength to choose an area of work – as a consultant in community organizing – in which I sought to regain my sense of self. My resilience to shift positions was the result both of my learning resistance – an indoctrination passed on by Caribbean women in my family – and the practical use I made of that education in my everyday adult life.

As Scott (1991:7) has argued, habits of surviving were familiar in postcolonial systems prevalent in the Caribbean, where women's responsibility for themselves and their families taught them strategies for structural adjustment. Women struggled for power and established community organizations to resist ongoing institutional exploitation. They constructed multiple subjectivities to accomplish roles in their public and private lives. They acted out of feminist consciousness about various social issues and attempted to remove patriarchal structures in law, education, health, and social services. They resisted a system that discounted the rights of their communities to experience a human quality of life (*Caribbean Contact*, 1993).

I met such a group of women also in Canada. They accepted the label 'Black' and used forms of resistance I was familiar with. Recognizing my own pain in transition, I became curious about the ways in which Caribbean women's agency could be reconstructed in a new configuration of power and knowledge. Hence, I chose to inquire into the survival strategies of women who are representative of Caribbean racial complexities,[11] whose construction of resistance I knew began at home – their country of origin.

### 'Home' as a Site of Resistance: A History

In this brief historical review of Caribbean women's resistance I make two points: that the histories of domination and resistance for Caribbean women of all races are interconnected; and that, owing to the common threads of domination, resistance by Caribbean women is a historical legacy. 'Home' is the place in one's mind where one learns resistance. This, I would argue, is a historical consciousness emerging out of histories of slavery and imperialism. For a Caribbean woman, the concept of 'home' began with the oppressions produced by capitalism, slavery, and indentureship in which peoples of diverse origins – African, Indian, Chinese, Portuguese, other European, Syrian/Lebanese, and others – were subjected to varying and severe forms of cruelty and labour enforcement to develop and populate the region. In addition, the uprooting and genocide for Aboriginal peoples cannot be ignored as part of that history, as well as the African and Aboriginal alliances of the survivors (Craton, 1986; Young, 1993).

On the whole, Caribbean women over the centuries have been conscious of the ongoing processes of racism and sexism that produced the racial and gender divisiveness upon which their chances of survival were constructed. They, in turn, constructed a legacy of resistance strategies to serve as a tradition for ways of survival. Aretha, of mixed race and African heritages, who has lived thirty-seven years in Canada, gave voice to this legacy by saying, 'I see being a Caribbean woman as being from a strong background, where I always worked in a community even though I was little [young]. I think that continues in me. Sometimes when I look at it I see what I am doing, I see the need to do it because my mother did it.'[12]

The survival of a Caribbean woman began with the history of slavery and continues in the current times. The experiences of African and Indian-Caribbean women have been taken up by historians in both edited and single works. Among other themes, they have focused on the nature of African women's rebelliousness in the slave trade and on women's role in their liberation from slavery and indentureship (see, for example, Reddock, 1994; Espinet, 1993; Bush, 1990; Beckles, 1989; Mathurin, 1975). Of the several scholars who are writing Caribbean women's history, however, I depend heavily on Bush (1990), Silvestrini (1989), and Terborg-Penn (1986). They have explored African-Caribbean and African diasporic women's experiences, thus directing our thinking towards the significance of various forms of resistance. Enslaved women resisted authority to protect their sexual integrity. For example, Mary Prince refused to do her duty of giving her master a bath and left his employment in spite of the beating he inflicted upon her. She reflected on this incident in her biography: 'He had an ugly fashion of stripping himself naked and ordering me then to wash him in a tub of water. This was worse to me than all the licks. Sometimes when he called me to wash him I would not come, my eyes were full of shame. He would then come to beat me. One time I had plates and knives in my hand, and I dropped both ... He struck me so severely for this that at last I defended myself ... I then told him I would not live longer with him' (quoted in Ferguson, 1993:67–8).'

Any display of talking back or otherwise refusing to do as ordered was often seen by Whites as bad character. One White woman writer, Gertrude Carmichael, recorded in her journal, with abhorrence, the bad behaviour, the grumbling, poor work, and petty theft present among African women during her encounter with women enslaved as domestics in the nineteenth-century Caribbean.[13] Caribbean women responded to their obligation to procreate to satisfy the slaveowner's need for an increased labour force by refusing to bear children, resorting to abortion and infanticide so that their offspring would not inherit the harsh difficulties of the slave system (Dadzie, 1990). They recreated their status and influence in African society[14] by organizing communities that were often disbanded because of migratory shifts in human sales and escapes (Bush, 1990:105–8). This form of resistance was effective in mobilizing group action towards maronage, a form of slave revolt which included guerrilla warfare. Generally speaking, African women in the context of slavery pursued resistance by engaging in activities that 'reflect the heritage and worldview of traditional women on the continent' and that were essential to her survival (Terborg-Penn, 1986:188).

While knowledge produced about African women in the nineteenth century makes visible this aspect of their identity, less information has been unearthed about Caribbean women of other heritages. However, documentation about East Indian women's experiences is becoming more available. They, next to African women, comprise the second largest group in the Caribbean. The indentureship system that replaced slavery, in spite of its relatively brief tenure, did not lessen the inhumanity of captivity and forced labour for capitalist gains. The few experiences documented show that Indian women were subjugated to field work like their African sisters, and received comparable punishment and gross indignities as human beings. Indentureship of Indian immigrants took place mainly in the English-speaking Caribbean – Guyana, Trinidad and Tobago, and Jamaica. During 1834/5–1839 six thousand men and a hundred women were exported from India to Guyana (Reddock, 1994:27); in Trinidad and Tobago, 206 men and 21 women arrived in the first shipment in 1845 (Look Lai, 1993:225); while in Jamaica between 1845 and 1847, the average of 11 per cent of the total recruited were women each year (Shepherd, 1995:237).

However, these figures were 'characterised by the numerical disparity between the sexes' in the continent of India. The few females who entered this system, were described 'not as wives or daughters but as individual women' (Shepherd, 1995:240). Possibly as some scholars speculate, they could have been resisting patriarchal systems that controlled them sexually such as arranged marriages and the 'sati' – widow burning. For instance, Reddock (1993:227) wrote that, 'Brahmin widows comprised a large proportion of those migrating. The remaining number usually comprised women who had left their husbands or been deserted by them for whom prostitution or destitution was the only remaining alternative in India.'

Indian women resisted these gendered conditions by taking up the option to be indentured. A classic example is given in the autobiography of Anna Mahase, whose mother was married to an older man at the age of twelve. She was afraid of his moustache, ran away to the Calcutta depot for indentured immigration, and was then shipped to Trinidad and Tobago (Brereton, 1995:82). Another way in which indentured Indian women resisted the stereotype of gender inequality was by working at more than one job, which made their earnings in the long run equal to that of men (ibid.:243, 244).

Indian women were also victimized by patriarchal rules that regulated their existence as wives, daughters, and workers.[15] In spite of the violence that was produced by the control of their sexual lives, many women in resistance made choices about marriage and forms of intimate relationships with men, so we find that 'Creolised Indian women abhorred this practice of early betrothal and expressed their disapproval in letters to the editor in the newspaper of the day' (Shepherd, 1995:248).

The system of indentureship included a small number of Chinese and Portuguese women who also replaced African women in the plantations. The little we know of their histories suggests an equal resistance, but we require more to expand the analysis of a Caribbean woman's resistance.[16] Of European women, some of whom were not raced, a history of their experiences indicates that the colonial system constructed them differently as women. They had their initial, but brief encounter with slavery and indentureship, followed by their positions as wives or in roles of power, yet they did not gain equality with European men.[17]

The period of emancipation at the end of the nineteenth century and onwards was marked by the emergence of a Creole culture, that is, the existence of people of all the heritages. They were born in the Caribbean with modified social stratification and a tiered system based on colour. The tradition of resistance among all groups appeared in various forms, counteracting the marginalization in leadership structures and repelling political and economic oppression inflicted on peasants and the labouring classes (Craton, 1993; Reddock, 1994; Shepherd, 1993. In the political sphere, Caribbean women's participation (Trinidad and Tobago) began in the early twentieth century, since 'women were not only organized as specific women's sections, but were members of occupational or regional branches. In this capacity quite a few reached executive positions but usually at a lower level' (Reddock, 1994:127).

This element of community organizing marks women's involvement in resistance against the traditional construction of woman as passive and against the division of gender roles. Community organizing directed women towards issues that threatened the working class in the labour economics system in Trinidad and Tobago. Labour union strikes in the post-emancipation society for the English-speaking Caribbean as a whole persisted. The few available accounts of women's organized experiences show their activism on issues of gender, economics, and diverse social relations, both in Trinidad and Tobago (Helena Manuel, Elmer Francois) and Jamaica (Daphne Rose Campbell, Adina Spencer, Satira Earle). These women, jailed for their radical politics, were among the first in the twentieth century to indicate in their activism a Caribbean feminism.[18]

Caribbean women's strategies to transform their roles as 'mistresses' into entrepreneurs was also a form of resistance. In her analysis of the historical situation in Jamaica, Paulette Kerr (1995) argued that women, some of whom were concubines, secured properties from White men, and took advantage of the increasing early nineteenth-century hospitality trade to obtain their economic independence. Kerr argued that Caribbean women 'strategised rather than gave into her (their) circumstances,' as they moved into occupations vacated by Whites and located themselves in another site of the struggle for survival. While the female role of inn- or tavern-keeper was highly evident and at times problematic, these women developed a lucrative business that increased their economic independence, and in the long run brought them a great deal of privilege and power. Kerr's article suggests that the significance of the business was not the gendered role of the women, but their empowerment as entrepreneurs. This business was not only prevalent in Jamaica, but lodging or boarding houses were also in evidence in other parts of the region, and were as successful (Kerr, 1995). For instance, in my study, Vanessa, of European, mixed race, and African heritage, whose birthplace was an island in the Eastern Caribbean, talks about the strategies of survival in the poor circumstances of her mother's birth, and told it this way, 'my mother was actually brought up by two aunts, one aunt in particular. Both were spinsters who had a boarding house.'[19]

Marginalized in the labour market during post-indentureship and victimized by patriarchal systems, Indian women left the rural areas of Jamaica and moved into the urban areas where they established their own market gardening and cottage industries that they peddled in the city. In spite of the race and gender discrimination they encountered in these areas, they resisted subjugation with their own strategies of survival (Shepherd, 1993).

My research made it clear that 'home' is the key to a Caribbean woman's survival, in spite of the option she has to romanticize the experiences of innocence in her childhood days. My study shows that the Caribbean woman must live with 'home' as an immigrant abroad and that there is no question of her letting home go. She may in her body periodically return or connect with a Caribbean fixed place, home, for a renewal of her social and cultural ties, but that physical return only serves as an endorsement of her past learning of how to resist to survive.[20] It is the use of recollections of resistance that has not altered her connection with 'home' while surviving in foreign critical situations.

I will now discuss how Caribbean women survive the identity of immigrant women in Canada, which homogenizes and pathologizes them, and which is in opposition to the diversity including traits of assertiveness upon which a Caribbean female identity was constructed. The discussion will include the voices of women in my study describing some details to illustrate the meaning of survival for Caribbean women.

**How Did Caribbean Women Survive in Canada?**

The stories of Caribbean women's survival in Canada contain many strategies that are consistent with their historical background. Three key strategies emerge from these stories: education, networking, and community organizing. Caribbean scholars have found that Caribbean women's strategies of survival, based on full household responsibility, have contributed largely to the socioeconomic and community life of the region (Barrow, 1986). In the diaspora, my study refers to strategies that are mainly used for the well-being of the woman herself, engaging her involvement in issues of race, gender, and sexual orientation. These are strategies that are used with an intensity to diffuse the effects of stereotyping and marginalization and to enable them to be subjects in the struggle (hooks, 1990).

## Education as a Strategy of Resistance

Caribbean women of all social classes and races place enormous significance on education. Parents, particularly mothers, implanted the idea that their own lack of knowledge, or their limits to basic education, was a setback, and therefore they struggled to prevent their own situations from being repeated for their daughters and sons. I recall being told that 'education opened doors to life,' which on reflection was a major piece of encouragement in a colonial world. Therefore, a Caribbean woman learned the emphasis the older generation placed on education as a serious and essential tool in the struggle for survival. Aita, of African heritage, who is currently very successful in her academic career, recalled her beginnings as follows: 'My mother did domestic work, and ... she picked up every piece of information that she could get from the white folks in terms of dress ... and one of the books she got religiously was the *Reader's Digest.* You would see her in the evening when she finished work, she would sit down and go through them and teach herself to read. And then in the night she would call us and she would say come bring your schoolbook and you start to read, and if you stumble over one word, she made you go back and read it, and spell the word out.'[21]

The African-American scholar Patricia Hill Collins (1990:157) wrote of African-American women, saying, 'Drawing on the model of education as empowerment, Black women routinely reject models of authority based on hierarchical relations.' This holds true for some Caribbean women like Anne (of African heritage), who, after having achieved higher education, moved to a position of authority in which she was able to initiate and establish liberal reforms in the organization's practices of both hiring and servicing clients. Ariel, of mixed race and African heritages, and a single mother, went on welfare because of ill-health during pregnancy and then did a mixture of paid and voluntary work in a Black community agency. She noted: 'But there was all this nagging. I still had to raise my boy and I still had to go to school and I couldn't do both together. And there I was forty-two, my life came crashing down. I developed very bad asthma. When my asthma became under control, and when my son graduated, I then applied to Concordia and McGill and got accepted at both.'[22]

Striving for education does not mean seeking gender equality. It means taking personal responsibility for one's own welfare, which in turn produces a degree of urgency in a female Caribbean migrant striving for security, either in the Canadian situation above, or in the Caribbean experience of Rey, who is a first-generation Chinese-Caribbean: 'My mother has no formal education. Probably in Chinese. But my dad did not want us (three daughters) to be abused, so he was very protective. His attitude was that you get the best education, be brought up ladylike as possible and be sensitive.'[23]

Sumanta, of Indian-Caribbean / South Asian heritages, who started university at seventeen years of age in Canada, similarly noted: 'My mother always pushed me to school. Like Mom was a teacher, and I started going to school with her before I was due for school. Both my parents encouraged me to learn. My mother more, she valued education a lot. I have thought of it recently. It kind of helped me to develop my strength, and my desire to get more education.'

**Networking as a Strategy of Resistance**

Networking was undertaken with the same sense of urgency as pursuing plans for education. I define networking as an act of forming bonds among Caribbean men and women to resist marginalization, to maintain a sense of identity, and to reduce feelings of alienation. While networking involves no apparent structure, it carries with it a reciprocal responsibility by persons participating in the network. Its purpose may or may not be to make women and men become 'aware of occupational and/other available opportunities' (Turrittin, 1976:306), yet by virtue of the intangible commitment, exchanges of that nature are acceptable. Networking has historical significance for Caribbean peoples who, as migrants within plantation societies, had their real kinship ties broken. They recreated new forms of family linkages with a mixture of kin, friends, and neighbours. The act of networking evolved as a subversive strategy of resistance, both because of the loss of lives in the harshness of slavery and indentureship, and because of the Westernized idea of the nuclear family. Embraced as a way of life in the colonial Caribbean, women in particular have used networking to provide support to each other, their families, and friends in circumstances that range from celebratory to needy.[24]

Transported to Canada, networking became another strategy of resistance against marginalization, and/or perhaps against losing 'home': the place that defines food, language, laughter, music, and other forms of communication. Maya, of African heritage, described how she became part of a network, when she said: 'What I found at university again was the whole alienation, a sense of alienation I felt from the time I came through the first two jobs and into university still. School friends that we had from home, a couple of them came up at the same time, so my friends and my sister's friends formed a network: we went to the market, the museum, to church among other places, and it was pretty well following the tradition as when we were home.'[25]

Many participants spoke about meeting Caribbean people accidentally and continuing the network into lasting friendships. For example, Bianca, of mixed race heritage, whose first place of residence was the 'Y' in Montreal, explained how she transformed networking to friendship: 'I soon found out what being different was all about. So it was natural for me to be with people from different parts of the Caribbean, in the way my grandmother was from all over. I met right there in the "Y" a young woman in the cafeteria on a Sunday morning. I smiled when she came walking towards me ... I could see that she thought she knew me ... anyway it was a woman from Tobago. We went to the Campus, and met another Black woman, Jamaican, and we hung out together, as the kids would say, and there were some guys, K ... and L ... Then the women moved out of the "Y," but I stayed because my mother felt I was safe there. They found a room close by – it happened so naturally – like we had a place to cook, we took it in turns, and then the guys came, so there was a community.'[26] I quote Bianca extensively in order to indicate clearly how in using ways of 'home' she empowered herself to resist an attempt to assimilate dominant cultural patterns of individualism popularly witnessed in Canadian lifestyles.

The opposite was true for Nisa, of European, mixed race, and African origins, who in some respects did not live entirely like 'home,' because her husband was not a 'joiner,' so networking was lost for her. She said: 'It always bothered me about my children, that they were brought up without close relatives, and I think it is the worst thing, it's like punishment for me.'[27]

Yet, Yelena, of mixed race, East Indian, Chinese, Portuguese heritage, who suffered extreme alienation in her own home in Canada when homophobia intensified her oppressions, relied extensively on networking: 'I just immersed myself on the lesbian scene in Toronto. One night I was on the phone line at LOOT[28] and a woman called and said she was kicked out from home, and she asked me if I was from the West Indies, and I said "Yes" and she came to the house, and it turned out that her parents were from Barbados. And, after her, another woman turned up from Jamaica, and another from St Lucia, and we formed a little group who used to 'lime' together in the lesbian bars, so way back then we had this Caribbean woman's thing!'[29]

## Community Activism as a Strategy of Resistance

As Caribbean women struggle with marginalization, and share their stories of networking, issues of discrimination emerge. One of the more repeated stories is about discrimination in housing accommodation, while another is about the omission of African-Canadian heritage from the curriculum of school boards. Many of the participants in my study in Toronto became active in community projects designed to fill the gaps brought about by race and gender discrimination. Several of the women in Toronto and Montreal got involved in advocacy for better education of children with African and Caribbean roots. Some of the activists began by aligning themselves with radical politics to confront practices of racism and sexism in housing and in immigration and refugee determination, while others got involved in resisting homophobia and racism in the lesbian community. In Montreal many Caribbean women became attracted on arrival to projects in social services and cultural and educational programs for the Black community. I think that Caribbean women's enthusiasm to get involved in social change is the imperative for community assertiveness ingrained in the teaching from 'home.'[30] Mobilizing community and engaging in struggles became a reality for Caribbean women, who rejected colonialist ideas and participated in 'the black radical discourse' (Mama, 1995).[31] Going beyond dependency on the dominant group, Caribbean women created self-defining alternatives and assertive modes of thought about liberation.

The following four stories illustrate the dynamics of community organizing as political and cultural resistance:

BIANCA : The first meeting I went to when I came in 1977 was through my brother-in-law who was involved in an activity around a community centre. I then got involved with the ... Association. I was founding member of the ... Society, and meetings used to happen at my house. And I was with various other groups, but the ones I spent most time working with were the Congress of Black Women, Toronto Chapter, and the Coalition of Visible Minority Women of Ontario. We used to meet at F ...'s kitchen table – a lot of work was done there on ... Street.[32]

NIKKI: I believe there was a resolution to draft the idea of a national organization for Black women, instead of having ad hoc meetings. I really got involved in 1976/77 in Windsor. The proposal was brought to Windsor in 1977. It was accepted. I called members and encouraged them to do work, so I saw myself getting involved in coordinating and the meeting to launch it was held in Winnipeg in 1980. So people applauded the job I did, and I was appointed the first President of the National Congress of Black Women of Canada.[33]

LENA: However, when Theatre Workshop Productions changed for the season, I was not one of them. So I made a joke with one of the actors, and I said 'You know what! I am going to start my own Theatre,' and we laughed. Black Theatre Canada started as a joke, although the starting of a Black organization is a very political thing, the motivation was cultural ... the impact of it was a most political one, and that is what happened with Black Theatre Canada, as I started it there was such an impetus to do it – I don't know where it came from, all I know is I wanted to act, I wanted to express myself, I am Black. It was a point I began to realize ... there are things that Black people stand for, there are things we express which show our culture and that could be done in drama, and that was my *raison d'être* for the theatre.[34]

USHA: I did volunteer work at the Royal Ontario Museum, and there I fell in love with the Kalimba. When the African/Black Heritage group started D ... asked me if I would do the Kalimba and with pleasure I did. After that I started to collect other small instruments from all around the world, and I went to schools with them. I can show you a letter of thanks from the ... Board of Education.[35]

Each of these stories indicates that work among Caribbean diasporic groups or within the wider community was woman driven and not woman centred. Activism is not dependent on ideas that focus on gender; it is derived from the sheer necessity for Caribbean women to survive race and gender domination and to protect their interest in the community. Their subject positions as migrant or outsider women with aims to access basic opportunities, and with the desire to make social and cultural contributions, define a difference in how they perceive feminism in the Canadian context.

## How Feminism Defines Itself for Caribbean Women in Terms of 'Home'

My research clearly stresses the difference between Caribbean women's approaches to feminism and ideas of Western feminism. The stories indicate that in the Caribbean some women's consciousness was raised by observing ways in which women and men in their families handled social issues; others participated with mothers and fathers in forms of community activism; and while messages were contradictory about personal relations with men, they did not exclude men, children, or any other issues of life from the struggle. Thus, for a Caribbean woman a feminism that seeks only equality for men and women offers an insufficient basis for action as the brand of feminism that was *learned* from 'home' was always rooted in wider social relations. Rhoda Reddock (1990:12) defines feminism as, 'The critical consciousness and awareness of women, a subordinated and/or exploited position in society and the commitment to do something to change it.'

Reddock reminds us that by definition feminism is not new for the Caribbean, as consciousness among women of their oppressions and a need to organize 'collective autonomy' was always evident. A Caribbean woman in Canada approaches feminism from what she has learned back 'home,' that is, she acts according to her conscience to resist injustice. When asked how she learned to be socially conscious, Lauretta, of European, East Indian, African, and Jewish heritage, replied: 'It was by doing. My mother was very people conscious, very political over what the government was doing for the people. So when she went to meetings we (her children) were there; when she held dances to raise funds, we were part of the preparations; when she visited poorer people, we were there.'[36]

As well, a Caribbean woman might yearn to maintain her position in the feminist discourse in Canada, only to discover that it is diametrically opposed to a Caribbean tradition of consciousness. Maya, of African heritage, claimed: 'I could see the oppression and yes, the sexism as the source of violence, yet it is never one of doing away with men in my community, because I recognize they are oppressed on the basis of race as well. So for me, it is a struggle when lesbians say feminism means you can't be supportive of men because you are a feminist. It is something I never agreed with.'[37]

A Caribbean woman seeking to find herself in a feminist context in Canada, feels either disempowered or marginalized in the white women's movement. Rowena, of mixed race and percentages of various races, tells her story about learning community consciousness through her mother's activism, followed by her own experience of participation in liberation politics in the Caribbean. She spoke of her experience with feminism in Canada: 'My initial foray into politics here was in feminist politics, 'The Women's Movement' in the seventies and early eighties which was *extremely* white. I dropped out because I wasn't taken seriously. I was tired of women who weren't getting it, and there were no women of colour. Me was tired of dey tekking me for a nice likkle brown girl.'[38]

Haniffa, of East Indian heritage, who insisted that community involvement is paramount to her life, said, 'I had done a few things in the women's movement but I felt closer to the anti-apartheid issue. At the time when the women's movement was taking off here (Toronto) women of colour felt excluded from the integral part of it. You were welcome to being part of the community and coming and doing this and that. The differences were like white women were trying to become equal to their partners in the public arena, whereas people of colour were just trying to find housing. So levels were vast!'[39]

These quotes tell us that Caribbean women's brand of feminism is being historically replicated. Their construction of an identity is based on involvement in multiple activities, with the result that issues other than gender are prominent. This type of feminism epitomizes the movement into a radical Black subjectivity that hooks (1990) wrote about. It is a movement that affects both Black men and women, encouraging them both to be critical about conservative political issues, and to 'explore revolutionary politics.' In order to participate in social change necessary for the well-being of migrant and marginalized communities (hooks, 1990:15–22). As the stories below reveal, Caribbean women shortly after their entry to Canada were conscious enough to take up community initiatives spontaneously, showing commitment to change:

MAYA: We tried to form an organization, Women in Support of Revolutionary Change, there was about eight of us. So we studied for a year, grappling with the whole issue of feminism which we didn't understand – the Germaine Greer type of feminism. The fact that you came from the Caribbean or wherever, and you experience the fact that your education wasn't valued, and all kinds of issues that immigrant women have to be confronted with – health, housing, education, children – so we talked about that and expressed the need to form an organization to deal with these issues.[40]

NAOMI: Along with the Congress of Black Women (Toronto Chapter), the Coalition of Visible Minority of Ontario built a 134-unit housing cooperative at Lakeshore. It was started by Aita, Annzinga, Delia, Barsa, and others. It started in 1983, and the groundbreaking was in 1993. I got involved in 1986, as a member of the founding board.[41]

CHERYL: When I came here at the first opportunity I got involved, the women's movement was just coming into vogue, names like Betty Friedan, Simone de Beauvoir, and Germaine Greer they were the bigwigs. I found a lot of women's groups. There was a lot of soul-searching, getting together ... and it was only white women. I don't know how they saw me, but I didn't take that on as an issue ... because I saw myself as a woman. I didn't see colour or race, the primary issue was what we as women were suffering, and what my mother was suffering, and my neighbours and the other people.[42]

These stories, I will repeat, indicate the preparedness of Caribbean women to take up social issues that are inclusive of the variety of existing oppressions, without losing sight of gender. They also show Caribbean women's knowledge and understanding of how their positions are racialized in the White women's movement so that their activist potential tends to go unrecognized.

**Conclusion**

There are possibilities that the past can be reconstructed in the present or can filter down to the present, by suggesting that 'home' is the learning institution from which values and standards are legitimized for the legacy of resistance and survival. I am arguing that Caribbean women brought 'home' with them to Canada and that this imagined construct enabled them to navigate the interlocking systems of race, class, and gender in politics and culture to institute community organizations of their own. Their feminist consciousness is deeply rooted in community. Their notion of 'home' is strictly about resistance: about how to survive.

NOTES

1 All names used in this essay are pseudonyms. Interview no. 36, 29 Aug. 1995.

2 Interview no. 10, 29 May 1995.

3 This is a study for my doctoral dissertation which began in 1994. I used the snowballing method to collect a sample of forty-five Caribbean women of multiracial heritages, residing in Toronto, Montreal, and Kitchener–Waterloo. All of them are identified with community work, from paid to voluntary. Two of them have academic status; a few are educators; many hold positions in the public, corporate, or community sectors; one owns a business; one is a homemaker; and one is self-employed home care worker. They entered Canada in three categories: domestic service worker, student, or with landed immigrant status. The study sought to enquire how Caribbean women survived in Canada.

4 Throughout this essay, I will list the heritages women have claimed with the pseudonyms used. This will erase the racial Westernized binary categories, Black and white, which are not appropriate to an analysis of Caribbean identity. Heritage will also include the racial and ethnic identities between the two extremes, as well as those commonly excluded from this identity. I use the term 'heritage' rather than race or ethnicity, because it suggests a linkage to origins of ancestors whom Caribbean women may have embraced through direct or indirect experience.

5 Interview no. 33, 23 Aug. 1995.

6 Interview no. 2, 18 Aug. 1994.

7 This woman identifies herself in the demographic profile in the category East Indian and has suffixed it with South Asian. The former is the colonial category for indentured people from India, while the latter is a modern term used to identify Indians in North America.

8 Interview no. 40, 19 Sept. 1995.

9 This expression is familiar to most Eastern Caribbean women, and it reflects the creative ability of these women to find strategies to survive in the limited opportunities provided for them to earn a decent living for themselves and their families. See Barrow (1986).

10 Interview no. 24, 24 June 1995.

11 To the best of my knowledge, these two themes – women's survival strategies and Caribbean racial complexities – have not been brought together in other scholarly work.

12 Interview no. 34, 29 Aug. 1995.

13 See Brereton (1995:69). Brereton regards the work of Mrs A.C. Carmichael as having a 'propaganda element in her descriptions,' which she believes reduces the worth of the evidence significantly.

14 See Wariboko (1995). This article, the editors state, though not Caribbean focused, informs us of the historical link before the middle passage to ascer-

tain what may be external influences on gender roles and experiences in the slave system.

15 My concern with the historical past before the middle passage for African women is echoed here for Indian women, to briefly expose the link in history that would account for women's strengths. H.C. Upadhyay (1991:1) made reference to the Vedic age in which Indian women's status was not objectified: 'In the Vedic period women participated in the fields like men and took active part in every sphere of life ... During the Vedic age women occupied a high position in society.' See also Uma Chakravati (1990) for understanding how an Indian woman's position was constituted and reconstituted in history.

16 In keeping with the colonial male-centred enterprise system of indentureship in the Caribbean, fewer Portuguese women than men were indentured immigrants; see Ferreira (1994). Howard Johnson (1987) makes no reference to women.

17 Barbara Bush (1981) uncovered some of the experiences of white women in which they negotiated their identities as sometimes equal to Black women and other times superior, yet envious of the exoticism constructed around Black women's sexuality.

18 Reddock (1988) recounted the biographical story of Elmer Francois, who was born in St Vincent, and her brilliant leadership of the Negro Cultural and Social Association in Trinidad and Tobago during a period of labour unrest. See also Lynette Vassell (1995), who wrote a personal narrative of Campbell's experiences and her negotiations with left politics in Jamaica.

19 Interview no. 25, 26 June 1995.

20 Christine Ho, in her study of Afro-Trinidadians in Los Angeles (1991), found that her sample showed the tendency for social networking and transcontinental and international visiting. These were the key themes in her findings of non-assimilation for this group.

21 Interview no. 20, 14 June 1995.

22 Interview no. 15, 6 June 1995.

23 Interview no. 39, 6 Sept. 1995. The Caribbean experience for Rey included her story as the child of Chinese immigrants. They struggled hard to fit into the structure: the first attempt was to have the children become Anglicans; after that her father came to believe that the Roman Catholic school was more prestigious, so he 'bribe[d] all the nuns' and sent his children there.

24 Networking is a major theme in Ho (1991), who theorized that networking, locally and internationally, eliminates marginalization and creates a new form of family to resist acculturation in the culture of the United States of America.

25 Interview no. 26, 27 June 1996.

26 Interview no. 2, 18 Sept. 1994.

27 Interview no. 14, 5 June 1996.
28 LOOT is Lesbian Organization of Toronto.
29 Interview no. 28, 29 June 1995.
30 My working definition of community activism is based on the actions that Caribbean women take because of their critical consciousness of levels of social and economic oppressions that are depriving groups such as designated-Aboriginals, immigrants, people of disabilities, Black women and men, women and men of colour, lesbians and gays of rights and opportunities.
31 See Amina Mama (1995:105–8). She has named two main themes that qualify as discourses: the colonialist-integrated discourse, that is, acting according to the dictates of the dominant group; and the Black radical discourse, which is just the opposite. I see the latter as applying throughout my investigation of resistance by Caribbean women.
32 Interview no. 2, 18 Aug. 1994.
33 Interview no. 22, 17 June 1995.
34 Interview no. 27, 28 June 1995.
35 Interview no. 1, 17 Aug. 1994.
36 Interview no. 21, 14 June 1995.
37 Interview no. 26, 27 June 1995.
38 Interview no. 37, 31 Aug. 1995.
39 Interview no. 4, 25 Aug. 1994.
40 Interview no. 26. 27 June 1995.
41 Interview no. 42, 24 July 1994.
42 Interview no. 3, 22 Aug. 1994.

REFERENCES

Anderson, Benedict (1991) *Imagined Communities*. London: Verso.
Barrow, Christine (1986) 'Finding the Support: A Study of Strategies of Survival.' *Social and Economic Studies*, 35(2):131–72.
Beckles, Hilary McD. (1989) *Natural Rebels: A Social History of Enslaved Black Women in Barbados*. London: Rutgers / Zed Books.
Brereton, Bridget (1995) 'Text, Testimony and Gender.' In Verene Shepherd, Bridget Brereton, and Barbara Bailey (eds.), *Engendering History: Caribbean Women in Historical Perspective*, 63–93. Kingston, Jamaica: Ian Randle.
Bush, Barbara (1981) 'White "Ladies," Coloured "Favourites" and Black "Wenches": Some Considerations on Sex, Race and Class Factors in Social Relations in White Creole Society in the British Caribbean.' *Slavery and Abolition*, 2(3):245–62.

– (1990) *Slave Women in Caribbean Society, 1650–1838*. Bloomington: Indiana University Press.

*Caribbean Contact* (1993) 19(10) Special Women's Issue.

Chakravati, Uma (1990) 'Whatever Happened to the Vedic *Dasi?* Orientalism, Nationalism and the Script for the East.' In Kumkum Sangari and Sudesh Vaid (eds.), *Recasting Women: Essays in Indian Colonial History,* 27–87. New Brunswick, NJ: Rutgers University Press.

Collins, Patricia Hill (1990) *Black Feminist Thought: Knowledge, Consciousness and the Politics of Empowerment.* New York: Routledge.

Craton, Michael (1986) 'From Caribs to Black Caribs: The Amerindian Roots of Servile Resistance in the Caribbean.' In Gary Y. Okihiro (ed.), *In Resistance: Studies in African, Caribbean and Afro-American History,* 96–116. Amherst: University of Massachusetts Press.

– (1993) 'Continuity Not Change: The Incidence of Unrest among Ex-slaves in the British West Indies, 1838–1876.' In Hilary Beckles and Verene Shepherd (eds.), *Caribbean Freedom: Economy and Society from Emancipation to the Present,* 192–244. Kingston, Jamaica: Ian Randle.

Dadzie, Stella (1990) 'Searching for the Invisible Woman: Slavery and Resistance in Jamaica.' *Race and Class,* 32(2):21–38.

Espinet, Ramabai (1993) 'Representation and the Indo-Caribbean Woman in Trinidad and Tobago.' In Frank Birbalsingh (ed.), *Indo-Caribbean Resistance,* 42–61. Toronto: TSAR.

Essed, Philomena (1990) *Everyday Racism: Reports from Women of Two Cultures.* Alameda, Calif.: Hunter House.

Ferguson, Moira (ed.), (1993) *The History of Mary Prince: A West Indian Slave – Related by Herself.* Ann Arbor: University of Michigan Press.

Ferreira, Jo-Anne S. (1994) *The Portuguese of Trinidad and Tobago.* St Augustine, Trinidad and Tobago: Institute of Social and Economic Research, University of the West Indies.

Grewal, Inderpal (1996) *Home and Harem: Nation, Gender, Empire and the Cultures of Travel.* Durham: Duke University Press.

Ho, Christine (1991) *Salt-water Trinnies: Afro-Trinidadian Immigrant Networks and Non-assimilation in Los Angeles.* New York: AMS Press.

hooks, bell (1990) *Yearning: Race, Gender and Culture.* Toronto: Between the Lines.

Johnson, Howard (1987) 'The Chinese in Trinidad in the Late Nineteenth Century,' *Ethnic and Racial Studies,* 10(1):82–95.

Kerr, Paulette (1995) 'Victims or Strategists? Female Lodging House Keepers in Jamaica.' In Verene Shepherd, Bridget Brereton, and Barbara Bailey (eds.),

*Engendering History: Caribbean Women in Historical Perspective*, 197–212. Kingston, Jamaica: Ian Randle.

Look Lai, Walton (1993) *Indentured Labor, Caribbean Sugar, Chinese and Indian Immigrants to the British West Indies.* Baltimore and London: Johns Hopkins University Press.

Mama, Amina (1995) *Beyond the Masks: Race, Gender and Subjectivity.* London: Routledge.

Mathurin, Lucille (1975) *The Rebel Woman in the West Indies during Slavery.* Kingston, Jamaica: African Caribbean Publications.

Puar, Jasbir K. (1996) 'Writing My Way "Home"; Travelling South, Asian Bodies and Diasporic Journeys.' *Socialist Review* 24(4):75–108.

Reddock, Rhoda E. (1988) *Elmer Francois.* London: New Beacon Books.

– (1990) 'The Caribbean Feminist Tradition.' *Womanspeak*, nos. 26/27:12–16.

– (1993) 'Indian Woman and Indentureship in Trinidad and Tobago: Freedom Denied.' In Verene Shepherd and Hilary Beckles (eds.), *Caribbean Freedom: Economy and Society from Emancipation to Present*, 225–37. Kingston, Jamaica: Ian Randle.

– (1994) *Women, Labour and Politics in Trinidad and Tobago: A History.* London: Zed Books.

Scott, Yvonne Kesho (1991) *The Habit of Surviving: Black Women's Strategies for Life.* New Brunswick and London: Rutgers University Press.

Shepherd, Verene (1993) 'Emancipation through Servitude: Aspects of the Conditions of Indian Women.' In Hilary Beckles and Verene Shepherd (eds.), *Caribbean Freedom: Economy and Society from Emancipation to the Present*, 245–50. Kingston, Jamaica: Ian Randle.

– (1995) 'Gender, Migration and Settlement: The Indentureship and Post-indentureship Experience of Indian Females in Jamaica, 1845–1943.' In Verene Shepherd, et al. (eds.), *Engendering History: Caribbean Women in Historical Perspective*, 233–57. Kingston, Jamaica: Ian Randle.

Silvestrini, Blanca G. (1989) *Women and Resistance: Herstory in Contemporary Caribbean History.* The 1989 Elsa Goveia Memorial Lecture. Department of History, University of the West Indies, Mona, Jamaica.

Terborg-Penn, Rosalyn (1986) 'Black Women in Resistance.' In Gary Y. Okihoro (ed.), *In Resistance*, 188–209. Amherst: University of Massachusetts Press.

Turrittin, Jane Sawyer (1976) 'Networks and Mobility: The Case of West Indian Domestics from Montserrat.' *Canadian Review of Sociology and Anthropology*, 13(3):305–20.

Upadhyay, H.C. (1991) *Status of Women in India.* Vol. 1. Daryaganj, New Delhi: Anmol Publications.

Vassell, Lynette (1995) 'Women of the Masses: Daphne Campbell and "Left"

Politics in Jamaica in the 1950s.' In Verene Shepherd, Bridget Brereton, and Barbara Bailey (eds.), *Engendering History: Caribbean Women in Historical Perspective*, 318–33. Kingston, Jamaica: Ian Randle.

Wariboko, Waibinte (1995) 'The Status, Role and Influence of Women in Eastern Delta States of Nigeria, 1850–1900: Examples from New Calabar.' In Verene Shepherd, Bridget Brereton, and Barbara Bailey (eds.), *Engendering History: Caribbean Women in Historical Perspective*, 369–83. Kingston, Jamaica: Ian Randle.

Young, Virginia Heyer (1993) *Becoming West Indian: Culture, Self and Nation in St Vincent*, 23–44. Washington: Smithsonian Institution Press.

# 9

# Coming to Terms with *Hijab* in Canada and Turkey: Agonies of a Secular and Anti-orientalist Émigré Feminist

## SEDEF ARAT-KOC

In the past decade or two we have seen the development of new veiling among some Muslim women in several countries. This has involved the adoption, usually by younger women, of various forms of head cover. What has made these forms of veiling 'new' and different from traditional veiling has been the fact that those who adopted various forms of *hijab* have often been young women, whose mothers had in most cases adopted western dress. These women typically state that they adopt this form of dress out of their own free will and often against the wishes of parents and husbands. 'New veiling' has occurred not just in predominantly Muslim countries, but also in Western countries, including Canada, which have minorities of Muslims.

As an émigré feminist from Turkey, who is observing this phenomenon both in Turkey and in Canada, I have felt compelled, both academically and politically, to respond to this development. My feminist, secular, and Western-oriented upbringing pulls me in an alarmist direction about the regressive, 'backward,' and anti-feminist nature of this development. On the other hand, as an émigré feminist, I am also sensitized to the dangers of a hasty conclusion in that direction. This essay is about the agonies of formulating a position and about self-critically reflecting over my position on new veiling in Turkey and in Canada.

The first section of the essay focuses on the agonies I face in formulating a position in Canada, a position informed by the sensitivities offered by being an émigré feminist, while avoiding the problems of an orientalist feminist position, on the one hand, and a liberal multiculturalist position, on the other. The second section focuses on my agonizing over the *hijab* in Turkey: How, on the one hand, I fear the partly real association and a very possible appropriation of this symbol by fundamentalism; and how, on the other hand, I have strong reservations about readily accepting what has become the dominant, 'secular' Turkish feminist position on this issue. The final section of the essay attempts to make sense of these agonies in light of the sensitivities given by my location as an émigré, which makes me an insider–outsider in both societies and feminist communities.

### Formulating a Position on the *Hijab* in Canada

Formulating a position on new veiling in Canada has been relatively straightforward, as in Canada the possibility of the issue being automatically and necessarily confused and collapsed with the issue of fundamentalism is not as great as in Turkey. Formulating a position for me is still only relatively straightforward, however, as it involves feminist questions and concerns over what the symbol of *hijab* means for women; as well as Middle Eastern and Muslim émigré concerns over the racism or orientalism so often involved in the interpretations of 'the' symbol. The challenge of an anti-racist, anti-orientalist feminist position is to formulate an analysis that, on the one hand, avoids an orientalist and patronizing feminist position by taking into account the voices of those women who have chosen to adopt the *hijab*. The other side of the challenge is to maintain a critical feminist questioning over what the symbol and the practical use of the *hijab* could mean in different and changing contexts and for different groups of women.

In formulating a position on the emergence of veiling in Canada, it has been important, first, to critique and resist the orientalism involved in interpreting the *hijab* as ultimately and necessarily a symbol of women's oppression and exclusion from the public sphere. In this regard, I agree with the observations and conclusions of Homa Hoodfar (1993) and Shahnaz Khan (1995), who attribute agency to the women who adopt the *hijab* and argue that *hijab* may be a sign that involves multiple meanings for the women who wear it.

Influenced by these interpretations, and based on my own reading of the voices of women who have adopted the *hijab* in Canada, I tend to interpret it as an identity marker, representing an assertion of and pride in an ethno-religious Muslim identity, which an earlier generation of Muslims have had to suppress. In an environment of orientalist racism, which has been perceived by Muslim minorities in Canadian society as hostile in the recent period since the Gulf War, assertion of such an identity has been important for women who might have otherwise felt pressured or encouraged to assimilate into a different notion of Canadianness.

Another interpretation of *hijab* attributes a potentially liberatory, rather than oppressive meaning to it. What is unique to some of the recent explanations by women for their adoption of various forms of veiling has been the use of a feminist language. Contrary to its interpretation as representing the exclusion or withdrawal of women from the public sphere, *hijab* may mean, according to some of the young women who have adopted it, the assertion of 'personhood' (that is, as opposed to femininity). It is interpreted as a way for women to maintain public presence and active public lives, while avoiding sexual objectification of their bodies and sexual harassment in the public world (Arat-Koc and Bezanson, 1996; MacLeod, 1992).

Attempting to avoid the pitfalls of both orientalism and a patronizing feminist position has been the first challenge in formulating a stand on new veiling in Canada. While being open to hearing and accepting the multiplicity of meanings associated with the new veiling, it is also important to keep in mind that women's exclusion and oppression may still be one of the meanings of *hijab* in some contexts, for some people. The recent literature on the immigrant and émigré experience, which associates immigrant cultures with hybridity,[1] and which attributes almost infinite agency to the minority immigrants in defining and shaping such a culture, may exaggerate the degree of individual and collective freedom involved in the construction of ethnocultures. Such a literature is, after all, the product of a specific group of immigrant intellectuals – such as Salman Rushdie – whose personal, social, and economic conditions and cultural environments may be much more favourable towards creativity and choice regarding cultural definitions and practices. Hybridity remains one of the possibilities for identity formation in diaspora. The other possibilities are the continuing pressures from the larger society for assimilation, or the tendency on the part of the individual or the ethnic community to retreat to 'tradition' or fundamentalism. The latter is an attempt to restore an imagined purity of ethnocultural identity and to recover a sense of unity and certainty in a rapidly changing and possibly hostile environment (Hall, 1992; Robins, 1991). When 'tradition' and fundamentalism *are* the responses to diaspora, it is important to note that such responses may lead to a creation of ethnocultural communities that may be particularly restrictive towards women (Yuval-Davis, 1994).

The second challenge in formulating a position on new veiling in Canada has been the need to differentiate my position from that of liberal multiculturalism. Infinitely and unprincipally pluralist, such a position would take an 'anything goes' approach to any kind of cultural practice and its implications. One of the problems with such an approach would be the indifference it would assume towards the causes – including a defensive reaction to racism – for the emergence of some cultural practices. Celebrating, or at least uncritically accepting any practice, but not asking questions regarding the emergence or re-adoption of that practice, would politically mean that nothing would be done to address the problems that may lie at the root of such a practice. Another problem with a liberal multiculturalist approach would be that in the name of 'respecting' any and all practices, such an approach would be unable to recognize and problematize situations when and where new veiling may, in fact, unquestionably be associated with the exclusion and oppression of women.

In cases where and when we find that the *hijab* is associated with women's oppression, an anti-orientalist orientation would require us to develop an analysis of such oppression which would overcome some of the problems of culturalism or cultural reductionism. Overcoming culturalism would involve refusing to reduce immigrant and minority women's problems to *hijab* or other aspects of the women's ethno-religious 'background.' It would involve rejection of a simple characterization of the cultural background as traditional, backward, and necessarily oppressive towards women, and a rejection of a simplistic characterization of modern 'Canadian' culture as necessarily being liberating for women. Overcoming culturalism would involve focusing on racism as one of the major determinants unfavourably shaping the status and conditions of certain groups of immigrant or minority women in Canada. If it is specifically immigrant women who are experiencing oppression, the analysis would also involve focusing on those characteristics of Canadian immigration and settlement policies that directly and actively contribute to a subordinate status for immigrant women. Among these are sponsorship conditions and (lack of or inadequate) access to language training that create and perpetuate relations of dependency for women. An anti-orientalist perspective, therefore, would focus less on the universal and mythical characteristics attributed to an ethnocultural 'background,' and more on the specific material, socioeconomic, and legal conditions that immigrants may face in the countries of settlement.

## Formulating a Position on the *Hijab* in Turkey

Formulating a position on the *hijab* in Turkey involves more agonizing than the one on Canada. The most important reason for this has been the fact that the connection between the *hijab* and fundamentalism is a far greater possibility in Turkey than it ever could be in Canada. First, Turkey is a predominantly Muslim country. Second, there has been a growth of Islamic fundamentalism in Turkey since the 1980s, a growth that may possibly lead to the capturing of state power. Even though multiple meanings of *hijab*, as well as a multiplicity of positions for women who wear the *hijab* are present in Turkey, as in Canada, the proximity of fundamentalists to political power in Turkey in the past decade has made real the potential for one single meaning to gain hegemony. One of the consequences of fundamentalists attaining state power would be the elimination of an element of choice in the adoption of *hijab* and the replacement of all the present meanings, some conformist, some protesting, women themselves attach to the symbol of *hijab* with one single meaning that fundamentalists would define. As a result of the actual differences and different potentialities the Turkish case represents, I am more apprehensive about taking the same approach to *hijab* in Turkey as I do in Canada.

Despite my apprehension about taking a more optimistic 'multiple meanings' approach, however, I have serious reservations about readily accepting what has been the dominant response among Turkish feminists to *hijab*. In the past decade, Turkish politics has witnessed a polarization between 'Islamists,' on the one hand, and self-proclaimed secularists or 'laicists,' on the other. In a polarized political environment, the laicists have returned to a cult of Kemalism to defend their position. Many feminists have also found this to be an effective weapon, as Kemalism seems to simultaneously provide what have been dominant discourses in Turkey both on secularism and on women's rights.

Despite the obvious advantages a readily and widely available discourse provides to defend a feminist, secularist, and a general democratic position against the dangers posed by fundamentalism, I question the political strategy of using a specifically Kemalist discourse towards this end. In the past decade, Turkish feminists have critiqued Kemalism for its limited conception of women's emancipation and for subordinating women's emancipation to the nationalist and modernization projects. I consider this critique very valuable for the development of an autonomous feminist thought and practice. Nevertheless, I believe that such a critique has to go beyond showing the ways in which Kemalism has not done enough. Such a critique has to critically engage with the orientalist, elitist, and authoritarian nature of the Kemalist modernization discourse and practice.

The historical association of Kemalism with these characteristics causes two major problems. First, it makes Kemalist discourse a problematic tool for secular democrats in general and feminists in particular. Second, the orientalist nature of Kemalism makes it counterproductive for feminists. This is because the definition and defence of women's rights through an orientalist discourse fuels fundamentalists' claims of authenticity and enables them defend their conception of women's place in society as *the* only one 'naturally' compatible with Turkish-Muslim values and traditions against a 'foreign' Kemalist one imposed upon society.

To be able to demonstrate the bases for my reservations about the problems and limitations of relying on a Kemalist discourse to analyse and critique the *hijab*, I will provide, in the following section, a short summary of the nature of the Kemalist discourse of modernization.

**The Kemalist Discourse of Modernization**

By Kemalism, I refer to the discourse – including the ideology and institutional practices – surrounding the modernization and nation-building projects of Mustafa Kemal Ataturk and his People's Republican Party – which ruled Turkey in a single-party regime from 1923 to 1945. Despite the growing complexity of Turkish politics in the postwar period, Kemalism has remained the official state ideology in Turkey.

One of the most defining characteristics of Kemalism has been the definition of ways to help Turkey to catch up with Europe. In this sense, Kemalism represented a continuation of anxiety among Turkish intellectuals since the nineteenth century over the military and general weakening of the Ottoman Empire in relation to Europe. To prevent Turkey from becoming another colony of Europe would require rapid industrialization and general economic development. As urgent as economic development, however, was the task to 'raise Turkey to the level of contemporary civilizations.' Change in this direction would involve using a singular, absolute concept of what 'contemporary civilizations' represented. Modernization was equated with Westernization. As Abdullah Cevdet of the Young Turks expressed early in the twentieth century: 'There is no second civilization: civilization means European civilization and it must be imported with both its roses and thorns' (cited in Jayawardena, 1986:30).

What was different about the Kemalist elite compared with the earlier Ottoman intellectuals was that they had political power. In the discourse of modernization that the Kemalist elite used, 'catching up' with 'civilization' would mean adopting all the forms 'it' assumed in recent Western history: in politics, administration, the legal system, culture, attire, and so on. The kind of 'modernizing' reforms introduced in Turkey in the 1920s and 1930s – ranging from the changing of the form of government and the legal system to the adoption of the Latin alphabet, the Gregorian calender, and the Western hat – demonstrate how the equation of modernization with Westernization was interpreted literally.

According to the Kemalist elite, Islam and the elements of 'Eastern culture' were the causes of the stagnation, backwardness, and the eventual collapse of the Ottoman Empire. Adoption of 'contemporary civilization,' therefore, would have to involve cutting ties with the past and getting rid of religious and Eastern influences in culture: 'We are going to be civilized and proud of it. Look at the rest of the Turks and Muslims! What catastrophes and disasters have come upon them, because their minds could not adjust themselves to the all-encompassing and sublime dictates of civilization! This is why we too remained backward for so long, and why we were stuck in the last swamp. If we have been able to save ourselves in the last few years, it has been because of the change in our mentality. We can never stop again ... We must go on; we have no choice. The nation must understand this clearly. Civilization is a blazing fire so powerful that it burns and annihilates all those who are indifferent to it' (Ataturk, 1959: 207).

The discourse of modernization involved a curious combination of nationalist sentiments with an acute sense of inferiority in relation to Western culture. The attitude towards indigenous culture was, at best, ambiguous. On the one hand, the urgency of reform was usually expressed as an attempt to protect Turkey from ever again falling into colonial or semicolonial status. On the other hand, the perceived dichotomy of modernity and tradition meant that a choice had to be made in favour of one and the exclusion of the other. In a way, however, there was no choice because the direction of history was towards 'civilization' as it was modelled in the West. In 1926, Mahmut Esat, then the minister of justice, commented on the adoption of the Civil Code from Switzerland: 'The decision of the Turkish nation is to accept contemporary civilization without any condition and reservation ... The Turkish nation which has been advancing with the decision to take and internalize contemporary civilization has to keep in step with its necessities at whatever the cost. This is mandatory for a nation that intends to survive' (cited in Yetkin, 1983:140). Ataturk's justification of the 'hat law' used the same sense of urgency and inevitability: 'The questions about whether we should wear the hat or not are meaningless. We shall wear the hat, and adopt all the products of civilization from the West. Those who are not civilized are doomed to remain under the feet of those who are' (Ataturk, 1959:223).

When women's place in society was discussed, the orientalist discourse suggested that improvements in women's conditions could only be achieved by replacing indigenous customs with practices borrowed from the West. The sense of cultural inferiority that such orientalism infused into the modernization discourse meant that there was a preoccupation among the modernizing Turkish intellectuals with what the West thought about Turkey. Ataturk's comments on women's veiling had more to do with this concern than with how the veil affected women and what kinds of gender relations it symbolized. Addressing a group of 'gentlemen' in 1925, Ataturk (1959:217) said: 'In some places I have seen women who put a piece of cloth or a towel or something like it over their heads to hide their faces, and who turn their backs or huddle themselves on the ground when a man passes by. Gentlemen, can the mothers and daughters of a civilized nation adopt this strange manner, this barbarous posture? It is a spectacle that makes the nation an object of ridicule. It must be remedied at once.'

In this discourse, a democratic approach to modernization would be naive, and even risky, because the majority of people in Turkey were seen as immersed in tradition, embodying the past which the reformists wanted to eradicate. They were also seen as ignorant masses whose ignorance would prevent them from seeing the 'light' of civilization. This approach to people led to an elitism on the part of the modernizing intellectuals who unapologetically used the motto 'for the people, despite the people' to characterize their approach to change.

In addition to elitism, the perception of the common people as traditional and ignorant masses led to authoritarianism. In introducing modernizing reforms, the Kemalist elite displayed a vigilant style, whereby the reforms were introduced as laws. When the fez was banned and replaced by the Western hat, through the 'hat law,' for example, hundreds were jailed and hanged because of their rejection of the new hat: 'We accomplished that under the Law for Maintenance of Order. We would also have done so without it. But if it is said that the proclamation of that law eased our task, that would be most correct. Indeed, the existence of the Law for the Maintenance of Order prevented the large-scale poisoning of the nation by certain reactionaries' (Ataturk, 1959:895).

In the context of the orientalism, elitism, and authoritarianism that framed the modernization project, some potentially liberating reforms did not necessarily have an empowering effect on the affected groups. To take the example of secularism, we can say that secularism no doubt brought more freedom to religious minorities, as well as to the Muslim population, who could now enjoy popular sovereignty instead of being ruled on the basis of an absolute transcendental power.

The single-handed, top-down, and authoritarian approach Kemalists took towards secularization has often been defended as having been inevitable given the strength of organized religion itself. However, there are aspects of the way secularism has been interpreted and carried out that made it different from a democratic measure limiting the absolutism of theocracy. Inspired by a positivist and rationalist cynicism towards all forms of religion, as well as a specifically orientalist distrust of Islam, Kemalism also took an uncompromising stand on popular, local forms of Islam, some of which had a heterodox approach towards Islam and a progressive interpretation of gender relations for Muslims. Significant among secularization reforms was a law passed in 1925 that practically outlawed all forms of popular Islam – religious brotherhoods, mystic orders, and dervish convents – and ordered the closure of holy places. What the specific approach of Kemalists to secularism did, in a way, was to treat 'Islam' as monolithic, instead of recognizing the relative amorphousness and heterogeneity of its practice (Sayyid, 1994).

In the case of reforms – from dress codes to legal reform regarding education, marriage, divorce, child custody, property ownership, work outside the home, suffrage, and access to legal and political office – and general support for 'women's emancipation,' the changes were positive, at least for a small group of urban, middle-class, educated women who benefited from them directly. The orientalist tone of the reforms, however, can be interpreted as having been one of the obstacles to a wider appeal and resonance for the larger population. The statist, top-down nature of the emancipatory project has also been detrimental for women's liberation in general, as it suppressed a history of autonomous feminist organizing among Ottoman women in the nineteenth and early twentieth century (Ahmed, 1984; Tekeli, 1982, 1988, 1991; Toprak, 1988; Sirman, 1989; Arat, 1994) and turned women's emancipation into a paternalistic, if benevolent, project of an authoritarian state (Kandiyoti, 1987, 1989, 1991).

As earlier mentioned, the Kemalist elite shared a general mistrust of the common people and introduced change with a 'for the people, despite the people' principle. The 'traditional,' 'ignorant' masses were not the only people who were suspect, however. As the Turkish state grew increasingly authoritarian in the 1920s and 1930s, all forms of autonomous organizing in a newly emerging civil society, including precisely those initiated by the modern, enlightened subjects of the Turkish nation, started to be suppressed. In a way, the reformers had 'identified their task negatively, as unseating, rather than constructing an alternative to community-based social life' (Keyder, 1988:209). Following a Kurdish rebellion in eastern Turkey started by a religious leader, Seyh Sait, 'independence tribunals' were established in 1925 under the Law for the Maintenance of Public Order. The tribunals targeted not just religious orders and ethnic organizing, but also opposition parties and trade unions.

By 1938, except for local sporting clubs, all forms of independent organizing were eliminated in anticipation of a new legislation on associations. Among the organizations forced to close was the Turkish Women's Federation, which was pressured to declare that there was no women's question in Turkey where women had been granted all their rights and where they, like men, were working under the leadership of their 'chief,' for the good of the country (Yetkin, 1983:84–6). Some of the other organizations that were closed or forced to abrogate themselves were the Students' Union, the Teachers' Union, the Press Association, and the Retired Officers' Society. The 1938 Law of Associations banned not only associations that 'aimed to destroy the territorial integrity of the state' or 'disrupt political and national unity,' but also 'groups' based on religion, confession, sect, region, family, congregation, race, sex, or class (Weiker, 1974:246).

**Problems of Using a Kemalist Discourse on the *Hijab***

The historical association of Kemalism with orientalism, elitism, and authoritarianism in its discourses on modernization in general and women's emancipation in particular limits the feasibility of its use, in my opinion, in a feminist analysis of *hijab*. One problem with the Kemalist discourse is that it has defined women's unveiling, as well as all the other modernizing reforms for women, in terms of the requirements of 'civilization,' and of nation-building. What has been done 'for' women has never been justified in terms of what women want or even what is in the best interests of women themselves. When Kemalism has defined women's emancipation in this way, it has failed to constitute an effective challenge to the way fundamentalist discourse defines women's place and proper behaviour, as the latter, in a way, replaces one paternalistic discourse with another, telling women what they need to do in order to meet the requirements of a Muslim identity, instead of a Western one.

Another problem with the Kemalist discourse is that this discourse automatically assumes and treats the *hijab* as always being connected with fundamentalism and as an ultimate and necessary symbol of women's oppression. Such an interpretation does not allow for an understanding of the multiplicity of meanings associated with the *hijab* and the differences among women who adopt it.

A Kemalist discourse is also limiting because, through the orientalist assumptions it makes about the *hijab*, it culturalizes women's problems in Turkey, reducing them to the effects of religious and cultural practices. Unfortunately, the extra attention the *hijab* has received among Turkish feminists has been at the cost of analysis and critique of other sources of oppression for women, for example, the effects of restructuring.

A final problem with the use of a Kemalist discourse is that it resonates too strongly with the historical divisions among women in Turkey along urban–rural and class dimensions and between the formally and Western-educated and the uneducated groups in the population, who have been identified by dominant discourses as 'enlightened' and 'Western–contemporary' or 'traditional.' As such, the *hijab* has the potential to become a populist symbol of dissent, even in face of its recent adoption by many urban, middle-class, and educated women. The resonance with major historical divisions in Turkish society also means that the adoption of a Kemalist-orientalist critique of the *hijab* may contribute to the definition of feminism being identified as a 'foreign' and elite perspective, thus creating a major obstacle for feminism becoming hegemonic among women.

Bobby Sayyid (1994) has argued that Kemalist discourse politicizes Islam by creating the 'other' in Turkish society. I would suggest that the fundamentalists are able to make claims to authenticity today by appropriating and framing in a populist way this 'other' of Kemalism. So, even though both fundamentalism and the *hijab* are modern phenomena in Turkey, the fundamentalists can present them as authentic and popular because they can associate them with the sentiments and practices of the underdog of Kemalism.

### Analysing My Agonies: What Constitutes 'Émigré Feminism'?

In this section, I will attempt to analyse how my position(s) on the *hijab* may be related to my location in Canada as an émigré feminist. In such an analysis, it is very important, first, to avoid a tendency to make essentialist claims as to what forms of representation may be possible and legitimate through the identity of émigré feminism. I cannot, and should not, for example, claim in the Canadian context, a licence to speak 'as a Turkish woman' or 'as a Turkish feminist.' As privileging as such claims to be the voice of Turkish women and Turkish feminists might be, I need to resist them as they can be irresponsible as well as dangerous. Such claims may let me go unaccountable to address very important questions such as what other representations of Turkish women are possible, what approach(es) to feminism have prevailed in Turkey, and what the relations (including real and potential tensions) are between Turkish feminists and other Turkish women.

One of the ways to de-essentialize émigré feminism – while still using it as a meaningful category that goes into constituting subjectivity – would be to treat it as involving not just a single location, but many. This would involve historicizing and contextualizing émigré feminism and explicating some of the multiple locations and the variety of theoretical–intellectual and political influences and unique personal trajectories of exile and migration that may go into its constitution.

In terms of the theoretical or intellectual and political influences on my analysis, an obvious one is feminism. Also important was the timing of my exposure to feminism: the fact that much of my exposure and interest occurred in the 1980s when women of colour contributed to feminist thought and practice through a critique of Western feminism. In addition to the critique by women of colour, feminist writing in the 1980s was also influenced by poststructuralist and postmodernist theory. Both Black feminist thought and poststructuralist and postmodernist theory have contributed to a problematization, on my part, of orientalism.

In addition to the impact of feminist theory and politics and poststructuralism, one of the significant influences on the formation of my analysis that needs to be accounted for are the political and theoretical developments in the radical democratic left in the 1980s. Among these developments what has been most influential on my thinking have been questioning of teleological, evolutionist conceptions of history and of the tendency to attribute a vanguard elite role to those intellectuals who possessed such conceptions of history.

In terms of developments in radical democratic theory and politics in the 1980s, particularly influential on my thinking were the rediscovery of and debates around Antonio Gramsci's concept of 'hegemony.' The concept of hegemony is useful because of the questions it opens up and the insights it provides as to why some ideologies gain support among people and others do not. The concept of hegemony may help us address why, for example, Kemalism or Western feminism may have failed to gain wider support among people whose interests, many may believe, they so obviously address and serve. The concept of hegemony can inspire a critique of orientalism that goes beyond the problems of the inaccuracy of its dichotomies (for example, orient–occident, tradition–modernity) and the racism in the hierarchy of cultures it assumes.

The concept of hegemony is also useful in the way it provides an understanding of why subaltern groups support certain ideologies and policies that may seemingly be against their interests. It replaces the concept of 'false consciousness.' So, in the case of *hijab*, instead of seeing it as a necessary antithesis of feminism, as an ultimate form of false consciousness for women, we have a conceptual tool that allows us to ask questions as to what *hijab* means to different people and why and how it resonates with certain popular interests and sentiments.[2]

So far I have argued for the necessity to de-essentialize an émigré feminist position. In addition to avoiding an essentialist use of the category, it is also important to avoid privileging an émigré feminist position, assuming that it may provide one with a unique epistemic advantage, a positionality that provides one with pure knowledge, a superior perspective in understanding the 'home country,' as well as the country of immigration, which the 'insiders' in either cannot have.

Having cautioned myself and my readers about the problems and dangers of essentialist and privileging perspectives on émigré feminism, I would nevertheless agree with others in this volume that there may be certain sensibilities and sensitivities that cross-cultural challenges may provide to émigré feminists. Regarding my position(s) on the *hijab*, one such sensitivity has to do with the high probability that I would have taken for granted the orientalism of most urban, middle-class, formal and Western-educated intellectuals – including most feminists – in Turkey, rather than problematizing it or being bothered by it, if I did not have the first-hand experience of belonging to the oriental 'other' as a Middle Eastern and 'Muslim' immigrant and a minority in a Western country. In Turkey, I was never the 'other' of orientalism. On the contrary, as an educated, urban, middle-class woman, I embodied the modern, Western identity that the Turkish Republic has been trying to strive for since its foundation. In Canada, however, by nationality and official religious status, I have at least partly belonged to the 'other.' Partly, because I 'pass' in physical features and in dress. And, partly, because my secularism and lack of direct personal affiliation and identification with Islam may have sometimes contributed to a partial freedom from some of the stigma attached to such an identity. Belonging to the 'other,' although partial, has nevertheless been very real in Canada, contributing, therefore to a sensitization that I would not otherwise have developed.

Belonging to the 'other' even in a partial sense means that in Canada I am always an insider–outsider to both the mainstream society and the feminist community. It also means that I start to think as an insider–outsider with respect to the feminist community in Turkey, not taking for granted a complete sense of 'we'-ness with them, and also not automatically thinking about 'Muslim women' or women in *hijab* as 'them.'

Being the insider–outsider in both Canada and Turkey may provide me with certain sensitivities that, for example, 'insiders' of neither the 'Islamist' nor the 'secularist' positions may be able – or allowed – to develop in a polarized political environment as in Turkey. It also contributes to great agonizing. This is because of what I would like to call the émigré guilt. It is guilt related to the issue of accountability. It is guilt surrounding any attempts to analyse developments in Turkey: especially those developments that may have direct political implications and consequences. My agonies are based on the lingering fear I have that despite the multiplicity of the meanings of *hijab*, and the diversity of women adopting it, it would be difficult to prevent its association with or appropriation by fundamentalism, especially if the fundamentalists assume state power, as could happen in Turkey. My guilt is based on the fact that, compared with the secular intellectuals and activists in Turkey, I may be able to afford to take a less polarized position, partly because, being an émigré, I would not ultimately have to live with the potential consequences of my analysis, in a potentially totalitarian society that fundamentalists would likely shape in Turkey.

The distance I have from the potential consequences of my analysis could be interpreted as undermining the credibility of my analysis. Whether it does so or not depends on what approach I and my readers take to émigré feminism. If I try to justify my position on the *hijab* on the basis of a mystified, essentialist, and singular meaning attached to an émigré feminist location, this may help privilege me with an unquestioned moral authority to speak 'as a Turkish émigré feminist living in Canada.' At the same time, however, the demonstration of my distance from the phenomenon and its consequences can automatically and totally undermine the value of my analysis. If I help to deconstruct my position, however, by being more explicit about and ready to defend the theoretical–intellectual and political influences on my analysis, I make myself more open to criticism, but avoid the ironically equal possibilities of total (uncritical) acceptance or total dismissal of my analysis.

NOTES

1 See Bhabha (1990), Gilroy (1987), Pieterse (1995), Rushdie (1991).
2 As an example of this kind of analysis, see MacLeod (1992).

REFERENCES

Ahmed, Leila (1984) 'Early Feminist Movements in the Middle East: Turkey and
Egypt.' In Freda Hussein (ed.), *Muslim Women*, 111–23. London: Croom Helm.
Arat, Zehra (1994) 'Turkish Women and the Republican Reconstruction of
Tradition.' In Fatma Muge Gocek and Shiva Balaghi (eds.), *Reconstructing
Gender in the Middle East: Tradition, Identity and Power*, 57–78. New York: Colum-
bia University Press.
Arat-Koc, Sedef, and Kate Bezanson (1996) 'Modernity, Nationhood and Woman-
hood: Debates Over "Hijab" and "Muslim Women" in "Multicultural" Quebec
and Canada.' Paper presented at the meeting of the Canadian Sociology and
Anthropology Association, Learned Societies Conference, St Catharines,
Ontario, June.
Ataturk, Mustafa Kemal (1959) *Ataturk'un Soylev ve Demecleri*. Vol. 2. (Speeches and
Declarations of Ataturk.) Ankara: Turk Tarih Basimevi.
Bhabha, Homi (ed.), (1990) *Narrating the Nation*. London: Routledge.
Gilroy, Paul (1987) *There Ain't No Black in the Union Jack*. London: Hutchinson.
Gramsci, Antonio (1971) *Selections from the Prison Notebooks*. Translated and edited
by Quintin Hoare and Geoffrey Nowell Smith. New York: International Publish-
ers.
Hall, Stuart (1992) 'The Question of Cultural Identity.' In Stuart Hall, David
Held, and Tony McGraw, *Modernity and Its Futures*, 273–325. Cambridge: Polity
Press in Association with the Open University.
Hoodfar, Homa (1993) 'The Veil in their Minds and On Our Heads: The
Persistence of Colonial Images of Muslim Women.' *Resources for Feminist Research*
22(3/4):5–18.
Jayawardena, Kumari (1986) '"Civilization" Through Women's Emancipation in
Turkey.' In *Feminism and Nationalism in the Third World*, 25–42. London: Zed
Books.
Kandiyoti, Deniz (1987) 'Emancipated but Unliberated? Reflections on the
Turkish Case.' *Feminist Studies* 13(2):317–38.
– (1989) 'Women and the Turkish State: Political Actors or Symbolic Pawns?' In
Nira Yuval-Davis and Floya Anthias (eds.), *Woman–Nation–State*, 126–49.
London: Macmillan Press.
– (1991) 'End of Empire: Islam, Nationalism and Women in Turkey.' In Deniz

Kandiyoti (ed.), *Women, Islam and the State*, 22–47. Philadelphia: Temple University Press.

Keyder, Caglar (1988) 'Class and State in the Transformation of Modern Turkey.' In Fred Halliday and Hamza Alavi (eds.), *State and Ideology in the Middle East and Pakistan*, 191–221. New York: Monthly Review Press.

Khan, Shahnaz (1995) 'The Veil as a Site of Struggle: The Hijab in Quebec.' *Canadian Woman Studies* 15(2/3):146–52.

MacLeod, Arlene Elowe (1992) 'Hegemonic Relations and Gender Resistance: The New Veiling as Accommodating Protest in Cairo.' *Signs* 17(3):533–57.

Pieterse, Jan Nederveen (1995) 'Globalization as Hybridization.' In Mike Featherstone, Scott Lasch, and Roland Robertson (eds), *Global Modernities*, 45–68. London: Sage.

Robins, Kevin (1991) 'Tradition and Translation: National Culture in its Global Context.' In J. Corner and S. Harvey (eds.), *Enterprise and Heritage: Crosscurrents of National Culture*, 21–44. London: Routledge.

Rushdie, Salman (1991) *Imaginary Homelands*. London: Granta Books.

Said, Edward (1978) *Orientalism*. Harmondsworth: Penguin.

Sayyid, Bobby (1994) 'The Sign O'Times: Kaffirs and Infidels Fighting the Ninth Crusade.' In Ernesto Laclau (ed.), *The Making of Political Identities*, 264–86. London: Verso.

Sirman, Nukhet (1989) 'Feminism in Turkey: A Short History.' *New Perspectives on Turkey* 3(1).

Tekeli, Sirin (1982) *Kadinlar ve Siyasal, Toplumsal Hayat* (Women and Political Social Life). Istanbul: Birikim.

– (1988) *Kadinlar Icin* (For Women). Istanbul: Alan Yayincilik.

– (1991) 'Tek Parti Doneminde Kadin Hareketi de Bastirildi' (The Women's Movement was Also Repressed in the Single-Party Period). In Levent Cinemre and Rusen Cakir (eds.), *Sol Kemalizme Bakiyor: Roportaj* (The Left Looks at Kemalism: Interviews), 93–107. Istanbul: Metis Yayinlari.

Toprak, Zafer (1988) 'Halk Firkasindan Once Kurulan Parti' (The Party That was Founded Before the People's Party). *Tarih Ve Toplum* 9(51):30–1.

Weiker, Walter (1974) *Political Tutelage and Democracy in Turkey*. New York: Hilmes and Meier.

Yetkin, Cetin (1983) *Turkiye'de Tek Parti Yonetimi, 1930–1945* (Single-Party Rule in Turkey, 1930–1945). Istanbul, Altin Kitaplar Yayinevi.

Yuval-Davis, Nira (1994) 'Identity Politics and Women's Ethnicity.' In Valentine Moghadam (ed.), *Identity Politics and Women: Cultural Reassertions and Feminisms in International Perspective*, 408–24. New York: Westview.

# 10

# Émigré Iranian Feminism and the Construction of Muslim Woman

## HAIDEH MOGHISSI[1]

The rise of Islamic fundamentalists to power in Iran made women the main target of the Islamic onslaught and the main contender against its project to turn Iran into an Islamic stronghold. The formidable resistance of women, starting with the massive anti-veil protests immediately after the revolution, has continued in hundreds of intriguing, creative ways, targetting the regime's re-Islamization project and the restrictions placed on women's public life. Women's resistance imposed certain compromises on the Islamic state and shaped developments in the state's gender politics. But the formidable power of the Islamists and their remarkable success in silencing open opposition drove hundreds of thousands of skilled and educated workers and Iranian intellectuals into exile, including the left, nationalists, and feminists.

The same cultural and political factors that moved women against Islamic fundamentalism continue to affect Iranian women in exile. Iranian women form a vibrant and highly politicized émigré community, which is actively and passionately involved with political and cultural developments of the home country. The number of independent, women-centred publications and radio stations and feminist conferences and events organized around guest speakers by exiled Iranian women in Europe and North America speaks eloquently to the mounting interest of émigré women in feminist analyses and discourses on the situation of women in Iran. In this dynamic and volatile setting, feminist academic writings provide distinct, unequivocal, and highly specific political meanings for Iranian women in exile, and they often provoke intellectual and political realignment and divisions within the émigré community. Indeed, one major, perhaps *the* major, political conflict is increasingly taking shape around the concept of Muslim woman. The notion of 'Islamic feminism,' which has recently found currency in feminist academic settings, has been even more contentious. In the past couple of years, for example, meetings of international scholarly groups such as the United States–based Foundation of Iranian Women's Studies or the Center for Iranian Research and Analysis, as well as country-based conferences, have been absorbed by sharp debates on this topic. Although unfolding in academic settings distant from Iran, the root cause of these conflicts is to be found in Iran's postrevolutionary experience, especially the defeat of the democratic hopes and the gains of the revolution by Iran's historically most undemocratic political force, the clergy. But it is also the result of the particular configuration or composition of Iranian émigré feminists.

Exiled Iranian women have been drawn powerfully to feminism, having experienced the rise of Islamic fundamentalism and felt the clutches of the Islamists over their personal lives, and having been disillusioned by the populist left and by nationalist forces, who through their silence or faint-hearted support of women's rights accelerated Islamization policies and the defeat of women's spontaneous movements. Exposure to feminist ideas and involvement in other, 'new' social movements, as well as liberation from the organizational or ideological discipline of the traditional left, have influenced Iranian feminists' self-perception and encouraged critical thinking. The past political experiences and new awareness about the complexity of, and the links between, struggles for gender equity and social justice have also made émigré feminists particularly alert to the new feminist discourses. Despite their radical claims, these new discourses push, in fact, for the most conservative – and disappointingly familiar – ideas about social change.

## Émigré Iranian Women: Who Are We?

It should go without saying that exiled and self-exiled Iranian women do not represent a homogeneous and easily recognizable community. Generally, exiled Iranian women share an urban, new[2] middle-class background, with secular, non-traditional life experiences and behavioural patterns. However, the experience of exile, the feelings towards the country we left behind, and the expectations of women for the future can be quite different depending on class background, education level, age, marital status, religion, cultural and ethnic affiliation, the length of our time in exile, and, most importantly, our political and ideological standpoints.

First, there are the more affluent, middle-class, and for the most part married, self-exiled women. These women left their homes and privileges in Iran because they had lost their jobs and social status and power in the 1979 revolution, because of cultural repression, and because of the uncertain future for their husbands and children. These women overall did not have many problems in adjusting to life in exile. Their plentiful economic resources continue to provide them with privileges similar to the ones they enjoyed in Iran. These women have created their own community of friends and associates from among those in the Iranian diaspora. They tend to deal with other citizens in their host countries selectively, as the need arises. The women-centred organizations, publications, and get-togethers of this group, are predominantly charity oriented.

By contrast, there is a second group of women, who consciously identify themselves as feminists or whose personal and political lives can ascribe to them this identity. This group comprises what one might, broadly speaking, call the politically engaged women who for various reasons were forced into exile, whether voluntarily or involuntarily. Some of them were driven to exile because their world-views, lifestyles, or professions were deemed counter-revolutionary in the anti-intellectual frenzy that the Islamists promoted. Many more left Iran to escape the political and cultural repression after the 1979 revolution and the Iran–Iraq war. Most members of this group, in one way or another, participated in the experience of the pre- and post-revolutionary oppositional politics of the revolution which brought Islamists to power. Some are former activists and members or supporters of various political parties and organizations in opposition to the Islamic government. The overwhelming majority of these women carry with them their commitments to secular values associated with human rights, social justice, and political democracy.

Finally, there is a third, small, but influential group of Iranian women academics with varied ideological orientations. Some in this group have a background similar to that of the women in the second group, while others are mostly old-time émigré women. The majority of these women have lived in the West almost all their adult lives. Some belonged to the pre-revolutionary anti-Shah movements of Iranian students in Europe and North America. Many of them returned to Iran immediately after the revolution, to have a taste of the revolution, or to put their skills and experiences at its service. However, disillusioned and defeated, they left Iran again. This last group is the focus of the present essay.

Although émigré academic feminists come from different schools of thought, and have had different political and theoretical persuasions, a growing number of them have moved towards what I have called neo-conservative feminism.[3] The central core of their ideas is that both the Islamic state and the Muslim women in Iran have been transformed in directions favourable to women. Hence, we should divert our attention from the 'rhetoric of fundamentalism' and 'its impact on women' to 'the dynamics of the relationship between the fundamentalists and women ... the complexity, and the humanity of women's lives within their own cultural context' and 'let women be the protagonists of their own life dramas.' From this very sound and defendable premise, Shahla Haeri (1995:131) set out to establish 'the long overlooked, agency of *Muslim women*' – that is, women who '*despite* the existing structural restrictions and cultural confinement, have found ways to empower themselves, to pursue their objectives, and to give meaning and direction to their lives.' The rise of fundamentalists to power, according to Haleh Afshar (1994:17), has not been all negative, and its practical consequences not so damaging to the cause of women. Indeed, it may be that all secular women and men, and many Muslim women whose understanding of Islamic laws does not match that of the Islamic state, have got it wrong. Fundamentalism for Iranian women 'has almost literally been a godsend.' Afshar acknowledged the fact that with the arrival of the Islamic Republic Iranian women lost all they had struggled for over a century. But women, 'as women and as believers,' showed remarkable resilience in dealing with this grim situation. That is because 'it was only as devout Muslims that women could counter the demands made of them'; the defenders of Women's rights took the Republic to task for failing to deliver Islamic duties 'and they won considerable ground and are continuing to do so' (Afshar, 1994:18–19).

Favourable changes in the lot of women are possible, perhaps even desirable, only through an Islamic frame of reference, argued another writer, Nayereh Tohidi (1994). Islamic feminism, as 'the spontaneous evolution out of women's own activism' is capable of opening up new prospects for Iranian women and 'chang[ing] the dimensions, conception, and definition of women's identity and the woman question for the younger generation of Iranian women and men' (Tohidi, 1994:141–2). Indeed, according to Homa Hoodfar (1993), the new Islamist feminism has advantages over secular feminism, which she identified as Western. In Hoodfar's view (1993:17), Islamic feminists 'challenge and reform the Islamic doctrine from within rather than advocating a Western model of gender relations.'

Some male academics have added their voices to these celebratory accounts of women's lives under fundamentalism. Akbar Mahdi (1995), for example, drew a rosy picture of the political situation in the religious-soaked Iran. Within the context of free-flowing political views and opinions, he posited, women speak in a much more colourful language than before, reflecting the diversity of views and opinions about their lives, and demonstrate a level of independence never before seen.

These analyses of the political conditions and feminist forces in present-day Iran and laudatory reports on the achievement of what they call *Muslim women* are, at best, simplistic and one-dimensional: they have no correspondence to the experiences of the majority of women in Iran. Yet, they can create confusing illusions about women's lives under fundamentalism, which is distinguished from other political–cultural movements of this century by its offensive against all legal and sociocultural institutions of women's 'empowerment.' Indeed, the sharp edges of fundamentalism are pointed at women, regardless of whether its point of reference is Islam, Hinduism, Judaism, or Christianity. By mystifying the activities of Muslim women and their sense of empowerment under Islamic rule, these neo-conservative feminists in effect make fundamentalism banal, by erasing its harshest and most characteristic features. At the same time, they present an indigenous version of feminism for the region, which does not include core feminist ideas and a commitment to human rights as they have so far been understood. As some in opposition to this group have put it: these neo-conservative women are not trying to make Islam feminist, but to make feminism Islamic.

What are the main reasons for this dramatic realignment and change of tone within Iranian academic feminism? Perhaps it is a combination of factors. These might include, for example, a genuine, though erroneously articulated, desire to challenge the stereotypical colonial images of Islam and of Muslim women that prevail in the West. The realignment may reflect actual developments in the gender politics of the Islamic regime in the post-Khomeini era. Finally, the new direction of émigré academic feminism may be influenced by the depoliticizing intellectual tendencies of identity politics and the postmodern mood dominant in Western, notably North American, academia.

Admittedly, for too long the 'oppressed' and 'passive' Muslim woman – presented as the inverse image of the civilized, knowing, and liberated Western woman – dominated academic and popular writing. But respect for the right of the previously silenced and misrepresented Muslim woman to speak for herself, so long overdue, is gradually being recognized, as a result of successful challenges by feminist scholars from the region and outside it, and by the continuing efforts of hundreds of thousands of secular and Muslim women, political activists, and libertarians in the region. Their agency is no longer invisible to outside observers. But I want to argue that the new imagery of the Muslim women constructed by some Iranian feminist academics as an alternative to the older, more passive image, is as stereotypical, as essentializing, and as disempowering as it was in the typical, orientalist writings.

The stated intention of neo-conservative, Islamic feminists is to challenge the '*generalities, images,* and *perspectives*' that have dominated images of Muslim women in the West. They wish to call into question an 'undifferentiated category which across [the] cultural divide and ethnic boundaries ... flattens out differences and homogenizes women in space and time' (Haeri, 1995:132). In their hands, however, the term *Muslim woman* turns into precisely the sort of 'one size fits all' concept that does, indeed, flatten the diverse material conditions and ideological configurations experienced by the Iranian female population. Haeri, for example, in the same fashion as the orientalists, implied that all women living in Islamic societies are Muslim women. This is a familiar, traditional notion, except that, in Haeri's account, all these Muslim women are actively, dynamically, seeking empowerment.

In Haeri's construction (1995:132), Muslim women include, for example, 'the unveiled, autonomous, independent, economically successful, educated, and articulate woman with whom [she] identifies.' She also used the term, more generally, for women who use an Islamic framework to defend women's rights because secular outlets are not available, or for the 'secular Muslim women' in Western universities, who, like Haeri herself, who *chooses* to call herself a Muslim woman in terms of her 'sense of cultural and religious identity.' Also included are Muslim women from the Islamic establishment who advocate legal reforms in the hope of softening the impact of specific, gender-based, legal and administrative policies, which they see as discriminatory.

Bringing such a range of women together within a single category is obviously problematic. It forgets the crucial difference between a woman who merely lives (and must live) in an Islamic society and women who have personally embraced Islam and practise its teachings. The Muslim women who are haphazardly assembled together to construct an imagery that serves specific intellectual goals have distinct and important differences that make the use of such an all-encompassing concept unwise and completely unjustified.

Several distinct kinds of women can be recognized among Muslim women. First, there are genuinely fundamentalist women with very rigid, traditional views on gender issues. They are themselves members of the elite: these women are the torch bearers of the Islamists. They belong to the female auxiliary of the Hezbollah and are used in periodic rallies to excite enthusiasm for a more rigid dress code (the Islamic *hijab*), or to attack, when convenient, the legitimacy of newspapers and journals that have been labelled as non-Islamic. Islamic feminist expression within this category includes the occasional comments made in favour of women's greater access to employment by leaders such as Ayatollah Khomeini's daughter and her associates in the Society of Women of the Islamic Republic. These interventions, of course, are purely political and often self-serving. The women involved accept Islamic shari'a (jurisprudence) and its provisions *tout court*.[4] For example, the daughter of Chief Justice Ayatollah Yazdi (his adviser on women's affairs) is an ardent supporter of men's right to unilateral divorce.

The second type of Muslim woman is also part of the established order, if only slightly more removed from the points of command. Recruited to help to promote the regime's gender politics, and related to male elites by marriage or blood, these women are the main beneficiaries of Iran's re-Islamization of public life. Some, like Maryam Behroozi and Marzieh Dabbagh, the Majlis (parliament) deputies, are devout Muslims who initially supported the flogging of unveiled women (Mojab, 1995a; Moghissi, 1995). After more than a decade of involvement in public life, numerous trips abroad, opportunities for the formal education that they previously lacked, and confrontations with their male counterparts' masculinist values and demeaning practices, they have very pragmatic, 'political' reasons for trying to improve women's status *vis-à-vis* men. Their activities, regardless of personal political intentions, are a hopeful sign; they may help get some gender-based educational and employment barriers removed by the regime they support.

Finally, there are those women who, while loyal to the Islamic regime and the values for which it stands, are critical of its treatment of women and try to soften its gender-oppressive policies. These women hope to reform Islamic shari'a in favour of women. These are the women who one may identify as *Islamic feminists*, that is, Muslim women who, while embracing Islamic ideology as liberating, are genuinely trying to promote women's rights within the confines of Islamic shari'a and to impose a more moderate and more female-centred interpretation of Orthodox Islamic text on the Islamists.

To cloud differences among these Muslim women and suggest that, because they are active on gender issues, they are 'feminist' activists is, at best, problematic. Except for the last group, the newly found voices of Muslim women echo the standpoint of the fundamentalist state. Their agency, if such it is, in support of male-defined gender roles is positively damaging to Iranian feminist struggles for gender equity, dignity, basic human rights, and democracy. Indeed, it should be clear that women can be used effectively in the production and exercise of the most undemocratic, misogynist values and social policies, and in the rise and consolidation of authoritarian movements and regimes. Indoctrinated by the ruling ideology, women can contribute to, if not take part in, the exercise of state violence and coercion and produce the harshest voices in support of repression. In her illuminating study of women in right-wing Hindu movements, for example, Flavia Agnes (1995) demonstrated the dangerous turn the mobilization of women can take in the hands of communal forces. Women's activism, manipulated by the right-wing communal forces, Agnes argued, was not directed against violence within the home and community as secular women's organizations had hoped, but was directed externally towards Muslims – both men and women. By the same token, through appropriating the symbols and slogans of women's organizations against obscenity in the media, the women's wings of Hindu fundamentalist movements used their newly found strength and voice for curtailing freedom of speech and expression on secular issues (Agnes, 1995:140–1).

Regretably, women's agency and activism do not always mean an improvement for women in the home or in society as a whole. It is simple-minded to suggest that, because previously secluded women have found access to public space, they are going to change gender and power dynamics within Iranian society or transform Islam's patriarchal character. Even more objectionable in the portrayals of neo-conservative feminists is their deliberate attempt to cloud the resilience of hundreds of thousands of young, secular women under fundamentalist rule. These women have demonstrated a remarkable effort to push back the Islamists' sociocultural offensive and to recapture, inch by inch, the legal, educational, and employment opportunities that they lost with the revolution. This is a wilful omission. It buries Iranian women's long history in the secular feminist tradition. It is a tradition whose voice, as articulated by women like Qurrat-ul Ain and Bibi Khanum, was heard as far back as the 1840s, although the women's campaign for gender equity did not become fully organized until the beginning of the twentieth century (Bamdad, 1977; Nashat, 1983; Afary, 1996). Iranian pioneers for women's rights also tried to negotiate change in women's legal and social status within the then permissable cultural and religious boundaries. They, too, had to emphasize their adherence to Islam to avoid the smearing accusations by religious fanatics of the day. But neither they nor the researchers who explored their experiences found it necessary to use the term Muslim feminism as a decorative marker for the women's movement in Iran.

Political repression and religious despotism, which mute open expression against the Islamic regime among secular feminists, have not, and could not possibly persuade secular women to accept that the path to social transformation and the recognition of women as full citizens passes through the corridors of the Islamic populist utopia. Secular women do not share the vision of their Muslim sisters about the existing social order, and they do not find Islam to be a liberatory ideology, an alternative to feminism. They have little hope that women can achieve much within the confines of shari'a. Their adherence to Islamic dress and moral codes is neither a matter of choice nor of ideological transformation. These women bear the brunt of re-Islamization policies. Through their quiet, effective, resolute efforts, they survive these policies, but always at a high cost and without the consolation of religious belief. These efforts draw energy from thousands of young women who grew up under the mullahs' rule, but who do not want their lives worked out for them by the old Islamic patriarchy. But resistance also comes from women whose education and professional skills derive from decades of social and economic development and legal reforms which, however class based and lopsided, have benefited the female population at large. Ironically, this group includes an impressive number of women writers, poets, and filmmakers who are often presented in the West as beneficiaries of the new relaxed mood of the Islamic state.

True, mandatory *hijab* has made secular women virtually indistinguishable. The Islamic regime would love, if it could, to make them invisible and it has done its best to turn the female population into undifferentiated and undifferentiable creatures, stripped of their sexuality, humanity, and voice. But, in this, the regime fails. Iranian women of diverse social and class backgrounds and ideological beliefs continue to resist the Islamic state. One case in point is the conflict over *hijab*, which Islamists celebrate as the symbol of Islamic womanhood, and which secular women reject as an outrageous ploy to control women's body and women's choice. After seventeen years of Islamic rule and the commitment of staggering resources to impose the Islamic dress code through indoctrination and coercion, adherence still must be forced on women through the efforts of 300,000 *basiji* (militia). In fact, the *basiji* merely supplement the efforts of locally organized teams. Periodically, these enforcers take over Tehran's streets and the streets of other cities. For a few days, at least, they drive *bad-hijabs* out of sight.

It may be, as Afshar (1994:16) has argued, that many 'Muslim women have *chosen* the veil as a symbol of Islamification' (emphasis added). Also, the veil may be presented as part of the 'lived experience of Muslim women,' which these women use to 'free themselves from the bonds of patriarchy,' as Homa Hoodfar (1993:7) has said they do. In fact, it has been suggested that not to recognize veiling as empowering is to 'deny Muslim women their agency.' Such interpretations, however, do not change the brute fact that the veil *accomplishes* the objectification of women. It represents chastity and modesty – as defined by men. It symbolizes male authority and control over the female body. Precisely for this reason, hundreds of thousands of Iranian women refuse to accept the veil as an expression of their adherence to Islam or to the political regime that it represents.

According to neo-conservative feminists, however, there is no secular feminist movement, indeed, perhaps no secular woman in present-day Iran. For according to Parvin Paidar (1996:59), 'Secular feminism was crushed and driven into exile.' This way, the neo-conservative feminists hear and celebrate the 'authentic' voices of Muslim women in favour of reforms within Islamic shari'a, but dismiss and marginalize the voices that demand removal of shari'a from the political and legal systems in Iran. The neo-conservative feminists also try to silence the secular exiled women, who refuse to celebrate their own suppression by making apologies for the Iranian government, by accusing them of, in the words of Nayereh Tohidi (1994:56–7), 'being Stalinists,' or being portrayed as 'increasingly individualistic,' as Paidar (1996:63) has done, and treat them as outsiders to their own culture. Not to recognize the legitimacy and the vitality or even the existence of secular views and voices in present-day Iran and privileging the voices of religion, even if done out of carelessness, is bad analysis. If done consciously and deliberately, it is bad politics.

Curiously, the writings we are discussing almost completely disregard the conditions and circumstances, and the cultural and political contradictions, which during the post-Khomeini era induced changes in the Islamists' policy and practice *vis-à-vis* women. This is an oddity, in view of the sound advice of their authors to distinguish between text and context when discussing the experience of Islamic women, and their insistence that we see the difference between fundamentalist *rhetoric* and the way in which fundamentalism works in practice (Haeri, 1995:130). Indeed, the *context* of these changes are the actual conditions and contradictions that forced certain compromises on the Islamists, moving them away (although never too far) from their religiously inscribed *text.*

Sociocultural and political contradictions arose from the conflict between the demands of a capitalist economy, which would normally lead to women's incorporation into the labour force as independent workers, and the Islamists' determination to maintain sexual segregation and the rigid regulation of female–male interaction. It was exactly this capitalist economic context that forced the regime to remove the barriers, at least on paper, to women's participation in some technical fields of higher education, notably, engineering and law, and to readmit women to professions from which they had been excluded after the revolution (Afary, 1996; Moghissi, 1995; Mojab, 1995b). Had the Islamists captured state power in, say, 1960 – prior to the economic, social, and cultural changes that, inevitably, changed women's social and legal status, gender roles and relations, as well as women's expectations and self perceptions – their backward *practice*, no doubt, would have been closer to their *text.*[5]

Moreover, as a result of economic and social changes of the previous decades, women had learned something about their rights and their lives that, much to the dismay of the religious establishment, could not be unlearned. This reality is ignored in much of the writings of neo-conservative feminists. For example, to argue, as Paidar (1996:64) has done, that 'it took about forty years for secular feminists of the Pahlavi era to change the family law ... [but] it took Ayatollah Khomeini one speech to demolish [it] ... and since then, it has taken Islamist feminists over twelve years to build it again bit by bit' is to assume that the revolution wiped out not only the *ancien régime,* but all the social and economic forces that promoted the introduction of reforms, including the family code. Aside from the characteristically one-sided presentation of Muslim women as the agents of change, this argument seems to suggest that Iranian feminists, whether Islamic or secular, started from a clean slate and learned to fight for their rights without having behind them the favourable material conditions, and the awareness, skills, experience, and struggles of the past.

Indeed, the campaign of Islamic feminists and Muslim women in the Majlis for the reinstitution of a new family law was only one link in the chain of socioeconomic and political pressures felt by the Islamists. These pressures included the practical difficulties that arose from Islamization policies, such as the increasing rate of divorce, prompted by the reinstitution of men's unilateral right to divorce (sometimes even discussed in the Majlis); the sit-ins of war widows in Ayatollah Montazeri's house, protesting women's lack of rights to child custody and guardianship (which goes to the grandfather when the father dies); and the gruesome murder of women by their husbands (often in order to remove an obstacle to their remarriage).

In addition to the mounting dissatisfaction and protests from within Iran, the Islamic government has had to face constant criticism from abroad for its treatment of women. To 'export the revolution,' efforts had to be made to counterbalance the negative propaganda of the world media. But, as is always the case, even cracking one door open and making one concession generated demands for other changes and openings.

Indeed, the Islamists' well-advertised political manoeuvres and change of tactics impressed academic feminists outside the country more than they did the Iranian women who actually had to endure Islamic rule. For example, in the winter of 1990, when President Rafsanjani in a sermon at the Friday prayer in Tehran spoke in favour of *mut'a* ('temporary marriage' for a set price) and encouraged young men to use *mut'a* to marry war widows, his speech sparked a commotion in Iran and was criticized by the state-sponsored women's magazines.[6] Even one of the most conservative women's organizations, headed by Khomeini's daughter, objected to *mut'a* as endangering family stability.[7] *Mut'a* is popularly understood to provide legal licence for prostitution and the sexual exploitation of young girls and women of the poor classes. Nevertheless, an Iranian feminist scholar in the West presented the institution as a channel of sexual gratification for women, a step towards their empowerment (Haeri, 1989). In the same way, during the late 1980s, Iranian state statistics reported a dramatic decline in the rate of women's participation in the labour force, and the president's adviser on women's affairs blamed it on postrevolutionary policies and the promotion of the culture of domesticity.[8] In contrast, an Iranian feminist scholar in the West insisted on the stability or even growth in women's labour force participation under Islamic rule (Moghadam, 1988).

Focusing on the achievements (or, perhaps, changes in perception) by one group of Muslim women who are negotiating for more space and a fairer share of social and economic resources should not cloud the overall disempowering impact of fundamentalist rule in Iran. Indeed, some of these favourable writings bring to mind the Persian proverb that 'A distant drum sounds pleasant' *(Aavaz-e dohol shanidan as dour khoush a'st)*, a popular proverb used by Persian poets and philosophers critical of the illusions created about the virtues of distant, remote, and improbable things, events, and phenomena.

The actual impact of fundamentalists' rule for women is horrifying. It should not be mystified. The feminist commitment to equity, justice, and humanism requires that the practical consequences of fundamentalist rule for women be exposed. These consequences include such practices as the inadmissibility of a woman's testimony in the case of her own rape (so ruled, because, legally, a woman's testimony is worth half that of a man); the stoning of women accused of adultery or prostitution; the horrific brutalization of women through so-called honour killing, which has alarmed even the chief justice (*Zan-e Rooz*, 1993); rape and sexual violence against young women, within marriage; the alarming rate of women's self-burning; the imposition of a mandatory dress code, even the colour of which is decided by Islamic bureaucrats; the arrest and torture of women who are considered as poorly veiled *(bad-hijab)*; and the cultural and political repression of female professionals, writers, and poets, who find it so difficult to survive outside the parameters of the acceptable Muslim woman. These difficulties have even led to actions of self-destruction, as in the case of Homa Darabi, a woman university professor and psychologist, who set herself on fire in public to protest political repression and the suppression of women's basic personal rights.[9] Grim realities, such as the widening gap between the rich and the poor in the 'government of the dispossessed,' have caused several major riots since 1993 in Tehran, Gazvin, Shiraz, and other major cities (Bayat, 1994). But one looks in vain for any reference to them in the writings of neo-conservative academic feminists.

For those of us who lived through the memorable experience of the revolution, and who have watched, in horror, the devastating consequences of the Islamization policies, and felt the clutches of the Islamists on our personal lives, the infatuation of academic feminists with 'Islamic feminism,' and their softening tone *vis-à-vis* Islamic fundamentalism, reminds one, uncomfortably, of the self-negating actions and discourse of the traditional left when it was thrust into the frenzy of 'anti-imperialist' populism during the post-revolutionary period. Then, enchanted by the sudden 'politicization' of the ordinary, uneducated masses, who were later used, devastatingly, by *Hezbollahi* gangs and the clergy, against whoever disagreed with the Ayatollah's 'anti-imperialist' vision, many on the traditional left abandoned their pre-revolutionary democratic goals, surrendering individual liberties. They fell for the Ayatollah's local, home-grown, concept of anti-imperialism; toning down their criticism of Islamic totalitarian acts, such as the summary 'trials' and gruesome 'revolutionary execution' of officials of the *ancien régime*, the left, and Kurdish nationalists. They did not object to forced veiling of women and to suppression of the free press. Reducing their expectations and paralyzed by the political situation made particularly complex after the takeover of the American embassy by the Islamists, many people belonging to the secular left placed their hopes in the Islamic forces. It did not matter that the Islamists' understanding of social and economic forces of change and development and their ideas about human rights, political and cultural democracy, gender equity, basic individual rights, and national and religious freedoms did not match the rest of the society. The left just had to 'correct' its understandings of these long aspired-for goals, to bring them in line with the 'native,' locally generated thoughts of the Ayatollah, completely pure of Western influence. In the writings of neo-conservative, academic feminists one hears again, tragically, an echo of this same romantic confusion, surrendering, at the same time, their own vocation (and obligation) to act as critical intellectuals.

**Conclusion**

Almost two decades have passed since the 1979 revolution in Iran. Contrary to the hopeful prognosis of various political analysts, and the equally wishful predictions of the opposition, the Islamic fundamentalist regime still rules. To survive amidst internal and external hostility and pressure, the Islamists depended on the continuing flow of oil revenues, used to appease the middle classes. They have demonstrated a remarkable ability in finding face-saving excuses for the failure to implement the social and economic projects in favour of the poor and the dispossessed (*mustazafan*) which earlier they had promised.

However, the unresolved social and economic conflicts and contradictions that led to the 1979 revolution are unfolding in directions unfavourable to the Islamists and their supporters. The class-based, self-defeating economic policies of the previous regime, presented back to the society in an Islamic cloak, together with political repression and the Islamists' heavy-handedness in executing their re-Islamization project, have sparked a serious challenge to the regime's legitimacy. The regime has succeeded in immobilizing, through intimidation, coercion, and terror both the moderate alternatives and the radical opposition to its rule. But political and cultural resistance persists in many forms. This is a nightmarish reality for the Islamic regime. Since 1993 Iran has witnessed several major uprisings, unprecedented since the revolution. In 1994, 134 Iranian writers and poets petitioned against the strangulation of freedom of expression and the harassment of secular intellectuals by the regime. Cultural and political expression in contemporary Iran constitutes a life-threatening activity – evidenced by the arrest and eventual murder in 1995 of Sa'idi Sirjani, prominent poet and educator (Karimi Hakak, 1994; Whitley, 1994); the victimization of the journalist and writer Faraj Sarkoohi, who 'disappeared' in Tehran Airport on his way to Germany, and the death of Ghaffar Hosseini, whose body was discovered in Tehran. Both Sarkoohi and Hosseini were signatories of the 1994 Declaration by 134 Iranian writers.[10]

Under Islamic rule, general discontent and urban unrest, as well as the remarkable ability of Iranian society to resist cultural and political repression and survive unthinkable economic hardships, are dominant features of life. Iranian newspapers report regularly on clashes in the streets of Iran's major cities between bystanders and the 'morality police' over the arrests of violators of the Islamic moral code and the rampages of the mob following sports and recreational events. But the irrepressible skill of Iranian women in surviving discriminatory policies and gendered moral rules, and their persistent attempts to recapture social space misappropriated by the Islamists after the revolution are, perhaps, the most prominent challenges faced by the Islamic state. The clear message of the young women who grew up under the Islamic regime and have passed through years of Islamic 'resocialization' and indoctrination processes, but who still defy the *hijab* code, is that they have not been won over to Islamic values or the Islamic world-view, as defined by the fundamentalists.

What does all this mean to the Iranian exiles and, more specifically to émigré feminists? As in other diasporic communities, more politically oriented Iranian feminists are attuned to political developments in the home country and how these will affect women. For many of us, the limited social space recaptured by women offers evidence of the effects of the remarkable energy and determined resistance of all Iranian women. We have reasons to believe that the struggle of women inside Iran was positively affected by the efforts of Iranian feminists outside Iran to bring to light the plight of women under fundamentalist rule, as well as by media reports on the subject and by the reports by U.N. rapporteurs.[11] The Iranian government, like other authoritarian regimes, is quite conscious that its human rights record, particularly its treatment of women, is known outside Iran. Indeed, it has done its best to contravene this impression in the West and to counterbalance the voices of Iranian political activists on the subject. Dispatching of women from the Muslim elite to international conferences and state visits,[12] and assigning a woman the task of carrying the banner of the Iranian athletes in the 1996 Olympics[13] demonstrate that the Islamic regime does not feel itself completely immune to outside pressures and criticism. In other words, it is reasonable to assume that activities of the exiled opposition, animating resistance inside Iran, may have prompted the much talked about changes in the Iranian state's gender policy. For this reason, exaggerated accounts of what women have achieved under Islamic rule and the role of Muslim women in promoting these achievements, are bound to ease the pressure the Islamists feel to make further compromises on the issues of women's rights. Consequently, the exaggerations actually work against the interests of Iranian women and their struggle for pushing back the Islamist offensive.

The task of secular émigré Iranian feminists is to support the resistance of Iranian women against fundamentalism and to provide them with the encouragement and appreciation they deserve, without, at the same time, causing confusion as to what is achievable under Islamic rule. An even more daunting task for secular feminists is to acknowledge and respect the activities of Muslim women who are trying to propose a more woman-centred interpretation of Islamic shari'a, without becoming complicit in the Islamists' propaganda campaign to present an 'Islamic solution' as a viable alternative to secular agendas and secular values. Secular feminists have a basic intellectual responsibility to sustain pressure on the Islamic state to make more space available for women and men to develop their own oppositional discourse and politics. This responsibility includes not reducing expectations for basic human rights, equity, justice, and dignity – to which all women, and men, are entitled.

NOTES

1 Support for this study by a Social Sciences and Humanities Research Council Small Grant, York University, is gratefully acknowledged.
2 I use the term 'new' to distinguish this section of the Iranian middle class, which was the product of the economic and social reforms of the 1960s and 1970s, from its 'traditional' counterpart with roots in the bazaar and long-standing connections with Islamic leaders and institutions.
3 The term 'neo-conservative' is useful to identify this group of Iranian feminists, despite the shortcomings of the broad and heterogeneous character of their

perspectives. Considering the long tradition of liberals' and reformers' advocacy of civil liberties, individual rights, and social reforms, both in Iran and in the West, the alternative title of liberal or neo-liberal would not suit neo-conservative feminists. Moreover, conservatism does not solely refer to advocating the status quo. It also refers to a preference for slow gradual development, as opposed to structural changes. Neo-conservatives are a moderate form of conservatism. Many of its early proponents, at least in the United States, were former liberals.

4 The shari'a, Islamic codes of law, sets rules of conduct in matters of daily life and in religious matters for the Muslim community. The shari'a is derived from the Quran, the *Hadith* (sayings attributed to the Prophet Muhammad and, in Shi'ism, to the twelve Imams), sunna, or practical traditions, and *Ijma*, the consensus among the *ulama*, the Muslim jurists.

5 The modernization project in Iran, the so-called White Revolution, carried out under the deposed Muhammad Reza Shah in early 1960s, included legal and socioeconomic changes favourable to the status of women. The most important change was, perhaps, the introduction of the Family Protection Act in 1967. The new family law did not make a radical break from the shari'a. However, it tried to modify the civil code in favour of women on such crucial issues as divorce (previously a unilateral right of men) and the custody of children (where previously, boys over the age of two and girls over the age of seven belonged to the father). Despite the limited scope of the law, it faced strong opposition from the clergy, who condemned the new family law for violating the Islamic shari'a and the words of God. Other reforms, such as women's enfranchisement and the legislation that allowed women to serve as judges, also faced clerical opposition. It should go without saying that the material rewards of Iran's modernization project were not enjoyed by the overwhelming majority of women, particularly in rural areas. Nonetheless, despite continued disparity between rural–urban and male–female life options and resources and the class character of the changes introduced by the Shah's regime, the economic growth and social and legal reforms of the period improved women's position and self-perception. That is, a large sections of the female population benefited from favourable changes in women's employment and particularly educational opportunities opened to them.

6 *Iran Times* (17 Azar 1369, Dec. 1990).

7 *Neda,* Society of Women of Islamic Republic, 1/3 (Aug. 1990).

8 *Iran Times,* 30 July 1993.

9 It is worth mentioning that after Homa Darabi's suicide, only a handful of Iranian women academic feminists agreed to join their voices with over seventy Iranian academics in exile who signed a petition in protest of the repression

that forces some intellectuals, like Homa Darabi, to take such dramatic steps to bring to the world's attention the plight of women under Islamic rule.

10 On 20 Nov. 1996, PEN released an open letter to President Rafsanjani on the cases of Sarkoohi and Hosseini, signed by writers Edward Albee, Jacques Derrida, Gunter Grass, Eric Hobsbawm, Milan Kundera, Arthur Miller, Edward Said, and Susan Sontag. Following the suprise election of Muhammad Khatami to the presidency in May 1997, and under continued international pressure, Sarkoolin was released from prison.

11 In its most recent annual human rights review, the U.N. human rights committee, reflecting on the findings of Maurice Copithorne, the new U.N. rapporteur on human rights in Iran, once more condemned Iran for its violations of human rights, continued executions, harassment of Iranians in exile, and discrimination against women. See *Iran Times*, 6 Dec. 1996.

12 Most recently, one of President Rafsanjani's daughters, Fatemeh, president of the International Union of Muslim Women's Non-Governmental Organizations, told an audience in London to ignore propaganda that describes Iranian women as oppressed. *Iran Times*, 6 Dec. 1996.

13 'Political expediency' furnished the decision to send a woman, Lida Fariman, to the Olympics and to assign her the task of carrying the Iranian banner. Fariman had found out about her banner-carrying assignment through the news on the radio, without ever being consulted. Yet, since 'it had been found advisable' for a woman to carry the banner, neither Fariman nor other Iranian athletes objected to this decision. See *Zanan*, no. 30, Mehr 1375, Oct. 1996, pp. 40–1.

REFERENCES

Afary, Janet (1996) 'Steering Between Scylla and Charybdis: Shifting Gender Roles in Twentieth Century Iran.' *National Women Studies Association Global Perspectives* 8(1) (Spring):28–49.

Afkhami, Mahnaz (1984) 'Iran: A Future in the Past – "The Pre-Revolutionary" Women's Movement.' In Robyn Morgan (ed.), *Sisterhood Is Global*, 330–1. Garden City: Anchor Press / Doubleday.

Afshar, Haleh (1982) 'Khomeini's Teachings and their Implications for Women,' *Feminist Review*, no. 12 (October):59–72.

– (1994) 'Women and the Politics of Fundamentalism in Iran,' *Women against Fundamentalism* 1(5):15–20.

Agnes, Flavia (1995) 'Redefining the Agenda of the Women's Movement Within a Secular Framework.' In Tanika Sarkar and Urvashi Butalia (eds.), *Women and Right-Wing Movements: Indian Experiences*, 136–57. London: Zed Books.

Bamdad, Badr-ul molouk (1977) *From Darkness into Light: Women's Emancipation in Iran.* Hicksville, NY: Exposition Press.

Bayat, Asef (1994) 'Squatters and the State,' *Middle East Report*, no. 191.

Haeri, Shahla (1989) *The Law of Desire: the Temporary Marriage in Shi'i Iran.* Syracuse: Syracuse University Press.

– (1995) 'On Feminism and Fundamentalism in Iran and Pakistan.' *Contention* 4(3):129–49.

Hoodfar, Homa (1993) 'The Veil in their Minds and on our Heads: The Persistence of Colonial Images of Muslim Women.' *Resources for Feminist Research* 22(3/4):5–18.

Karimi Hakak, Ahmad (1994) 'Ali Akbar Sa'idi Sirjani: A Storyteller and His Times.' *Middle East Journal* 48(3):533–6.

Mahdi, Akbar (1995) 'Reconstructing Gender in Post-revolutionary Iran: Two Perspectives on Women in Islamic Republic,' *Middle East Insight* 11(5).

Moghadam, Valentine (1988) 'Women, Work and Ideology in the Islamic Republic of Iran.' *International Journal of Middle East Studies* 20:221–43.

Moghissi, Haideh (1994) *Populism and Feminism in Iran: Women's Struggle in a Male-defined Revolutionary Movement.* London: Macmillan Press.

– (1995) 'Public Life and Women's Resistance.' In Saeed Rahnema and Sohrab Behdad (eds.), *Iran After the Revolution: Crisis of an Islamic State*, 251–67. London: I.B. Tauris.

Mojab, Shahrzad (1995a) 'Islamic Feminism: Alternative or Contradiction?' *Fireweed*, no. 47.

– (1995b) 'Education and Human Rights: Iran.' In *Academic Freedom*, Vol. 3, *Education and Human Rights*, 19–25. London: World University Service, Zed Books.

Nashat, Guity (ed.), (1983) *Women and Revolution in Iran.* Boulder: Westview Press.

Paidar, Parvin (1996) 'Feminism and Islam in Iran.' In D. Kandiyoti (ed.), *Gendering the Middle East: Emerging Perspectives*, 51–67. Syracuse: Syracuse University Press.

Tabari, Azar (1986) 'The Women's Movement in Iran: A Hopeful Prognosis.' *Feminist Studies* 12(2):343–60.

Tohidi, Nayereh (1994) 'Modernity, Islamization, and Women in Iran.' In Valentine Moghadam (ed.), *Gender and National Identity: Women and Politics in Muslim Societies.* London: Zed Books.

– (1995) Letter written to *Zanan*, no. 29, Tir 1375, July.

Whitley, Andrew (1994) *Middle East Report*, no. 191, Nov.–Dec.

*Zan-e Rooz* (Women of Today), Tehran, 3 July 1993.

*Zanan* (Women), Tehran, July 1996.

# 11

# My Journey as a Woman across Continents

## YESHIM TERNAR

As a novelist and essayist, I agonized over what to write for this book. Yes, I was once an academic, and my doctorate has not expired, but I no longer read much in the social sciences, except when I have to at my part-time job as an associate editor for a psychiatry journal. I am no longer up to date on the latest debates in feminist theory or cultural criticism. This does not mean that I have stopped thinking or that I have suddenly become hopelessly ignorant. On the contrary, I read more and more widely than I ever did as a graduate student. It's just that I am no longer concerned about proving myself or defending my ideas in front of the reigning academic powers.

For this reason, I decided to write a testimonial, saying it as it is and has been for me as a woman. The emotion that popped up most frequently when I thought about this essay was anger. It was not anger at men or the patriarchy, but anger at how Western feminists have created a discourse that defines the reality of women in general, the nature of our struggles, who our enemies are, and what are our weaknesses and vulnerabilities. For the most part, these arguments have been so eloquently constructed, bolstered by such dramatic statistics, motivated by such heartfelt rage, that I felt that if I spoke my mind, I would be branded as a traitor to the sisterhood and classified as yet another un-enlightened female.

But if I do not speak up, I continue to endorse a reality I do not fit into; I comply with the patronizing assumptions of those who could not know how it has been for me as a female. Granted, I have learned through the writings of feminists how to pinpoint situations of abuse, power inequality, and victimization. I have been able to analyse the world I inhabit from a fresh angle. However, I have not been able to find through feminism the means to be at peace with the world, with my own body and my own spirituality, with my iconoclastic creativity.

That resolution has come through a synthesis of several ideologies and a mature acceptance of paradox and irony in the world and in my own life. Given the limitations of length for this essay, I have decided to focus on my experience of my body in society across cultures so far because it was through the vehicle of my body that I have transported myself from one country to another, from one lover to another, from one creative project to another.

Contrary to general expectations, I have often felt just as threatened by women as by men, both emotionally and physically. I experienced these threats because I come from an abusive family background and was born in a culture where overt displays of power struggles between people are not limited to encounters across genders. Living in North America exposed me to other forms of aggression such as emotional aggression through passive aggressive behaviour, which Canadians excel at, and intellectual aggression, which is an undercurrent in most academic encounters whether between women or men. Through all this, I have had to navigate my body, which this time around, is in the form of a female.

I was born in Istanbul, a city that straddles two continents: Europe and Asia. I was conceived in Europe, went back and forth between Europe and Asia many times on ferries and boats while still in my mother's womb, and was delivered in Admiral Bristol Hospital (the American hospital) in Europe on a day in November when icebergs had floated down from the Russian rivers into the Bosphorus, creating footholds for daredevils to skip across the channel that separates the West from the East.

It was a cold winter that year, they say, and perhaps the icebergs were not really as numerous and wide to accommodate daredevils, but I like to believe that they were because all my life I have been doing just that, skipping across continents, ideologies, languages, and gender roles.

My mother tells me I had the biggest cranial circumference of all the newborns in the maternity ward, and I was a hungry and curious child from the moment I emerged. I had grabbed the sheet the nurses were attempting to wipe me with and brought it to my mouth. She tells me I was quiet, but distinctive in my size and hunger. This is her way of telling me I demanded my fill from a world that was cold, slippery, unstable, and wondrous.

From the Admiral Bristol Hospital I was taken to an apartment building called Yasha, which means 'live!' in the district of Cerrahpasha, which means 'the surgeon general.' A militaristic self-discipline and a surgeon-like mental incisiveness have served me well all my life. In 1990, when I visited the apartment I was taken to as an infant, I saw that there were pigeons roosting on its window-sills, adamantly cooing and clucking in that doleful, complaining way that pigeons do in all cities. Everywhere I have lived, pigeons search for a better place to roost, for the perfect hole where they will not be disturbed.

My relationship to feminist ideology could be compared to the pigeons that always perch on the window-sills and rooftops of the apartment buildings that I inhabit; close, yet noisy and irritating. I prefer the company of doves, who are related to pigeons, but I find that I always have to search for them in the wider skies beyond the ready proximity of pigeon-holes.

As a teenager, I was voluptuous, with full thighs and buttocks, and fleshy arms. My hair was long, my lips vulnerable, my eyes anxious. I was growing into a woman too rapidly in a world where men took for granted their right to claim a woman's body for recreation or procreation and considered their desires more important than a woman's right to keep her body for herself. My body betrayed me by reaching out to a world where my mind and my dreams would not be respected simply because I was young and nubile.

Those were the years of mini-skirts, tight-knit dresses, net stockings, and hot pants. I wanted to wear them because they were fashionable, and also because I wanted to be Western in every possible way. I was already travelling abroad in my mind, and I wanted to wear the clothes teenagers in the West were wearing. The summer I was sixteen, I worked as a tourist guide and interpreter for a group of American students who had come to Tarsus American college in the south of Turkey to do volunteer maintenance work and small construction projects on the school property. After spending a month with them in the south and west of Turkey, we came to Istanbul, my native city. I wanted to show my American friends around Istanbul, and I thought I could behave like a foreigner, dare to walk through back streets, explore my city with tourist eyes.

I was leading a small group through the winding back streets of Beyoglu (the Pera district) up a steep hill paved with cobblestones, when a couple of young men swaggered towards us. As they approached, they ogled us all and made lewd comments. Being the only one who understood Turkish, I squirmed and must have grown defensive and defiant at the same time, perhaps taking bigger strides towards them as I glared at them. Just when I thought I had successfully countered their verbal and psychic assault on our fresh flesh; the man passing by closest to me reached out and grabbed my left breast, palming it as if it were a peach he was sizing up for firmness. He had won. I was property. The streets belonged to men. I could not pretend to be a Western woman in Turkey.

During those years I played tennis as often as I could to forget about the turbulence that seemed to be a permanent fixture in my family. My parents separated when I was fourteen, and I was left to live alone with my father who rarely came home. The next year, it was decided that I would become a boarding student at Robert College, the American high school I attended, although my home was too close to the school for me to properly qualify as a boarding student. The woman in charge of the dormitory made me feel from the beginning that I was taking up space in the dormitory which should have been available to a more needy student whose family lived far away. She never considered the fact that my parents were far away although my home address was close.

I played tennis with a vengeance, throwing my body around the courts, wearing a short skirt and an old T-shirt. The more I played, the better I got at the game, and the more my body developed. I got so good at tennis that the best of the boys and the physical education instructors wanted to play with me. I felt I was getting acceptance in a genderless game, but I was mistaken. The dormitory superintendent, Enise O. had been watching, unhappily, as I ran across the courts, waving my racket.

She called me into her office one Saturday. I had no idea why she wanted to see me. Nothing unusual had happened as far as I could tell. She hissed at me from behind her desk, with a mysterious pain whose meaning I could not fathom for years to come.

'The male dog does not follow if the bitch does not wag her tail,' she said to me. I repeated it as if it were a riddle. I had no idea what she meant. Because I did not respond with shame, as she had expected I would, but with total bewilderment, her plans went awry. 'Is this all?,' I asked, 'I'll think about what you said.' She stared at me as if to say, 'I accept my defeat because you are far shrewder than I thought and a true slut.' I remember being hurt and thoroughly confused.

My confusion regarding my body in society, what to reveal and what to not disclose, where and how, what the proper gender attitudes were that would please older women and keep away predatory men, while hopefully attracting my true love, was not limited to interactions with people outside my family.

My own mother hurt me with her violence and her inability to hold and comfort me in my times of need. She was both fragile and cruel, alternatively violent and emotionally withdrawn, her psychic energy focused on her own pain which she believed, and convinced all of us to believe, was larger than anyone else's. She refused to see how much of her pain I shouldered, hoping it would lighten her load. She refused to see how many times I threw my body in front of her to impede her violence so that she would not have the energy to go on to my younger sisters whose bodies and bones were more fragile.

I was a clown and an entertainer. My mother liked to laugh, so I was prepared to do anything as long as it would lighten anxious times in the household, of which there were many. My mother was a physician who had chosen to be a full-time mother. She loved literature and music. I pleased her with my desire to read and learn. She supported my favourite escape from her and my family and a world bereft of human reassurance by buying me all the books I wanted.

I had an aunt, my mother's sister, who grew incapable of offering love to her nieces as soon as she had her own children. My father's mother, a huge boisterous woman who was uneducated but full of hugs, who cooked well and loved to feed her grandchildren, was not welcome in our home. Whoever could provide love to me was often at odds with my mother and therefore distant from me.

This is not the place to condemn or judge my mother. I have included these details here to demonstrate that growing up in a Third World country does not necessarily mean that a female child will find mother surrogates or the support of other females. I have written about my family and my mother in bits and pieces in other places, disclosing details in my fiction and non-fiction. I will not delve into it much further here.

I have also written about my father in my fiction and feel compelled to continue to do so, for I am inspired by his difference and eccentricity. For the purposes of this essay, it will suffice to state that he was an angry man when I was a child, and, in retrospect, I realize that he was quite depressed, perhaps bewildered by the demands of his enormous creative talent and the family he had engendered. He remained distant from us and from my mother. He womanized indiscriminately. He behaved as if it were his civic duty to service lonely women. He was a man who loved food, sex, and travel. He was never there as a barrier between the women of his family and the rest of the world which is the proper function of a man in Turkey and in any other Islamic country. My father encouraged us to wear the skimpiest bikinis so we could get the full benefit of the sun, but he was never around to scare the men who eyed us ravenously on the beach. He was either swimming away towards the horizon or sleeping off a huge lunch, oblivious to the world.

Then there was my maternal grandmother. She loved me, but with reserve. She gave me a sense of security and belonging, but always with some uneasiness. She was orphaned as a child and had suffered in ways that were similar to how I feel I have suffered as a young girl and a young woman. And perhaps in the same way I have learned to be slightly suspicious of affection, she was as well, of her own and of others'.

She was a sexy woman even throughout her sixties and seventies. She would often sit on the living-room couch like a pretty cat and twirl her bare feet which were plump and well shaped. She liked to leave the two bottom buttons of her dresses undone so that she had more leg room to move about when she walked with vigourous steps. She had no qualms about showing her beautifully shaped alabaster legs through the slit in the front of her knee-length dresses.

Her mother had been a member of the Ottoman harem before she was liberated from the palace to marry and give birth to my grandmother. My grandmother reminded us that although her mother had been a tutor of calligraphy and reading at the harem, she had been admitted to the palace also because she had been very attractive. When my grandmother was orphaned at the age of eight, she was left in the care of her father, a judge in Aleppo, who was never kind to her and sent her away to boarding school in Istanbul. My grandmother had wanted to become an actress before Turkish women of Muslim origin were allowed to appear on stage, and she had wanted to become a medical doctor before the social reforms of the Turkish republic in the late 1920s when Turkish women were allowed to continue on to higher education.

As her graduation from high school approached, my grandmother was faced with the choice of either returning to Aleppo or quickly finding a husband in Istanbul who would shield her from her father. She explained to us that her father may have married her off to someone against her will in Aleppo, an Arab most likely (which is the worst fate for a liberated Turkish woman even now), or, even worse, she might have been sold to a rich Arab woman. She said that her father was unscrupulous enough to do that.

To my sisters' and my innocent ears, this option seemed better than marrying a fat Arab merchant who would likely have a set of gold teeth. But my grandmother would insist that being sold to a wealthy older woman with a taste for young female flesh was even more repugnant. My mother would always cut her off so that we never quite figured out what would have been in store for my grandmother had she been sold to a woman by her own father.

My grandmother praised my beauty. Unlike my mother, she perceived me as an attractive young woman. But even this was fraught with some anxiety for me. I will never forget that awkward moment, the evening I graduated from high school when my mother, my two younger sisters, and I were seated around my grandmother's dining-room table, sharing wine and food in celebration of the event. My grandmother looked at me across the table and said that my lips were beautiful. 'I would kiss those lips if I were a man,' she said. None of us quite knew what to say then. I tried to smile, but could not. I passed out under the table that night, my head swimming with one more doubt and a little bit more anxiety and confusion than most high school graduates.

During my formative years, there were always more women than men around me. Most of the women who left an impression on my psyche were women of my grandmother's generation, perhaps because my maternal grandmother was the most socially stable person in my immediate environment and was therefore able to keep her friends. Many of these women were widows who had been married to generals and colonels in the Turkish army. They lived on widows' pensions and devoted their lives to the study of spiritual matters and neighbourhood gossip, offering each other home-made brandies whatever the hour of the visit. There was no limit to their booming eccentricity. I often write about such women in my fiction.

A truly feminist personality was my grandmother's best friend, Hatice B., a former professor of chemistry who, in her old age, still kept her private chemistry lab going. Ms B. was professionally successful and unmarried. She was a short wiry woman with extremely dark skin, 'like a raisin,' as my grandmother called it. She had bright green eyes that burned like a chemical fire in her small dark face. She epitomized the duality of beauty versus intellect, since the reason for Ms B.'s unmarried state was attributed by herself and by my grandmother to her unattractive looks. However, that judgment was always modified in all accounts of her life by the fact that several men had in fact found her attractive and had asked to marry her. Ms B. had been unconvinced by their interest; she believed she was unattractive and therefore undesirable. She had done the sensible thing by choosing not to delude herself or others.

Ms B. was freer and livelier and more energetic than any other woman I remember from my childhood. She travelled, she skied, wearing a long dark skirt, nonetheless, instead of ski pants, and had no qualms about changing her clothes in front of an open window or walking around in a swimsuit. I regarded her freedom as a curse and a blessing because the ease her body afforded her in the social sphere was also what kept her from a romantic attachment.

What complicated my assessment of her life was the envy my grandmother felt for her best friend's professional achievements. Failing to achieve a similar professional success in her own life, my grandmother had wanted my mother to become a career woman like Ms B. But my mother had rebelled against this plan and chosen to become a mother of three girls after becoming a medical doctor. She remained exclusively a housewife until her divorce, albeit in emotional turmoil. The unresolved tension between career and beauty was then passed on to my generation, with myself, as the eldest girl, expected to fulfil the script. This is a tension with which I have struggled until now.

When I ran away to the United States to do my liberal arts degree, this conflict between beauty and intellect coloured my assessment of the women I met in North America as well as my assessment of my own developing femininity. Bennington College was where a new element was added to the conflict because there I learned as a young female to be sexually liberated, to accept my right to have sexual desire, and to express it in socially unconventional ways. Yet, the lingering desire to mate successfully remained unresolved. There was not much hope of resolving it at Bennington College because the female-to-male ratio among heterosexual students was about four-to-one.

At Bennington, in 1975, I met the now-famous Camille Paglia. She was brilliant and provocative even then. I remember a classmate pointing her out to me as the angry lesbian teacher who had gotten into trouble with the school administration for kicking a student lover in a moment of fury. There were many lesbians at Bennington College, and most of them were angry. I remember associating female independence with anger and instinctively becoming suspicious of the whole enterprise because I had already been wounded by so much rage in my home environment. How could more rage solve the problems already created by rage? The axes that adorned the book covers of Mary Daly's books did not entice me, either. The fact that I came from a culture where men knifed each other and their women out of spontaneous rage, and where axe murders made front-page news every day, hindered my appreciation of a certain feminist symbology.

I came to Canada, specifically, to Montreal, at the age of twenty-three. I have been based there since. I obtained a master of arts and then a doctorate in cultural anthropology at McGill, followed by a one-year special bachelor's degree in social work. Most importantly, I evolved into the fiction writer that I am today. Most of this was achieved in loneliness. In the process, as I explored philosophy, history, feminism, and literary theory, I learned how not to feel threatened by the ideological positions of others, however forceful they might be. In Montreal I became the adult I am now and gained the self-knowledge and the intellectual strength that liberated me from my previous experiences of victimization. In Montreal I also had several years of psychotherapy, explored alternative therapies such as hypnotic regression, trance dance, and spiritualism, and read intensively on spirituality.

My doctoral thesis, which was subsequently published in revised form in 1994 as *The Book and the Veil*, contains many of the insights I accumulated as a young woman intellectual who was born and raised in the East and has travelled and lived in the West. Through the lives of Zeyneb and Melek Hanoums, two Turkish sisters who lived in Istanbul at the turn of the twentieth century, and who escaped to Europe to experience freedom, as defined by Western feminists then, I explored the soul of émigré feminism, as well as the influence of class and culture on gender identity. I learned who I am as I wrote this book. *The Book and the Veil* was an exploration of my Turkish cultural roots, the influence of Islam on my identity as a woman, as well as the influence of Western culture on my identity as an intellectual. Finally, I was able to put into place and synthesize all that had previously baffled me in the behaviour of both Turkish and non-Turkish men and women.

When I sent a copy of *The Book and the Veil* to my friend Eileen from Bennington College, who had never forgiven me for my rejection of Mary Daly, she responded by saying that she found it ironic that my book was classified under women's studies. Where else did she expect it to belong? Being a woman is never simple.

Now that the intellectual and the emotional concerns that preoccupied me regarding my female identity are no longer as numerous or onerous, I feel an incredible sense of freedom. I feel I can now be much more spiritual and much more creative. I am no longer embarrassed by my desire to seek and find true love. I no longer feel I have to repress my physical and sensual desires in the name of social and political conformity.

In many ways, I feel fresh and newborn, and ready to really explore what it is to be a woman who desires to love and to be loved. I am more hopeful than I used to be that I will encounter my true soul mate and have a successful marriage, although North American marriage and divorce statistics warn me that my chances at forty are slimmer than before. Perhaps it is time to hit the road once again and explore other continents, where other states of mind and body are more likely to be found.

In Turkey, marriageable young women are visited in their homes by the mothers of young men or by their appointed matchmakers. This encounter is called *gorucuye cikmak*, which means, 'to appear in front of the inspector.' It is a traditional custom that urban bourgeois families claim they have no use for. However, it still goes on. It is one thing to reject the custom when people are trying hard to convince you to follow it, and quite another when no one considers you a likely mate for their son, and therefore does not bother to inspect you. I have the dubious honour of never having been visited by an inspector.

Was I too liberated? Too ugly? Too Westernized? Too boyish? I had to be rebellious because I did not have much of a choice to be otherwise, given my family background and my personality. I had to be boyish because it was the only way I could protect myself in that country where every woman has to have at least one male relative who protects her socially. In the absence of a father, uncles, brothers, or male cousins in this role, I had to integrate masculine qualities into my self-presentation.

There was also the fact that I was simply too big, top to bottom, to fit into female clothes. Out of necessity, I became a cross-dresser, wearing men's shirts and jeans, men's hush puppies and jackets. I became accustomed to the comfort of the cut of men's clothes and to the manner in which they made me appear androgynous, so that my body did not detract attention away from my mind. I enjoyed the protection that men's clothes offered me in the absence of men who protected me. Then I began to feel like a fake each time I put on nylon stockings or a skirt.

To this day, I enjoy observing the exaggerated styling and body language of transvestites. I feel that they are the ones who really know how to make the best of women's clothes. I think I would have enjoyed being a gay queen so that I could indulge my desire to dress with real flair. The problem is that I was born a woman.

Humour aside, I have been trying to fit into my own body with ease for many years now. Feminism has helped me analyse how my body has been desired, how it may be assaulted or invaded, how it has been socially controlled and monitored, how it has been judged and assessed by males and females, but it has not given me the key to how I can be happy in it, in peace with my soul, in peace with the world and the members of my own gender as well as the members of the opposite gender. That growth has come through ongoing personal reflection as to what my own specific desires and needs are for joy, love, and friendship, for spirituality and creativity.

In time, through my own brand of faith and trust in the world of the spirit and the creative process, I have come to feel more at ease with who I am, so that, finally, I can accept that what feels right for me may not conform to the tenets of a politically correct ideology, the customs of the country I happen to be living in, or the socially expected norms of behaviour from my gender. All this varies according to the dictates of the social and historical context one happens to be living in. To be a woman is a journey in itself, to be a creative female travelling across continents is yet another journey. And I am willing to travel much further, geographically, culturally, artistically, and spiritually. I hope to learn from both men and women along the way, for I want to be a fully realized human being by the time my transit on earth this time around is completed.

# 12

# Transnational Subjectivities: Travelling to Greece with Karen Connelly

## SMARO KAMBOURELI[1]

Only a study at once theoretical and localized can address the paradoxes inherent in transnational feminist practices. Frequently employed as a concept offsetting the abstracting and universalizing tendencies of such discourses as those of feminism and postcolonialism, transnationalism has recently achieved considerable currency. Yet the term as I understand it remains perilously close to globalism, the very condition it seeks to challenge, or, at best, it exacerbates the political ambivalence characteristic of global formations. If *trans* signifies a gesture *beyond* a given field, transnationalism can function easily as a figurative substitute for globalism, suggesting a movement beyond certain specificities and localisms, a tendency to transcend history, even to do away with the vexing opposition between the global and the local, thus becoming yet another totalizing configuration. On the other hand, if we take trans to mean *across, on the other side, through,* the desired political efficacy of transnationalism, manifested in such recent studies as Inderpal Grewal and Caren Kaplan's edited collection of essays (1994) *Scattered Hegemonies: Postmodernity and Transnational Feminist Practices,* is potentially restored. With trans read this way, transnationalism signifies intercultural exchanges that occur across distinct locations through specific discourses while foregrounding and problematizing the particularities involved.

Discussions of transnational feminism do not address the semantic ambivalence of transnationalism, although we often find that ambivalence inscribed in the ways the term is employed. Thus, Caren Kaplan (1994:139) deployed transnationalism in the double sense I outlined above. She called for 'a transnational feminist politics of location [which] in the best sense of these terms refers us to the model of coalition or, to borrow a term from Edward Said, to affiliation. As a practice of affiliation, a politics of location identifies the grounds for historically specific differences and similarities between women in diverse and asymmetrical relations, creating alternative histories, identities, and possibilities for alliances.' Transnational has a delimiting function here. As an adjective, it designates the field where a politics of location operates. A remedial term, it elucidates the concerns to practice a politics of location while enunciating the promise that the seeming contradiction between its encompassing meanings and locations need not have a debilitating effect, need not result in what Kaplan called 'magisterial relativism.'

In the concluding section of Kaplan's essay, however, transnational appears as a figure heedful of troubling circumstances: 'In a transnational world where cultural asymmetries and linkages continue to be mystified by economic and political interests at multiple levels, feminists,' Kaplan (1994:148) argued, 'need detailed, historicized maps of the circuits of power.' Her circumspection indicates that to speak of transnational feminist practices does not automatically entail 'an effort to deconstruct hegemonic, global universals.' Kaplan did not pause to consider the semantic ambivalence of transnationalism, yet her argument intimates that transnational, even as a descriptive qualifier similar to the various equivocations of the postcolonial, does not by itself address the crisis facing the study of cultural differences. Instead, it augments the pool of heuristic terms through which we approach this crisis.

I have begun by teasing out the double signification of transnationalism because of my anxiety concerning the issue at hand: what characterizes a transnational feminist practice, or émigré feminism, as the issue was framed by the colloquium organized in anticipation of this volume of essays? That the participants in this project are all transnational subjects is obviously not coincidental; less obvious, however, is what this correspondence suggests or is meant to accomplish. Our identification with transnationalism, although understood and materialized in different ways, begs the questions of positionality and the politics of self-location.

I am fully aware that any discussion of transnationalism I undertake will inadvertently put into motion, reactivate as it were, the trajectory of my life story. Yet my immigrant experience, the kind of relocation entailed in certain transnational practices, is not in itself the source of my anxiety; rather, it is a fact of an ontological order. Instead, my unease concerns what I can possibly do with this fact, where to put the personal. Acknowledging this fact engages me in the debate about whether personal references resolve the politics of addressing otherness or further aggravate how we conceptualize, and understand, the materiality of difference.

My concern, then, is how a diasporic critic can address transnationalism without necessarily either suspending her life story or allowing that
life story to determine, at the expense of other contingencies, her critical
project. This matter is not peculiar to diasporic feminist subjects alone.
Angela McRobbie (1982), Jane Tompkins (1993), Nancy K. Miller (1991),
Sara Suleri (1992), bell hooks (1989), Trinh Minh-Ha (1989), and more
recently Elspeth Probyn (1993) have addressed, in various contexts, the
importance of experience and articulated in different ways the imperative to explore how experience can stall investigation or serve to mediate
some of the issues under study. These methodological and political
debates suggest that simply disclosing the personal achieves nothing
besides naming what has long been considered to be a vexing problem.

My transnational experience may pose difficulties when declared, let
alone elaborated on, in critical discourse because of the perilous possibility of letting my diasporic subjectivity function as a mirror of sorts, a
spurious allegory of the object of my study – perilous because of the
risks involved in rendering '"lived" experience' (Althusser, 1971:204)
and all the emotionality attached to it into a paradigm of theoretical
investigation or a radical departure from what the problem is at hand. It
is precisely this practice that Suleri (1992:761) critiqued: 'When feminism turns to lived experience as an alternative mode of radical subjectivity, it only rehearses the objectification of its proper subject.' Here
Suleri identified an extreme position, which elsewhere (1995:175) she
called 'a confessional mode,' but I also find extreme the opposite incli-
nation, namely, the complete disavowal of the personal in critical practice because it might taint the disembodied formulations of theoretical
discourse.

To pretend I could easily brush aside my personal experience, suspend
or exceed its emotional and political ramifications, would be a fallacious
and hypocritical gesture, and it would raise a new set of nettlesome questions. If the deletion of the personal is predicated on the assumption
that reliance on one's experience can single-handedly invalidate one's
project, then we should be reminded of Althusser's words (1971:204):
'Ideology slides into all human activity ... it is identical with the "lived"
experience of human existence itself.' Holding the personal in abeyance
becomes a rhetorical gesture, a trope of simulation that pretends it is possible to bar completely the personal from permeating critical discourse.
As Althusser (1971:205) reminded us, 'This "lived" experience is not a
*given*, given by a pure "reality," but the spontaneous "lived experience" of
ideology in its peculiar relationship to the real.' It is the privileging of the

personal on the assumption that it faithfully mirrors a larger category of experience that is the problem.

If, however, we re-articulate the personal in terms of how it refracts, not just reflects, what it points to, then the personal can function as a medium facilitating analysis. Employing the personal not as a privileged paradigm but as a means of deflecting facile identifications involves a critical shift from the putative disengagement of theory while veering away from an unadulterated notion of reality. Thus, the inscription of the personal can operate as a strategy that dispenses with any reified locus from which the self might speak, while not cancelling out that 'a speaking position is always tied to the practices and politics bound up with daily life' (Probyn, 1993:86). Because the strategic inscription of the personal disassembles claims to authenticity or authority, it does not posit alterity as an immutable sign; instead, it exposes the liminality of a subject that finds itself in a constant circuit of exchanges.

In what follows I deal with the liminal aspects of transnational subjectivity by reading Karen Connelly's *One Room in a Castle: Letters from Spain, France and Greece* (1995). I deliberately focus on her chapter on Greece, which bears the same title as her book, in order to explore the strategic deployment of the personal while thematizing transnational feminism in the double sense I discussed above. The contiguities between Connelly, a Canadian writer who lived in and wrote about Greece, and myself, a Greek relocated in Canada, call for a supple approach, an approach that ought to be vigilant. My reading of 'One Room in a Castle' should be understood as a mode of travelling – travelling to Greece by reading Connelly – that follows a double itinerary. I travel back to Greece by reading Connelly's account of Greek culture, but travelling in this instance also amounts to self-reading: reading about my country of origin, encountering, as it were, a figuration of myself as an object of writing. The effect of this reading-as-travelling is that of *mise en abyme*: my self-reading discloses my figuration as cultural object, but in the process I perform a reading that becomes self-writing, an apposite act that records my understanding of Connelly's cultural codes while mirroring my response to them.

As a transnational subject, my reading of any text about Greece is bound to take the form of embedding. Embedding, according to Ross Chambers (1984:35), 'allows for relatively intense interpretive involvement on the part of the reader'; it 'defines and limits but defines and limits a *range* of reading options.' It is seeing my figural self encoded as a Greek in Connelly's text that calls into play my lived experience as a transnational subject, an experience mediated by my reading act. I hope that, in what follows, this congruence of relations and differences will result in what Probyn (1993:146) called a 'geography of the possible in which our lines of analysis, of thought, of difference may be made to connect.'

## Lesbos: The Nature and Origins of Metaphors

Living according to nature needs a lot of designing, organized effort and vigilant monitoring. Nothing is more artificial than naturalness; nothing less natural than throwing oneself at the mercy of the laws of nature.

Zygmunt Bauman (1991:7)

Nature is the set of images we have been supplied in television specials.

Alfonso Lingis (1995:45)

Karen Connelly opens 'One Room in a Castle' with a scene that describes her arrival on the island of Lesbos.

This place begins with poetry.

Nothing is obscure here: the world is highly visible in every direction. If I stand on a low mountain, I see the hills of Turkey jostle beneath the clouds like a purple caravan.
   I'm speechless, awed by this place in a way I wasn't expecting. (313)

The metaphors of poetry promise that everything is connected everywhere. That is why this place begins with poetry. Because here, on the island, the bonds between objects and landscape, between people and history, are visible and over-whelming. I am the blind woman who wakes one morning and sees, for the first time, her naked feet ... So I wade, amazed, through the union between trees and stones and their shadows, between air and sun-fire. (318–9)

Metaphor, in its figurative and literal senses, is the central trope that unravels Connelly's travel memoir. It is metaphor that reveals Lesbos to her in all its 'brilliance' (315), and it is metaphor, too, that seems to be the essence of what is revealed. Metaphor, Connelly has a Greek man remind both her and her readers, is 'a Greek word.' By returning meta-phor to its 'origin[s]' (373), she marks her narrative, saturated as it is with metaphors, with a signature that feigns to be not her own but that of Greece. Metaphor as a 'found' trope speaks of a reciprocity between

Greece and Connelly's narrative, a cooperative exchange intended to diminish the cultural distance between Connelly and Lesbos.

Relying on a poetics of visuality supplied by her metaphors, Connelly is seduced by the very transparent terms with which she constructs the landscape she visits for the first time. Lesbos, her text suggests, offers itself to Connelly like an open book whose form and aesthetics emanate from nature. At the same time that she naturalizes – and nationalizes – metaphor, she assumes that nature-as-text is written in a universal language whose meaning she can intuit, hence the apparent ease with which she interprets the landscape and its people. Constructed this way, the Lesbos landscape-as-book shifts Connelly's position from that of a writer to that of a reader. During her stay in Greece, 'poetry is the only sound [she] can make' because 'this place begins with poetry' (313). The logic of her writing method seems to be synonymous with her understanding of Lesbos's nature. Her task then as reader and writer is to translate the image of this place as poetry into a discourse that records her pleasure in Lesbos as a register of knowledge. The latter register, though, corresponds to Lesbos only as what Shoshana Felman (1983:31) has called 'a *referential illusion*,' an illusion produced by 'an utterance that is by its very nature *self-referential*: the illusion or a real or extralinguistic act of commitment created by an utterance that refers only to itself.' This self-referential register of knowledge works against Connelly's desire to communicate to her readers that her seduction by Lesbos indeed relies on the objective reality her 'found' metaphors convey. The reality of her pleasure becomes conflated with the reality of this island. Her notion that nature is the single source from which the meaning of Lesbos originates accounts for her elation upon encountering rural Lesbos: the poeticality of Lesbos articulates and is itself triggered by what Connelly takes to be the essence of Greek culture, an essence whose 'principles of structure must derive from nature' (Leontis, 1995:197). The circularity of Connelly's writing method raises many questions about how she practices her gaze as traveller.

The Lesbos landscape-as-book cuts a paradoxical figure. Purportedly uncontaminated by Greek history and the modernity of Greek culture, it is a script that remains equally untouched by any non-Greek cultural elements. Yet this 'communion of language and soil' (Leontis, 1995:197) is far from being a natural Greek phenomenon that Connelly has happened upon. Quite the contrary, as Artemis Leontis (1995:199, 197) showed, it is a construction, often 'programmatic,' that attempts 'to determine what relationship binds Neohellenes to the Hellenic *cosmos*.' An aesthetic and ideology that was eventually adopted and promoted by the fascist regime of General Ioannis Metaxas in 1936, it was countered by a liberal aesthetic which advocated a 'Greekness [that] embodied the foreign and the local, the traditional and the new. It harmonized modernity with indigenous traditions. It represented an autochthony without the ethnocentrism of ... the Hellenolatry of the Metaxas dictatorship' (Jusdanis, 1991:80). Far from being spontaneous or natural, Connelly's response to nature, together with her adoption of a naturalistic discourse allegedly elicited from the Greek landscape, is conditioned by the Western stereotypes of Greek culture whose scholarly as well as popular history is too complex to recite here.

Seen through the eyes of this Canadian traveller, Lesbos's nature has a double economy: on the one hand, it is a rustic landscape where 'dusk's honey dripping from the olive trees' (315) overwhelms Connelly; on the other, the same landscape, perceived through her romanticizing perspective, doubles as the culture of a people whose 'myster[y]' is 'how much the shepherds resemble their donkeys, or, possibly, how much the donkeys resemble their shepherds' (420). On Lesbos, according to Connelly, humans mirror the natural environment, and nature mirrors humans. She attributes the transparency of the place to this ongoing play of reflections, notwithstanding that reflections create a semblance of lucidity, that they displace and distort the images formed. In 'One Room in a Castle,' culture circulates as merely the product of such reflections, the result of the incestuous relationship between humans and nature, between Connelly's metaphors and anthropomorphisms. She finds humans and animals to be in a binding relationship whose value and signification are one and the same thing, two sides of the same coin – nature. Nature-as-culture.

In Connelly's text the economy of this nature-as-culture circulates not as commodity, but as gift. Indeed, one of the epigraphs to *One Room in a Castle*, from Lewis Hyde's *The Gift* (1979:4), announces Connelly's travel-writing method: 'Whatever we have been given is supposed to be given away again, not kept ... The only essential is this: *the gift must always move.*' The local inhabitants Connelly meets practise this 'natural' law: Thanasee gives her 'free grapes and, occasionally, free melons' (316); Andreas gives her feta cheese and bread; Maria, eggs; Yiorgos, a metaphor; Fotis, stories and myths; Isadora, her life story. There is no reference to money being exchanged. Thus, a so-called primitive economy emerges whereby natural objects, including life stories, are passed on to Connelly freely and without prejudice. Yet, as Hyde (1979:158) remarked on 'the destruction of the spirit of the gift ... all cultures and all artists have felt the tension between gift exchange and the market, between the self-forgetfulness of art and self-aggrandizement of the merchant.' If Connelly practises Hyde's dictum and lets the gifts she receives circulate, she does so by repackaging them as the commodity that her book is. The narrativized configuration of these Greek gifts becomes her capital as a Canadian writer. But in the cultural economy Connelly practises, the circulation of these gifts as capital is devoid of the reciprocity that characterizes the exchange of gifts. 'Tributes made, gifts given, impose claims on the receiver. A regime of gifts is a regime of debts ... It is an economy of rigorous reciprocity; each gift proffered requires the return of the equivalent' (Lingis, 1995:8). In the narrative context of her book, Connelly does not give the islanders anything back; her only acknowledgment of indebtedness to them is that she cannot 'stop writing' (431) about them, that she is 'alive' (432).

The produce, myths, and life stories that Connelly receives from these Greeks are all imaged in natural terms. Perhaps it is because Connelly considers metaphors to be one of the natural products of this island's economy that she demands that Yiorgos give her one: 'Give me a metaphor,' she says, and he complies by giving her metaphors, including the one she uses as the title of her book and its chapter on Lesbos (373–4). What she gives him in exchange is hair that 'is a wilderness' (356) and an identity that is other than what he is: he is 'a misplaced sultan' (339), 'a stunning cross between Lawrence of Arabia going to battle and Genghis Khan going to bathe,' a 'Greek Bedouin' (340). While Connelly takes Yiorgos's metaphors to be authentic, her own metaphors depict him as a contaminated subject, a fate shared by Fotis who is 'like a Tasmanian devil' (333). The textuality of 'One Room in a Castle' announces that metaphors grow naturally on this Aegean island – as naturally as thyme, oregano, and its eleven million olive trees – but Connelly fails to divine any local figures to describe the inhabitants. She articulates their Greekness by drawing from an international repertoire of metaphoric – and exotic at that – labels.

'In classifying metaphors according to their native regions,' Jacques Derrida (1982:220) wrote, 'one would necessarily ... have to reduce the "lending" discourses, the discourses of the origin – in opposition to the borrowing discourses – to two major types: those which precisely appear more original in and of themselves, and those whose object has ceased to be original, natural, primitive.' Derrida proposed this opposition 'of *physis* to *tekhne*, or of *physis* to *nomos*' as a principle that 'is at work everywhere.' In Connelly's employment of metaphor, the tenor of her figural

tropes (the Lesbos Greeks) is securely lodged within a natural order, the
*physis* she has come upon; this *physis* begins to acquire social meaning and
to gravitate towards culture, *techne*, when she intervenes, that is, when she
transports vehicles specific to other cultures into this natural order. That
the particularity of a bedouin, a sultan, and Lawrence of Arabia has
already been diffused and expropriated in history through orientalist
practises undercuts the spontaneity of her discourse, the authenticity she
strives to capture.

If 'metaphors speak of what remains absent' (Harries, 1979:82), then
Connelly's metaphors supplement an absence she finds on Lesbos. The
vehicles of the metaphors she imports suggest that culture is what Lesbos
lacks. Her failure to talk about the Lesbos people in local terms belies her
initial claim that on Lesbos 'nothing is obscure.' Conversely, if these people's Greekness can be articulated in different ways – what metaphoricity
implies – then it lacks a proper name, the precise essence Connelly is so
intent on attributing to those Greeks. While the vehicles of metaphors are
supposed to deliver the meaning of their tenors, hers reveal less about
their subjects than they do about her. She intends her metaphors to
express the singularity of these Greek subjects, but the figurative transnational qualities she applies to them only serve to illustrate the derivative-
ness of her metaphors. Her first encounter with Lesbos reproduces the
ideology that informed the Europeans' first contact with indigenous peoples outside the West. Connelly's textual amalgamation of historical references – which are far removed from their origins and relate, instead, to
the legacy of orientalist practises – are not metaphors organic to Lesbos;
in contrast, they are the tropes that facilitate the transport of Connelly's
own cultural baggage.

The readiness with which Connelly draws her metaphors from diverse
historical, national, and cultural periods discloses the method of her
transnationalist practise. It yields a structure whereby transnationalism
relies on the principle of a putative universality, a structure reproducing
the culture-versus-nature paradigm in a disturbing fashion: nature is what
Connelly believes she encounters on Lesbos; culture is what she produces. The Lesbos mountains, for example, are 'piled in the manner of
broken columns. From the distance, some of the ridges are like ruined
temples' (328); there is no direct reference to any of the ancient sites of
the island. Broken columns are an image without an origin or a particular
reality. If, as Derrida (1982:221) suggested, 'metaphor play[s] exclusively
the role of a pedagogical ornament, no matter how the author would
have it,' we can infer from the metaphoricity of Connelly's text that cul-

ture is both what she imports into the Greek world of this island and what she exports from Lesbos by packaging her perceptions of the island and its people into the book we read. Culture, then, operates through the technology of her specific kind of transnational practise.

**Innocence and Experience as Transnational Tactics**

The technology of Connelly's transnationalism involves her stance as an experienced traveller yet a naive subject. Her life and writing patterns declare her travelling experience: according to her book's dust-jacket, 'When she's not travelling, Karen Connelly lives in Greece.' A year spent in Thailand, at the age of seventeen, resulted in her first non-fiction book, *Touch the Dragon: A Thai Journal* (1992). As she says in its preface, written on Lesbos, that volume 'took over five years and four countries to become a book' (n.p.). The travels referred to in *One Room in a Castle* include a sojourn of a year and a half in northern Spain, a few months in southern France, and her stay on Lesbos. Connelly approaches the sites she visits with an apparent spontaneity and innocence that have become her trademark.[2] At the same time that these qualities are meant to validate her role as witness to the lives of people represented as being more innocent than she, they demonstrate the tactics by which she derealizes Greece. Hers is a mythology of travel that feeds on the enthusiasm with which she approaches a foreign culture. Connelly negotiates her passages through these cultures through a series of tropes that assure her instrumentality as travel writer is always in excess of the survival value and cultural difference of the places and people she visits and writes about.

Connelly's innocence as traveller might be the result of the spontaneity with which she approaches these foreign sites, but it marks her writing as yet another trope, one that shows in relief her transnationalist practises. Connelly's performance as traveller vouches for her innocence while ensuring, ironically, that her travelling experiences, however enriching they might be, do not affect her wonderment when she enters a new culture. In her text, innocence assumes a privileged function. By means of this tactic she is able to effect three things: she is able to aver the purity of the Greeks she encounters, to guarantee the authenticity of her representation of them, and to pose nostalgia as a mode that privileges at once lived experience as the singular source of unmitigated meaning and the compulsion to re-enter a world unadulterated by modernity. Thus, Connelly's transnational practise does not disclose a discursive field of experiences. Her departures from Canada seem to be motivated by a desire to remove herself from a worn-out Western world so that she can live in countries like Greece where '"people have an incredible dignity that's becoming increasingly difficult to find in the Western world"' (cited in Andrews, 1995:H1). In this context Lesbos appears caught in a time-lag – exactly the frozen, fossilized site that functions as both the bait and alibi galvanizing the imagination of an 'innocent' cultural traveller. In contrast to her public image and the publishing record she has established for herself as an experienced late twentieth-century traveller, the *mise en scène* of 'One Room in a Castle' shows how badly Connelly wants the thrill afforded an explorer, how she aspires after the delight of an ethnographer who happens upon a people previously undiscovered by Westerners.

Thus, Connelly admits that she 'read [Greek myths], but it was a while ago. I don't remember exactly' (331) – a tactic that allows her to posit Fotis as a native informant. Accepting the bait, he proceeds to tell her the myth of Orpheus whose decapitated head, according to tradition, was washed up on a Lesbos shore. If her 'found' metaphors and innocent stance are tropes promoting at once an aesthetics of a simulated reality and a cultural *mythos* of Greece, she fails to detect the ironic mode of Fotis's storytelling. Thus, her misreading of his rhetoric and body language undercuts her wish to present him as a native informant, an authentic source of information. For Connelly, who hardly ever questions the truthfulness or honest intentions of her Lesbos interlocutors, the authenticity of native informants is determined by their supposed lack of irony.

'Where is Orpheus' head buried?' The skepticism in my voice insults Fotis.

'*Where, where, where?* Just like a foreigner, all these goddamn questions. How do I know where, exactly? Leave the story alone! Can't you see? That's the beauty, no one knows exactly where ...'

He seems so genuinely angry that I apologize. 'It was a beautiful story.'

He growls in a small but ferocious way, like a Tasmanian devil. 'It's not over yet.'

'Oh. What else happens?'

'Nothing else *happens*. But there is an important detail.'

Instead of saying anything, I cautiously put the last piece of feta in my mouth.

'We know that Orpheus' head was buried on this island because the nightingales here sing more beautifully than anywhere else in Greece.' He gives me a significant look. 'Because Orpheus was a great musician. You see?'

'Yes, I see. You don't have to explain that.' We exchange almost angry looks.

'Don't they tell stories in Canada?'

'Yes.'

'Then you know you're supposed to believe the storyteller, right?'
'Yes. I suppose so.'
'No *suppose*. Definitely. If I tell you another story, you can't say, Is this true? Is that true? And if you're going to stay here, learn Greek. It gives me a headache to tell stories in bloody English.' (333–4)

For Connelly, the effectiveness of this passage depends on her persuading the readers that Fotis believes the myth to be real. And he does, but not in Connelly's sense of reality. Fotis's self-reflexiveness about storytelling discloses the reality of the myth to be the reality of his speaking act. For this storyteller, the Orpheus myth is not unlike a simulacrum, a copy with no precise referent or original, and its veracity is the kind that demands constant play with and against various realities, including the capacity of language to mobilize constructions of the real. By calling Connelly a foreigner, Fotis draws attention to her inability to understand the social, cultural, and rhetorical codes that generate his storytelling. Connelly takes his 'significant look' at her to be a transparent declaration of his belief in his story's veracity, a readiness to denounce her scepticism. But the look, I would like to argue, is Fotis's most telling and deliberate strategy, one doubly encoded and therefore ironic: it signals his belief in the lack of a definite reality and dramatizes the fictionality of his role as native informant. Connelly's belief, though, that Fotis's story is free of cunning reveals how she comes to discover a clear reality principle in Lesbos.

Connelly attributes irony to herself – her scepticism, the coolness of her posture versus the anger of Fotis, her refraining from verbalizing her bemusement – and this attribution is supposed to provide the contextual evidence that Fotis delivers his narrative in a straightforward fashion. Yet the irony in this passage, at least for this reader, lies in how Connelly's intention to be ironic at Fotis's expense is subverted by the effectiveness of his own irony. Fotis gets annoyed not because she doubts the credibility of the story but because she does not understand that he tells her a *story*. While Connelly's irony is of the 'elitist' kind, implying 'the assumption of superior knowledge' (Hutcheon, 1994:94), Fotis's seeks to establish '"amiable communities"' (Wayne Booth cited in Hutcheon, 1994:93), the kind that 'come into being in "contact zones" as the "social spaces where cultures meet, clash, grapple with each other, often in contexts of highly asymmetrical relations of power"' (Pratt cited in Hutcheon 1994:93). Thus, the textuality of this narrative episode and Fotis's performance as storyteller – a performance suspending the singularity of truth – change Connelly's self-attributed role as ironist to that of the target of Fotis's irony.

That Connelly is obviously not the first foreigner Fotis encounters also belongs to this series of ironic inversions. Greece has long been a popular destination for tourists, and many islanders, including those from Lesbos, immigrated to North America and Australia, among other places, many of them returning to or maintaing close ties with their mother country. By not paying attention to this tourist and diasporic traffic, Connelly stresses her desire to discover on Lesbos an unmediated reality, a nature that dazzles her with its purity, a culture that can hardly be distinguished from the nature that produces it.

## The Elision of History, or the Lure of Unmodernity

Might not what lures us ensnare us, might not the strings we pull enmesh us, might not the path before us end in an impasse? The abyss lurks behind the connections of things and beneath the paths where they beckon.

Alfonso Lingis (1995:931–2)

Connelly's overdetermined reading of Lesbos depicts a veracity that can be confirmed only by its 'aesthetics of the hyper-real, a *frisson* of vertiginous and phony exactitude, a *frisson* of simultaneous distancing and magnification, of distortion of scale, of an excessive transparency' (Baudrillard, 1994:28).

Implicit in this double function of Connelly's narrative is the virtual absence of cultural or historical inscriptions, an absence implying she is interested exclusively in the modernness of this island. Indeed, her references to historical sites or local historical figures are few. There is, for example, a casual reference to Sappho, born on Lesbos, 's[inging] ... centuries before any of us were born' (336). The omission of references to such cultural sites on Lesbos as museums, art galleries, various architectural styles, a university, and Byzantine churches suggests Connelly's consistent reluctance to contextualize historically and culturally the world she encounters. Whether by design or by default, the lack of any references to the historicity of Lesbos points to Connelly's intense look on the modernity of the island, a modernity that, paradoxically, has no relation to history whatsoever. In 'One Room in a Castle' modernity is synonymous with the meaning derived from Connelly's lived experiences on location.

Thus, she claims we can 'see the entire agrarian culture of the island at a glance': 'We would see people who only recently acquired electricity.

Most still live without telephones. We would see thousands of gates made of baling-wire, tonnes of hand-mixed cement, countless women working in kitchens and courtyards, superstitions born thousands of years ago still alive and breathing. We would see the evil eye' (331).

The repetition of 'still' impresses on readers the historical continuity of life on Lesbos, but it discloses, all the same, Connelly's ahistorical method. The economy of Lesbos relies on agriculture, but it depends as much on its tourist, commerce, and shipping industries. And if not every village house has a telephone, the island has an international airport and a capital city, Mitilini, with a population of 25,000 people,[3] that hardly suggest a society that has remained untouched by the exigencies of history. Connelly's hyper-real image of Lesbos cannot afford such intrusions. Instead, she proceeds to register present-day Lesbos by studying its gates. This is not a study she details for the reader, but she shares with us the conclusion she reaches: 'I discern something of the nature of the island, something of the nature of Greece itself' (323). Gates are signs that mark thresholds; they suggest a crossing through, preferably on invitation, and they evoke mediation, negotiation. Crossing through the 'gate' into this island, to appropriate Connelly's metaphor, is synonymous with exiting the modernity of the West.

What the modernity of the West entails for Connelly becomes clear in her interviews with the Canadian media. While Connelly employs the trope of innocence in her narrative, in interviews she assumes the role of a well-informed writer, a traveller who knows what she is after. Here is one example: 'Greece is a wonderful place to live ... because of its remoteness ... Part of the fascination with Greece is it's still a relatively agrarian society, if you live in the countryside or on the island. Things haven't really changed that much in 2,000 years. Even though there is a lot of mechanization in Greece, the social mores and the economic stability of the region are still very local, very community-based. The peasant way of life still exists' (cited in Andrews, 1995:H1).

The historical, economic, and social perspectives that Connelly brings into this and other such statements are virtually absent in 'One Room in a Castle.' Nevertheless, their distortion of Greece's geographical location, lack of economic stability, and historical development is characteristic of her text. More importantly, journalists like Andrews and media personalities like Peter Gzowski[4] treat her comments as authoritative statements on the subject of Greece, thus leaving them unchallenged.

Connelly's exit from the West affords her the opportunity to see the world afresh. Thus, she looks at Lesbos with a gaze that transcends the island's history at the same time that it suspends her own: 'I wake up to the contradictions and complexities of this world, some of which I can't even properly articulate yet. It *is* like being a child: I live by my senses here, I comprehend the islanders' world by intuition, understanding nothing completely' (369). This statement suggests that becoming a transnational subject for Connelly has a corrective function at best, an escapist one at worst. As Elaine Kalman Naves (1994:19), one of Connelly's interviewers, commented (on Connelly's passage from Thailand back to Canada and then off to Spain), 'once again, she was rescued by another country and culture.'

Modernity, for Connelly, is inextricably related to Europe, it is a by-product of Western culture that does not exceed its cultural borders. Connelly finds 'modern day Greece' to have an 'ephemeral nature' whose 'beauty ... is distinctly unmodern' (324). Since, as she says, 'Greece is not Europe' (331), the only way for Greeks to become modern is to become other. Significantly, this is not a fate she wishes on them. Connelly's text makes it clear that the enthusiasm with which she embraces Lesbos is motivated by her desire to discover a world she can image in premodern terms, terms measured here in opposition to industrial progress, urbanism, the production of culture, and the commodification of nature. What gives her text its impetus is not a desire to escape from what we have come to call the crisis of modernity, the realization that the 'dysfunctionality of modern culture is its functionality,' that the 'modern powers' struggle for artificial order needs culture that explores the limits and the limitations of the power of artifice' (Bauman, 1991:9); rather, it is a desire to avoid this very crisis. Unbeknownst to its author, 'One Room in a Castle' recreates some of the conditions that have led to the crisis of modernity. Connelly denies, or represses, the Western narratives of modernity but embraces their myth of progress – a necessary embrace if she is to declare the unmodernity of Greece. Hence Connelly's function as a transnational subject is posited at the periphery of Greek culture but at the centre of her narrative about it.

### The Tourist as 'Freak'

The tourist does not merely place himself 'at one point' on the surface of his sphere of experiences, but ... he places himself at its center ... [T]ourism operates less to palliate than to exacerbate alienation as the tourist in his insatiable desire for immediacy and authenticity finds himself enmeshed in the very web of mediacy and inauthenticity from which he is trying so hard to flee.

Georges Van den Abbeele (1980:6–7)

'One Room in a Castle' admits no critical disjunction between Connelly's language and the world she describes. As she says in an interview with Claire Goulet (1995:13): 'Languages are about construction, about evolution, and I don't think, for me at least, that I could discover (or perhaps I'm just not interested in discovering) whatever truths or surprises or interesting tidbits are to be found in deconstructing my language. I'm interested in creating worlds with my language, and I'm interested in creating paintings with my language, in creating sensual scenes and stories and moments. I'm not interested in going backwards and taking it apart.' Connelly's positivist approach to language may explain why she moves so easily from lived experiences to cultural generalizations. Her discourse about Lesbos and Lesbos itself are held together in a mimetic relationship. What conjoins the two seems to be Connelly's lived experience, which guarantees that 'nothing is obscure here.' Yet the complacency evoked by her reliance on experience, and the assuredness with which she employs language to write about another culture are undercut but the anxiety permeating 'One Room in a Castle,' her need to avoid being a tourist at all costs.

'I do not believe I am a tourist,' she says. 'But when I go up to the village, I realize what I am. A freak. A tourist who hasn't left yet. A tourist who is learning Greek. A tourist who should get married' (349). These statements reflect Connelly's self-consciousness as a transnational subject, an awareness she applies to how she is viewed by locals but not to how she perceives them. She admits, with great reluctance, that she is a tourist, yet metaphor comes to her rescue: she is a 'freak' of a tourist. Because she stays after the tourist season is over and attempts to learn the Greek language, Connelly exceeds a tourist's normative function. By virtue of being the only foreigner around she supersedes the technology of tourism. If tourism evokes a standardization of behaviour, a submersion of individuality, Connelly's 'freakishness' speaks of her uniqueness. Her self-appellation as 'freak' thus points to her desire to occupy an eccentric position in that she is a foreigner, and a woman at that, when no other foreigners are around. Socially and textually, this eccentricity is immediately translated into a central position.

Connelly's resort to metaphor to disavow the tourist label is a telling example of how she constructs a mythology about her transnational position. As Dean MacCannell has written (1992:45), in tourist discourse and exchanges, 'metaphor always involves suppression: a veiling of the obvious through which the outlines of the obvious can be seen. The tourist's historical dependence on metaphor necessarily produces something like an unconscious.' The touristic unconscious, for MacCannell (1992:41, 25), instigates a tourist's ready avowal of 'primitive modalit[ies]' that challenge the social and cultural codes of the West. Thus, condoning a cultural practise or a mode of living not valued in the West reflects the Western subject's repression of her ancestors' various cultural 'savager[ies].' Connelly's touristic unconscious would explain why she does not personally renounce modernity but becomes fascinated with, and temporarily tries to adopt, what she takes to be the unmodernity of Lesbos.

Connelly admits to a certain 'awkward[ness]' when Greeks tell her things like '"Tourism came to Greece and the gods left"': 'what am I?,' she wonders, 'I am not a tourist, am I? I am a traveller. This is what I tell myself. I am actively engaged in the life of this place. But who ever admits she is an ugly, grasping tourist?' (385). The contradiction between 'I am a traveller' and being 'actively engaged' with Lesbos is emblematic of how Connelly operates as a transnational subject. She interacts on a daily basis with people like Fotis, Andreas, Thanasee, Panagos, Maria, and Yiorgos – people she treats as specimens of Lesbos's unmodernity – but it never crosses her mind that these people have already become part of the technology of tourism, their island having long been enmeshed in the networks of modernity. In different degrees and ways, these people practise 'a kind of performative "primitive"' (MacCannell, 1992:26). 'The term "primitive,"' in this context, refers to 'a mythic necessity to keep the idea of the primitive alive in the modern world and consciousness' (MacCannell, 1992:34). Connelly is anxious to dispel the effects of tourism from herself, but she remains oblivious to the impact of tourism on locals.

This asymmetry allows her to maintain the fallacy that the people of Lesbos are unmodern and informs her desire to become one of them. If Connelly is only vaguely aware of her 'touristic unconscious,' she definitely wants to understand the 'unconscious' of the people she encounters. In a short section she titles 'A Greek Lesson,' we read:

*EXO. MESA.*
   Out. In. *Eime exo. Eime mesa.* I am out, I am in.
   *Thelo na eime mesa.* I want to be in. *Eime mesa.* I am in. The Greek expression to denote belonging, intrinsic understanding of a given place, event, or situation. *Eime mesa.* (342)

If Connelly wants to realign the boundaries defining who is in and who is out, she does so with great ambivalence and curious results. Fotis is someone who, she believes, lets her 'in.' He is 'a strange character': 'Secretive, though he tells me some of his secrets, some of the secrets about his place' (330). Yet Fotis, though he might 'possess an intelligence that is, in essence, frightening,' does not facilitate her desire to be 'in.' As she says, 'When I see him, I think: I am not in Europe, this is a separate continent' (330). She evokes the power structure of Occident versus Orient, but she does not question the implications of its binary logic. Greece is a member of the European Union, but its development out of Ottoman rule as a modern state has always involved, both internally and externally, the question of whether or not it is part of the West.[5] Connelly takes the sign of Europe to be homogeneous and therefore lacking any ambivalence; in a similar gesture, she discards cultural and historical hybridity as a reality principle. Since she does not find Greece to be European enough, it must be oriental, an order of reality implied (because taken to be natural) rather than clearly articulated or closely examined. Thus, the only time in 'One Room in a Castle' when Connelly ventures into 'civilization,' she thinks of 'the small town' she visits as '[being] Istanbul to me' (383). This is not a reference to a city Connelly knows[6] but to the symbolic and social imaginary of orientalism that Istanbul has become. 'Civilization has its perks,' Connelly says of Istanbul-like Talloni;[7] 'There are women out in the streets here, even young women!' (383). This comment, together with her declared intentions to 'take a hot shower' in a friend's home, visit the town's bookstore, 'go to the shop with the best almonds,' and 'eat souvlaki' (383–4), operates as a slippage with regard to her image of Lesbos's unmodernity. Not unlike some of the tourists MacCannell talks about, Connelly can assimilate the place and people she so desires to be part of by consuming, among other things, local food. Her text makes it abundantly clear that she does not want to belong to a continent that is not Europe. The function of the Greek subject as a European/non-European other reinforces Connelly's privileged position as a Western woman.

If she is not a tourist, as she claims, what is she then? Connelly might very well be a nomad, for she posits herself as a young writer who can write primarily while living under nomadic conditions. But hers is not the nomadic consciousness as defined by Rosi Braidotti (1994:25), a 'consciousness ... akin to what Foucault called countermemory ... a form of resisting assimilation or homologation into dominant ways of representing the self'; if 'the nomadic trajectory is controlled speed ... [if t]he nomad's relationship to the earth is one of transitory attachment,' then, in Braidotti's terms, the nomad is 'the antithesis of the farmer: the nomad gathers, reaps, and exchanges but does not exploit.' In contrast, Connelly is a different kind of nomad, one who valorizes her presence by attaching herself to Lesbos with the shrewdness of the kind of 'parasite' that can consume the 'host' on which it feeds. Her desire to be 'in' relies on the same logic that Michel Serres's study (1982:81) *The Parasite* brilliantly sets out to deconstruct: 'There is always,' Serres wrote, 'the same mystery of the guest of the master who becomes the master of the master.'

Connelly appears to function as an expatriate writer, the kind that belongs to the 'bands of permanently displaced tourists' that Caren Kaplan (1996:47) wrote about: 'They exist precisely through a form of voluntary homelessness, yet their lack of commitment or roots limits them to a role as witness ... More and more like voyeurs of the decadent and exotic, the expatriates *see* "others" or "otherness" but do not yet divine their own role as actors in the production of the world they believe they are simply observing.' If expatriate writers travel because, as Kaplan (1996:44) argued, they 'fe[el] their own cultures [are] exhausted and drained of significance,' they do so because they seek to mine other cultures for their traditions, but also because they fantasize about escape. In this regard, *A Room in a Castle* enacts the intent of expatriate writing to 'mask[] and submerge[] all references to commerce or popular culture by promoting artistic concerns' (Kaplan, 1996:45–6). Hence, Connelly's resorting to 'found' metaphors, her locating the source of her writing in a locus that is other to her, her cosy relationship with a culture she 'comprehend[s] ... by intuition' (369).

## Between Here and There: The Text as Vehicle

One cannot retreat behind one's opaqueness and travesties, and still retain intact one's perception of the other. For the other, in his alterity, is not a datum of perception, but is present only as an appeal answered, a contestation recognized, in an *apologia pro vita sua*.

Alfonso Lingis (1983:136)

If reading *One Room in a Castle* for the first time was a difficult experience for me, it was so because Greece appears in it as a cultural sign that is at once present and absent, a sign produced by various historical and discursive contingencies that Connelly's text decidedly disavows. How her text,

as I have tried to argue, both derealizes and posits a hyper-real image of
Lesbos is not something I attribute exclusively to her not being Greek.
Indeed, there are examples of Greek authors who have produced cultural
narratives advocating a 'natural' portrait of Greece akin to Connelly's.
Thus, I have not set out to contest her view of Lesbos as a pristine rural
society or offer a counter-representation of her image repertoire. Instead,
I have tried to respond to her text by way of exploring how my approach
to it is simultaneously a matter of theory and of praxis, at once a critical
response and a self-creating gesture that performs – acts out, as it were –
my history as a diasporic person.

My reading is a kind of historiography: it submits a record of my interest in how we articulate cultural differences while registering a metanar-
rative of sorts, how I travel back to Greece by reading Connelly. My
writing is then 'a mode of "travelling theory" that involves displacement
in time and space' (Behdad, 1994:1). I am at once subject and object, a
writer and the written.

For Connelly, travelling to Greece is part of an itinerary in which residing on Lesbos is just one long stop among others. Greece, she discovers,
is a place that exceeds its geography – it is neither in Europe nor anywhere else – as much as it transcends its history. She is enthralled with
Lesbos because, to her, it appears immutable, untainted by modernity,
and therefore pure and authentic. For me, travelling to Greece implies a
return to my birthplace where I lived the first half of my life. Return, however, belies the notion of homecoming: homecoming is experienced
through an oblique gaze. While Connelly goes to Greece intending to
find the otherness of modernity, I cannot go back planning to encounter
that same otherness, nor do I discover a sameness that speaks of my
authenticity as Greek, the kind that might lend my return a certain ease.
If anything, I have learned over the years to tread cautiously. It is because
my return to Greece 'calls for a dwelling in language, in histories, in identities that are constantly subject to mutation' (Chambers, 1994:5) that my
reading of Connelly's text functions as a vehicle that conveys me to
Greece. Author and reader become travelling companions – two Canadians visiting Lesbos. A likely couple, it would appear, a couple that fulfils
the plot conventions of certain films and novels: away from home, they
discover they have very little in common, and so they go their own ways,
intersecting only now and then.

This is, I think, what sets us apart: Connelly goes to Lesbos impelled by
the romantic idea that the island is a separate entity, a world awaiting her
watchful gaze, a place that is her diametrical other; I go to Lesbos (as in

fact I did in 1993) neither to test a nostalgia for difference nor to discover any pre-established reciprocities, nor, for that matter, expecting to encounter a rural haven. Reading 'One Room in a Castle' as well as visiting Greece signal a '"return of the question of identity"' (Hall, 1989:9). When homecoming is understood as a return to the *question* of identity – not a way to identity itself – then it entails not only a re-entry into the mother country, but a recitation of the departure from it. At once a point of entry and exit, the place revisited can only be a palimpsestic territory, the corollary of a transnational subject's hybrid self.

Connelly's sojourn in Greece is driven by a desire to be in. Her narrative is written with the fervour of someone who has succeeded in breaking through a wall of incomprehension, who has mastered 'the secrets about this place' (330), be they intuited from gates and baling-wire or harboured by people. This is a desire that speaks of both memory and amnesia as it recites the cultural economy of colonial travel, of earlier ethnographic practises, of orientalism. It is a nostalgia for the present, only it is disguised as a nostalgia for the past. When she repeats one of her Greek lessons, this desire writes itself unequivocally in both languages: '*Thelo na eime mesa*. I want to be in. *Eime mesa*. I am in ... *Eime mesa*' (342). While she wants to be in (and her narrative conveys the impression that she does get in), I find myself circumscribed by a similar binary: I am both in *and* out, a quandary, a liminal position that has given me over the years as much trouble as delight. This is why my reading of Connelly's text dramatizes the ambivalence of my transnational position, an ambivalence accompanied by what appears to be the privilege of being a native.

My reading act – in itself a transnationalist practise – addresses some of the possibilities of how I negotiate my position as native informant, how I might practise my privilege of having access to certain kinds of knowledge. This is not knowledge possessed naturally or intuitively, but acquired through a fluctuating reproduction of reality, by means of an identity that is mutated, that complies with and disobeys the laws of simulation. It is the kind of knowledge that immediately alerts me to the many social and cultural slippages punctuating Connelly's representation of Lesbos and of its inhabitants. '"Five years ago [circa 1989–90], you couldn't find a television in a Greek bar"' (385); 'sometimes, it is impossible to know when a man and a woman are together here, because they seldom touch each other in public. Often a man will speak to his wife or girlfriend as if he were speaking to a casual acquaintance' (389): these are just a few, among many, examples which either belie social reality on Lesbos or fail to convey an image of the island that is distinctly indigenous. For example, while in Canada television and video screens are pervasive in bars and pubs in rural as well as urban areas, in Greece one encounters them only in some *kafenia*, the coffee-houses where, traditionally, men gather to watch sports. Slippages of this kind, however minor they might be in themselves, are more likely to be noticed by Greek rather than non-native readers. Interestingly enough, it was this kind of detail that distressed me in her book when I first read it.

Reading Connelly's text as native informant involves my ability to practise my own gaze by testing hers. Yet my readerly and writerly responses engage me in a double way: I am a native-as-object, but I am also a native-as-subject, a subject with a transnationalist agency. As Chow (1993:51) has written, the 'agency of the native cannot simply be imagined in terms of a resistance against the [objectified] image ... It needs to be rethought as that which is at once image and gaze, but a gaze that exceeds the moment of' objectification and reduction. My reading of Connelly's text is, then, an act of 'writing diaspora,' an act of practising my diasporic agency. To put it differently, I practise my diasporic subjectivity by writing about an other while at the same time confronting my otherness as it is indirectly imaged in Connelly's text, and as it is experienced in Canada *and* in Greece. Seen this way, my reading of Connelly should not be considered as synonymous with a reaction to the infidelity of her narrative *vis-à-vis* Greece, but rather as a complex act in which dispersed subjectivity, the self as object, and gender constructions converge. Thus, while Connelly can claim for herself an astounding capacity to understand Lesbos and Greek culture as a foreigner, I accomplish only the certainty that my identity as a transnational subject can never be resolved. It develops as a series of unstable points, those interstices formed when travel accounts like Connelly's, cultural narratives, and personal histories meet.

## The Gender Question, or Reading with 'Attitude'

Will I speak the truth to you? To you, Devika?

Alfonso Lingis (1983:135)

'Isadora at Talloni' and 'Isadora of the Red Dress' are two sections in Connelly's 'One Room in a Castle' where the contingencies of transnational subjectivity, native informant, and gender specificity converge *and* disperse in the subjunctive mode. These narratives stand out for me because they intend to delineate the formation of the female Greek subject at a microsocial level. Their gender specificity as well as their formal modalities militate a readerly response on my part that reconfigures the liminality of my transnational position; I find myself situated at an extremely acute angle to Connelly's particular articulations of Greek women. This position does not simply reproduce the inside–outside opposition I addressed earlier, which often tends to be reductive, but brings to the fore the fallacious naturalness of the cultural categories and gender boundaries characterizing 'One Room in a Castle.'

These narrative sections make a woman, Isadora, their exclusive focus in an otherwise male-focused text. While Connelly's daily interactions with Greek males speak of how she romances Lesbos, the 'Isadora' sections, although they deal with the perils and allurement of seduction, attempt to do precisely the opposite: they disperse Connelly's Lesbos romance, spoil her fantasy of an unmediated reality. Furthermore, they offer the most intimate portrait among the characters focalized in 'One Room in a Castle.' In 'Isadora at Talloni,' Isadora's voice is embedded in Connelly's own narratorial voice. Hearing Isadora speak from inside quotation marks, we find that she is feisty and embittered at the same time. Isadora is a woman who 'speaks freely' (384), which endears her to Connelly and explains why she is the only woman on Lesbos at whom the author gazes intently: 'I [Connelly] am happy to have her company. Perhaps what I miss most here is the company of women. There are plenty of tourist women on the island now, but I want to know Greek women – not an easy thing to do ... Almost immediately, I like her [Isadora] very much. Why? Because, unlike most of the young women here, she speaks freely. She does not whisper' (384). Connelly does not consider the possibility that there might be something about herself – among other things, her social performance of gender and cultural differences, her own ambivalence about being or not being a tourist – that stops the local women from opening up to her: 'Maria and I are on speaking terms, but like most of the younger women I've met here, she is still reluctant to get close. Generally, the men here are flamboyant, noisy, vital, while the women are withdrawn, watchful, quiet. It is hard to speak to any of the young women because I can hardly ever find them' (350). Connelly finds these women aloof, their sexuality non-existent: 'Sex is something Greek men anxiously try to get from foreign women, because Greek women have to answer to their jealous fathers until the old tyrants are six feet under' (350). The gender roles she perceives on the island perpetuate a conventional understanding of patriarchy, one befitting the manner in which she fashions Lesbos's unmodernity:

men occupy public spaces, while women are relegated to the domestic sphere.

What is not visible to Connelly's eyes is conveniently described as non-existent. How gender differences are enacted in the privacy of the domestic sphere, how domestic and public spaces intersect in discursive ways, how cultural particularity and gender roles inform each other, where and how local young women socialize, how the patriarchal elements of Greek culture intersect with matriarchal values – all these Connelly does not consider, primarily because it is difficult for her as foreigner to access them. Yet she takes the territory she occupies herself – the country fields and public spaces – to be the paradigmatic sociocultural arena that determines the presence or absence of the Lesbos women's agency.

It is Isadora's visibility that makes her a notable exception to the rule of gender roles as Connelly forges them; it makes her a native informant who shares her insider's knowledge with the author. Significantly, in 'Isadora of the Red Dress,' the quotation marks are removed, and Isadora ostensibly becomes the subject of her own discourse. The section's title specifies that this is 'a story,' marking a departure from Connelly's autobiographical travel mode. 'Isadora of the Red Dress' is Isadora's own autobiography, only this life-writing narrative violates 'the autobiographical pact': the signator and the narrator are not the same person (Lejeune, 1989). Thus, 'a story' is not intended to suggest the fictionality of Isadora's narrative but Connelly's role as mediator.

That Isadora tells her life story for Connelly's benefit as travel writer and as woman is made clear in 'Isadora at Talloni': '"I cannot imagine your life. You see?," Isadora tells Connelly. '"You are the lucky one, because you see me here, today, and you know what the peasant women and village girls are like. But I have no idea what it must be like to live in Canada. No idea"' (384). Similar to Yiorgos's metaphors and Fotis's myths, Isadora's life story is yet another 'gift' to Connelly. And this 'gift' is as much Isadora's life 'story' as her authentication of Connelly's understanding of Lesbos women. In this respect, 'Isadora of the Red Dress,' as the title insinuates, reveals Connelly's appropriation of Isadora as a research site, testifies to her authority over Isadora's story. Thus, the title works against the story's (and Isadora's) autobiographical mode. Ironically, the red dress Isadora wears was given to her by a German tourist, who stayed at the hotel where Isadora works as a part-time maid, a sign reinforcing how this Greek woman's subjectivity is eclipsed by the meta-narrative of cultural assumptions and values Connelly brings to Lesbos.

As with some of the other gifts she receives, Connelly solicits Isadora's story. Isadora may be positioned as the subject of her own discourse, but she still remains an other (an informant), for her story emerges only when she is addressed by and herself addresses Connelly. If Connelly offers Isadora's story – and I think she does – as a heuristic device, a strategy meant to further legitimize her perception of things Greek, it is a device that loses its efficacy for me when I read the text in terms of both what it says and how it says it. Connelly reassembles this life-writing narrative as a discourse that circulates within the cultural and media economy of Canada. If Connelly's own narrative returns to these Greeks at all, it is only in an oblique fashion and in a transnational context such as the one within which I find myself to be a reader.

There is yet another element that distinguishes Isadora's role as character in 'One Room in a Castle.' She is an outsider. She is from Athens, a university-educated woman who has lived on Lesbos for three years, has a boyfriend, Gavrilo, and makes a living as a maid and by selling jewellery.

Constructed as it is around her gender difference, urbanism, roles as informant and outsider to the island, Isadora's character (perhaps more than anything else in Connelly's text) functions as my textual double, compelling me to test the liminality of myself as a Greek urban woman, as native informant. Yet no sooner do I recognize these affiliations than Isadora is strangely separated from me or, more accurately, our affiliation fades away. The more confessional Isadora becomes, the more compelled I feel to respond to her 'with attitude': 'Attitude cannot be expressed by looking back at myself; speaking with attitude means being thrown forward onto a terrain of other selves. This terrain holds both my self and her self but we remain distinct; we are spoken in compatible registers but we do not collapse into an amorphous and indifferent state. This attitude must be grounded in the profound recognition of the deep structure of difference' (Probyn, 1993:143). The difference that surfaces when Isadora's narrative converges with Connelly's in my reading act speaks of an epistemological movement, not of the drift that occurs in the gaps between truthful representations and fictional modalities, but in the different ways of knowing. Reading Isadora's story with attitude, then, means inhabiting a discursive field that is already there, that precedes my performative present, that becomes a re-enactment of my cultural performance.

Isadora's story is itself a cultural performance, one impelled by Connelly's desire to supplement her narrative with an 'authentic' Greek voice, to write over her perceived invisibility of Lesbos women through Isadora's gender performance. Gender, as Judith Butler (1990:270–1) said, is a '*stylized repetition of acts* ... which are internally discontinuous ... [so that] *the appearance of substance* is precisely that, a constructed identity, a performative accomplishment which the mundane social audience, including the actors themselves, come to believe and to perform in the mode of belief.' In the case of Isadora's story, this make-believe is the double result of the performativity of her gender and of her own living performance as a Greek woman disenchanted with Greek urban life and modern Greece itself.

Isadora's gender performativity and living performance are grounded in the content and style of her discourse. Her narrative offers a crude cultural and social history of modern Greece that includes the occasional foray into the island's past under Ottoman rule (402, 408). At once self-exposure and cultural exposure, it complements Connelly's intent gaze at Lesbos's present. Against Connelly's romanticization that arrests the passage of time, Isadora's style is moralistic, often melodramatic, and steeped in temporality. This, together with the racy tone and ribald (in comparison with Connelly's) language, creates a sense of immediacy instrumental to the impact that her living performance is to have.

While a university student in Athens, Isadora '"got sick of Greece, sick of patriotism, sick of politics"' (384–5). She bemoans the rising consumerism of Greeks, laments the arrival of tourists (385), feels '"disgust"' at Greece for joining the European Community (385), and longs for the old days when people like her grandparents '"lived off their trees ... but it had nothing to do with getting rich"' (387), whereas now '"peasants are all dying [but] just like animals don't know when they're dying out"' (385). Her frustration with Greek urban living as well as with the quotidian life on Lesbos mimics Connelly's own nostalgia for a rural Edenic-like place. Yet there is no correspondence between Isadora's concern for the peasants in general and the banality of her cliché images about them. Thus, the portrait Isadora draws of rural Lesbos men is reductive because it is devoid of a social, economic, and cultural context that would account for their behaviour: 'They tease me a great deal, the old farmers and shepherds, because I am from Athens ... When I st[i]ck out my tongue, they all laugh aloud ... Horny old men with rotten teeth and goat-leather hands. They're narrow-minded, backward; they gossip and drink all day ... But they're good people, mostly, and their wives have the hearts of giants. A few of them would break their own bones to keep you from harm' (392). Here Isadora's cultural performance is mediated by her gender performativity and, more specifically, by what she presents as the normative sexual behaviour of these men. Her descriptions of them reinforce the literality of Connelly's 'found' metaphors. Seen from the educated and urban perspective of this modern woman, the image of these 'horny old men with rotten teeth' is the conduit of Connelly's notion of Lesbos's unmodernity. Isadora's narrative, then, lends Connelly's outsidedness a certain insidedness: it recites Connelly's own cultural and linguistic mannerisms. Both women embrace the image of the foreign (here imaged as what they lack and therefore desire) and do so with the same fervour with which they reject it.

Isadora's loathing for these men and for the mode of life in Athens as well as on the island soon takes the form of self-loathing. The social imaginary she creates debilitates as much the local people as it does herself. When she arrives at the island, Isadora wants the sea 'to hold [her] in her blue arms,' and proceeds to burn her clothes (391). Whether true or false, the latter act illustrates the hyper-reality of Isadora's cultural performance: now she can 'dress simply, like the people who live here' (391). Yet she remains persistently and painfully aware of her appearance and poverty. Her account of a simple way of life is regularly punctuated by her translating her social interactions into economic transactions: '*Posso kanei?* How much is it worth?' (401), she wonders all the time about the treats she receives from men like Nikos or about 'the exchange rate for human skin' (401). Isadora's anxieties stem from her precarious social and economic position on the island. While Connelly discovers Lesbos to be a healing and inspiring place, Isadora finds herself in situations that remind her that the island bears the social and cultural residue of the very things she wants to shun, that it is not the polar opposite of sophisticated urbanism that Connelly thinks it is. For Isadora, living on Lesbos conveys a sense of her agency, but it also constructs a scenario that involves her as a victim of herself as well as a sexual prey of others. Although Isadora lives with Gavrilo, it is not through her relationship with him that her gender performativity materializes. As soon as Gavrilo is mentioned, he is rendered as invisible as the local women. It is Nikos, a rich man cast in the role of the stereotypical Greek male, an urbane version of the man that seduces Shirley Valentine in the same-title film, who figures prominently.

At the same time that Isadora presents a hackneyed image of the Greek male as sexual predator, she also casts herself in the role of a woman who willingly, if not wilfully, becomes prey to his desires: 'I would like to have a good reason for Nikos, but I don't. I'm not hungry ... Certainly I'm not in love. A dozen times I've told myself that lust is not a good reason, although it's better than no reason at all ... As I fold my red dress and find my silver earrings and toss my lipstick into my stained leather bag, I say to myself: I must remember what I am doing now, so that I will not do it again. But I'm afraid I'll do it again anyway, because the habit stays with me even though everything else is finished' (393). Isadora fails to locate a logic in her behaviour as it resists both the pragmatics of her life and the extent to which she can understand and articulate her desires. In this context, reading this passage with attitude does not mean determining the psychoanalytic and social reasons that inform Isadora's promiscuity; instead, it discloses why 'Isadora of the Red Dress' must become the woman that the social and cultural semiotics of a 'red dress' signifies.

When Connelly first introduces Isadora, we are told that she makes a living by selling jewellery; later, Isadora refers to her work as a hotel maid. While she narrates her overnight stay in Nikos's house, she talks about yet another source of income: 'If you do it well, the money can be very good. I thought I was a mechanic, for them, but also for myself. The brain is like an engine. You can lift it out of the car, put it back in later, make some adjustments, and things run again. But you cannot do this with your soul. That was my discovery' (403–4). Why does Connelly insert into her narrative the story of a jaded urban woman who gradually reconstructs herself as a part-time prostitute with a presumably discerning mind? Isadora's body and brain, neatly separated from each other and realigned only as a binary pair, function as a replica of the exchange value system regulating Connelly's text. Isadora's body, like her story, has no other value than that necessitated by Connelly's transnational tactics.

Isadora's aleatory sexual behaviour reveals the ludic function of her story. 'The ludic,' Baudrillard (1990:158) has written, 'encompasses all the different ways one can "play" with networks, not in order to establish alternatives, but to discover their state of optimal functioning.' In this respect, Isadora's gender performativity and cultural performance put her self forward without reworking the ways in which Connelly fashions Greekness. Thus, Isadora's body becomes the embodiment of Connelly's transnational method. Capitalizing on the double meaning of story – story as personal narrative that has a certain historicity and documentary value and story as fictive construct – Connelly grafts Isadora's narrative into her own in order to mask her desire to demystify Lesbos's 'secrets.' But neither Isadora's body nor her story inscribe in 'One Room in a Castle' the cultural intelligibility that Connelly craves.

Significantly, 'Isadora of the Red Dress: A Story' has no direct impact on how Connelly responds to Lesbos. In 'I read *The Guardian*,' the section that immediately follows Isadora's life story, Connelly continues to muse about her life on the island as if she has never met Isadora, let alone heard and written down her story: 'Because I live without electricity, a television or a radio are useless to me. The newspaper is my only real connection to the active life of my century. The way I live now is also part of my century, but, as a friend recently explained to me, it has nothing to do with the modern age ... But like you, like Isadora, like each individual in every separate country, I am the invention of my century' (414). In Connelly's wish to maintain the illusion of unadulterated reality, both Isadora and the islanders are declared absent and are therefore silenced. Connelly declares that the particularity of their lives has no room in modernity; modernity, for her, has only one face. It is that of the liberalist sentiments she expresses in a casual fashion – 'What of the carpet children in India ... I remember Africa without ever having been there, a continent of people slaughtered by greed' (415) – the casualness testifying to her normative function as a typical modern woman. When she asks rhetorically, 'Is Greece really a laughing old man with a donkey / tattooed on his chest? Is such happiness legal?' (417), her answer is unabashedly positive. In instances like this one, when Connelly inscribes her image of Lesbos on the shepherd's body, her text drops all pretences of being authentic, thus showing her to be an author misreading her own narrative. The more sharply defined the barriers she raises between the reality of Lesbos and her own media-disseminated reality, the more her text belies her overall intention.

Connelly misreads, too, Isadora's story, thus obliterating the cultural, social, and gender ambivalences Isadora introduces. By ridding her own narrative of ambivalence, Connelly uses Isadora's story as a relay for the circulation, and verification, of her own discourse. Thus, she purges ambivalence: 'Purging ambivalence means above all delegitimizing all grounds of knowledge that are philosophically uncontrolled or uncontrollable. More than anything else, it means decrying and invalidating "common sense" – be it "mere beliefs," "prejudices," "superstitions" or sheer manifestations of "ignorance"' (Bauman 1991:24). The paradox of disclosing *and* suspending ambivalence, of producing ambivalence only to submerge it in the desire to maintain a semblance of order, is key not only to what characterizes modernity but also to what makes the emancipatory project of modernity problematic. The credibility of Connelly's narrative of Lesbos lies precisely in this paradox, in how 'One Room in a Castle' is at once a representation of Lesbos and the scandal of its own representational devices.

When Connelly says that 'like you, like Isadora, like each individual in every separate country, I am the invention of my century,' she expresses only momentary 'distrust' at how she fetishizes her inventional tactics: 'There are no time machines here; there is no other world. Only this place exists, this globe of canaries and demons' (414–5). She embraces the fictionality of the real she invents not as a fiction but as a paradigmatic, global reality. Her apostrophe to her readers thus invites me to disbelieve what she believes. Her bracketing of Isadora's life story and its ambivalences performs her capacity for forgetting. It is this kind of performative act that enables Connelly to conclude 'One Room in a Castle' through circular repetition: 'Yiorgos. Poetry is a country, and Yiorgos lives there' (431) – an image of Lesbos that is at odds with my response to Isadora's story.

And this is why the ending of her narrative has become the beginning of my performative act here. A response, measured by my transnational location, cadenced by the liminality of my doubleness as reader of her text: at once subject and object, Greek and Canadian, I have read 'One Room in a Castle' by embracing the scandals of its ambivalences.[8]

To be and function as a transnational subject, one must first encounter one's own image as object, be it an image one presents to oneself or an image forged by others. The practice of transnational subjectivity, then, means navigating through the turbulent waters of liminality. This does not mean liking the objectified image one encounters of oneself or setting out to dispel all its evocations. What it means is making an inventory of gains and losses, redefining one's understanding of subject and object formation, confronting (instead of eliminating) inassimilable elements, above all learning how to live with differences.

NOTES

1 This essay was researched and written with the support of a Social Sciences and Humanities Research Council of Canada research grant.
2 See, for example, Elaine Kalman Naves (1994), and the review of *One Room in a Castle* by Mark Abley (1995) and Valerie Fortney (1993).
3 This figure is based on the 1991 census.
4 For example, Connelly was interviewed live on 'Morningside,' the CBC Radio program hosted by Peter Gzowski, on 13 Oct. 1995.
5 There is a plethora of studies on this issue by Greek as well as non-Greek scholars. See, for example, Jusdanis (1991) who discusses some of these debates.
6 Not one of the publications by or about her mention a trip to Turkey. The most recent reference to her travels includes a visit to Burma.

7 No Lesbos town bears this name. Talloni could be an alias of Kalloni or Mitilini.
8 I have in mind here Bauman's chapter 'The Scandal of Ambivalence.'

REFERENCES

Abley, Mark (1995) 'Owning the Place,' *Books in Canada*, Oct. 30–1.
Althusser, Louis (1971) *Lenin and Philosophy and Other Essays*. Translated by Ben Brewster. New York: Monthly Review Press.
Andrews, Marke (1995) 'Rural Beauty and Charm: It's Greece to Her.' *Vancouver Sun*, 14 Oct. H1 and H2.
Baudrillard, Jean (1990) *Seduction*. Translated by Brian Singer. Montreal: New World Perspectives.
– (1994) *Simulacra and Simulation*. Translated by Sheila Faria Glaser. Ann Arbor: Univeristy of Michigan Press.
Bauman, Zygmunt (1991) *Modernity and Ambivalence*. Cambridge: Polity Press.
Behdad, Ali (1994) *Belated Travellers: Orientalism in the Age of Colonial Dissolution*. Durham: Duke University Press.
Braidotti, Rosi (1994) *Nomadic Subjects: Embodiment and Sexual Difference in Contemporary Feminist Theory*. New York: Columbia University Press.
Butler, Judith (1990) 'Performative Acts and Gender Constitution: An Essay in Phenomenology and Feminist Theory.' In Sue-Ellen Case (ed.), *Performing Feminisms*, 270–82. Baltimore: Johns Hopkins University Press.
Chambers, Iain (1994) *Migrancy, Culture, Identity*. London: Routledge.
Chambers, Ross (1984) *Story and Situation: Narrative Seduction and the Power of Fiction*. Minneapolis: Univeristy of Minnesota Press.
Chow, Rey (1993) *Writing Diaspora: Tactics of Intervention in Contemporary Cultural Studies*. Bloomington: Indiana University Press.
Connelly, Karen (1992) *Touch the Dragon: A Thai Journal*. Winnipeg: Turnstone.
– (1995) *One Room in a Castle: Letters from Spain, France and Greece*. Winnipeg: Turnstone.
Derrida, Jacques (1982) *Margins of Philosophy*. Translated by Alan Bass. Chicago: University of Chicago Press.
Felman, Shoshana (1983) *The Literary Speech Act: Don Juan with J.L. Austin, or Seduction in Two Languages*. Translated by Caherine Porter. Ithaca, NY: Cornell University Press.
Fortney, Valerie (1993) 'In the Wake of a Dragon.' *Quill and Quire*, 59(2).
Grewal, Interpal, and Caren Kaplan (eds.), (1994) *Scattered Hegemonies: Postmodernity and Transnational Feminist Practices*. Minneapolis: University of Minnesota Press.
Goulet, Clare (1995) 'Death of the Tragic Female: A Conversation with Karen

Connelly.' *Studies in Canadian Literature / Études en littérature canadienne* 20(22):111–22.

Hall, Stuart (1989) 'Ethnicity: Identity and Difference.' *Radical America* 23(4): 9–20.

Harries, Karsten (1979) 'Metaphor and Transcendence.' In Sheldon Sacks (ed.), *On Metaphor,* 71–88. Chicago: University of Chicago Press.

hooks, bell (1989) *Talking Back: Thinking Feminist, Thinking Black.* Boston: South End Press.

Hutcheon, Linda (1994) *Irony's Edge: The Theory and Politics of Irony.* London: Routledge.

Hyde, Lewis (1979) *The Gift: Imagination and the Erotic Life of Property.* New York: Random House.

Jusdanis, Gregory (1991) *Belated Modernity and Aesthetic Culture: Inventing National Literature.* Minneapolis: University of Minnesota Press.

Kalman Naves, Elaine (1994) ' "Tales of a Traveller": Profile/Karen Connelly.' *Books in Canada* 23(7):17–21.

Kaplan, Caren (1994) 'The Politics of Location as Transnational Feminist Critical Practice.' In Interpal Grewal and Caren Kaplan (eds.), *Scattered Hegemonies: Postmodernity and Transnational Feminist Practices,* 137–52. Minneapolis and London: University of Minnesota Press.

– (1996) *Questions of Travel: Postmodern Discourses of Displacement.* Durham and London: Duke University Press.

Lejeune, Philippe (1989) *On Autobiography.* Translated by Katherine Leary, and edited by Paul Eakin. Minneapolis: University of Minnesota Press.

Leontis, Artemis (1995) *Topographies of Hellenism: Mapping the Homeland.* Ithaca, NY: Cornell University Press.

Lingis, Alfonso (1983) *Excesses.* Albany, NY: SUNY Press.

– (1995) *Abuses.* Berkeley: University of California Press.

MacCannell, Dean (1992) *Empty Meeting Grounds: The Tourist Papers.* London: Routledge.

McRobbie, Angela (1982) 'The Politics of Feminist Research: Between Talk, Text and Action.' *Feminist Review,* 12:46–57.

Miller, Nancy K. (1991) *Getting Personal: Feminist Occasions and Other Autobiographical Acts.* New York: Routledge.

Minh-Ha, Trinh (1989) *Women, Native, Other: Writing Postcoloniality and Feminism.* Bloomington: Indiana University Press.

Probyn, Elspeth (1993) *Sexing the Self: Gendered Positions in Cultural Studies.* London: Routledge.

Serres, Michel (1982) *The Parasite.* Translated by Lawrence R. Schehr. Baltimore: Johns Hopkins University Press.

Suleri, Sara (1992) 'Woman Skin Deep: Feminism and the Postcolonial Condition.' *Critical Inquiry* 18(4):756–69.

– (1995) 'Criticism and Its Alterity.' In Mae G. Henderson (ed.), *Borders, Boundaries, and Frames: Essays in Cultural Criticism and Cultural Studies*, 171–82. New York: Routledge.

Tompkins, Jane (1993) 'Me and My Shadow.' In Diane P. Freedman, Olivia Frey, and Frances Murphy Zauhar (eds.), *The Intimate Critique: Autobiographical Literary Criticism*, 23–40. Durham: Duke University Press.

Van den Abbeele, Georges (1980) 'Sightseers: The Tourist as Theorist.' *Diacritics* 10(4):2–14.

# 13

# Western Feminism? Problems of Categorizing Women's Movements in Cross-national Research[1]

## VAPPU TYYSKÄ

Sexual difference is a political alliance of women, in recognition of their respective differences.

Braidotti (1994:207)

The impact of feminism is connected upon the insistence upon agency, subjectivity, self-determination and self-transformation.

Eisenstein (1991:112)

The relative merits and dangers of postmodernism have been subject to much debate within feminist discourse. There has been debate over the pitfalls of relativism, idealism, abandonment of theory, agency, and action. Yet there has also been a reluctance to completely reject postmodern lines of inquiry. For all the problems involved, it is generally (albeit sometimes reluctantly) acknowledged that feminism can benefit from an accommodation of some aspects of postmodernism.

This benefit is perhaps the most discernible in reinforcing the feminist tendency to problematize the general category of 'woman.' I would like to emphasize that this insight is not unique to postmodernism. However, the latter's resistance to universals and essentialism of any kind has reinforced a tendency towards a critical evaluation of the significance of cultural and geopolitical differences (Nicholson, 1990; Evans, 1995; Grewal and Kaplan, 1994; Hekman, 1990). In acknowledging and analysing 'difference' within the category of 'woman,' feminists are self-conscious about both their own position and delivery of information and analysis and about the reception and interpretation of information by different audiences (Mani, 1990). This sensitivity to multiple subjects and audiences encourages feminists to be accountable for what are possibly hegemonic practices. It has been claimed that 'such accountability can begin to shift the ground of feminist practice from magisterial relativism (as if diversified cultural production simply occurs in a social vacuum) to the complex interpretive practices that acknowledge the historical roles of mediation, betrayal, and alliance in the relationships between women in diverse locations' (Kaplan, 1994:139).

Thus, the concepts of 'location' or 'politics of location' (Probyn, 1990; Kaplan, 1994; Mani, 1990) and the construction of 'the other' (Yeatman, 1990: Braidotti, 1994) are central to the feminism and postmodernism debate. Again, although not original, this postmodern rewording brings attention to a previously acknowledged dilemma in the social sciences, related to the position of the researcher as an interpreter of selected aspects of lived reality. In doing so, we are constantly creating ideas about 'others,' or those who we are researching.

My essay centres on this discussion of the problem of exclusion and silencing and construction of subjects and subalterns as 'the other.' I will base my discussion on the empirical experience gained from my own comparative research project delving into the impact of the women's movements on the child care policy process in Canada and Finland from 1960 to 1990. This is a very practical and very personal undertaking. I want to outline the problems I faced during the course of my research, and the consequences of the choices I made, regarding the construction of general typologies of women's movements in cross-national comparative research in the Western context.

Following the postmodern vocabulary, I also want to raise the question of 'location' as a 'transnational' issue (Grewal and Kaplan, 1994; Kaplan, 1994; Mani, 1990). This has two components. The first one concerns a transnational audience, that is, the tendency of audiences in different geopolitical locations to focus on different aspects of feminist work as significant (Mani, 1990). More germane to my discussion is the second aspect of transnationalism, that is, that alongside the transnational movement of capital and culture, there is movement, or 'world travelling' of the researcher[2] (Lugones, as in Kaplan, 1994:11; see also Mani, 1990).

It is customary in the postmodernist feminist (and postcolonial) debate to focus on the problems this multiple positioning of the researcher creates for relationships between 'Western' and 'non-Western' women. For example, Rich (1986, in Probyn, 1990:176–7) refers to this as the 'ontological conceit of the Western subject,' that is, that in 'creating our own centres and our own locals, we tend to forget that our centres displace others in the peripheries of our making.' This generalization is certainly valid in relation to some general aspects of global and post-colonial arguments, especially as they relate to the Western position of hegemony. However, in my estimation, this very category is curiously contradictory in terms of the emphasis on diversity and difference within the feminist postcolonialist position.

Based on both my research and personal experience, I would like to call into question the construction of the concept of 'Western' feminism and make an argument about the plurality of identities in that context. My position, as a 'White' middle-class immigrant woman within the general 'Western' context, is based on the complexities of the insider–outsider status I hold in both Western countries where I have engaged in research. I will suggest that the local–periphery or inclusion–exclusion dichotomies have to go beyond the Western versus non-Western analysis to acknowledge the diversity within each of these socially created categories.

## Selecting and Constructing Typologies of Women's Movements

Briefly stated, my sociological study was focused on discovering the female agency in the child care policy developments in Canada and Finland between 1960 and 1990. I wanted to find out how women, through organized collective action, participated in the child care debate, and what their impact was on the process and the outcomes. In this essay, my concern is not with the process or the outcomes, but rather with the agents of change, that is, the women's organizations. The two issues are (1) the selection of the organizations and (2) the development of typologies or categories of organizations.

As pointed out by Probyn (1990), we construct categories from a specific location. Categories imply hierarchies, because they carry 'preferred' labels and exclude other categories. There are problems inherent in constructing categories in relation to one location. This presumes a certain body of knowledge, or a research tradition. In the modernist context, this usually means that you have to make a choice between prevailing 'schools of thought,' within one main paradigm (Foucault, as discussed by Probyn 1990:185). Thus, I will discuss how my research project was guided by (1) the existing research traditions of my discipline, (2) the goals of my research, and (3) personal ideological preferences.

## Inclusion–Exlusion

In relation to the research traditions, I was first guided by the overriding norm in sociology as a discipline that any meaningful analysis has to involve general categories and conclusions (Yeatman, 1990:186). Second, as a feminist embedded in the Western, North American and European context (locale), I was informed by a socialist feminist (materialist) analysis. This tradition has been criticized by some postmodern feminists (for example, Nicholson, 1990:1) as repeating the problems of Marxism in its tendency to overgeneralize and present overarching categories. However, in contradiction to this statement, it is from this tradition of analysis that I learned a historical method that encouraged me to be respectful of and alert to cross-national differences and my position as a researcher, even within the context of generalizations. I found these concerns echoed in my reading of postmodern feminist research.

The selection of specific organizations implies an articulation of the field (Probyn, 1990:178) in which some categories are excluded. Because the goal of my comparative research project was to discover how the women's organizations influenced government and state policy, I wanted to choose the larger and presumably more influential women's organizations involved in the political process on the issue of child day care. I consciously excluded 'radical' feminists from my study on the grounds that these groups (1) were not numerically very large or significant and (2) generally avoided involvement with mainstream – that is, male – politics based on their focus on woman-centred culture and community. Frankly, behind this choice was primarily the consideration of accessibility of information and data within my limited budget. These groups themselves lack resources, and consequently they do not have the extensive archival collections of the larger and better funded women's organizations. This in itself speaks volumes about the acts of inclusion and exclusion in society at large, which was repeated in my research by virtue of my personal financial and time limitations.[3]

I wanted to be as inclusive as possible within my 'exclusive' category of 'mainstream,' larger women's organizations, aiming to incorporate a range of major women's organizations, not only those that are deemed to be feminist organizations. Feminist organizations are distinguished from others that are called 'woman-centred' in their approach. The difference is that the latter accept the prescribed limits of patriarchal practices, whereas feminists want to transcend those limits (see, Dominelli, 1991:272).

In this general selection of women's organizations, I was guided by an interest in both ideology and structure (see Table 13.1). In terms of the latter, I chose mainstream women's organizations that are more institutionalized in relation to the official political system – insiders. These included women's factions of mainstream political parties and labour

TABLE 13.1 Selected women's organizations in Canada and Finland, 1960–1990.

| Ideology | Canada | | Finland | |
|---|---|---|---|---|
| | *Insiders* | *Outsiders* | *Insiders* | *Outsiders* |
| Equality | Liberal women | CCDCF | | Nytkis National Council of Women |
| Equality/ Liberation | | Women in CCF/NDP Union women NAC CDCAA | Social Democratic Women Socialist women Union women | Association 9 |
| Equal value | PC Women | REAL Women | Centre Women Coalition Women | Martha Association |

*Key to abbreviations*
CCDCF – Canadian Child Day Care Federation
CCF/NDP – Canadian Commonwealth Federation / New Democratic Party
CDCAA – Canadian Day Care Advocacy Association
NAC – National Action Committee on the Status of Women
Nytkis – Women's Organizations in Cooperation
PC – Progressive Conservative
REAL Women – Realistic, Equal, Active, for Life Women

unions. They are generally called 'women's rights' groups that 'work the system,' as opposed to the 'women's liberation' groups which represent the independent women's movement, including single-issue organizations (Dahlerup and Gulli, 1985:6–7, 12–13). In my study, the latter are represented by the umbrella organizations of women's groups and child care advocacy groups – outsiders. My final selection amounted to a total of nine organizations from each country.

Canadian women's organizations were represented by the women's associations of the major political parties, the Liberal Party of Canada, the Progressive Conservative Party, and the New Democratic Party. Union women were represented by women in the Canadian Labour Congress as the central labour union. From among independent women's organizations, I included the National Action Committee on the Status of Women, as well as three child care advocacy organizations: the Canadian Day Care Advocacy Association, the Canadian Child Day Care Federation, and the Ontario Coalition for Better Child Care.

From among the women's organizations of Finnish political parties, I included the Social Democratic Women, the Democratic League of Finnish Women (socialist), the Centre Women (centre–agrarian), and the Coalition Women (conservative). Union women were represented by the women's sections of the two largest central labour unions in Finland: the Central Organization of Trade Unions in Finland and the Confederation of Salaried Employees. The independent women's movement was represented by the National Council of Women in Finland as the umbrella of women's groups and Association 9, a significant feminist and child care advocacy group that flourished in the late 1960s and early 1970s. I also included the new, loosely knit Women's Organizations in Cooperation that emerged in the late 1980s as a forum to represent the interests of women across the partisan political spectrum.

In an attempt to create both diversity and inclusiveness, I included selected non-feminist and anti-feminist organizations in my research, in order to understand the dynamics and debates within the wider women's movement, not only the feminist movement. In addition to the non-feminist Progressive Conservative Women, the anti-feminist faction in Canada is represented by the Realistic, Equal, Active for Life (REAL) Women. In Finland, the Martha Association represents a mass movement of agrarian women and housewives; it is non-feminist but not anti-feminist in nature. At the time (see Table 13.1), I categorized non-feminist and anti-feminist organizations together. In retrospect, I realize the importance of distinguishing between the two, especially when one considers both the possibilities for alliances and cooperation and divided solidarities within the women's movement.[4]

**'Western' Feminism?**

My next aim was to extract the ideological tendencies of each of these organizations, in order to create viable analytical categories of the women's organizations for the purpose of cross-national comparison. Because I was dealing with political issues, I considered three different options with regard to politics-based categories and associated labels.

The first choice I faced was to use the generally accepted categories of left, centre, and right-wing politics. But, since I wanted to steer consciously towards a more woman-oriented vocabulary and content (that is, to capture some core or essence of the variety of specifically women's politics), I rejected the left–right–centre labels.[5] In the end, this option can be perceived to be transnational, but the vocabulary excludes a 'women's' perspective and agency.

A second option would have been to use the categories called liberal and socialist feminism and the conservative conceptualization of womanhood. In my study, I focused on the North American and Canadian feminist literature where there is a tradition of identifying categories in this manner. As I chose to include conservative women in the study, I grappled with the concept of 'feminism.' It is not possible, in my estimation, to use the words 'conservative' and 'feminism' jointly. Therefore, I entertained using the term 'conservative concept of womanhood' (following the previously discussed distinction between feminist and woman-centred approaches).

I faced two further problems. First, I was increasingly aware of the tendency in the Canadian tradition of feminist scholarship, since the 1980s, to move away from self- or other-identified labels like liberal or socialist and to favour more eclectic approaches to feminism. In the 1990s this approach has been emphasized even more, as feminists try to come to grips with the postmodern challenge of inclusion–exclusion. This led me to approach the above labels with caution.

The second problem arose from the comparative context itself. It is apparent that this categorization is neither transnational nor inclusive, because it is based on an Anglo-American typology. I became acutely aware of how inappropriate these typologies were as labels for the Finnish women's organizations. For example, the categories 'liberal' or 'conservative' have limited applicability in the Finnish context. Liberalism has never been a major current there. Conservatism of the extreme kind is not prevalent either, in that even the political parties and women's organizations of the conservative wing of politics in Finland are significantly more moderate than the conservatives in Canada. Even the most conservative Finnish women's organizations, such as the Martha Association, acknowledge women's right to break out of their traditional family role, while in Canada this is denied by the most conservative and anti-feminist organizations, such as the REAL Women. On the other hand, I was also aware how socialist tendencies in the feminist movement in Canada were much more muted than the longstanding and more extreme traditions in Finland.[6]

In the end, the matters of typologies and labels got ever more complicated as I immersed myself in the literature on the Nordic countries. The first problem here had to do with mediating between two distinct research traditions, labelled 'Anglo-American' and 'Nordic' (Waerness, 1989; Siim, 1987; Hernes, 1987). This distinction between geopolitical groupings was an improvement in that it overcame the all-encompassing 'Western' label. However, it still posed its own problems of overgeneralization between groups of countries that are in significant ways quite distinct from one another. Nevertheless, this level of generalization was to me acceptable, based on the two different geopolitical locations created within the research tradition centring on women and the welfare state.

Thus, while reading the Nordic literature on the women's movement, I came across categories by Norwegian researchers Eduards, Halsaa, and Skjeie (1985) which seemed to capture the woman-centred approach I was after. These categories bore the labels of politics of equality, equality–liberation, and equal value.

In short, the politics of equality promotes increasing women's public (that is, in the formal economy and politics) responsibilities, but not at the expense of their freedom to choose. Thus, in the area of public child care policy, options should be available to allow women to either stay at home or to engage in their public responsibilities. In comparison, those organizations that fall within the equality–liberation perspective emphasize women's right to employment, and thus to public child care services. In this framework, this type of state intervention is a way out of women's oppression, as it is a step towards removing the sexual division of labour. In contrast, the equal value position accepts the sexual division of labour and believes in the complementarity of men's and women's traditional roles. These organizations would discourage the development of public day care services. In the end, I chose this typology to classify women's organizations in both countries (Tyyskä, 1995; see Table 13.1).

However, as neat as the picture appeared to me at the time, the final typology is still ridden with complexities, and it has resulted in distortions of what is 'real' in the context of historical developments in each of these countries.[7] Thus, for example, the vocabulary of 'equal value' (a conservative view in the typology) is highly misleading in the Canadian context, where the term is applied to phrases and slogans such as 'equal pay for work of equal value,' which more adequately falls within the context of equality or equality–liberation politics in my framework. In other words, although this typology is transnational in character, it is linguistically exclusive in that it is derived from the Nordic context, and it is not relevant to the discourse in Canada.

## Accountability: Transnational Researcher as a Nomad

A further problem arose in relation to my position as a researcher engaged in transnational excursions into areas that are both familiar and foreign. In this regard, Probyn's (1990:185–7) caution to be 'vigilant to the submerged conditions that silence others and *the other of ourselves* [emphasis added],' strikes a poignant chord. As a woman who has immigrated into the 'Anglo-American' culture from the 'Nordic' one, I am at the same time an outsider and an insider in both realms. I feel myself truly constructed as 'the other' both in Canada and in Finland. Despite my long stay (now over twenty years) in Canada as a landed immigrant, my experience is very much of one of an outsider. Similarly, after such a long stay away from Finland, I cannot make any claim to being an insider in that environment either.

This kind of position is traditionally viewed as a benefit in my academic discipline, in that I am expected to be more able to maintain my 'objectivity' in both realms and prevent personal biases from contaminating my research. From a personal point of view, this tension between an insider and outsider status poses an ongoing problem in my attempt to mediate both my own identity and to struggle with the contradictions posed by different research traditions. In other words, there are divided loyalties as well as contradictions in 'making sense' of the world, based on this 'mixed-up' locale (both in the concrete and subjective–psychological sense).[8] As stated previously, this problem was compounded by (1) the pressure towards creating all-encompassing, comparable categories for the purpose of my research (based on the general pressure in sociology towards creating generalizations), and (2) differences in the research traditions, categories, and labels between the two countries.

## Conclusions

After the long process of searching for general typologies of women's organizations in cross-cultural research, I am forced to conclude that the generally complex and intricate culturally and historically specific differences between the two countries and their women's organizations defied the level of generalization I forced upon them. Although I wrote these up as a self-criticism of the study at the time I did the study, I was not fully aware of the implications until much later. I will summarize and outline some of these implications here, based on the preceding discussion, and with reference to the feminist postmodernist discourse.

Most of these following thoughts open up questions rather than offer firm answers.

Based on established research traditions in a discipline, the research question of interest, and the subjectivity of the enterprise of social analysis, I believe that everyone is faced with decisions about inclusiveness and exclusiveness. I also believe that it is not possible, nor is it necessarily fruitful, to be completely inclusive in all research. The main aim of my study was to bring to light the importance of gendered practices by the women's movement in the interpretation of social policy outcomes. I feel that the study was successful in this task and that it brought out the voice of (some) women's organizations that had been 'silenced' (Probyn, 1990:185) through omission.

However, the previous conclusion is not completely unambiguous. There are at least three major categories of questions that arise from the above discussion. The first has to do with the transnational scholar. One question here is: How does the choice of categories affect the results? In my research, I struggled with the different typologies arising from different traditions, with an end result that still holds limitations. How would my results have been different had I made a different choice? In sociology, the research question guides us towards inclusion and exclusion. In my case, a focus on government policy dictated a level of analysis that was exclusive of some grass-roots organizations that may have had significant input. Would this exclusion alter my results? In the end, I do not think it would. My general conclusion was that it was important to consider the gender dynamics embedded in the formal political process in relation to the government and the state. That conclusion would not be altered. However, were I to ask a different question, it would perhaps be necessary to widen the scope of my categories, or move to a different level of analysis with different organizations altogether. If we are to understand these gender dynamics in the transnational context, both levels of analysis are likely required.

Furthermore, as researchers we are sometimes unduly criticized for the choices we make. My point here, based on personal experience, is that the choice of categories fundamentally illustrates the serious difficulties in obtaining funds for research on topics related to women. Few feminist scholars command generous funds that would allow us to engage in long-term research of large numbers of uncharted and undiscovered women's organizations. Therefore, the level of analysis is often decided for us, by these constraints, and in no way reflects any conscious attempt to exclude specific groups.

The second set of questions has to do with the transnational audience: What is the value of particular research traditions and scholarly discussions in different countries or geopolitical areas? How can a more diverse audience be reached, considering the limitations of the researcher? In my study, I drew upon two different and quite distinct traditions. In the end, my study is more understandable to (and perhaps subconsciously more directed at) the Finnish, rather than the Canadian audience. The divided loyalties that are embedded in my research are probably reflected in the greater degree of interest in my work in Finland and the Nordic countries than in Canada.

This realization leads into my third and final question, related to the issue of 'researcher as a nomad' who has to practice 'accountability' (Braidotti, 1994:196). Accountability means that it is essential to engage in 'politics of location,' that is, to be aware of your position and the limitations of your position both in the ideological and geographical sense (Eisenstein, 1991:106–7). In raising the issue of accountability, my last question also relates to the ongoing need to examine the political value of diversity in relation to agency. Feminist scholarship extends beyond scholarly boundaries. Women respond to information and analyses and get politicized. The question is: How do categories affect the politicization of women? In other words, if you cannot find yourself in a category, or your category has been 'silenced' or constructed as 'the other,' what impact does it have on the politicization process? This question bears implications for the construction of transnational alliances among women, and it is ridden with the complexities outlined above, including both pragmatic considerations (resources) and ideological differences. Accountability is ultimately a question of pushing these pragmatic and ideological limits to allow for an ever-increasing range of voices to be heard.

An additional problem related to this category of questions is faced by most or all transnational scholars, namely, the resistance to comparative work on two specific and interrelated grounds. The main problem is a tendency towards 'orientalism'[9] arising from an 'outsider's' supposed unfamiliarity with the actual conditions in the 'foreign' setting. The past track record – going back to its imperialist and colonialist roots – of transnational research has led to a complete rejection of comparative research in some quarters. It has also led to a second and related problem of pressure upon researchers to focus on 'their' country and setting.[10] This is especially problematic in the context of transnational feminist scholarship where large numbers of us acknowledge several countries and areas as 'our own.'

Thus, my final point related to the last question is to problematize certain categories emerging from the postmodern and postcolonial discourse. Researchers engaged in these discourses make decisions about exclusion–inclusion, categories, and limits. And in doing so, they categorize and juxtapose 'schools of thought' identified with particular geopolitical areas. One such common typology is Western (or Eurocentric) as opposed to non-Western approaches. Based on my own research, I suggest that this is a limiting categorization that does injustice to the variety of positions *within each category*. I concur with Grewal and Kaplan (1994:11) that the notion of homogenizing the West is problematic. If anything, it sets an initial 'us against them' scenario between feminists rather than opening up dialogue towards potential cooperation and understanding. The professed aim of feminism, as influenced by postmodernism, is to increase awareness of one another's positions (political, geographical, cultural, and subjective). This would aid us in finding enough common ground for the creation of transnational connections (Kaplan, 1994:139). This goal is not attainable if the positioning begins with preconceived notions of 'Western' feminism and feminists, without making allowances for the diversity that exists within that category as well.

NOTES

1 The author would like to thank the following individuals for their valuable comments on earlier drafts of this paper: Allen Tyyskä; attendants at the Conference on Émigré Feminism, Peterborough, Ontario, 3–6 Oct. 1996; attendants at the Graduate Student Seminar Series, Department of Sociology, University of Toronto, 1 Oct. 1996.

2 This is also articulated as the question of 'hybrid' or 'nomadic' subjects (Braidotti, 1994).

3 Comparative research is an expensive undertaking, and it often leads to situations of little or no choice in relation to our data collection. The question of poor resources, especially where feminist research is concerned, should not be underestimated in passing judgment about acts of inclusion and exclusion in research projects. This problem applies both to the research subjects and the researcher. I found that my study was seriously hampered by the comparative lack of archival materials in Canada, compared with Finland. Finnish women's organizations have significantly better resources and can afford good record-keeping. In contrast, the Canadian data were more difficult to obtain, and I was forced to rely more on the personal files of individuals rather than on well-organized files of organizations.

4  I would like to thank Margrit Eichler, Ontario Institute for Studies in Education, University of Toronto, for her criticism which prompted a clarification of
   my thinking in this area.

5  I have used these categories in some publications on the topic (e.g., Tyyskä,
   1994).

6  In our discussion at the Conference on Émigré Feminism, it was also noted
   that aside from vocabulary describing political currents, other words are contentious in the transnational context. One such word is 'gender' which has no
   equivalency in some cultures or languages.

7  Among these historically specific contingencies are different paths of development of the welfare state in the two countries, including women's incorporation into welfare state regimes. As more 'institutional' welfare regimes, Nordic
   states are unique in that they are more egalitarian than other types. This is
   based on a long history of socialist and social democratic movements and governments. In contrast, political parties of the left are weak or missing in Canada. The prevalent ideology in Canada is traditional liberalism, which exerts a
   more hands-off approach to the welfare state, along the lines of the 'residual'
   model of a welfare state. Additional restrictions to extensive policy development arise from the Canadian federalist state structure which is more conservative than the unitary state structure of Finland. Moreover, the Finnish system
   of multiparty coalition governments has resulted in a politics of consensus
   which contrasts with the Canadian system where essentially two main political
   parties have been locked in a situation of political conflict. These features
   result in different ideological climates which frame women's participation and
   influence in the government arena. Women's participation itself is a matter of
   different historical pathways. Finnish women have been a major force in the
   development of state and government as well as the formal economy. This is
   because of a history of external and internal warfare, leading to women's early
   entry into the wage labour force and politics, long before the Second World
   War. In Canada, women were incorporated into the economy in the post–
   Second World War era, in the aftermath of their role as a 'reserve army of
   labour' in wartime industries and during the postwar economic boom. For a
   more detailed discussion of these conditions, which are beyond the main aim
   of this chapter, see Tyyskä (1995).

8  This problem was raised by several of the participants at the Conference on
   Émigré Feminism, some of whom discussed the pain they had had to deal with
   in analysing their countries of origin, having been involuntarily uprooted.

9  This problem was raised and extensively discussed at the Conference on Émigré Feminism. For a fuller discussion, see other chapters in this collection.

10 I have personally been 'pigeon-holed' in this fashion. Although comparative

research is easier when you command the language or are familiar with the culture, I question this forcible confinement of researchers to what is 'familiar.' If we are to reach an understanding of one another, I think it is necessary to explore the 'unfamiliar' through our own eyes.

REFERENCES

Braidotti, Rosi (1994) *Nomadic Subjects: Embodiment and Sexual Difference in Contemporary Feminist Theory.* New York: Columbia University Press.
Dahlerup, Drude, and Brita Gulli (1985) 'Women's Organizations in the Nordic Countries: Lack of Force or Counterforce?' In Elina Haavio-Mannila et al. (eds.), *Unfinished Democracy: Women in Nordic Politics,* 6–36. Oxford: Pergamon Press.
Dominelli, Lena (1991) *Women across Continents. Feminist Comparative Social Policy.* London: Harvester Wheatsheaf.
Eduards, Maud, Beatrice Halsaa, and Hege Skjeie (1985) 'Equality: How Equal?' In Elina Haavio-Mannila et al. (eds.), *Unfinished Democracy: Women in Nordic Politics,* 134–60. Oxford: Pergamon Press.
Eisenstein, Hester (1991) *Gender Shock: Practicing Feminism on Two Continents.* Boston: Beacon Press.
Evans, Judith (1995) *Feminist Theory Today: An Introduction to Second-wave Feminism.* London: Sage.
Grewal, Inderpal, and Caren Kaplan (eds.), (1994) *Scattered Hegemonies: Postmodernity and Transnational Feminist Practices.* Minneapolis: University of Minnesota Press.
Hekman, Susan J. (1990) *Gender and Knowledge: Elements of Postmodern Feminism.* Cambridge: Polity Press.
Hernes, Helga (1987) *Welfare State and Woman Power: Essays in State Feminism.* Oslo: Norwegian University Press.
Kaplan, Caren (1994) 'The Politics of Location as Transnational Feminist Critical Practice.' In Inderpal Grewal and Caren Kaplan (eds.), *Scattered Hegemonies: Postmodernity and Transnational Feminist Practices,* 137–52. Minneapolis: University of Minnesota Press.
Mani, Lata (1990) 'Multiple Mediations: Feminist Scholarship in the Age of Multinational Reception.' *Feminist Review,* no. 35: 24–39.
Nicholson, Linda J. (ed.), (1990) *Feminism/Postmodernism.* New York: Routledge.
Probyn, Elspeth (1990) 'Travels in the Postmodern: Making Sense of the Local.' In Linda Nicholson (ed.), *Feminism/Postmodernism,* 176–89. New York: Routledge.
Siim, Birte (1987) 'Vertaileva näkökulma naisten ja hyvinvointivaltion suhteeseen'

(A comparative approach to the relationship between women and the welfare state). In Aino Saarinen et al. (eds.), *Naiset ja valta: Näkökulmia 'hyvinvointivaltioon'* (Women and power: Approaches to 'the welfare state'), 65–75. Jyväskylä: Gummerus.

Tyyskä, Vappu (1994) 'Women Facing the State: Childcare Policy Process in Canada and Finland, 1960–90.' *Nora: Nordic Journal of Women's Studies* 2:95–106.

– (1995) *The Politics of Caring and the Welfare State: The Impact of the Women's Movement on Child Care Policy in Canada and Finland, 1960–1990.* Helsinki: Finnish Academy of Science, Ser. B, tom. 277.

Waerness, Kari (1989) 'Dependency in the Welfare State.' In Martin Bulmer et al. (eds.), *The Goals of Social Policy*, 40–55. London: Unwin Hyman.

Yeatman, Anna (1990) 'A Feminist Theory of Social Differentiation.' In Linda Nicholson (ed.), *Feminism/Postmodernism*, 283–95. New York and London: Routledge.

# 14

# Antipodean Feminisms

## JACQUI TRUE

From the other side of the world,
From a little island cradled in the giant sea bosom,
From a little land with no history,
(Making its own history, slowly and clumsily
Piecing together this and that, finding the pattern, solving
the problem,
Like a child with a box of bricks),
I, a woman

Katherine Mansfield, 'To Stanislaw Wyspianski' (1909 [Poland], 1916)

Then too there was that *word* – and Brixton knew that Antipodes meant opposite feet.

Frank Sargeson, *Sunset Village* (1976)

In her introduction to an Australian international forum (and edited monograph) on feminism and poststructuralism in cross-cultural studies, Susan Sheridan (1988:1) characterized 'antipodean feminism' as an inherently creative form of feminism that receives and transforms theories and practices elaborated elsewhere: 'Australian feminism has always provided fertile ground for the transplantation of "international" (U.S. and U.K., and lately, French) feminisms, has certain indigenous features, notable among them being its capacity to graft those others on to its own growth and at times to produce new species. Antipodean feminism may be imaged, as the Australian novelist Christina Stead represented the continent itself, not as an island colonial outpost but positioned at the crossroads of world trade routes and inhabited by settlers who are, para-doxically, born travellers. More precisely, the importation of ideas should be considered as a rewriting of their discourses in different circumstances rather than Australian comments on what would remain American, British, and French events.'

Could this Antipodean articulation of feminism as adaptive and eclectic be relevant to our understanding of feminisms elsewhere, that is, to those feminisms also on the margins of Europe, but that may not even refer to themselves as feminist, as such? In this essay I explore how antipodean feminisms, namely, those located in the New Zealand and Australian antipodes, are rewritten from an assortment of transnational discourses and practices, specifically for the local (post)colonial context. This antipodean context is one where the colonized (indigenous peoples) and colonizers (White settlers), unlike the European Occident–Orient, share the same physical and social field. White settler subjectivity, in particular, is 'a subject position that oscillates uneasily between identities as colonizer and colonized' (Ang, 1995:69).[1] In his text *Culture and Imperialism*, Edward Said (1994) deconstructs the polarities of Occident and Orient, East and West, metropole and colony. He argues that there is another, contrapuntal way of conceiving history, where stories of self and other, power and resistance, the colonizer and the colonized, are told as inextricable from each other and intimately related. Here I develop Said's contrapuntal method, as I describe the struggles over race, class, and gender in the formation of feminism in New Zealand. In this way, this essay gives substance to Susan Sheridan's idea that antipodean feminisms are 'Janus-faced' insofar as they reconstruct feminisms received from *outside* and mobilize them in the indigenous discourses that contest gendered power relations *inside*.

This negotiation of inside and outside discourses of feminisms in New Zealand illuminates some of the questions of feminism and feminist issues that I have confronted in my research and travels in that other antipode of Europe – Eastern Europe. In the second part of this essay, then, I argue that a similar dynamic process of 'antipodean feminism' is occurring in the wake of Soviet Communism's collapse as a system and with the liberalization and democratization of Central and Eastern European societies. My discussion of these postcommunist feminisms is inspired by my reflections on experiences in Central and Eastern Europe, particularly in Czechoslovakia and the Czech Republic. There also, Western feminisms are transformed in the course of translating them to make meaningful sense in a different cultural and historical context. Transnational feminist ideas and institutions are strategically used for the purpose of gaining legitimacy for local innovations and struggles. Because there is currently less political space for exchanging and elaborating feminist ideas within Central and Eastern European civil societies, this transnational dialogue has been all the more important in introducing new ways of thinking and acting. However, these processes of emulating and adapting feminist discourses and practices from outside are not without conflict. They also involve negotiating power relations between genders and among women that may have previously gone unchecked and unchallenged in the local context, as well as in the transnational context.

In this essay I define the phenomena of émigré feminism as part of the rich and contested, historical circulation of feminist ideas, institutions, organizing, and cultural and scholarly production more frequently referred to as transnational feminism. It is often overlooked that feminisms, both in terms of their normative claims and practical struggles, have to a great extent always been transnational and that feminists have often acted as bridges among different social movements, ideologies, and cultures. As Deborah Stienstra stated (1994:xii), 'Women have been organizing [autonomously] at the global level for at least 150 years.' It is also typically forgotten that feminism has been embedded, and indeed emerged from within a Western imperial and Enlightenment context, and it is therefore not benignly outside of prevailing political and economic frameworks and power relations. In spite of this transnational orientation, however, feminist gains and losses in this century have been primarily expressed and experienced in national and/or state-based contexts, which are for the most part also Western. Thus, I suggest that such terms as émigré or transnational feminism maintain these tensions between nationalism, imperialism, and internationalism, while those such as 'international feminism,' 'global feminism,' or 'feminist internationalism' tend to elide them.[2] Feminism is a powerful social force that is formed within particular historical, cultural, and political contexts but that transgresses state sovereignties. Feminism does not aim to capture the state, or that form of centralized power, rather, feminist ideas and movements aim to transform the civil societies, the very sources of social power that states and other formal, collective institutions operate within[3] (True, 1996a).

Antipodes are places on the Earth diametrically opposite to one another. Literally, New Zealand is regarded as the notional antipodes, geographical, cultural, and seasonal, of Britain or Europe (Orsman, 1997). However, antipodes is also a metaphorical figure of speech that refers to tropes of otherness or difference in modern European thought

(McLean, 1997). Figuratively, thus, 'antipodean feminism' conveys the bottom-up, grass-roots impetus of feminisms as well as their transnational diffusion and negotiation. The idea of antipodean feminism allows me to compare and contrast the development of feminist consciousness in ostensibly opposite contexts, in liberal democratic New Zealand / Aotea-roa and Australia and postcommunist Central and Eastern Europe.[4] Both places are the antipodes of Europe to the extent that they have been ambiguously on the periphery of continental European civilization. Both have to some degree been subject to colonial and imperial rule, and, as little players, their indigenous histories have been mostly marginalized by the grand narratives of great powers and conquerors. I begin this contra-puntal narrative with the antipodean feminism that is most familiar to me. Starting with first-wave frontier feminism, as it may be coined, I trace the contours of feminism in the antipodes in relation to the international context of feminism and the historical formation of a settler state based on race and class hegemony.[5]

**Feminism in the Antipodes**

Like many people I grew up taking my surroundings for granted and assumed that where I was located must indeed be the centre of the uni-verse. It was a surprise, then, when the actual geographical situation of my country on a world map was pointed out. New Zealand was not only but a small group of islands, it was incredibly far from all the great and colourful land masses, isolated, in what seemed an endless amount of uninhabited blue ocean. I remember this moment well, which was proba-bly akin to the Lacanian mirror stage where the infant recognizes the dis-tinction between itself and the (m)other and experiences the lack or absence of the other or mirror image. This initial experience of the 'tyr-anny of distance' is all too common for twentieth-century New Zealand-ers. Perhaps this explains why connections to the world, between European settlers and the western, European hemisphere, especially the British mother country, have been so eagerly sought after and main-tained. Rollo Arnold (1976:5) wrote that: 'New Zealanders have sustained a strong awareness of the outside world because, of the new countries, they need it most. Their colony was too small, its population too scat-tered, its social origins too deprived, for the community to feel that it could in any sense aspire to being culturally complete in itself. Maybe that is why [New Zealand] ... has produced the world's most avid readers; pos-sibly, too, the world's greatest travellers.'

Until recently, it was hoped that superior European civilization would 'show us these islands and ourselves ... give us a home in thought' (Renwick, 1987:197), and thus endow New Zealanders with a sense of identity and meaning in spite of their separation from Europe. This is why issues concerning New Zealand/Aotearoa's national representation on a global scale are particularly sensitive. Like most modern states, engagement with the world outside is both crucial to the definition of New Zealand national identity and feared as a source of threat to this identity. As Simon During (1985) has noted, in New Zealand, tensions or lack of conformity between the individual and society have been perceived in the past as a tension between New Zealand society and external forces. This is the nationalist–isolationist terrain together with the social forces associated with (post)colonialism, settler state capitalism, and frontier masculinity, upon which feminism in the antipodes has developed and has had to struggle.[6]

New Zealand is internationally lauded as the first self-governing country to extend the suffrage to women citizens, in 1893. Historical accounts of New Zealand feminism typically begin with the events that led up to this political victory for women citizens. The competitive national 'desire to hold the [women's suffrage] record runs deep' in the Anglo-American world (Daley and Nolan, 1994:4). Women suffragism, as Ellen Carol Dubois (1994:224) stressed, was an international protest movement that relied upon international cooperation, resources, and ideological inspiration to sustain a long struggle and marginalization by the national governments and politics of the time. The achievement of the franchise by New Zealand women was said to give 'new hope and life to all women struggling for emancipation' in Europe, Britain and her colonies, and the United States (Page 1993:1). Indeed, the largest international academic conference to take place in New Zealand was that held in 1993 to commemorate 100 years of New Zealand women's suffrage and suffragist movements worldwide.

Conventional national history, however, downplays rather than celebrates this comparatively early achievement of female suffrage and the collective organization of women that was its prerequisite. All too frequently, the conservative, morally superior nature of the suffragists is what is noted, as well as the lack of political activism by women after the vote was gained. William Pember Reeves, social reformer and first historian of the suffrage movement, regarded woman suffrage as an achievement and gift from self-interested, but chivalrous male politicians. In his well-known monograph, *State Experiments in Australia and New Zealand*,

Reeves wrote, 'One fine morning of September 1893, the women of New Zealand woke up and found themselves enfranchised. The privilege was theirs – given freely and spontaneously, in the easiest and most unexpected manner in the world.' He chastised further, 'It is well to face the truth and to dissipate any vision that may still be in the air of an intellectual uprising by enslaved Woman against the ancient and fraudful rule of tyrant Man' (quoted in Spearitt, 1992:329).

This historical explanation went largely uncontested until the second wave of feminism in the 1960s and 1970s. New Zealand's achievement of woman suffrage was typically explained by referring to the progressive nature of the settler state and the rational actions of its statesmen. Women themselves were (often) charged with the radical subversion of this social liberal state. Indeed, the strongest argument against woman suffrage was articulated by Prime Minister Robert Stout in 1887 (New Zealand Parliamentary Debates, 12 May 1887:248; Sawer, 1996:120), who was actually in support of passing the franchise bill: 'I believe that there is only one danger in passing this bill ... That danger is, that if we have women voters and women representatives, they would strive to extend the functions of the State.' Thus, women's collective struggle and autonomous organization against this state, and its male representatives who resisted the enfranchisement of women for over twenty years in parliamentary debate, was rendered invisible in the public record. However, revisionist feminist history that documents the internationally mobilized and informed nature of women's suffrage activism, as well as its involvement in alliances with male politicians, disrupts this 'malestream' narrative of democratic reform in New Zealand and Australia.

As noted, the historical record stresses the civilizing impulse of first-wave antipodean feminism. Separation from Britain triggered nationalist sentiments in New Zealand and Australia. Indeed, the hostility towards the outside civilization of the *mother country* and its attendant class system produced virulent, nationalist assertions of egalitarianism. It also produced masculine resentment towards civilized habits, such as domesticity and respectability, embodied by women subjects inside the 'White dominions' of Australia and New Zealand. Thus, as these new nation states developed they institutionalized inside–outside and public–private boundaries, coded as masculine and feminine respectively. As a result, New Zealand and Australian political cultures were characterized in their very beginnings by exclusively male–masculine activities and representations in a 'public' realm (True, 1996b).

Colonial settler society, however, was considered barbaric by metropolitan citizens back in the mother country. Emigration was perceived in Britain, for instance, as 'only for Godhoppers and country-bumpkins and not for civilized beings' (John Logan Campbell quoted in Graham, 1988:137). William Morgan, a visiting English gentleman, commented in 1860, 'I certainly pity the unfortunate individual who lives in the bush all alone. What indeed is the bush without female society!' (Graham, 1988:120). Conditioned by outside (British imperial) standards of civilization, however, women suffragists did sometimes emphasize the moral improvement that their political enfranchisement would achieve. Equal rights for women, they argued, were inseparable from the task of morally reforming society by civilizing its social dispositions, welfare system, workplace, and religious practices. Suffragists did not see the equality of the sexes as incompatible with women's sexual and moral difference. For them, the extension of citizenship rights meant extending traditionally defined womanhood into new realms, and it did not perforce require New Zealand women to become 'like men.'

Nevertheless, this feminine frontier was subordinated to a state-building project in which a class compromise was manifest. If New Zealand was not 'the lucky country' (Australia), it was 'God's own country,' Godzone, as a result of radical state reform in the late nineteenth century. It was both a paradise for working men, because of high wages and easy property acquisition, and a laboratory for social welfare. Egalitarianism was the dominant social disposition in the early days of New Zealand and Australia. It set their new world settlements apart from the class inequality of the old world and the impoverishing industrialism of Britain. It inverted the British class system, turned the world upside down, in a way.

After the first wave of feminism in New Zealand, the social forces that had been oriented towards women's equal rights, regrouped in various social reform organizations, especially those pertaining to the improvement of women's and children's situation. If civilizing men and parliament had been one of the rhetorical aims of the suffragists, then civilizing settler capitalism was the intrinsic goal of these later reform movements. Eminent New Zealand economic historian J.B. Condliffe (1930, 1959), who taught at the University of California at Berkeley in the interwar years, argued controversially that the various statutory entitlements to public health, education, elderly pensions, and employment compensations that effectively enacted the New Zealand welfare state were traceable to the activism of the women's suffrage movement. The historiography has made no such direct linkage. Nevertheless, it is clear that the nature of the state based on the mandate and interests of propertied male citizens did change when women and non-propertied subjects became citizens. Their inclusion confirmed the legitimate political interest of the state in redistribution and the socioeconomic welfare of citizens, not merely in the classical liberal task of protecting the wealth of propertied male heads of households. It changed the field of political forces and helped create social rights to ensure the economic security necessary for effective citizenship.

Similar to other Western welfare states, in interwar New Zealand a bargain was struck between labour and capital that structured the duties of the state, the market, and the family around the needs of industrial 'productivity' and growth, profit, capital investment, and the working capabilities of a full-time, paid, male labour force. Thus, the welfare state created distinctive, gendered citizens: breadwinners and housewives, workers and mothers. The New Zealand welfare state embodied contradictory liberal equal-rights and republican mother-right discourses of women's citizenship (Pateman, 1989). The social provisions of postsuffrage welfarism included both practical benefits and strategic costs for women's citizenship: while motherhood-related financial and health benefits, social services, and rights to child custody assisted women's care-giving, and reproductive regulation, the 'family wage,' gender-segregated education, occupations, and protective labour legislation all increased the state's role in shaping 'womanhood' according to bourgeois gender roles. In the interwar period, thus, Maureen Molloy (1992:296–7) argued, 'woman-in-the-family' not 'woman-for-herself' became the subject of the New Zealand welfare state. Maori women, in particular, were subject to public discourses about their reproductive and moral fitness and therefore to state interventions.[7] 'Support for motherhood, although characterised as the first duty of the State, was not a right of mothers but a responsibility of State' (Molloy, 1992:301).

As already argued, the legitimation of the New Zealand and Australian states was ideologically based on egalitarianism – essentially reduced to the previous frontier ideal of a 'classless' society. However, referring to Australia, Bruce Kapferer (1988:179) has argued that contrary to 'legends of people, myths of state' (the title of his book), 'egalitarianism establishes the ideological terms for the existence of inegalitarian distinction.' In other words, egalitarianism is defined around a set of universal norms that demand sameness and conformity and otherwise justify unequal or differential treatment. Women and Maori who were typically not identified as members of a 'class' (as either workers or capitalists) were beyond the pale of postwar egalitarianism. Ironically, the inegalitarian exclusion of women – as colonial helpmeets (to men) – and Maori – as noble savages – was the necessary foundation for egalitarian mateship among Pakeha men and the incorporation of the working classes in national hegemonic unity (Gramsci, 1971). In 1900 the American socialist Henry Demarest Lloyd reckoned that the task of absorbing all classes into the middle class was the dominant political force in the dominion of New Zealand (the 'Newest England'). In 1952, after the last official colonial ties with Britain had been severed (1947 ratification of 1932 Act of Westminister), Bill Pearson more acutely criticized New Zealanders for 'hiving off the threats of communism, the coloured races, and the bland terror of infinite space, trying to give their customs a universal validity flouted by life, time and the multiplicity of planets. They huddle to reassure themselves that their habits are beyond question, and difference and unconformity questions them. It is a dream too, of the middle class wanting to compensate for the daily routine of competition: life is cruel, business forces you to shoddy tricks, but on our dream let us relax and be jolly good fellows.'

This dream of a classless society led by and for the middle class profoundly shaped the New Zealand welfare state and class compromise that emerged in the interwar and subsequent postwar era. Postwar Western hegemony in New Zealand supported a culture of conformity together with a frontier tradition of anti-intellectualism. This culture suppressed the development of social alternatives, including feminist alternatives. Models and norms developed elsewhere were merely translated to fit the New Zealand context. Indigenous thinking was not encouraged, and social hierarchies therefore went mostly unquestioned. Examples of this can be found in the way New Zealand foreign policy was conducted as an extension of the British home office until at least the 1960s, if not the early 1970s, the insensitive treatment of local New Zealand artists and writers, and the extremely narrow range of roles for women in society, collectively and condescendingly known as 'Sheilas' (True, 1996b). Paradoxically, in an apparently egalitarian, democratic society, an almost entirely white, well-bred, male elite dominated official modes of thinking and acting.

This political and cultural conformity that underpinned New Zealand national hegemony was cemented by cold war ideology and a particular world order configuration led by the United States and based on the universalization of the nationalist welfare state in the West and the authoritarian socialist state in the East. This was the background against which second-wave feminism rose up in 1960s New Zealand. It caused a radical rupture in cultural conformity and was part of a feminist comeback across the Western part of the world, especially strong in the United States.

The beginnings of women's work and equality legislation had been established in New Zealand with the Equal Pay Act of 1962. However, it was not until the mid-1960s that the social status of most women (especially the female gender roles of housewife and mother) was critically examined, influenced by American Betty Friedan's *The Feminine Mystique* and other revolutionary international texts. Women began to collectively challenge their prescribed postwar life-chances. Liberal feminists fought for the fundamental equality of women with men. In New Zealand and Australia, as in other Western countries, major legal and social achievements resulted from this movement that has been instrumental in substantially transforming women's expectations and opportunities. However, liberal feminism did not challenge other factors that structurally disadvantage women, such as the regulatory social control of women by welfare states, the standard of equality based on normative male experience, the masculine values of competition and individualism, or the masculine public sphere that tends to render private inequalities invisible. In retrospect, Christine Dann (1985:3) argued, New Zealand feminism had not died with the suffragettes, but was finding new forms in relation to major socioeconomic shifts. Liberal feminism evolved in the 1960s and 1970s as one political expression of feminism that attempted to progressively shape the forces (for example, the social liberal state and the postwar economic boom) that were changing and shaping women's lives in the postwar era.

In their account of second- and third-wave feminisms in Australia, Shane Rowlands and Margaret Henderson (1996:10) pointed out that 'the sources of key texts for the Australian women's movement' were from the United States and that the sensationalist media coverage of feminist activism, that is, the identification of feminist gurus, was largely American instigated. The visit in 1972 to New Zealand by the Australian-British feminist Germaine Greer made the local women's liberation movement, 'women's lib' as it was coined, a household name (albeit derided in many). Although 1970s feminism in New Zealand was strongly influenced by the development of liberal, radical, and socialist feminisms internationally, the struggle to articulate them was engaged nationally. For example, the celebration of Suffrage Day (19 September) in 1893 was revived by second-wavers in 1970 as an annual celebration. The women's liberation movement combined socialist thinking and experience in New

Zealand left movements with new radical feminist ideas and agendas that cut across the class and national boundaries of traditional political parties and organizations (Dann, 1985).

Radical feminism advocated raising women's consciousness outside male institutions, that is, the state and its apparatuses, and in separation from men. It validated women's 'truths' and experiences but in opposition to singularly identifiable oppressors, namely, men and the state. On New Zealand terrain, radical feminists aggressively confronted the masculine frontier culture and 'real men' aggressors. They stormed public bars and clubs reserved for men only, protested against sexist advertising, beauty contests, and male violence, fought for equal pay and abortion rights, spoke in workplaces and on the streets, and were even voted into the national parliament (Dann, 1985). Successful in many respects in challenging masculinist norms, radical feminism nevertheless did not always empower women whose lives were so embedded in these norms, and its aggressive strategies often alienated these women from feminism. By the 1980s, Guy, Jones, and Simpson (1990) have argued, radical feminists became increasingly, avidly anti-theoretical, proclaiming the utility of simplistic binary categories of 'us and them.' By producing a clear-cut theory of women's sexual oppression and sexual oppressor, radical feminism did not pay sufficient attention to the complexity of women's gender oppression in specific cultural, class, race, and national contexts and excluded possibilities for women's empowerment through market opportunities, democratic institutions, and social solidarity with men.

It could be argued that the United States liberal feminist movement for equal rights historically arose out of the radical women's liberation movement and a sense of frustration with their revolutionary, rather than reformist goals. In contrast, in the social democracies of Australia and New Zealand the historical development of liberal and radical feminism seems to be reversed; radical feminism having emerged from the limitations of prior equal rights (legal) gains. New Zealand and Australian liberal feminisms themselves have evolved quite indigenously in the spaces in-between women and the state. A close relationship has developed between state institutions and the women's movement. 'Femocracy,' a term coined by Australian feminist sociologist Anna Yeatman (1990), among others, to express the reality of feminist 'penetration' of bureaucratic state apparatuses, has been both an agent and structural outcome of alliances between feminists and the state. 'Femocrats' in Australia and New Zealand have institutionalized comparatively progressive women's policy machinery, including gender-equity legislation and executive policy-making institutions. Arguably, the culminating femocrat achievements were the introduction of an Office of a Women's Advisor to the Australian Prime Minister in 1975 and, in New Zealand, an autonomous Ministry for Women's Affairs with its own cabinet minister in 1984–5.

In more recent years femocrats have become embroiled with neo-liberal discourse and the economic restructuring of the state. In the very same year that the women's affairs ministry was established, the New Zealand Labour government began to legislate a program of neo-liberal reforms. These eventually included trade and price liberalization, financial and labour market deregulation, the privatization of public assets and services, and drastic reductions in state expenditures. Over the past fourteen years this reform has intensified the role of the market mechanism, in everybody's lives, albeit unequally and unevenly. This structural change has gravely affected most women, because of their greater dependence on state employment, public services, and the welfare support system (Kelsey, 1993). Maori and Pacific Island women have been especially negatively affected by social welfare and public service cuts and the shift to individual employment contracts. Rolling back the state has had the effects of further differentiating New Zealand women in terms of race and class; feminizing the flexible labour force and, to a lesser extent, the ranks of corporate and government leadership.

'Woman' was always a strategic unifying subject of feminist movements, and much of the impetus of feminist theory and practice has been to differentiate women and their variety of oppressions as well as to illuminate commonalities. Yet the heightened fragmentation of women by contemporary socioeconomic transformations would seem to undermine these efforts. Moreover, New Zealand politics appears to have been superseded by neo-liberal individualist anti-politics, whose constituencies are no longer men, women, children, Maori, Pakeha, and so on, but politically neutral consumers, clients, taxpayers, and even citizens. Neo-liberal reform has created new constituencies in New Zealand. They include what Wendy Larner (1996) called the 'new boys' – a comparatively elite group of managers and entrepreneurs who are the globalizing agents of the internationalization of the New Zealand state and economy and who have greatly benefited from the recent structural transformation (Gill, 1995). Another is a new underclass of unemployed persons and working poor, among whom Maori and Pacific Islanders are overrepresented.

Women who have experienced the household and community costs of economic restructuring at the hands of a woman finance minister, and cuts to social welfare benefits and public services under the knife of a woman minister of social welfare, know that wearing a 'navy-blue skirt' does not ensure that one is sensitive to the needs and situation of women or of society generally. The fact that conservative women politicians are at the 'cutting edge' of restructuring is not lost on the New Zealand public. Second-wave feminists have also been co-opted as agents of the neoliberal state and market sector, and they do not necessarily support other women or the collective interests of women (Kedgley and Varnham, 1993). The illusion that being a woman qualifies one to be a superior civil servant, victim, or spokesperson for women has been dispelled. The question that must be posed, then, is how might feminism in the antipodes and elsewhere be reconstituted to address these structural transformations, which have changed the relationship between national and global political economies, states, and civil societies and therefore the terrain for feminist politics and organizing (Brodie, 1995)?

**Feminism in the Other Antipodes? Central and Eastern Europe**

The fact is that a gigantic eastern 'appendage' was also attached to the formula [of Russian expansion], forming in a sense a partner of the western (North American [and antipodean]) appendage to the Occidents.

Szucs (1988:312).

Like Australia and New Zealand, Central and Eastern European countries have feminist histories that run deep, although they have often been lost or forgotten at different times. In my travels to and studies of the Czech lands, for example, I have learned that first-wave feminism emerged there in the context of the movement for Czech national self-determination in the late Habsburg monarchy at the turn of this century. Unlike first-wave feminism in the antipodes, however, Czech feminism did not struggle for greater democratization of an existing state. Rather, it struggled to found a state that would protect the distinctive culture and political expression of the Czech nation, men and women both. Czech feminism, though, developed in the context of transnational feminism, as did the suffrage movements in Australia and New Zealand.[8]

After socialist regimes came to power in Czechoslovakia, and other Central and Eastern European countries, however, women's emancipation became the state project of the Communist party and not of an organic feminist social movement. Across the East bloc communist regimes based on the dictatorship of the proletariat or working class by a vanguard Communist party attempted to eliminate bourgeois social forces and create a classless society. Class solidarity in these socialist states was forged against bourgeois states and the capitalist world system. National identities and interests were subordinated to Soviet communism and the goal of international socialism. Further, emancipating women meant incorporating women in this class project by forcibly integrating them into the paid industrial labour force and, therefore, the working class. Feminist movements in the West that fought for women's rights *vis-à-vis* the patriarchal state and men as a group, were reviled as bourgeois political forces in the communist East. The potential for the development of autonomous women's organizations, as with all other forms of independent association and movement, was systematically supressed in socialist states.

Today, after the fall of communist regimes in Central and Eastern Europe, the politics of feminism and anti-feminism are once again key sites of struggle over the democratization of these societies and the formation of new political subjects. Although *woman* was not a legitimate political identity in socialist states (or only in the overarching context of working class and Communist party membership), the identity of woman is paradoxically now tarnished as a result of its association with the state discourses of emancipation (from above). Postcommunist women remember and despise those Communist party spokeswomen who were seemingly oblivious to the reality of the communist regime for most people, and particularly the hardships for women, working a double shift in the household and in the workforce. In her biography of Václav Havel, President of the Czech Republic, Eda Kriseová (1993:254–5) shares a particularly telling anecdotal experience she had with the chairwoman of the Women's Union of the Communist party in November 1989, at the time of the Velvet Revolution and the negotiations between party apparatchik and Civic Forum dissident representatives: 'After the parley, Mrs Němcová came up to me. She asked me what I did ... Perhaps she asked me the question because she thought I would want her job. Then, as woman to woman she confided her concern. I ought to take action in the name of morality, she said. We are, after all, a cultured nation and the singer Dědeček has used vulgar words in the [revolutionary] song he had sung last night on Letna Plain. As women, we should be able to see eye to eye and take action, for, after all, we know what morality is. I looked at her with panicked eyes. She had signed that loathsome proclamation against the students [and allowed the riot police to attack them in Wenceslas Square], and now she was concerned with morality [!].'

Western observers frequently comment on the prevalence of anti-feminism in postcommunist societies. They note, in particular, the anti-feminist and anti-Western sentiments expressed by women involved in postcommunist professional, humanitarian, ecological, motherhood, or traditional women's organizations. However, these organizations can also be interpreted as collective attempts to cope with massive social change and to delimit the scope and character of partisan politics. They may be understood as responses to the contradictions between the theory and practice of women's emancipation in the past, and to the present context of uncertainty, where technocratic models of transition politics predominate. As we saw in the case of New Zealand and Australia, feminisms evolve in the context of particular historical formations and their contradictions in terms of gender, race, and class inequality. Hana Havelková (1997) argues, for instance, that Czech women's resistance to adopting Western feminist ideas and struggles reflects their determination (in contrast to elite Czech men who uncritically accept Western expertise and models) to defend their unique subjectivities in the process of mediating Westernization.

Czech women have good reason to be sceptical of Western feminism. Unmediated Western feminisms may not be the best way to resist the formation of a postcommunist political subjectivity that is both conditioned by Western norms and constructed through the symbolic and material exclusion of women. In the first instance, liberal strands of Western feminism tend to unreflectively accept masculine subject positions, while radical feminisms celebrate an oppositional but equally generic, Western female subject. Second, as markers of the West not organically rooted in the local culture, Western feminist concepts can easily be used in the former East to discredit women's rights and bolster masculinist and nationalist identities.

Let me outline further why I think postcommunist women have good reason to be sceptical of the global diffusion of Western feminism. As a result of my involvement in East–West feminist conversations, I see this scepticism as a constructive process of local translation and innovation with respect to feminist concepts and organizing. De facto feminisms are emerging out of Central and Eastern European women's encounters with Western feminists and their cultural production and organizational forms (Smejkalova-Strickland, 1995). After the experience of forty years of Soviet-mandated communism, many Central and Eastern Europeans are acutely aware that collective identities and strategies developed in another historical and cultural context cannot be easily transplanted.

They understand that social movements must evolve spontaneously within their own cultural conditions and contradictions. For example, Jiřina Šiklová (1993:9) discussed the women's organization Prague Mothers, 'an informal, spontaneously-arisen organization of women who are interested in ecological problems and stand up for the interests of women.' Šiklová explained that 'they outright reject feminism and even refuse to discuss it,' which they believe is for intellectual, university women. Nevertheless, Prague Mothers have set up networks of drop-in centres for mothers across the Czech Republic, in transnational collaboration with a German women's organization.

Activists and scholars in Central and Eastern Europe committed to women's rights realize that an indigenous language with which to articulate these rights must also evolve locally. *Gender*, an Anglophone word and concept distinguished from biological sex difference, is used in the name of the Kiev, Krakow, and Prague Centres for Gender Studies – centres of resources, research, and networking for women's organizations – but is explained in relation to the activities, problem solving, and critical thinking that develop in and around each centre in each country (Hradílková, 1993). The analytic category of gender does not have an ahistorical or universal meaning. Ann Snitow (1994) recounted her experience in opening a bank account for the Prague Gender Studies Centre with Jiřina Šiklová, on behalf of the Network for East–West Women: the teller asked her if the organization these ladies were representing was a brothel! Concepts and discourses are not always understood in the same ways in different cultural contexts, and, moreover, they undergo change in their translation from other languages and contexts.

Czech women typically reject Western feminist discourses that collapse them into a homogeneous bloc reminiscent of communism, as 'Eastern European women' (see Jung in this volume). In the course of her questioning of where 'Europe' ends and therefore where the frontiers of European concepts of woman and feminism lie, Jiřina Šiklová comments that, for Czechs, the problems and status of women two thousand kilometres East of their Central European country seem as remote as those of Western women (Šiklová, 1994). She notes, however, that six years after the fall of communism Western feminism continues to be spread further eastward, in her view, by missionary-like Western feminist activists.

Postcommunist women are also equivocal about the touted individualism of Western feminism. They often perceive feminism in an undifferentiated way, as a contradictory embrace of masculine power and politics with implicit biases towards families, men, and social solidarity. Šiklová (quoted in Hauser, 1993:239) went as far as to suggest that Western women's movements are narcissistic: 'Sometimes women in the West abandon their traditional positions in society, rooted in their own culture, and give up the typical social roles of women without asking who will take over their tasks.' Hana Havelková (1997) has also commented on the real resistance of Western societies to feminist achievements. She seemed to be alluding to the failure of Western feminism to improve the relative material conditions and social status of very many women. This incredulity towards liberal feminist goals of equal male and female participation in the labour market, and especially in political life, derives in part from postcommunist women's experience of the impotency of politics and representative gender quotas in communist states. It could also be explained by the affinity of many women, who might be sympathetic to feminism, for the kind of civic and moral politics practised by Central and Eastern European dissidents in the independent movements that toppled communism.

Many postcommunist women's organizations share the former Charter 77, Solidarity, and other civic movements' desire to expand spaces for citizen participation and independent initiative. They also seek to transform civil societies from below in order to transform political societies, that is, the state and the nature of power itself. In Central and Eastern European societies, Western analyst Stephen Heintz (quoted in Woodard, 1995) observed, there is 'democracy at the macro level ... but a lack of decentralisation of political power.' The strategy of cultural transformation from below is therefore especially salient and may serve to challenge the accountability and democracy of formal political institutions. This East–Central European form of 'politics from below' is also remarkably similar to the practical philosophies of women's movements worldwide, the networking and cooperation between which I have coined 'transnational feminism.' Indeed, the so-termed 'anti-political' associations and organizations of Central and Eastern European women are regarded by the few scholars of gender issues in the region as virtual or de facto feminisms, in spite of the fact that many of the women involved state themselves to be 'anti-feminist,' or simply 'not feminists.'

In my view, popular analysis that perceives Central and Eastern Europe as anti-feminist because the region has not established feminist movements fails to acknowledge 'the different forms that feminisms take and the different practices that can be seen as feminist movements' in distinctive cultural, geographical, and historical contexts (Grewal and Kaplan, 1994:20). Why should feminism or de facto feminist equivalents follow the same historical formation as antipodean feminisms, when they clearly emerged in relation to a specific political culture and state form? Furthermore, political expressions of 'anti-feminism' in Central and Eastern Europe are a precondition for publicizing and expanding the discourses of feminism beyond the small-scale initiatives of a few scholars and activists. As Kumkum Sangari and Sudesh Vaid (1990:18) wrote, 'The history of feminism ... is inseparable from the history of anti-feminism.' At the same time, to speak and act effectively at the transnational level, I realize that we must seek some common understanding of what 'feminism' stands for. Yet, that understanding, as Karen Offen (1988:119) has heeded, 'cannot be derived exclusively from our own culture, it must be not only historically sound but comparatively grounded' and, I would add, receptive to differences among women across class, race, and state sovereignties.

## Antipodean Feminisms: East and West

The adjacency of Eastern Europe, its relative accessibility compared to the remoteness of the South Pacific, rendered it peculiarly susceptible to a cultural construction that partook of both fact and fantasy.

Wolff (1994:359).

Just as the antipodes – Australia and New Zealand – are historically and culturally constructed in relation to, and distinguished from, Europe and Great Britain, Eastern Europe is a political construction of competitive modernity and has been a cultural repository for Enlightenment identity and difference.

Today, however, in both antipodean places, New Zealand and Australia and postcommunist Europe, the political identities of *worker, woman,* and *European* are sceptically viewed in popular discourse and by radical reforming governments. In postcommunist societies, attempts to fix language and reality to these ideological categories and their emancipatory projects are vigorously resisted. Certainly such categories and projects construct and have constructed the way we perceive and produce reality. Until recently, in former communist regimes, as Ivan Klíma (1995:136) stated, 'Truth was what you found in pockets of worker's overalls, under miners' helmets, and in the heavy gloves of steelworkers.' Or equally, in antipodean feminist communities, truth was personally defined by the quantity of oppressions or degree of victimization one could claim, for example, as disabled, lesbian, single mother on welfare, or woman of colour. Collective identities have been produced and reproduced through classification and exclusion; the exclusion of non-workers and peripheral and unpaid workers from political and social recognition, and in opposition to so-called enemies, bourgeois, heterosexual White men, for example. A workers' international or global sisterhood are now thoroughly discredited, based on our experience and critical reflections on the exclusionary and falsely universalizing nature of identities and identity politics.

Nevertheless, feminist discourses are an integral aspect of current globalization processes. Intensified global flows of feminist ideas, publications, activism both 'down under' and in the former East, have produced more self-aware local feminist identities. It is an irony, then, that an important effect of so-termed globalization has been the increased presence and assertiveness of national or indigenous (that is, New Zealand, Australasian, Czech, Polish, Central and Eastern European) feminisms in international venues, publications, and debates (see Larner, 1995; Molloy, 1995; Smejkalova-Strickland, 1995). These feminisms are definitely cosmopolitan, but they mostly resist the universalizing, global pretensions of feminism.

At the same time, as globalizing processes provoke indigenous articulations of feminist identity and politics, they also transform the very grounds of critical feminist analysis. Studies of women and the causes and consequences of global economic restructuring can no longer be confined to the national level of analysis. Contemporary transnational feminist flows of ideas and interactions, however, are not always analytically sophisticated in helping us chart this world of overlapping identities and scattered hegemonies. Nor are transnational feminisms inherently transformative, in that they open the world to more critical voices that defy professionalization and commodification. Contemporary feminist texts and cultural forms are generally produced in the United States, yet are globally consumed, with little reference to the local specificity of feminisms. Rowlands and Henderson (1996) controversially regard the current array of (anti)feminist texts and media representations as forms of United States neo-imperialism that are entirely global market-led and *status quo* maintaining. They are highly critical of the presence of this 'blockbuster feminism' in Australia and its capacity to co-opt and de-politicize local feminisms. In *Culture and Imperialism*, Edward Said (1994:319) observed that 'rarely before in human history has there been so massive an intervention of force and ideas from one culture to another, as there is today from America to the rest of the world.' Western feminist ideas, which emanate largely, but not exclusively, from the United States are part of this massive global cultural flow.

Academic feminism, which one would presume to be a critical, intellectual source of transformative politics, is also inextricably linked to the production of specialized knowledges located for the most part in the academic enclaves of North America. Transnational feminist research still depends, to a large extent, on an institutional context where the West provides the models, the sophisticated theoretical frameworks, and the knowers, while the rest of the world provides the objects of research, the playground for making known and becoming known in the West. In colonial times, Said (1994:186) said, 'going native, playing the great Game,' like Lawrence of Arabia or Kipling's Kim, 'depend[ed] upon the rock-like foundations of European power.' Similarly, in a U.S.-led postcolonial era much transnational academic feminist research, like other institutionalized knowledge production, depends upon the foundations of American hegemony that make the world easily accessible and imperatively knowable to elite Westerners.

I do not mean to imply that transnational feminist cooperation and reciprocal, equitable exchange does not exist. There are many transnational feminist encounters that as an ethical requirement contest the very power relations that are their actual condition of possibility (True, 1995). East–West feminism, in my experience, is beginning to develop networks and relationships based on this critical reflexivity. There is also transnational feminist scholarship that critically analyses changing relationships among women and men in global divisions of labour and documents the pervasiveness of gender ideology within global social relations (see Peterson, 1992; Tickner, 1992; Sylvester, 1994).

**Conclusion**

For Westerners and Easterners entering the emerging postcommunist dialogue on gender issues, it is crucial to represent the many feminisms and de facto feminisms that have developed in both Western and former East European countries. In this essay I have tried to approximate such a representational strategy by using my own eclectic, personal experience as a starting point. Making connections between and among feminisms that are open, dynamic, and in this way transformative is all the more important when there is a Western tendency to diminish diverse and multilayered feminist discourses by collapsing them into a singular universal, liberal discourse, usually derivative of the Anglo-American postwar context (see Caine and Pringle, 1995; and also Du Plessis et al., 1993). Moreover, the non-existence of a feminist movement, per se, in former East bloc countries does not mean that the form that feminism might take there now, as these new states struggle to integrate into the global political economy and define their identities anew, must emulate the development of feminisms in the West. It is clear, though, that the plight of feminisms East and West is, more than ever before, intimately related and mutually contingent. This does not, however, negate the need for indigenously produced feminist theories to help different members of distinct societies to shape and interpret their own gender, postcommunist, and global transitions. Indeed, histories of imperial dominance and anti-intellectualism, as well as a contemporary context of political–economic transformation that privileges pragmatism, make local theorizing in Central and Eastern Europe as well as Australia and New Zealand especially critical (Šmejkalová-Strickland, 1995; Molloy, 1995).

The fall of communism and the diffusion of democracy open up new possibilities for the un-gendering of world politics. Émigré, expatriate, and exiled feminists are ideally located, intellectually and practically, for recognizing and building on these recent transformations in identity and community. Their cross-cultural and often highly contested experiences of feminism compel feminists everywhere to come to terms with their own hybridity and appropriation of transnational and local practices. We are all émigré feminists now, grounded in several social and political contexts, and responsible for the needs of others in a radically interdependent world. The third wave of feminism, therefore, is at once transnational and local, contrapuntal and antipodean.

NOTES

1 Ien Ang (1995:69) made a similar important point that 'the fact that Australia [and New Zealand] itself is on the periphery of the Euro-American core of the West (and as such is often forgotten or ignored by that core) produces a sense of non-metropolitan, post-colonial whiteness whose structure of feeling remains to be explored.' White settler subjectivity, Ang continues, is 'a subject position that oscillates uneasily between identities as colonizer and colonized.'

2 Like Inderpal Grewal and Caren Kaplan (1994:13), I prefer to the use the term 'transnational' because it problematizes a 'purely locational politics' and allows us to situate feminism within the contradictions of state formation in a global political, economic, and cultural system. Transnationalism also incorporates hegemonic and counter-hegemonic movements: there are transnationalisms of

the powerful and of the powerless, transformative and order-maintaining forms of transnationalism (Cox, 1992). Transnationalism emerges from economic globalization and from the political multilateralism of states, but it also emanates from local social movements that respond transnationally to the contradictions of development and unaccountable power that are a result of this very transnationalism 'from above.'

3   Gender – and social mobilization based on gender identity – cuts across state sovereignties. Feminist approaches to international relations note that there is an integral relation between the struggles of women and feminists both within and across nation-states. When viewed from the perspective of gender inequalities and hierarchies, world politics is based less on the power of core states over more peripheral states than on the power of a transnational elite that is overwhelmingly male and Western. Feminisms, therefore, are no different, they exist in and around, below and above the state, and seek not to displace particular states but to change their gendered form within a global context of gender hierarchies. For an introduction to feminist perspectives on international relations, see Peterson (1992), Tickner (1992), and Sylvester (1994). See also Cox (1987).

4   Aotearoa – which translates as the land of the long white cloud – is the indigenous Maori name predating New Zealand – the name coined by the Dutchman, Abel Tasman in his 1642 voyage to the South Pacific. Aotearoa/New Zealand is the official name of the state registered at the United Nations. In this chapter I refer to New Zealand more often as the specific name for the colonizing settler state.

5   No doubt there are many similarities between the development of antipodean and Canadian feminisms given their similar settler state and British dominion origins. However, this is a discrete subject for study – and I believe there are several researchers currently engaged in just this type of historical comparison.

6   It should be noted, as Simon During (1985:370–1) stressed, that New Zealand 'can be characterised by the equilibrium of its postcolonising and postcolonial forces. In no other country are they so equally balanced ... It has never been sufficiently recognised that New Zealand has a different, and more complex discursive community than Australia because the post-colonial/post-colonising forces are balanced here as they are not there.' During is referring here to the balance of forces of cultural representation, production, and identity, not to the balance of material and political forces.

7   The terms 'Maori' and 'Pakeha' refer to the two main ethnic groups and/or political identities in Aotearoa/New Zealand. Maori is the name for the indigenous people of Aotearoa. Pakeha is the Maori name for foreigner or white man. It is still a controversial and politicised term for white New Zealanders of British origin, distinguishing them from non-New Zealand Europeans.

8 In 1865 an American Ladies Club was established in Prague. The club developed Czech linkages with American and English feminisms, sponsored visits by eminent feminists of the time, published a monthly women's journal that reported on women's movements elsewhere, and included a library and technical museum devoted to objects useful to women's work (David-Fox, 1991:28). In 1890, Charlotte Garrigue Masaryková, the American-born wife of Tomáš Masaryk, the future president of the First Czechoslovak Republic, translated into Czech John Stuart Mill's *On the Subjection of Women*. She is known to have strongly influenced Masaryk's feminist ideas on 'the woman and social questions.' Czech feminists also belonged to an international alliance of woman suffragists, and in 1913 Prague women's organizations hosted a contingent of delegates from ten countries en route to the International Suffrage Alliance conference in Budapest (David-Fox, 1991:30). First-wave Czech feminism had a distinctly national consciousness. Somewhat in contrast to antipodean suffragists, who struggled against male-dominated states mediated by partial alliances with progressive men, Czech feminists established relationships of solidarity with Czech men and a future Czech nation-state. This nationalist solidarity was privileged over solidarity with German-speaking feminists in the Habsburg multilingual state. Czech feminists fought (successfully) for women's rights to education, civil liberties, and the vote as an essential part of Czech national progress and liberation.

REFERENCES

Ang, Ien (1995) 'I'm a Feminist But ... "Other" and Post-National Feminisms.' In Barbara Caine and Rosemary Pringle (eds.), *Transitions: New Australian Feminisms*, 57–73. New York: St. Martin's Press.
Arnold, Rollo (1976) 'The Village and the Globe: Aspects of the Social Origins of Schooling in Victorian New Zealand.' *Australian and New Zealand History of Education Society [ANZHES] Journal* 5(1):1–12.
Brodie, Janine (1995) *Politics on the Boundaries: Restructuring and the Canadian Women's Movement*. Halifax: Fernwood.
Caine, Barbara, and Rosemary Pringle (eds.), (1995) *Transitions: New Australian Feminisms*. New York: St Martin's Press.
Condliffe, J.B. (1930, 1959) *New Zealand in the Making: A Study of Economical and Social Development*. London: Allen and Unwin.
Cox, Robert W. (1987) *Production, Power and World Order: Social Forces in the Making of History*. New York: Columbia University Press.
– (1992) 'Multilateralism and World Order.' *Review of International Studies* 18(2):161–80.

Daley, Caroline, and Melanie Nolan (eds.), (1994) *Suffrage and Beyond: International Perspectives*. Auckland: University of Auckland Press.

Dann, Christine (1985) *Up from Under: Women and Liberation in New Zealand, 1970–1985*. Wellington: Allen & Unwin.

David-Fox, Katherine (1991) 'Czech Feminists and Nationalism in the Late Hapsburg Monarchy: 'The first in Austria.' *Journal of Women's History* 3(2): 26–45.

Dubois, Ellen Carol (1994) 'Woman Suffrage Around the World: Three Phases of Suffragist Internationalism.' In Caroline Daley and Melanie Nolan (ed.), *Suffrage and Beyond: International Perspectives*, 257–77. Auckland: University of Auckland Press.

Du Plessis, Rosemary, Phillida Bunkle, Kathie Irwin, Alison Laurie, and Sue Middleton (eds.), *Feminist Voices: Women's Studies Texts for Aotearoa/New Zealand*. Aukland: Oxford University Press.

During, S. (1985) 'Postmodernism or Postcolonialism.' *Landfall* 152, 39(1): 366–81.

Gill, Stephen (1995) 'Structural Change and Global Political Economy: Globalising Elites in the Emerging World Order.' In Yoshikazu Sakamoto (ed.), *Global Transformation: Challenges to the State System*, 169–99. Tokyo: United Nations University Press.

Graham, Jeanine (1988) 'Settler Society.' In W.H. Oliver with B.R. Williams (eds.), *The Oxford History of New Zealand*, rev. ed., 112–40. Oxford: Clarendon Press; Auckland: Oxford University Press.

Gramsci, Antonio (1971) *Selections from the Prison Notebooks*. Translated and edited by Quintin Hoare and Geoffrey Nowell Smith. New York: International Publishers.

Grewal, Inderpal, and Caren Kaplan (eds.), (1994) *Scattered Hegemonies: Postmodernity and Transnational Feminist Practices*. Minneapolis: University of Minnesota Press.

Guy, Camille, Alison Jones, and Gay Simpson (1990) 'From Piha to Post-Feminism: Radical Feminism in New Zealand.' *Sites: A Journal for Radical Perspectives on Culture*, 20:7–20.

Havelková, Hana (1997) 'Transitory and Persistent Difference: Feminisms East and West.' In Joan Smith et al. (eds.), *Transitions, Environments, Translations: Feminisms in International Politics*, 56–62. New York: Routledge.

Hauser, Eva (1993) 'Mind the Gap! Women from Post-communist Countries: Conservatism or Progressivism?' *Women: A Cultural Review* 3(3):238–43.

Hradílková, Jana (1993) 'The Discipline of Gender Studies.' *Jedním Okem/One Eye Open* 1(1):39–45.

Kapferer, Bruce (1988) *Legends of People, Myths of State: Violence, Intolerance, and*

*Political Culture in Australia and Sri Lanka*. Washington: Smithsonian Institution Press.

Kedgley, Sue, and Mary Varnham (1993) *Heading Nowhere in a Navy Blue Suit: And Other Tales from the Feminist Revolution*. Wellington: Daphne Brasell Associates Press.

Kelsey, Jane (1993) 'Engendering Poverty: Rolling Back the State on New Zealand Women.' *Victoria University of Wellington Law Review* 23, Special Issue:59–76.

Klíma, Ivan (1995) *Waiting for Light, Waiting for Dark*. Translated by Paul Wilson. New York: Grove Press.

Kriseová, Eda (1993) *Václav Havel: The Authorized Biography*. New York: St Martin's Press.

Larner, Wendy (1995) 'Theorizing "Difference" in Aotearoa/New Zealand.'' *Gender, Place, and Culture* 2(2).

– (1996) 'The "New Boys": Restructuring in New Zealand, 1984–1994.' *Social Politics: International Studies in Gender, State and Society* 3(1):32–56.

McLean, Ian (1997) 'Europe's Antipodean Others.' *Thesis Eleven*, no. 48:69–90.

Molloy, Maureen (1992) 'Citizenship, Property and Bodies: Discourses on Gender and the Inter-War Labour Government in New Zealand.' *Gender and History* 4(3):293–304.

– (1995) 'Imagining (the) Difference: Gender, Ethnicity, and Metaphors of Nation.' *Feminist Review*, no. 51:94–112.

New Zealand Parliamentary Debates, *Hansard Reports*, 12 May 1887.

Offen, Karen (1988) 'Defining Feminism: A Comparative Historical Approach.' *Signs* 14(1):119–157.

Orsman, H.W. (ed.), (1997) *The Dictionary of New Zealand English*. Auckland: Oxford University Press.

Page, Dorothy (1993) 'Introduction.' In Dictionary of New Zealand Biography (eds.), *The Suffragists: Women Who Worked for the Vote. Essays from the New Zealand Dictionary of Biography*, 1–24. Wellington: Bridget Williams Books and Dictionary of New Zealand Biography.

Pateman, Carole (1989) *The Disorder of Women: Democracy, Feminism, and Political Theory*. Stanford: Stanford University Press.

Pearson, Bill (1974) *Fretful Sleepers and Other Essays*. Auckland: Heinemann Educational Books.

Peterson, Spike V. ( ed.), (1992) *Gendered States: Re-visioning International Relations Theory*. Boulder: Lynne Rienner Publishers.

Renwick, W.L. (1987) 'Show Us These Islands and Ourselves ... Give Us a Home in Thought. Beaglehole Memorial Lecture.' *New Zealand Journal of History* 21(2):197–214.

Rowlands, Shane, and Margaret Henderson (1996) 'Damned Bores and Slick

Sisters: The Selling of Blockbuster Feminism in Australia.' *Australian Feminist Studies* 23(11):9–16.

Said, Edward (1994) *Culture and Imperialism.* New York: Vintage Books.

Sangari, Kumkum, and Sudesh Vaid (eds.), (1989) *Recasting Women: Essays in Colonial History.* New Delhi: Kali for Women.

Sawer, Marian (1996) 'Gender, Metaphor and the State.' *Feminist Review,* no. 52:118–35.

Sheridan, Susan (1988) *Grafts: Feminist Cultural Criticism.* London: Verso.

Šiklová, Jiřina (1993) 'McDonalds, Terminators, Coca Cola Ads and Feminism: Imports from the West?' In S. Trnka with L. Busheikin (eds.), *Bodies of Breads and Butter: Reconfiguring Women's Lives in the Post-Communist Czech Republic,* 7–11. Prague: Prague Gender Studies Centre.

– (1994) 'Feminism and Citizenship.' *Helsinki Citizens Assembly Quarterly,* nos. 11–12:11–12.

Šmejkalová-Strickland, Jiřina (1995) 'Revival? Gender Studies in the 'Other' Europa.' *Signs* 20(4):1000–6.

Snitow, Ann (1994) 'Feminist Futures in the Former East Bloc.' *Peace and Democracy News* 7(1):40–4.

Spearitt, Katie (1992) 'New Dawns: First Wave Feminism 1880–1914.' In K. Saunders and R. Evans (eds.), *Gender Relations in Australia: Domination and Negotiation,* 325–47. Marrickville, NSW: Harcourt Brace Jovanovich.

Stienstra, Deborah (1994) *Women's Movements and International Organizations.* London: Macmillan Press.

Sylvester, Christine (1994) *Feminism and International Relations in a Postmodern Era.* Cambridge: Cambridge University Press.

Szucs, Jeno (1988) 'Three Historical Regions of Europe: An Outline.' In John Keane (ed.), *Civil Society and the State: New European Perspectives,* 291–333. London: Verso.

Tickner, Ann J. (1992) *Gender in International Relations: Feminist Perspectives on Achieving Global Security.* New York: Columbia University Press.

True, Jacqui (1995) 'Successions/Secessions: Identity, Gender Politics, and Post-Communism.' *Political Expressions* 1(1):31–50.

– (1996a) 'Feminism.' In Scott Burchill and Andrew Linklater (eds.), with Richard Devetak, Matthew Paterson, and Jacqui True, *Theories of International Relations,* 210–51. London: Macmillan Press.

– (1996b) '"Fit Citizens for the British Empire"?: Class-ifying Racial and Gendered Subjects in "Godzone" (New Zealand).' In B.F. Williams (ed.), *Women Out of Place: The Race of Nationality and the Gender of Agency* 103–28. New York: Routledge.

Wolff, Larry (1994) *Inventing Eastern Europe: The Map of Civilisation on the Mind of the Enlightenment.* Stanford: Stanford University Press.

Woodard, C. (1995) 'Czech Republic Strives to Keep "Velvet Recovery,"' *Christian Science Monitor,* 24 May.

Yeatman, Anna (1990) *Bureaucrats, Technocrats, Femocrats: Essays on the Contemporary Australian State.* Sydney: Allen and Unwin.

# Index

Aboriginal-Caribbean heritage 149, 154, 169n30

aboriginal people 154

abortion 81, 100, 110, 126; Hungary 100; New Zealand 277; slave women 155

academic feminism 61n9, 191–2, 286; Iranian 193; poststructuralist 18; third wave 287

academic feminists 209; Hungarian 100; interaction with male academics 209; Iranian émigré 191–2; neoconservative 192; North American 286; South African 33, 61n9; transformative politics and 286

accessibility to education 75, 89n4, 199

accountability: hegemonic practices 253; of post-exiles 14; transnational feminism 49; transnational researchers 260, 262

acculturation 15; United States 168n24

Act of Westminster (1932, 1947) 275

*Actividades Femininas en Chile* 89n6

activism 55, 88, 157; African-Canadian feminism 141, 143; community 149,

162–4; — definition 169n30; negative aspects 196; social, Catholic Church and 78; solidarity 35; welfare state and (New Zealand) 273

activists: anti-apartheid 61n9; Black 166; Central and Eastern Europe 282, 284; Chileans abroad 75, 90; feminist 102, 126; women 37, 38, 75, 84, 105–6, 157

advertising, sexist 277

advocacy: child care 256, 257; for better education 162

*Afastada* 30–66; apprehensions 32–7; definition 53, 60n1

affirmative action legislation 140

Africa: gender relations 141. *See also* East Africa

African-American women 159

African/Black Heritage group (Canada) 163

African-Black vs Canadian-white 143–4

African-Canadian feminism 14, 131–48; activism 141, 143; coalition politics 142–3, 145; conceptualization 137–9; emergence, nature, vitality 140–5; grass-roots action 141, 145;

# Date Due

| OCT 06 2005 | | | |
|---|---|---|---|
| | | | |
| | | | |
| | | | |
| | | | |
| | | | |
| | | | |
| | | | |
| | | | |
| | | | |
| | | | |
| | | | |
| | | | |
| | | | |
| | | | |
| | | | |
| | | | |
| | | | |
| | | | |
| | | | |
| | | | |
| | | | |
| | | | |
| | | | |

PRINTED IN U.S.A.     CAT. NO. 24 161     BRO DART